Islami

Brian Kettell

First published in the United Kingdom in 2009 by Brian Kettell, Islamic Banking Training, 9a South End Road, London NW3 2PT
www.islamicbankingcourses.com

ISBN 978-0-9558351-1-7

Cover design by HBA, York

Edited and typeset by Diane Evans, Bradford, UK

Printed by Harcourt Litho, Swansea

Dedication

To my wife Nadia, our son and daughter Alexei and Anna. Nadia keeps the whole fleet on an even keel with only the occasional shipwreck.

Also published by the author

Introduction to Islamic Banking and Finance, Published by Oxford Press. Email the author, brian.kettell@islamicbankingcourses.com

Islamic Sukuk: a Definitive Guide to Islamic Structured Finance, Published by Oxford Press. Email the author, brian.kettell@islamicbankingcourses.com

Islamic Banking and Finance in the Kingdom of Bahrain, Published by the Bahrain Monetary Agency

Financial Economics, Published by Financial Times-Prentice Hall. This was translated into Chinese

Economics for Financial Markets, Published by Butterworth's-Heinemann

What Drives Financial Markets? Published by Financial Times-Prentice Hall

What Drives the Currency Markets? Published by Financial Times-Prentice Hall

Fed Watching: The Impact of the Fed on the World's Financial Markets, Published by Financial Times-Prentice Hall

The Valuation of Internet and Technology Stocks, Published by Butterworth's-Heinemann

The International Debt Game: a Study in International Bank Lending (Co-author), Published by Graham and Trotman

A Businessman's Guide to the Foreign Exchange Market, Published by Graham and Trotman

Monetary Economics, Published by Graham and Trotman

Foreign Exchange Handbook, (Co-author), Published by Graham and Trotman

Gold: An Analysis of its Role in the World Economy, Published by Graham and Trotman

The Finance of International Business, Published by Graham and Trotman

Acknowledgements

The author would like to thank Ahmad Chaudry from the Royal Bank of Scotland, Failaka Advisors and the Dow Jones Islamic Indexes for their generous assistance in writing this text.

I would also like to thank Shaykh Yusuf Talal DeLorenzo, Sharia'a Scholar and member of the AAOIFI Sharia'a Board, for permission to reprint Appendix 8.2 and to *The Banker* for permission to reprint their Top 500 Islamic Financial Institutions.

Introduction

Publication of this book takes place at a time when the conventional banking and financial systems of the world are facing threats to their very existence. These threats have focused attention on an alternative system of financial intermediation, Islamic finance, a sector largely insulated from the banking collapses taking place around the world. The world is, of course, a global marketplace so it is impossible to claim that any one single financial system can remain totally unscathed. However there is no doubt that the Islamic financial system has not suffered the devastating consequences of the sub-prime credit market collapse that has ensued elsewhere.

This book discusses in detail the system of Islamic financial intermediation as taking place through Islamic capital markets. The concept of an Islamic capital market refers to the market where financial intermediation activities are transacted applying principles that do not conflict with the conscience of Muslims and the religion of Islam. In other words, the Islamic capital market represents an assertion of Islamic religious law (the *Sharia'a*) in capital market transactions where the market should be free from the involvement of prohibited activities by Islam, as well as free from elements such as usury (*riba*), gambling (*maisir*) and ambiguity (*gharar*).

Objectives of an Islamic capital market

In principle, the objectives of the Islamic capital market are based on the *Sharia'a* law, which in essence should be treated as an important and necessary vehicle to transfer funds from surplus to deficit units. This is to ensure the equitable allocation of capital to sectors which would yield profitable returns to the owners of capital and hence contribute towards the overall growth and expansion of the economy. A clear objective of an Islamic capital market is to ensure that a means of attracting surplus funds for worthwhile investments exists in accordance with the owners' preferences. As with conventional investors this investment must allow for the preferences regarding risk investors, rate of return, as well as the period of investment preferred.

Without a capital market, surplus fund owners would not find sufficient opportunities to invest for the short-term. Most investments have gestation lags and are of long-term in character. Emergency needs may arise from time to time which cannot be easily met. The role of the Islamic capital market is to ensure that the needs of both surplus and deficit units are met, to the benefit of both parties.

It is un-Islamic to hoard wealth. There are numerous *Qur'anic* citations to that effect. It is therefore necessary to provide a mechanism for wealth owners to invest their funds in order to meet the needs of both themselves and society. An Islamic stock market should ideally be characterised by the absence of interest-based transactions and stocks of companies dealing in Islamically unlawful activities. It should also be free from any form of unethical or immoral transactions, such as market manipulation, insider trading and short selling.

Current market environment

Islamic capital markets are now gaining the momentum to grow into a vibrant marketplace, especially for emerging market borrowers in the regions of the Middle East, South-East Asia, South Asia and North Africa.

On the supply side, the volume of Islamic investors – with a preference for *Sharia'a* compliant instruments – has grown to form a critical mass that can support a well-functioning and efficient capital market. The market is evolving into a truly international market. Not only highly rated borrowers such as the Multilateral Development Banks (MDBs) (for example, the World Bank), but also developing country borrowers with lower credit ratings, such as Pakistan, have successfully raised a considerable volume of funds in this market.

On the demand side, countries in the developing world, especially the middle-income countries, will require a significant volume of investments in infrastructure over the next decade. To illustrate, taking the case of the GCC, additional infrastructure investments in coming years are expected to be massive.

Furthermore, Muslim stakeholders in middle-income countries are increasingly expressing their preference for *Sharia'a* compliant financing. Borrowers, especially public-sector institutions, are starting to reflect their stakeholders' voices in the implementation of financial operations. In turn, financial intermediaries, including private-sector commercial and investment banks, as well as development finance institutions, paying more attention to such 'non-financial' needs of their clients – in addition to satisfying these borrowers' funding needs, in order to stay successful in the marketplace.

For the MDBs, such as the World Bank, the development of Islamic capital markets has become a highly relevant topic. Firstly, MDBs are deeply involved in infrastructure finance in their borrowing member countries and are therefore naturally interested in the emerging Islamic capital market as a new and alternative source of financing. Secondly, by channelling the funds available in Islamic financial markets, which are mostly based in the countries with high savings such as the GCC countries and Malaysia, to finance investments in developing countries, MDBs are creating a new model for international development co-operation while responding to the stakeholders' voices on both sides. Thirdly, MDBs are promoting financial stability by encouraging the development of Islamic capital markets to enhance liquidity and enabling Islamic financial institutions to have more diversified portfolios and sound risk management. Furthermore, this should provide the momentum to integrate the Islamic capital markets within the framework of the international financial system.

The rapid growth of the industry raises some key issues, many of which are discussed in the text. This text will certainly not provide answers to all these issues but at least readers will grasp the flavour of the excitement this industry is generating in both Muslim and non-Muslim financial communities worldwide. A brief summary of the issues needing resolution are provided below:

- How do you create the critical underpinnings of dynamic Islamic capital markets?
- What constitutes a *Sharia'a* compliant product?
- To what extent are the diverging schools of Islamic jurisprudence converging towards a consistent view of *Sharia'a* compliant capital markets?
- Is standardisation really desirable, or necessary, or is the flexibility which current divergence affords the essential lifeblood of innovation in the industry?
- Will Malaysia, with its more liberal interpretation, streamlined structures, recent tax and other incentives become the model investment location for Islamic finance? Or will the Gulf model become the prevalent model by virtue of its current liquidity and stricter rules on *Sharia'a* compliance?
- What will be the role of international banks in driving convergence? To what extent are increased trade, finance and business links in the Middle East and Asia driving this convergence?

Islamic tranches are becoming the norm for project financings in the Middle East and elsewhere. In some cases deals are now being financed Islamically in their entirety. This creates benefits and challenges of Islamic finance for project deals from the issuers' perspective.

The essential role of innovation

- Is it enough for Islamic products to mirror conventional products, or should Islamic finance also aim to be qualitatively different from conventional finance?
- Is Islamic finance equipped to reproduce the entire range of products needed by issuers and provided by conventional banks?

Islamic capital markets in practice – corporate capital raising

The burgeoning *sukuk* market has established new benchmarks in Islamic finance. However many issues still remain:

- What are short- medium- and long-term prospects for the *sukuk* market? There are issues of performance, returns and so on.
- What are the essential limitations of *sukuk* as a fund raising and investment vehicle?
- Innovations: for example the role of convertibles and other innovations in broadening international appeal.
- The role of ratings in stimulating market growth.
- Creating a transparent and credible secondary market for *sukuk* – challenges and progress.
- What are the challenges in creating a trading culture from today's buy-and-hold investor practice? To what extent will regional and international co-operation, for example cross listings, serve to stimulate the market?
- Resolving the critical infrastructure issues such as lack of market makers.
- To what extent are differing cultural attitudes to trading an impediment to the development of secondary trading?
- What are the prospects for growth of *sukuk* issuance in the non-Islamic world?
- How suitable are *sukuk* and other Islamic instruments as fund raising instruments for international companies?
- What are the advantages, limitations and challenges for *sukuk*?

Opportunities, challenges and pitfalls in Islamic asset and fund management

- The mechanism of Islamic investing: documentation and approval process – the role of the *Sharia'a* Boards and organisational structures.
- What are the drivers for the current interest in Islamic investment?
- To what extent are Islamic investments essentially ethical investments, and what are the prospects for attracting both other ethical investors, and non-ethical investors to Islamic funds?
- Virtue versus vice – performance and returns: what is the outlook for Islamic fund performance given the constraints imposed on Islamic investment portfolios?
- Market growth potential: role of Islamic indices in growing the market.

- Prospects for *Sharia'a* funds in real estate, equities, commodities etc.
- How are different schools of Islamic thought converging on the definition of what is *Sharia'a* compliant with regard to derivatives?
- What constitutes acceptable mechanisms for Islamic derivatives, and how does documentation differ from more conventional products?
- Are derivatives a bridge too far – can derivatives really be considered *Sharia'a* compliant?

Private equity and venture capital

- Opportunities and limitations of Islamic private equity and venture capital investments.
- Meeting the legal, regulatory and judicial requirements.
- What are the limitations to growth of Islamic private equity and venture capital?
- To what extent will companies agree to *Sharia'a* Board scrutiny?

Islamic securitisation: an emerging asset class in Islamic capital markets

The use of Islamic securitisation and the range of assets being securitised are on the increase. Practitioners believe that, in the future, securitisation may well replace traditional bank lending as the preferred funding option for many companies. Vast opportunities for originators accrue from a liberated balance sheet, a high profile deal for both the originator and issuer and a healthy investment for the buy side. Not surprisingly Islamic securitisation is on the increase. The growing enthusiasm and receptiveness for these issues has led to a widening of the accessible asset base for securitisation and has stimulated innovation by issuers.

- How do Islamic securitisations compare to conventional structures? Are they essentially more secure than conventional structures by virtue of the additional credit enhancements required?
- What are the legal and other obstacles to the development of Islamic securitisations?
- To what extent is the growing prominence of international banks, with their lower cost of capital, and hence competitive pricing proposition squeezing out the local Islamic banks for the provision of Islamic finance, and what are the consequences for the market going forward?
- To what extent can international banks take a lead by virtue of their superior distribution network and broader capital markets expertise?
- How can international banks overcome the fact that they are not Islamic?

- How can local Islamic markets respond, for instance, by becoming more competitive, or by developing a unique 'value proposition' through community initiatives and so on?
- To what extent will access to much needed skills, such as *Sharia'a* competency, determine the competitive positions of local versus international Islamic banks?
- What is the most effective route to success in Islamic banking – international banks acquiring Islamic know-how, or Islamic banks acquiring international capital markets expertise?

London and the growth of Islamic capital markets

London is becoming a rival Islamic financial centre to the likes of the GCC countries, South-East Asia and Pakistan. British Prime Minister Gordon Brown has stated that he would like to see the city of London taking the appropriate steps to becoming a prominent Islamic finance centre. In the past few years whether you look at the retail market or the wholesale market, the UK government has been pro-active, especially in changing tax regulations to facilitate Islamic finance. It changed the ***sukuk*** rules in 2007 so that they are treated as bonds rather than leasing products.

But is London really going to emerge as a threat to the GCC or South-East Asian centres? Many consider London has now left even New York behind as the global financial hub, with its own advantages of a solid infrastructure, a favourable tax regime and the people and systems in place. There is no doubt the capabilities are there. And there are politics, too. The UK Government is keen to promote contact with the Islamic population. So, how much competition will London be for the Gulf? Participants recognise that the local players will still be based in the region. The secondary market potentially may become London because it will be centralised that way. The trading desks are already in situ. As the world of Islamic finance evolves there will be competition between the financial centres.

Contents

Chapter 1
Muslim beliefs

Islam is the name of the religion transmitted by the Prophet Muhammad as revealed to him by God (Allah). Central to Islamic beliefs is The *Qur'an* which may be defined as 'the book containing the speech of God revealed to the Prophet Muhammad in Arabic and transmitted to us by continuous testimony'. It is deemed a proof of the prophecy of Muhammad, is the most authoritative guide for Muslims, and is the first source of the *Sharia'a.* The *ulama* (religious scholars) are unanimous on this, and some even say that it is the only source and that all other sources are explanatory to the *Qur'an*. The salient attributes of the *Qur'an,* that are indicated in this definition, may be summarised as five: it was revealed exclusively to the Prophet Muhammad; it was put into writing; it is all *mutawatir* (universally accurately reported); it is the inimitable speech of God; and it is recited in *salah* (ritual prayer).

Five pillars of faith

The structure of Islam, like any other structure, is founded on pillars. Just as the strength and stability of any structure depends on the strength and stability of its pillars, the strength and stability of Islam depends on its pillars. Muslims are duty-bound to acquaint themselves with the nature of Islam's pillars.

During the 10 years between his arrival in Medina and his death in AD 632, Mohammed laid the foundation for the ideal Islamic state. A core of committed Muslims was established, and a community life was ordered according to the requirements of the new religion. In addition to general moral injunctions, the requirements of the religion came to include a number of institutions that continue to characterise Islamic religious practice today.

Foremost among these institutions were the five pillars of Islam. These are the essential religious duties required of every adult Muslim who is mentally able. The five pillars are each described in some part of the *Qur'an* and were already practiced during Mohammed's lifetime. They are the profession of faith (*Shahada*), prayer (*Salat*), almsgiving (*zakat*), fasting (*sawm*), and pilgrimage (*hajj*).

Although some of these practices had precedents in Jewish, Christian, and other Middle Eastern religious traditions, taken together they distinguish Islamic religious practices from those of other religions. The five pillars are thus the most central rituals of Islam and constitute the core practices of the Islamic faith.

1. Profession of Faith

The absolute focus of Islamic piety is *Allah*, the supreme, all knowing, all-powerful, God. The Arabic word *Allah* means 'the God,' and this God is understood to be the God who brought the world into being and sustains it to its end. By obeying God's commands, human beings express their recognition of and gratitude for the wisdom of creation, and live in harmony with the universe.

The profession of faith, or witness to faith (*Shahada*), is therefore the prerequisite for membership in the Muslim community. On several occasions during a typical day, and in the saying of daily prayers, a Muslim repeats the profession, 'I bear witness that there is no God but Allah and that Mohammed is his prophet'. There are no formal restrictions on the times and places these words can be repeated.

To become a member of the Muslim community, a person has to profess and act upon this belief in the Oneness of God (*Tawhid*) and the prophethood of Mohammed. To be a true profession of faith which represents a relationship between the speaker and God, the verbal utterance must express genuine knowledge of its meaning as well as sincere belief. A person's deeds can be subjected to scrutiny by other Muslims, but a person's utterance of the profession of faith is sufficient evidence of membership of the Muslim community.

2. Five Daily Prayers

The second pillar of Islam is the religious duty to perform five prescribed daily prayers or *Salat*. All adult Muslims are obliged to perform five prayers, preceded by ritual cleansing or purification of the body at different intervals of the day. The *Qur'anic* references also mention the acts of standing, bowing, and prostrating during prayers and facing a set direction, known as *qibla*. Muslims were first required to face Jerusalem during prayer, but already during Mohammed's lifetime they were commanded to face the *Kaaba*, an ancient shrine in the city of Mecca.

The most detailed descriptions of the rituals for prayer derive from the example set by the prophet Mohammed and are preserved in later Islamic traditions (*ahadith*). Some details of these rituals vary. However all Muslims agree that there are five required daily prayers to be performed at certain times of day: dawn (*fajr* or *subh*), noon (*zuhr*), mid afternoon (*asr*), sunset (*maghrib*) and evening (*isha*). The dawn, noon and sunset prayers do not start exactly at dawn, noon and sunset; instead, they begin just after, to distinguish the Islamic ritual from earlier pagan practices of worshipping the sun when it rises or sets.

A prayer is made up of a sequence of units called bowings (*rak'as*). During each of these units, the worshipper stands, bows, kneels and prostrates while reciting verses from the *Qur'an*. Wherever Muslims live in substantial numbers throughout the world, the call to prayer, or *adhan*, is repeated five times a day by a *muezzin* (crier) from a mosque, the Muslim place of worship.

The Friday noon prayer is led by an *imam*, who is a prayer leader in the Sunni division of Islam. This prayer differs from the usual noon prayers of the other days of the week. As a required part of the ritual at this congregational meeting, two sermons precede the prayer. On other days, Muslims can pray anywhere they wish, either individually or in groups. They must observe the rituals of praying at certain times of day, facing in the direction of Mecca, observing the proper order of prayers, and preparing for prayer through symbolic purification.

3. Zakat or almsgiving

The third pillar of Islam is *zakat* or almsgiving. A religious obligation, *zakat* is considered an expression of devotion to Allah. It represents the attempt to provide for the poorer sectors of society, and it offers a means for a Muslim to purify his or her wealth and attain salvation. The *Qur'an*, together with other Islamic traditions, strongly encourages charity and constantly reminds Muslims of their moral obligation to the poor, orphans and widows. However it distinguishes between general, voluntary charity (*sadaqa*) and *zakat*, the latter being an obligatory charge on the money or produce of Muslims.

4. Sawm or fasting

The fourth pillar of Islam is *sawm*, or fasting. Clear *Qur'anic* references to fasting account for the early introduction of this ritual practice. The *Qur'an* prescribes fasting during the month of Ramadan, the ninth month of the 12-month Islamic lunar year. The month of Ramadan is sacred because the first revelation of the *Qur'an* is said to have occurred during this month. By tradition the month starts with the sighting of the new moon by at least two Muslims. For the entire month, Muslims must fast from daybreak to sunset and refrain from eating, drinking and sexual intercourse. Menstruating women, travellers and sick people are exempted from fasting, but have to make up the days they miss at a later date.

According to various traditional interpretations, the fast introduces physical and spiritual discipline, serves to remind the rich of the misfortunes of the poor, and fosters, through this rigorous act of worship, a sense of solidarity and mutual care among Muslims of all social backgrounds.

5. Pilgrimage to Mecca

The fifth pillar requires that Muslims who have the physical and financial ability should perform the pilgrimage, or *hajj*, to Mecca at least once in a lifetime. The ritual of pilgrimage was practiced by Arabs before the rise of Islam and continues from the early days of Islam.

The *hajj* is distinct from other pilgrimages. It must take place during the 12th lunar month of the year, known as *Dhu al-Hijja*, and it involves a set and detailed sequence of rituals that are practiced over the span of several days. All pilgrimage rituals take place in the city of Mecca and its surroundings, and the primary focus of these rituals is a cubical structure called the *Kaaba*.

According to Islamic tradition (*hadith*), the *Kaaba*, also referred to as the House of God, was built at God's command by the prophet Ibrahim (Abraham of the Hebrew and Christian Bibles) and his son Ismail (Ishmael). The *Qur'an* provides detailed descriptions of various parts of the ritual, and it portrays many of these rituals as re-enactments of the activities undertaken by Ibrahim and Ismail in the course of building the *Kaaba*. Set into one corner of the *Kaaba* is the sacred Black Stone which, according to one Islamic tradition (*hadith*), was given to Ibrahim by the angel Gabriel.

Once pilgrims arrive in Mecca, ritual purification is performed. Many men shave their heads, and men and women put on seamless white sheets. This simple and common dress symbolises the equality of all Muslims before God, a status further reinforced by the prohibition of jewellery, perfumes and sexual intercourse. After this ritual purification, Muslims circle the *Kaaba* seven times, run between al-Safa and al-Marwa, two hills overlooking the *Kaaba*, seven times, and perform several prayers and invocations.

After these opening rituals, the *hajj* proper commences on the seventh day and continues for the next three days. Again, it starts with the performance of ritual purification followed by a prayer at the *Kaaba* mosque. The pilgrims then assemble at Mina, a hill outside Mecca, where they spend the night. The next morning they go to the nearby plain of Arafat, where they stand from noon to sunset and perform a series of prayers and rituals. The pilgrims then head to Muzdalifa, a location halfway between Arafat and Mina, to spend the night. The next morning, the pilgrims head back to Mina, on the way stopping at stone pillars symbolising Satan, at which they throw seven pebbles.

The final ritual is the slaughter of an animal (sheep, goat, cow, or camel). This is a symbolic re-enactment of God's command to Ibrahim to sacrifice his son Ismail, which Ibrahim and Ismail duly accepted and were about to execute when God allowed Ibrahim to slaughter a ram in place of his son. (In the Hebrew and Christian Bibles, Abraham is called to sacrifice his son Isaac rather than Ishmael.)

Most of the meat of the slaughtered animals is to be distributed to poor Muslims. The ritual sacrifice ends the *hajj* and starts the festival of the sacrifice, *'id al-adha*. The festivals of breaking fast (*'id al-fitr*) at the end of Ramadan and *'id al-adha* are the two major Islamic festivals celebrated by Muslims all over the world.

During the pilgrimage most Muslims visit Medina, where the tomb of the Prophet is located, before returning to their homes. If the pilgrimage rituals are performed at any time of the year other than the designated time for *hajj*, the ritual is called *umra*. Although *umra* is considered a virtuous act, it does not absolve the person from the obligation of *hajj*.

Six Islamic Creeds

As mentioned above the Prophet Mohammed declared that one of the five pillars is the principle that, 'There is no god but Allah; Mohammed is the Apostle of Allah'. To Muslims this principle is known as *Iman*.

Definition of Iman

Iman (faith) is to proclaim the following *Kalimah* (principle) and affirm its truth. By proclaiming the *Kalimah*, Muslims express their beliefs in the following Articles of Faith:

1) existence and Attributes of Allah;
2) destiny (*Qada'ar*);
3) angels;
4) prophets;
5) revealed books;
6) The Hereafter.

Belief in these six Articles together forms the Creed of Islam. Belief in any one of these implies belief in the others as well, and rejection of one implies rejection of all.

Iman as basis of righteous deeds

Iman is the basis of acts of worship and righteous deeds in Islam. Without the firm foundation of *Iman*, no act of worship and no deed, however sincerely and devotedly performed Muslims believe, will be acceptable to Allah.

1. Belief in Allah and his attributes

The Islamic reasoning behind the first Article of Faith is as follows:

1) The unimaginably vast universe around us, which contains millions of stars and planets and galactic systems, cannot have come about by mere chance, by material and physical accident or by a chain of accidents, but has been created by Allah in accordance with His will and design.
2) Allah is the creator of each and every thing in the universe. Nothing has come into being of its own accord; and everything depends on Allah for its existence and survival.
3) Allah is eternal: He is ever-living and will never cease to be.

4) Allah is one: everything depends on Him, but he depends on none. He is All-Powerful, and none has the power to change or evade His will or verdict. He has neither parents, nor offspring, nor clan.
5) Allah is unique both in His essence and attributes. He exists by Himself and is Self-sufficient, and does not stand in need of anybody else's aid to establish His rights and powers.
6) Nothing is beyond Him: nothing conceivable is beyond His control and power. He is above every conceivable defect, weakness or fault.
7) Allah is the real sovereign of the whole universe: He is the source of all sovereignty: everything is functioning according to His will.
8) Allah is the real source and centre of all power: no power exists besides His.
9) Allah is omnipresent: He watches over everything: nothing is hidden from Him either in the depths of the earth or in the limitless vastnesses of the heavens. He is the knower of the unseen and is fully aware of man's intentions, thoughts, feelings, even hidden motives. He possesses full and exact knowledge of what has happened in the past, or will happen in the future.
10) Life and death are completely under His control: He grants life to whomsoever He wills and brings death to whomsoever He wills.
11) The treasure houses of everything are with Allah: none can bestow anything on anyone whom He wills to deprive, and none can withstand anything from anybody whom He wills to favour.
12) Bestowing of gains or inflicting of losses is entirely in Allah's hands: none can ward off a misfortune that He wills one to suffer, and none can stop a good life that He wills one to enjoy.
13) Allah is the provider of every creature: all provisions of life are under His control. He is fully aware of the needs of His creations and provides them accordingly. He restricts His provisions or gives generously to whomsoever He wills.
14) Allah is just, all-knowing, all-wise: His decrees are just. He does not deprive anyone of his due. For Him good and evil are not equal: He will reward and punish everyone according to his deeds. He will neither punish a sinner unduly nor deprive a righteous worker of his rewards.
15) Allah has great love for His creatures: he forgives their sins, accepts their repentances and is ever merciful to them. A believer should never lose hope of His mercy and grace.
16) Allah alone deserves to be loved: one should seek only His pleasure and approval.
17) Allah alone deserves to be thanked, worshipped, adored and none else.

18) Allah alone has the right to be worshipped and His law obeyed unconditionally.

19) Allah alone deserves to be feared: He alone can fulfil hopes and grant prayers and give help and succour in difficulties and hardships.

20) Allah alone can show guidance: none can misguide the one whom Allah wills to guide, and none can show guidance to the one whom He has deprived of guidance.

Muslims would further reason that the worst people on the earth are those who disbelieve in Allah, reject His guidance, make others His associates and worship their own selves and desires instead of Him. Accursed are the ones who die as disbelievers, because they only earn the displeasure of Allah and the everlasting torment and ignominy of the Hereafter. Holding others as partners in Allah's Godhead is a falsehood and a most heinous sin. This is known as ***shirk*** (blasphemy). Allah will forgive all other sins but not the sin of ***shirk***. As it says in the *Qur'an*:

> '***Shirk*** is the only sin that Allah does not forgive. He may forgive whosoever He will, other than this sin, for whose associate's partners with Allah does, in fact, go far astray into deviation'.
>
> (S4: 116)

2. Belief in Destiny (*Qada'ar*)

The second Islamic Article of Faith is the belief in one's destiny is an integral part of one's belief in Allah's existence and His Attributes, and the *Qur'an* mentions it as such. The traditions (***hadith***) of the Holy Prophet mention it as a separate and independent article of the faith.

Belief in destiny implies that all good and evil that takes place in the world, or will take place in future is from Allah and in His knowledge. His knowledge is all-comprehensive and nothing of good or evil is outside it. Allah's knowledge comprehends all the good or evil deeds that man will commit after his birth. Not a particle moves anywhere in the universe but its movement is within Allah's knowledge and in accordance with His will. No power can deprive or withhold from a creature anything which has been pre-ordained for it by Allah, and none can provide a creature with anything of which Allah has deprived it. Allah is the Maker of all destinies, good or otherwise.

The teaching of Islam, in this regard, is that one should continue doing as much good as one can. One should avoid violating or neglecting religious commands and injunctions.

3. Belief in angels

The Islamic reasoning behind the third Article of Faith is as follows:

1) Angels have been created from light and are invisible, are of neither sex, and have been appointed by Allah to carry out His Commands.

2) Angels are helpless creatures and cannot do anything out of their own will. They carry out, without question, all the Commands of Allah and dare not oppose or neglect them in any way.
3) They are engaged day and night in praising and glorifying Allah and are never tired of this.
4) They remain in awe of Him and can never so much as think of disobeying or revolting against Him.
5) They carry out their respective functions honestly, efficiently and responsibly and are never guilty of shirking work.
6) The number of angels is only known to Allah Himself; four of them, however, are well-known, being nearest to Him in status and position. They are:

   Gabriel: whose duty has been to convey Allah's revelations and messages to the Prophets. He no longer performs this duty given that the institution of Prophet has come to an end with the arrival of The Holy Prophet Mohammed.

   Israfil: who by Allah's Command will blow into the trumpet on the Day of Judgment and bring the present system and order of the world to an end.

   Michael: whose duty is to arrange for rainfall and supply provisions to the creations of Allah, with His Command.

   'Izra'il: who has been appointed to take the people's souls.
7) Two angels have been attached to every human being: one to record his good deeds and the other his bad deeds. They are called *Kiraman Katibin*.
8) Two angels, called Munkar and Nakir, are sent to the grave to question a person after his death.

4. Belief in apostles

The Islamic reasoning behind the fourth Article of Faith is as follows:

1) The arrangement made by Allah to convey his messages and commands for the guidance of mankind is called Apostleship and those chosen for the mission are known as Apostles, Messengers or Prophets.
2) The Apostles have been conveying the Divine messages most scrupulously without tampering with them in any way.
3) Apostleship is God-given and cannot be acquired by effort and will.
4) All the Apostles have been men, and none of them was an angel, or *jinn* (evil spirit), or any other creature. Their only distinction was that God had chosen them as His Messengers and sent down His revelations to them.
5) The Apostles have faithfully practised what they presented and preached. They have been a perfect and true practical model of their teachings.
6) The Apostles were sent in every age and to every community and country. Muslims must believe in all the Apostles and reject none. They have to

express complete faith in those of them who have been mentioned in the *Qur'an* and *Hadith* and hold them in the highest esteem.

7) All the Prophets gave the same message and invitation. Therefore rejection of one will indeed be rejection of all.
8) Belief in a Prophet implies that one should follow him in life faithfully and completely.
9) The institution of prophethood came to an end with the arrival of The Prophet Mohammed. He was the Last of the chain of Prophets. No Prophet is to appear after him. His prophethood, therefore, will last and remain effective until the Day of Judgment.
10) The personal example set by the Prophet Mohammed is the most perfect model for all his followers in all spheres of life. His verdict is decisive in all religious matters. A Muslim has to follow faithfully and sincerely all that he has enjoined and to avoid all that he has forbidden.
11) Obedience to the Prophet is obedience to Allah and disobedience of the Prophet is disobedience of Allah. Love of Allah, therefore, demands that one should obey the Prophet for that alone is the test of one's firmness in the faith.
12) Another proof of one's faith is the extent of honour and esteem in which one holds the Prophet generally. Any insolence or impudence shown with regard to the Prophet is destructive of all one's works of the lifetime. The *Qur'an* says:

    > 'O you who believe! do not raise your voices above the Prophet's voice, nor speak loudly to him as you speak loudly to one another, lest your deeds become null, while you know not'.
    >
    > (S.49: 2)

    Muslims are honour-bound to regard the Holy Prophet dearer than their own parents, children and near and dear ones, even oneself. The *Qur'an* is explicit on this point:

    > 'The Prophet is closer to the Believers than their own selves'.
    >
    > (S.33: 6)

13) The belief in prophethood demands that Muslims should invoke Allah for His mercy and blessings on the Holy Prophet:

    > 'O believers! Call for blessings on him and salute him with a (becoming) salutation'.
    >
    > (S.33: 56)

5. Belief in the Revealed Books

The Islamic reasoning behind the fifth Article of Faith is as follows:

1) Allah sent down Scriptures for the guidance of mankind to teach man how to lead life in the right way. The Prophets demonstrated, by personal example, the meanings of these Scriptures.

2) Belief in all the revealed Books is necessary, for basically they all taught one and the same creed, viz to worship and serve Allah alone and to avoid ***shirk***.

3) Five of the Scriptures revealed to five of the well-known Prophets are:
Sahifah Ibrahim: revealed to Prophet Abraham
The *Torah*: revealed to Prophet Moses
The Psalms: revealed to Prophet David
The Gospel: revealed to Prophet Jesus
The *Qur'an*: revealed to Prophet Mohammed

4) Out of these revealed Books Muslims believe that only the *Qur'an* is intact, exists in its original form and will remain so until the Last Day. Muslims believe that Allah has taken it on Himself to preserve it:

   'Surely We have sent down the *Qur'an*, and surely We are its Preserver'.
   (S.15: 9)

5) The other four revealed Books have, Muslims reason, been irrevocably tampered with and none exist in their original form today. These Books were compiled long after the passing away of the Prophets and, Muslims reason, people inserted many things into them, which were opposed to their actual teachings. Thus the *Qur'an* is the only authentic and safe guide today in order to know, and understand the practice of the original guidance sent down by Allah.

6) No one has the authority to effect any alteration in the *Qur'an* in any way. The Prophet himself was not authorised to do so; his only mission was to follow and practise it faithfully. To interpret the *Qur'an* according to one's personal whims and reading one's own meaning into its verses is highly sinful.

7) The *Qur'an* gives clear guidance for the solution of all human problems, personal and collective. Muslims believe that ignoring its guidance in any sphere of life or adopting and following other laws in preference to the *Qur'anic* Laws is sinful.

6. Belief in the Hereafter

The Islamic reasoning behind the sixth Article of Faith is as follows:

1) Life is not only this worldly life but the real and eternal life is the life of the Hereafter which starts after death. The next worldly life will be blissful or painful and grievous depending on what one has earned and done in this worldly life. Belief in such a life is called belief in the Hereafter.

2) Every person is visited after death by two angels, called Munkar and Nakir, in the grave, who put to them the following questions:
Who is your Lord?
What is your religion?

What do you say about this man (pointing to the Holy Prophet Mohammed)?

This is the first of the tests in the accountability of the Hereafter.

3) On the first blowing of the Trumpet, the event which Muslims believe precedes the Day of Judgement, the present system and order of the universe will be upset and brought to an end. The earth will be shaken by a terrible earthquake, the mountains will be uprooted and shattered, the sun and the moon will collide, the stars will lose their brightness, and all living creatures will cease to live and the universe will be totally destroyed.

   The Day of Judgment, Muslims believe, is the final day of life on earth and for the universe. At the same time it is the beginning of the eternal life in the Hereafter.

4) Then, on the second blowing of the Trumpet, all the dead will be brought back to life by Allah's Command. This is the Day of Resurrection. A new order will be created in which all human beings will have eternal life and there will be no death. This will be a terrible and dreadful Day. Men will be in awe with downcast heads and eyes, awaiting the Divine verdict.

5) The whole of mankind will be gathered together before their Lord, Who will be the sole Judge and Ruler on that Day. As it says in The *Qur'an* :

> 'The day when all people will rise up (from their graves), nothing about them will remain hidden from Allah. (It will be asked): To whom belongs the sovereignty on this Day? (The whole world will cry out): To Allah, the One, the Almighty'.
>
> (S.40: 16)
>
> 'The sovereignty on that Day rightly belongs to the Beneficent, and it will be a hard Day for the disbelievers'.
>
> (S.25: 26)

   No one will have the heart to utter a word except with Allah's permission. He will call upon each individual separately to account for all his deeds. Then Allah will deliver His verdict in full knowledge, justice and wisdom. Each individual will be recompensed justly and equitably for all his deeds and no-one will be done any injustice whatever.

6) The righteous will be handed their life-scrolls in their right hand, and the sinners will be handed their life-scrolls in their left hand. The former will attain true success and the latter meet with failure. The former will exult in their success with bright and shining faces, while the latter will be burning inwardly with gloomy and dark faces. The righteous will be admitted to Paradise where they will enjoy Allah's favours and life of eternal bliss and peace. The criminals will be cast into Hell to suffer Allah's wrath and displeasure.

7) The Divine verdict on that Day will be final. None will be able to escape it by any trick, device, or design; nor will any saint or prophet intercede for anyone, for intercession will not be possible except by Allah's leave and permission. Nor will it be possible for anyone to return to the world so as to work again to earn one's salvation.

8) All one's deeds and actions, verbal and practical, are being recorded by the angels of Allah in a manner that nothing escapes their notice.

9) None of anyone's doings, big or small, remains hidden from Allah's sight.

10) The Believers will be blessed with such favours and bliss in Paradise that the like of these will never have been conceived by any eye, ear or mind.

11) The rebels of Allah will be cast into the blazing Hell from where they will have no escape. They will neither die to get rid of the everlasting torment nor live to enjoy the good things of life. They will desire death but death will disappoint them. The blaze of Hell will be ever brightening and unquenched. The dwellers will cry with thirst and be given molten metals for drink, which will scald their mouths and throats. They will have heavy collars around their necks and dresses of tar and fire on their bodies. They will be served with thorny bushes for food and will face Allah's wrath at every moment.

12) Who will be admitted to Paradise and who will suffer in Hell is known only to Allah. The Prophets of Allah, however, have clearly indicated and pointed out the works and deeds that enable one to deserve Paradise and the works that will lead one to Hell. It is, therefore, not possible in this world to predict with certainty as to who will be admitted to Paradise, except those who were given the good news of admission into Paradise by the Holy Prophet himself. One may, however, expect this from Allah that He will admit one to Paradise on the basis of the good works that one is performing in this world.

13) Allah in His mercy will forgive any sin that He pleases, but, according to the *Qur'an*, He will not forgive the sin of ***shirk*** and outright rejection of the Truth.

14) A person may believe and repent of sins any time in life; Allah is Gracious and Compassionate to His creatures and accepts their repentance most mercifully. No belief or repentance, however, is acceptable at the time one has reached the point of death and discerned, unmistakably, one's approaching end.

Given this background to Islam the next chapter turns to the legal principles underlying Islamic banking and financial relationships: The *Sharia'a*.

Chapter 2

Sharia'a law and *Sharia'a* Boards: roles, responsibility and membership

> I heard Allah's Messenger say 'The Halāl (permissible) is clear and the Harām (forbidden)' is clear. Between these are matters that are doubtful. Most people do not know whether these are from the Halāl or from the Harām. So, he who leaves it (such matters) to guard his religion (against adulteration) and his integrity has indeed saved himself. He who engages (to any degree) into any of these (doubtful matters) would soon engage in the Harām just as he who grazes (animals) around (another's) territory is likely to enter into it. Be cautious! Each king has a territory. Be cautious! And the (prohibited) territory of Allah is His prohibitions.
> *Hadith* narrated by an bin Bashir R.A.

Objectives of the *Sharia'a*

The flavour of the principles, underlying *Sharia'a* law, can be illustrated by the *ahadith* below:

> 'The basis of the Sharia'a is the wisdom and welfare of the people in this world, as well as the hereafter. This welfare lies in complete justice, mercy, well-being and wisdom. Anything that departs from justice to oppression, from mercy to harshness, from welfare to misery and from wisdom to folly, has nothing to do with the Sharia'a.' (Ibn Al-Qayyim)

> 'The very objective of the Sharia'a is to promote the welfare of the people which lies in safeguarding their faith, their life, their intellect, their posterity and their property. Whatever ensures the safeguard of these objectives serves public interest and is desirable.' (Al-Ghazali)

Sharia'a: the framework of Islamic banking

The origin and basis of Islamic banking is the *Sharia'a*, or Islamic laws, sometimes referred to as Islamic Jurisprudence. In the faith and belief of a Muslim, Islam is the religion revealed by Allah to his last prophet, Mohammad. It is a complete religion, embracing all facets of his mundane activities in this world and his state of affairs in the world hereafter. The teaching of Islam encompasses the essence of economic well-being and development of Muslims at the individual, family, society, state and *Ummah* (or Islamic universal community) levels. Figure 2.1 illustrates the Islamic view of life of a Muslim and the place of his economic activities, including banking and financial activities, within the framework of such a view.

As shown in figure 2.1, Islam may be perceived as comprising three basic elements. The first element is *Aqidah*, which concerns all forms of faith and belief by a Muslim in Allah and His will, from the fundamental faith in His being to the ordinary beliefs in His individual commands (*ahkam*). The second element is *Sharia'a*, which concerns all forms of practical actions by a Muslim manifesting his faith and belief. The third element is *Akhlaq*, which concerns behaviour, attitude and work ethics, within which a Muslim performs his practical day-to-day activities.

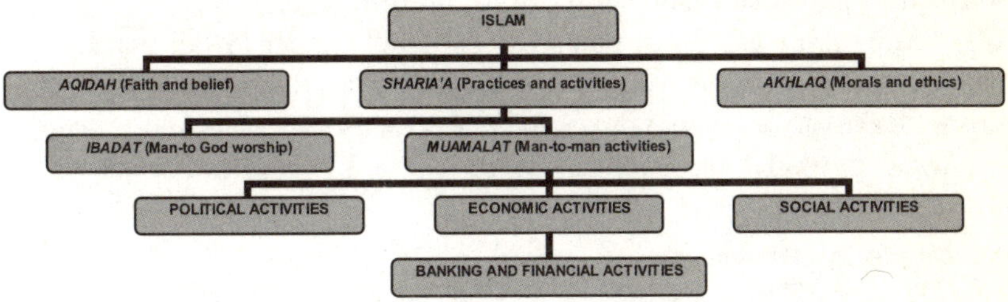

Figure 2.1. Islam, *Sharia'a*, *Muamalat* and banking and finance

Sharia'a, being the practical aspects of a Muslim's daily life, is then divided into two categories: *Ibadat* and *Muamalat*. *Ibadat* is concerned with the practicalities of his worship to Allah, in the context of man-to-Allah relationship. But *Muamalat* is concerned with the practicalities of his mundane daily life, in the context of various forms of man-to-man relationships.

A significant segment of *Muamalat* is the conduct of a Muslim's economic activities within the economic system. Within the economic system one finds the banking and financial system, the place where he conducts his banking and financial activities. Thus, in the Islamic scheme of life and *Sharia'a* framework, a Muslim's banking and financial activities can be traced through his economic activities, back to *Muamalat*, to *Sharia'a*, to Islam, and finally to Allah. This is the root of Islamic banking and finance.

Sharia'a is the religious law of Islam. As Islam makes no distinction between religion and daily life, Islamic law covers not only the rituals but every aspect of life. The actual codification of canonic law is the result of the concurrent evolution of jurisprudence proper and the so-called science of the roots of jurisprudence (*usul al-fiqh*).

A general agreement was reached, in the course of the formalization of Islam, as to the authority of four such roots: the *Qur'an* in its legislative segments; the example of the Prophet as related in the *hadith*; the consensus of the Muslims (*Ijma*), premised on a saying by Muhammad stipulating 'My nation cannot agree on an error;' and reasoning by analogy (*Qiyas*).

Another important principle is *Ijtihad*, the extension of *Sharia'a* to situations neither covered by precedent nor explicable by analogy to other laws. These roots provide the means for the establishment of prescriptive codes of action and for the evaluation of individual and social behaviour. The basic scheme for all actions is a fivefold division of categories and encompasses obligatory, meritorious, permissible, reprehensible and forbidden Islamic modes of conduct.

Numerous schools of jurisprudence (*Madhabs*) emerged in the course of Islamic history. Four co-exist today within Sunni Islam, with one or more dominant in particular areas; Maliki (North and West Africa), Hanafi (Turkic Asia), Shafii (Egypt, East Africa, South-East Asia) and Hanbali (Saudi Arabia). Shiite jurisprudence is often referred to as *Jafari*. While these schools of jurisprudence vary on certain rituals and practices, they are perceived as being complementary rather than mutually exclusive. Box 2.1 provides an explanation of *Sharia'a* terminology.

Box 2.1. *Sharia'a* terminology

Sharia'a: A *Sharia'a* product must meet all the requirements of Islamic law. To facilitate this, a *Sharia'a* Board is usually appointed. This board or committee is usually comprised of Islamic scholars available to the organisation, for guidance and supervision, for the development of *Sharia'a* compliant products.

***Sharia'a* advisor**: This means an independent professional, usually a classically trained Islamic legal scholar, appointed to advise an Islamic financial organisation, on the compliance of its products and services with Islamic law, the *Sharia'a*. While some organisations consult individual *Sharia'a* advisors, most establish a committee of *Sharia'a* advisors.

***Sharia'a* compliant**: This means ensuring that the requirements of the *Sharia'a* law are being observed. The term is often used in the Islamic banking industry as a synonym for Islamic. For example, *Sharia'a* compliant financing or *Sharia'a* compliant investment.

Compliance with the scheme of Sharia'a laws

Within the Islamic scheme of life, Islam imposes its *ahkam* (laws), in modern terminology norms or values, on its believers. These laws or values are not man-made. Instead they are ordained by Allah. These laws are derived from the sources of *Sharia'a*. The two primary sources are:

1) *Qur'an*
2) *Sunnah*

These laws, as derived from the above sources, are arranged into the following five level scheme of:

1) *Fard* or *Wajib*: an obligatory duty, the omission of which is punishable Islamically.
2) *Mandub* or *Mustahab*: an action which is rewarded Islamically, but the avoidance of which is not punishable.
3) *Jaiz* or *Mubah*: an action which is permitted, with the law being indifferent.
4) *Makruh*: an action which is disliked Islamically yet not punishable, but the avoidance of which is rewarded.
5) *Haram*: an action which is absolutely forbidden and punishable Islamically.

Banking and financial activities, being part and parcel of Islamic *Muamalat*, are therefore subject to the *Sharia'a* law on *Muamalat.*

Sharia'a Islamic investment principles

It is forbidden for any Islamic institution or investment fund to deal in the following goods:

- alcoholic drinks and related activities;
- pork, ham, bacon and related by-products;
- dead animals (or those not slaughtered according to the rules of the *Sharia'a*);
- products associated with gambling such as gambling machines;
- tobacco and other drugs;
- activities associated with pornography;
- gold and silver except for spot cash;
- armaments and destructive weapons.

According to the principles of Islamic jurisprudence the payment and receipt of interest is a grave sinful act, for which the participant is responsible in the Hereafter. Since almost all companies deal with some form of interest or otherwise prohibited activity, some *Sharia'a* Advisory Boards have determined an upper limit as to what percentage of a company's income can be earned through interest and/or such activities. It would be unacceptable to invest in a firm that exceeds these limits. These limits are evolving and, as a result, becoming more sophisticated and nuanced. Companies that may have been excluded under simplistic models a few years ago (for example, due to large cash holdings) may now be acceptable under newer *Sharia'a* models.

Conditions for investment in shares

In the light of the foregoing discussion, dealing in equity shares can be acceptable in *Sharia'a* subject to the following conditions:

1) The main business of the company is not in violation of *Sharia'a*. This means that it is not permissible to acquire the shares of companies providing financial services associated with interest, such as conventional banks and insurance companies. Companies involved in some other business not approved by the *Sharia'a*, such as companies manufacturing, selling or offering alcohol, pork, *haram* meat, or involved in gambling, night club activities, pornography and so on are forbidden.

2) If the main business of the companies is *halal,* such as computers, cars and textiles but the companies involved deposit their surplus amounts in an interest-bearing account or borrow money paying interest, a Muslim shareholder must express his disapproval against such dealings. This should preferably be done by raising his voice against such activities in the annual general meeting of the company.

3) If some income from interest-bearing accounts is included in the income of the company, the proportion of such income in the dividend paid to the shareholder must be given to charity, and must not be retained by the investor. For example if 5% of the total income of a company has come out of interest-bearing deposits, then 5% of the dividend must be given to charity.

   In other words where profits are earned through dividends, a certain proportion of the dividend, which corresponds to the proportion of interest earned by the company, must be given to charity. Islamic scholars have termed this process 'purification'.

   Sharia'a Scholars have different views about whether purification is necessary where the profits are made through capital gains (such as by purchasing the shares at a lower price and selling them at a higher price). Some scholars are of the view that, even in the case of capital gains, the process of purification is necessary because the market price of the share may reflect an element of leverage so interest payments have boosted the performance of the company. Other scholars reason that no purification is required if the share is sold, even if the activity results in a capital gain.

4) The shares of a company are negotiable (and can be freely invested in) only if the company owns some non-liquid assets. If all the assets of a company

are in liquid form, or in the form of money that cannot be purchased or sold, except at par value, then these shares cannot be purchased. In this case the share represents money only and, Islamically, money cannot be traded except at par.

What should be the exact proportion of non-liquid assets of a company enabling the negotiability of its shares? Contemporary scholars have different views about this question. Some scholars are of the view that the ratio of non-liquid assets must be 51% at the very least. They argue that if such assets are less than 50%, then most of the assets are in liquid form, and therefore, all its assets should be treated as liquid, on the basis of the juristic principle: 'The majority deserves to be treated as the whole of a thing.' Other scholars have opined that even if the non-liquid assets of a company are 33%, its shares can be treated as negotiable.

Sharia'a Supervisory Board (SSB)

To ensure that their financial activities are in conformity with the *Sharia'a* law, religious supervisory boards are mandatory for Islamic banks and Islamic financial institutions. Also called the *Sharia'a* supervisory committee or sometimes *Sharia'a* Supervisory Board (SSB), the SSB examines contracts, dealings and transactions to assure that Islamic beliefs are being implemented.

The SSB guarantees, and certifies, that the banking activities are *halal* (permissible). The SSB is merely an advisory body, but nevertheless it has an authoritative and respected function as the bank entrusts the SSB with questions as to the permissibility of its activities.

Function and responsibilities

The three central responsibilities of an SSB are:

1) to make sure that banking facilities and services are in accordance with Islam,

2) to guarantee that the bank's investments and involvement in projects are *Sharia'a* compliant, and

3) to ensure that the bank is managed in concordance with Islamic values.

In its articles of association the Faisal Bank of Egypt stated that, 'A Religious Supervisory Board shall be formed within the Bank to observe conformance of its dealings and actions with the principles and rulings of the *Sharia'a*.'

The International Association of Islamic Banks (IAIB) has chosen a more scrupulous clarification of the duties imposed on its supervisory committee.

In Article 2 of the Board's Statute, IAIB has entrusted its SSB with the following duties:

1) to study *fatawas* previously issued, assess its constituency with the *Sharia'a* and, when appropriate, base its own rulings on these decisions,

2) to supervise the activities of the bank in order to guarantee conformity with the *Sharia'a* law,
3) to issue religious opinions on banking and financial questions, and
4) to clarify legal religious rulings on new economic issues.

Sharia'a Boards: roles and scope of responsibilities

Sharia'a advisors have both supervisory and consultancy functions. Categorically, the overall applications of the *Sharia'a* by *Sharia'a* advisors have a two-fold objective. Firstly, the *Sharia'a* advisors review the operations of the institutions participating in the Islamic financial markets, ensuring that they comply with the requirements of the *Sharia'a*. This is, to a large extent, equivalent to a supervisory role.

Secondly, in the increasingly complex and sophisticated world of modern and dynamic Islamic finance, *Sharia'a* advisors endeavour to answer any issues or concerns for a particular transaction or product conformation with the *Sharia'a*. Where deemed necessary, they offer constructive, creative and/or alternative recommendations. This is, to a large extent, a consultancy role.

Institutions participating in the Islamic financial markets are required to establish operating policies and procedures to ensure that their activities, investments or operations, are undertaken in line with *Sharia'a* requirements. *Sharia'a* advisors are expected to participate and engage themselves actively in deliberating the *Sharia'a* issues put before them. Amongst the duties and responsibilities of the *Sharia'a* advisors that are prevalent in the Islamic financial markets are to:

- ***Review the products and services to ensure conformity with Sharia'a requirements***. In the Islamic investment industry *Sharia'a* advisors are responsible for ensuring that the funds they oversee are managed and administered in accordance with the principles of the *Sharia'a*. This also includes the responsibility to provide expertise and guidance, to the investment management companies and fund managers in all matters relating to the principles of the *Sharia'a* pertaining to the fund, including the trust deed, the prospectus, the investments of the fund and other operational and administrative matters.
- ***Review and endorse relevant documents.*** In order to be *Sharia'a* compliant, Islamic financial market products and services need to undergo a pre-defined vetting and endorsement process by *Sharia'a* advisors. The *Sharia'a* advisor's role is to advise on all aspects of Islamic securities, including documentation, structuring, investment as well as other administrative and operational matters and to ensure compliance with applicable *Sharia'a* principles and relevant resolutions. In the course of

reviewing and endorsing the documentation the basic principle that must be adhered to, is that no other person is competent enough to ensure that the documentation conforms and is consistent with the contemplated *Sharia'a* transaction, other than the *Sharia'a* advisor.

- ***Supervise investments made by the institutions in the Islamic financial markets***. Another integral role of the *Sharia'a* advisor is to supervise and ensure that the investments made by these institutions, comply with the *Sharia'a*. In this case, the *Sharia'a* advisor must ensure that the fund managers invest only in securities classified as *Sharia'a* approved by the *Sharia'a* Board.
- ***Deliberate on Sharia'a issues pertaining to the day-to-day operations of the institutions and provide advice accordingly***. In the day-to-day operations of these institutions, there are various *Sharia'a* issues that the practitioners will come across, particularly those with regard to the practice and implementation of financial transactions. These issues are usually not covered by text books or the theoretical framework of a particular transaction. Thus, *Sharia'a* advisors are compelled to understand and resolve these issues. By and large, this requires them to be closely involved with the actual practice and implementation side, as this gives them a more comprehensive and deeper understanding of the issues that they are dealing with.
- ***Conduct research and development of new products***. As the financial system advances, the need for Islamic financial institutions to compete, not only with the existing but also upcoming conventional products, requires *Sharia'a* advisors to develop or approve innovative new products which are competitive and acceptable to all. Some of the more complex financial areas requiring *Sharia'a* compliant innovation, are risk management, hedging tools, derivatives and hybrid financing facilities. When *Sharia'a* advisors are equipped with the essentials of both the *fiqh* and the *Muamalat*, especially concerning capital and asset management principles, it is intended that they develop Islamically acceptable financial products.
- ***Provide training and education on Muamalat, based on Sharia'a contracts***. The large growing pool of Islamic-finance practitioners must be well informed and systematically educated in order to prepare them with the necessary knowledge for managing Islamic financing activities. In the course of developing the Islamic financial market its dynamic nature must be recognised and complacency should be avoided. The dissemination process must be continuous, in order to train as many practitioners as possible, so as to provide successors who are well trained prior to succeeding their superiors. Since the *Sharia'a* advisors are those who possess the knowledge in *Muamalat*, it is pertinent that they lead the way in imparting knowledge

to these practitioners as well as to society in general. This is vital towards achieving a true and accurate understanding of the *Sharia'a* and the application of the nominate contracts in *Muamalat*.

- ***Assist related parties on Sharia'a matters and provide advice upon request***. The related parties of the institutions in the Islamic financial market, such as their legal counsels, auditors and consultants, may seek advice on *Sharia'a* matters from the *Sharia'a* advisors. These are expected to provide the necessary assistance so that full compliance with *Sharia'a* principles can be assured. Over and above this, they must also explain the *Sharia'a* issues and the recommendations offered for a particular decision. These opinions must be supported by the relevant *Sharia'a* jurisprudential literature from established sources.

Dubai Islamic Bank (DIB)

At DIB the *Fatwa* and *Sharia'a* supervision board oversees the application of different aspects of *Sharia'a*. It also ensures that all the transactions are in strict compliance with the *Sharia'a* principles. The board is further empowered with the right of contradicting any violating procedures, if found. The board of directors is obligated to obey the *fatawas*, irrespective of whether a unanimous or a majority consensus secured the decision (clause 78 of the Bank's Memorandum & Articles of Association). *Sharia'a* Board meetings are held periodically or whenever the need arises. The rights of the board are enshrined in Article Seven of the Bank's Memorandum & Articles of Association (Clauses 74-84). Box 2.2 provides details of the functions of the DIB's *Sharia'a* Board.

Sharia'a Board scholar qualifications

The qualifications necessary to become a *Sharia'a* Scholar are not defined in any formalised manner from, say, some central institution, as one would find in most professional bodies such as solicitors, architects etc. However a glance at the CVs of some of the better known scholars, listed below, provide a flavour of the qualifications needed to be a *Sharia'a* Board Scholar. The nine abbreviated CVs of prominent *Sharia'a* Board Scholars listed below indicate the depth of experience needed by *Sharia'a* Board members. The *Sharia'a* Board requirements for the State Bank of Pakistan are also described.

Box 2.2. Duties of the DIB *Sharia'a* Board

As an expert source on Islamic principles (including *fatawas*), the board, through a representative, usually the general secretary of the board, supervises the *Sharia'a* compliance of all the transactions in the bank.

To devote time and effort to devising more *Sharia'a* compliant transactional procedures, templates and banking products that enable the bank to adapt to market trends, while maintaining a competitive edge in deposit procedures, investments, and banking services. At the same time, the board gives its opinion on proposed new templates and banking transactions.

Analysing unprecedented situations that are not covered by *fatwa* in the bank's transactional procedures or those reported by different departments, branches and sometimes the customers. This is to ensure *Sharia'a* compliance before the bank develops any new products or implements any new procedures.

Analysing contracts and agreements concerning the bank's transactions, as submitted by the chairman of the board of directors or any department or branch within the bank or requested by the board itself in order that *Sharia'a* compliance can be evaluated and maintained.

Ensuring *Sharia'a* compliance in the implementation of all banking transactions and correcting any breaches.

Analysing administrative decisions, issues and matters that require the board's approval.

Supervising *Sharia'a* training programmes for the bank's staff.

Preparing an annual report on the bank's balance sheet, with respect to its *Sharia'a* compliance.

The *Fatwa* and *Sharia'a* Supervision Board submits a complete annual report for the board of directors, summarizing all the issues referred to the board, as well as its opinion on the bank's transactional procedures.

Source: *DIB*

Dr Hussain Hamid Hassan

Dr Hussain Hamid Hassan received his PhD from the Faculty of *Sharia'a* at Al Azhar University in Cairo, Egypt in 1965. He also holds two degrees in law from the International Institute of Comparative Law, University of New York and two degrees in Law and Economics from Cairo University. He served as Assistant Professor, Associate Professor and Professor of *Sharia'a* in the Faculty of Law and Economics at Cairo University between 1960 and 2002.

Dr Hassan chairs, or is member of the *Sharia'a* supervisory committees of many Islamic financial institutions, including Emirates Islamic Bank, DIB, National Bank of Sharjah, Islamic Development Bank, Dubai Islamic Insurance and Re-Insurance (Aman), Tamweel, AMLAK, the Liquidity Management Centre and the Accounting and Auditing Organisation for Islamic Financial Institutions. Dr Hassan is the author of 21 books on Islamic law, finance, economics, social studies and art. In addition to this he has also written more than 400 research articles on these subjects.

Dr Ali AlQaradaghi

Dr Ali AlQaradaghi received his PhD in the area of contracts and financial transactions from Al Azhar University in Cairo, Egypt in 1985. He is currently a Professor of Islamic financial contracts and heads the Department of Islamic jurisprudence in the College of *Sharia'a* and Islamic studies at the University of Qatar.

Dr Ali Qaradaghi presently serves on the *Sharia'a* Boards of many Islamic financial institutions in and outside Qatar including Emirates Islamic Bank and DIB in the UAE, Investment House and Investors Bank in Bahrain and First Investment in Kuwait.

In addition, he is a founding member of many charitable organisations and international Islamic jurisprudence bodies. He is the author of many research articles in contemporary issues in Islamic finance and banking. He has more than eight books published.

Dr Mohamed Elgari

Dr Elgari received his PhD in economics from University of California (USA), and is currently serving as a Professor of Islamic economics at King Abdulaziz University (Jeddah), Saudi Arabia. He is a *Sharia'a* advisor to many Islamic financial institutions including HSBC Amanah, Abu Dhabi Islamic Bank, Bahrain Islamic Bank, Dow Jones Islamic Index, National Commercial Bank, Saudi American Bank and Saudi Fransi Bank. He is a prolific writer and has published in a number of scholarly journals and authored several books.

Dr Mohd. Daud Bakar

Dr Mohd. Daud Bakar received his PhD from the University of St Andrews, UK. He was the former Associate Professor in Islamic law and Deputy Rector at the International Islamic University Malaysia. Dr Bakar is the Chief Executive Officer of the International Institute of Islamic Finance. His areas of specialisation include Islamic legal theory, Banking and Finance, Law of Zakat and Medieval Law. Dr Bakar is a member of the *Sharia'a* supervisory committees of many financial institutions in Malaysia and around the world, including the Central Bank of Malaysia, Securities Commission of Malaysia, International Islamic Financial Market, Accounting and Auditing Organisation for Islamic Financial Institutions and numerous other institutions. He has published more than 30 articles in academic journals and presented more than 120 papers in various conferences.

Sheikh Nizam M.S. Yaquby

Sheikh Nizam M.S. Yaquby received a BA from McGill University Montreal, Canada in Economics and Comparative Religion. He has studied traditional Islamic studies under the guidance of eminent scholars, including Sheikh Abdulla al-Farisi, Sheikh Yusuf al-Siddiqi, Sheikh Muhammed Saleh al-Abbasi, Sheikh Muhhamed Yasin al Fadani (Makkah), Sheikh Habib-ur-Rahman A. Zaini (India), Sheikh Abdulla bin Al-Siddiq Al-Ghumar (Morocco), and others.

His areas of specialisation are Khatib in Bahrain Mosques (1981-1990). He also taught *Tafsir*, *Hadith* and *Fiqh* in Bahrain. He is a member of the *Sharia'a* Supervisory Boards for the Islamic Investment Banking Unit of The Ahli United Bank (UK) PLC London, Abu Dhabi Islamic Bank and numerous other Islamic banks and institutions. He has participated in many Islamic, *Da'wah* and *Fiqh* international meetings. His publications include *Risalah fi al Tawbah* (in Arabic), *Qurrat al-Ainayn fi Fada il Birr al-Walidayn* (in Arabic), *Irshad al-Uqala ila Hukm al Qira h min al-Mushaf fi al-Salah*. He has also participated in over 500 lectures, sermons and training sessions and audio cassette recordings. He speaks Arabic, English and Persian.

Sheikh Muhammed Taqi Usmani

Sheikh Muhammed Taqi Usmani earned an MA in Arabic with distinction from the Punjab University in 1970 and was awarded an LLB with distinction from Karachi University in 1967. His BA was from Karachi University in 1964. In 1961 (1381 AH) he earned Takhassus in Ifta from Darul Uloom Karachi. He was awarded an Alimiyyah from Darul Uloom Karachi in 1959 (1379 AH) and the Fazil-e-Arabi with distinction from the Punjab University in 1958. He recently retired as Judge *Sharia'a* Appellate Bench, Supreme Court of Pakistan (where he had been since 1982). He is deputy chairman/permanent member of the International Islamic Fiqh Academy Jeddah (sponsored by the Organisation of

Islamic Countries (OIC)) and Vice President of Darul Uloom Karachi. He has been chairman of the Centre for Islamic Economics Pakistan since 1991 and the chairman of the *Sharia'a* Boards for: Saudi American Bank, Jeddah; Robert Fleming Oasis Fund, Luxembourg; *Sharia'a* Council, AAOIFI. He also worked for the Citi Islamic Investment Bank, Bahrain and Amana Investments Ltd, Sri Lanka. He was vice chairman of the *Sharia'a* Board of the Abu Dhabi Islamic Bank, Abu Dhabi. He was also a member of the *Sharia'a* Boards for: The Ahli United Bank (UK) PLC, London; Al-Baraka Group, Jeddah; First Islamic Investment Bank, Bahrain. His other accomplishments include:

- Being a member of the Commission for Islamization of Economy, Government of Pakistan.
- Teaching several branches of Islamic studies for over 40 years.
- Participating in many Islamic, *Da'wah* and *Fiqh* meetings across the world.

His publications include over 50 works published in English (including *Islamic Modes of Financing*), Arabic and Urdu. He speaks Arabic, English, Urdu and Persian.

Sheikh Abdullah Bin Suleiman Al-Maniya

Sheikh Abdullah Bin Suleiman Al-Maniya has been a member of the Senior Ulema Board since its inception in 1971 (1391 AH). He was formerly Judge of the Cassation Court in Makkah Al Mukarramah. He has supervised a number of PhD theses. By delegation he was appointed president of the courts of the Makkah Al Mukarramah. He has compiled a number of *fatawas* (interpretive opinions) and published several books.

Sheikh Dr Abdullah bin Abdulaziz Al Musleh

Sheikh Dr Abdullah bin Abdulaziz Al Musleh established the branch of Al-Imam Muhammad bin Saud Islamic University in Abha (Saudi Arabia) and was its rector from 1976 (1396 AH) until 1994 (1415 AH). He was Dean of the Faculty of *Sharia'a* and Principles of Religion at the Imam Muhammad bin Saud Islamic University, in addition to his work as rector of the University's branch in Abha. At the Faculty he also established the Islamic Economics Division. He was also Director General of the Panel of Scientific Miracles in the *Qur'an* and *Sunnah*. He has published numerous research studies and books including:

- Restrictions on Private Ownership under Islamic Sharia'a
- Murabaha from Fiqh (Jurisprudence) Heritage to Contemporary Applications in Islamic Banks
- A compendium of provisions of leasing and sharikah provisions.

Sheikh Dr Muhammad Al-Ali Al Qari bin Eid

Sheikh Dr Muhammad Al-Ali Al Qari bin Eid was Professor of Islamic Economics at King Abdulaziz University in Jeddah and was an expert at the Fiqh Academy of the Organisation of Islamic Conference in Jeddah. He was also director of the National Administrative Consultancy Centre in Jeddah. He has published several publications and books, which include:

- Financial Markets, Contracts and Transactions.
- Credit in the Form of a Card and a Proposed Formula for a Credit Card with no *Sharia'a* violations.
- Shares, Options and Futures: Types and Transactions carried out on the basis thereof.
- 'Letters of Credit', a chapter in the *Economic Fiqh Encyclopaedia* of the Islamic Fiqh Academy.

State Bank of Pakistan (SBP): proper criteria for appointment of *Sharia'a* advisors

According to the State Bank of Pakistan, a *Sharia'a* advisor needs the following minimum qualification and experience:

- A minimum of five years experience giving religious rulings.
- A knowledge of, or familiarity with, the banking industry.
- A minimum qualification of Dars-e-Nizami. In higher education a qualification such as an MA in Islamiat, economics or in the discipline of banking and finance may be an added bonus.
- In the case where the *Sharia'a* advisor has experience as a teacher of Islamic *Fiqh* in a reputable institution, other than banking institutions, for a period of not less than three years with a proven track record, the number of years of experience necessary may be relaxed.

As well as the above qualifications and experience, the *Sharia'a* advisor must have an impeccable track record in the companies he/she has served either in the capacity of an employee or director or chief executive or as chairman. He must not have had his employment terminated or dismissed in the capacity of employee, director or chairman of a company.

Solvency and financial integrity

A *Sharia'a* advisor must not be associated with any illegal activity relating to banking business. He must not have been in default of payment of dues owed to any financial institution and/or default in payment of any taxes individual capacity or as proprietary concern or any partnership firm or in any private unlisted and listed company. He must also have sufficient means to discharge financial obligations.

Integrity, honesty and reputation

A *Sharia'a* advisor must be honest and have no criminal convictions or be involved in fraud or forgery or any other financial crime. He must not have been subject to any adverse findings or any settlement in civil or criminal proceedings particularly with regard to financial or business investments, misconduct, fraud, formation or management of a corporate body and so on. He must not have contravened any of the requirements and standards of regulatory system or the equivalent standards of requirements of other regulatory authorities. He must not have been involved with a company or firm or other organisation that has been refused registration or licence to carry out trade or business. Nor must he have been involved with a company or firm whose registration or license has been revoked or cancelled or gone into liquidation. He must not have been debarred for giving religious rulings by any religious institution or body.

The *Sharia'a* advisor must have no conflict of interest. He must not be a *Sharia'a* advisor for any other financial institution. The term financial institution will include any bank, investment finance company, non-banking finance company, venture capital company, housing finance company, leasing company or *Mudaraba* Company. The conflict of interest does not apply if a *Sharia'a* advisor is nominated by the SBP to its own *Sharia'a* Board.

***Source.* State Bank of Pakistan**

Chapter 3

Conventional and Islamic financial intermediation

Functions of a financial system

The development of a financial system is closely related to the economy within which it evolves. There are certain features of a modern economy which necessitate the evolution of a parallel financial system:

1) the increasing specialisation of the work-force and therefore a greater necessity for a medium of exchange;
2) the fact that it takes a period of time for the results of production to appear on the market, such as agricultural products, consumer durables etc;
3) the need to provide resources for investment for future production;
4) the desire to save whilst still working, e.g. on the part of employees;
5) the desire to consume currently on the basis of *expected* future income.

The behaviour of financial institutions within the financial system is influenced by the structure of financial markets in which they participate, by the financial instruments in which they trade, and by the behaviour of the sectors of the economy from which they borrow and lend.

The financial system is a complex network embracing payments mechanisms and the borrowing and lending of funds. Though they also have other important functions the key role, played by financial institutions in the system, is to act as financial intermediaries channelling funds from those with income in excess of their needs to those wishing to borrow.

A useful way to analyse a financial system is to distinguish between deficit and surplus economic units.

A *deficit unit* has a desire to spend (i.e. make a claim on current output) of an amount greater than its income in a given time period.

A *surplus unit* has a desire to spend less than its current income in a given time period.

This matching of needs is achieved in two ways:

1) *Directly*–surplus units hold direct claims on deficit units.
2) *Indirectly*–by surplus units lending to financial institutions who then lend to deficit units.

Each sector within an economy issues financial liabilities and holds financial assets which represent claims on the other sectors. In a modern conventional financial system the range of these assets/liabilities is considerable. Usually each has its own characteristics reflecting the requirements of the lender and the borrower. The structure of the financial system is illustrated in figure 3.1 below.

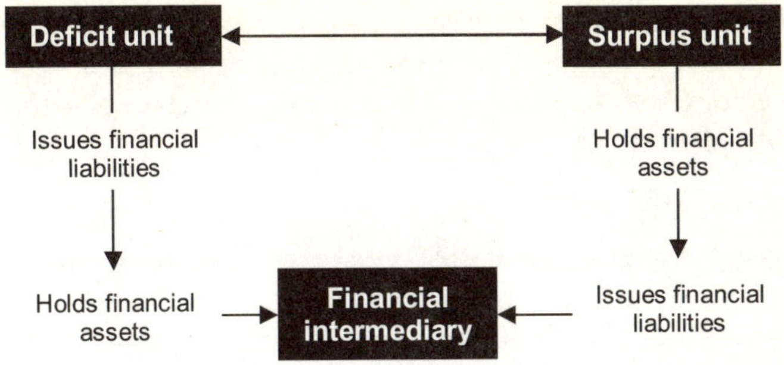

Figure 3.1. Conventional financial intermediation

Surplus saving and deficit spending units

All economic units can be classified into one of the following groups:

1) Households.
2) Business firms.
3) Governments.

Each economic unit must operate within a budget constraint imposed by its total income receipts and expenditures for the period. Households typically receive income in the form of wages and salaries and make frequent expenditures for durable and nondurable consumer goods and services and for housing in the form of mortgage payments. Businesses sell goods and services to households and businesses for revenues, and their expenditures are for wages, inventory purchases, and other production costs. Occasionally, businesses make capital expenditures in the form of new buildings and equipment. Governments obtain income by collecting taxes and fees and make expenditures for a myriad of services, such as health, welfare, education and defence.

Budget positions create the need for a financial system

For a given budget period, any unit within a group can have one of three possible budget positions:

1) a *balanced budget* position where income and expenditures are equal,
2) a *surplus* position where income for the period exceeds current expenditures, or
3) a *deficit* position where expenditures for the period exceed receipts.

The financial system is concerned with funnelling purchasing power from surplus saving units (SSUs) to deficit spending units (DSUs). DSUs include some households, government and local governments, the government in most periods, and a large number of businesses. Other economic units may be SSUs. Taken as groups, however, business firms and governments are typically DSUs and households are SSUs.

Financial claims

The problem is how to transfer the SSU's excess purchasing power to the DSUs that wish to borrow to finance current expenditures.

The transfer can be accomplished by an SSU lending money to, and accepting an IOU from, a DSU. An IOU is a written promise to pay a specific sum of money (the principal) plus an interest rate fee for the privilege of borrowing the money over a period of time (maturity of the loan). IOUs are called *financial claims.* They are claims against someone else's money at some future date.

To a DSU a financial claim is a liability, and the interest rate payments are the penalty for consuming before income is earned. To the SSU the financial claim is an asset, and the interest earned is the reward for postponing current consumption. The fact that financial claims (IOUs) are liabilities for borrowers (DSUs) and are simultaneously assets for lenders (SSUs) illustrates the 'two faces of debt'. That is, total financial liabilities outstanding in the economy must equal total financial assets.

Once a financial claim is outstanding, the lender (SSU) may hold the claim until it matures. Alternatively, the SSU may sell the financial claim to someone else before it matures. The DSU continues to have use of the funds even though the lender is now a different party.

The ability to resell financial claims allows the SSU to purchase claims with maturities that do not exactly match its own time preference. If an SSU purchases a financial claim with a longer maturity than its investment period, the claim can be resold to another SSU at the appropriate time. Likewise, an SSU can purchase a financial claim with a maturity shorter than its time horizon if additional claims either new or outstanding can be easily purchased. The ease with which a financial claim can be sold and resold is called its marketability.

There is a wide variety of financial claims all designed to meet the preferences of both SSUs and DSUs. Financial claims differ according to maturity, risk of default, marketability, and tax treatment.

Transferring funds from SSUs to DSUs

The purpose of the conventional financial system is to channel funds from SSUs to DSUs in the most efficient manner possible by either:

1) Direct financing and/or

2) Indirect financing.

Direct financing

In *direct financing,* DSUs and SSUs exchange money and financial claims directly. DSUs issue financial claims on themselves and sell them to the SSUs directly. The SSUs hold the financial claims in their portfolios as interest-bearing assets. The transactions appear as changes in the balance sheets (asset and liability holdings) of the two parties as shown in figure 3.2 below.

SSU		DSU	
Assets	**Liabilities**	**Assets**	**Liabilities**
– Money		+ Money from SSU	+ Direct claims issued
+ Direct claims of DSU			

Figure 3.2. Asset and liability holding of SSUs and DSUs

The claims issued by the DSU are called *direct claims* and are typically sold in direct credit markets, such as the money or capital markets. Direct financing provides SSUs an outlet for their savings, providing an expected return, with the effect that DSUs no longer need to postpone current consumption or forgo promising investment opportunities for lack of funds. Thus direct credit markets increase the efficiency of the financial system.

There are some problems, however, with the direct credit markets. Firstly because they are traditionally wholesale markets, the denominations of securities sold are very large (usually $1 million or more), and thus few consumers can transact in the market. Secondly DSUs must find SSUs that want direct claims with precisely the characteristics they themselves are willing to sell. The flow of direct claims from SSUs to DSUs by way of direct financing is illustrated in the top portion of figure 3.3.

Indirect financing

Until now we have considered only the direct flow of funds from SSUs to DSUs. Flows can be indirect if financial intermediaries are involved. Financial intermediaries include commercial banks, savings banks, life insurance companies, and pension funds. These and other financial intermediaries emerged because of inefficiencies found in direct financing, some of which were mentioned earlier.

For direct financing to take place, the DSU must be willing to issue a security with a denomination, maturity and other security characteristics that coincides exactly with the desires of the SSU. Unless both SSU and DSU are satisfied simultaneously, the transfer of money will probably not take place. A household with a six-month temporary excess cash balance of say $400 will have very little interest in buying a $5,000, 20-year bond issued by Microsoft.

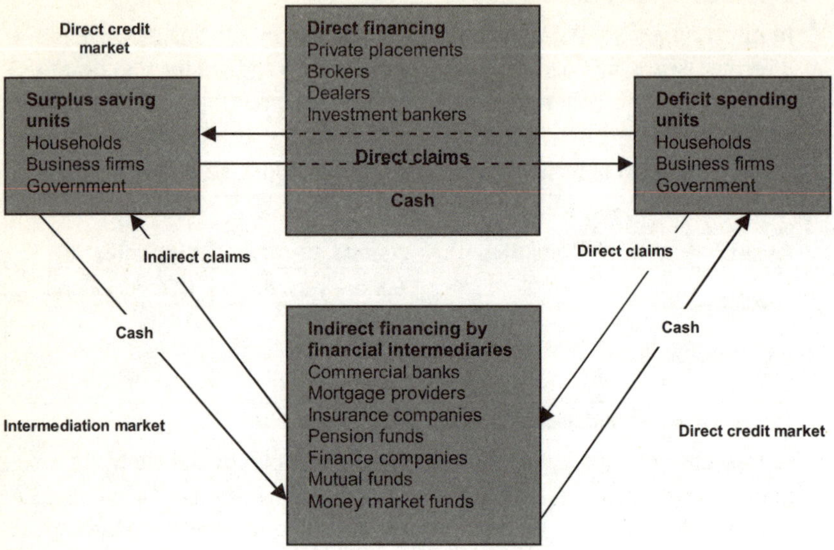

Figure 3.3. Transfer of funds from surplus saving to deficit spending units

To overcome these problems, financial intermediaries intervene between the borrower (DSU) and the ultimate lender (SSU). Financial intermediaries purchase direct claims (IOUs) with one set of characteristics (e.g. term to maturity, denomination) from DSUs and transform them into indirect claims (IOUs) with a different set of characteristics, which they then sell to the SSU. This transformation process is called financial intermediation. Firms that specialise in this intermediation are called financial intermediaries. The effects on the balance sheets of financial intermediation are summarised in figure 3.4.

SSU		Financial intermediaries		DSU	
Assets	Liabilities	*Assets*	Liabilities	*Assets*	Liabilities
– Money		+ Direct claim	+ Indirect claim	+ Money	+ Direct claim
+ Indirect claim					

Figure 3.4. Financial intermediation effects on balance sheets

Notice that in the financial intermediation market the SSU's residual claim is against the financial intermediaries rather than the DSU as would be the case with direct financing. The financial intermediation market is typically a retail market, and the indirect financial claims issued by financial intermediaries are often savings accounts, or varieties of unit trusts (mutual funds).

The bottom half of figure 3.3 illustrates the flow of money through the intermediation market and identifies the more important financial intermediaries.

Some examples of intermediation transactions include:

1) Households (SSUs) deposit excess cash balances in savings accounts of a building society (financial intermediary), which in turn makes home finance loans to other households (DSUs).
2) Households (SSUs) purchase life insurance policies from an insurance company (financial intermediary), which in turn invests the funds in bonds of a corporation (DSU).
3) Corporations (SSUs) purchase the commercial paper of a consumer finance company (financial intermediary), which in turn makes personal loans to households (DSUs).

Benefits of financial intermediation

Financial intermediaries transform claims in such a way as to make them more attractive to both DSUs and SSUs. If they did not serve this function, financial intermediaries would not exist. How do they accomplish this seemingly impossible task?

It is useful to view financial intermediaries as firms that produce specialised financial commodities such as business loans, life insurance policies and pension fund shares. Financial intermediaries will produce these commodities whenever they can sell them for prices that are expected, to cover all of their costs of production. In doing so, intermediaries enjoy two sources of comparative advantage over others who may try to produce similar services.

Firstly, financial intermediaries can achieve economies of scale because of their specialisation. Because they handle a large number of transactions, they are able to spread out their fixed costs. Also the use of specialised computer systems allows them to lower operating costs further.

Secondly, financial intermediaries can reduce the transaction costs involved in searching for credit information. A consumer who wishes to lend directly can also search for credit information, but often at a higher cost. Financial intermediaries are usually more familiar with credit markets, and their participants, than are outsiders.

Intermediation services

For the above reasons, financial intermediaries are often able to produce financial commodities at a lower cost than individual consumers. If they did not, individuals would produce their own financial commodities, and thus would transact in the direct credit markets. Financial intermediaries exist because of the high transaction costs involved in producing many financial commodities in small quantities.

Financial intermediaries, therefore, tailor the characteristics of the indirect securities they issue to the desires of SSUs. They engage in one or more distinct types of intermediation:

1) Denomination intermediation,
2) Maturity intermediation,
3) Risk intermediation, and
4) Liquidity intermediation.

They provide these and other services to earn a profit. Consumers use these services as long as the cost of doing so is less than those of direct credit markets.

So in producing financial commodities financial intermediaries perform four basic services:

1) **Denomination divisibility.** Financial intermediaries are able to produce a wide range of denominations, from $1 to many millions. They can do this by pooling the funds of many individuals and investing them in direct securities of varying sizes.

   Of particular importance is accepting the deposits of small savers who do not have an adequate amount of money to engage in the large denomination transactions found in direct financial markets.

2) **Maturity flexibility.** Financial intermediaries are able to create securities with a wide range of maturities, from one day to more than 30 years. Thus they are able to buy direct claims issued by DSUs and issue indirect securities with precisely the maturities (usually shorter) desired by SSUs. For example, building societies obtain funds by issuing a variety of savings accounts and certificates and invest the funds in long-term consumer mortgages.

3) **Credit risk diversification.** By purchasing a wide variety of securities, financial intermediaries are able to spread risk. If the securities purchased are less than perfectly correlated with each other, the intermediary is able to reduce the fluctuation in the principal value of the portfolio.

   Portfolio diversification is an application of not putting 'all of your eggs into one basket', where they might be 'broken' simultaneously. For example, the return on a portfolio with a large number of securities would not be affected much if one security were to go to bankrupt. However, an individual investor, who held only the defaulted security, could be wiped out financially.

4) **Liquidity.** For most consumers, the timing of revenues and expenses rarely coincide. Because of this, most economic units prefer to hold some assets that have low transaction costs associated with converting them into money. Many of the financial commodities produced by intermediaries are highly

liquid. For example holding a bank current account permits consumers to purchase an asset or repay a debt with minimal transaction cost.

Direct credit markets, efficient capital markets and Islamic capital markets

Efficient capital markets are commonly thought of as markets in which security prices fully reflect all relevant information that is available about the fundamental value of the securities. Because a security is a claim on future cash flows, this fundamental value is the present value of the future cash flows that the owner of the security expects to receive. The cash flows anticipated for stocks consist of the stream of expected dividends paid to stockholders plus the expected price of the stock when sold. In the present value calculation, future cash flows are discounted by an interest rate that is a function of the riskiness of those cash flows. The riskier the cash flows, the higher is the interest rate used in discounting.

As will be seen in *Chapter 4* the use of interest rates in Islamic capital markets is, however, not permitted.

Theoretically, the profit opportunities represented by the existence of 'undervalued' and 'overvalued' stocks motivate competitive trading by investors that moves the prices of stocks toward the present value of the future cash flows. For example, new information about the fundamental values of securities will be reflected in prices through competitive trading. Thus, the search for mis-priced stocks by investment analysts and their subsequent trading make the market efficient and make prices reflect fundamental values.

Researchers of capital market efficiency examine how much, how fast, and how accurately available information is incorporated into security prices. Financial economists often classify efficiency into three categories based on available information – the weak, semi-strong and strong-forms. In order to analyse the efficiency, or otherwise, of Islamic capital markets it is necessary to know how efficiency can be classified.

Weak-form efficiency

Weak-form efficiency exists if security prices fully reflect all the information contained in the history of past prices and returns. The return is the profit on the security calculated as a percentage of an initial price. If capital markets are weak-form efficient, then investors cannot earn excess profits from trading rules based on past prices or returns. Therefore, stock returns are not predictable, and so-called technical analysis (analysing patterns in past price movements) is useless.

Semi-strong-form efficiency

Under semi-strong-form efficiency, security prices fully reflect all public information. Thus, only traders with access to non-public information, such as some corporate insiders, can earn excess profits. Under weak-form efficiency, some public information about fundamentals may not yet be reflected in prices. Thus, a superior analyst can profit from trading on the discovery of, or a better interpretation of, public information. Under semi-strong-form efficiency, the market reacts so quickly to the release of new information that there are no profitable trading opportunities based on public information.

Strong-form efficiency

Finally, under strong-form efficiency, all information – even insider knowledge of apparent company secrets – is incorporated in security prices. Thus, no investor can earn excess profit trading on public or non-public information.

Informational efficiency matter and constrained portfolios

The capital markets channel funds from savers to firms, which use the funds to finance projects. Informational efficiency is necessary if funds allocated through the capital market are to flow to the highest-valued projects. Shareholders want management to maximise stock prices and thus will attempt to ensure that their managements undertake only projects (decisions) that increase the value of their stock. Management compensation packages tied to stock performance are one way in which stockholders align management's interests with their own.

However, maximisation of stock prices can result in the capital market directing funds to the most valuable projects only if stocks are efficiently priced, in the sense of accurately reflecting the fundamental value of all future cash flows. Thus, for example, if capital markets are efficient, there is no reason to expect managements to emphasise the short run at the expense of long-term projects. Additionally, efficient capital markets make it easier for firms to raise capital because the markets determine the prices at which existing and potential security holders are willing to exchange claims on a firm's future cash flows.

A related reason for caring about efficiency is that investors who do not have the time or the resources to do extensive analysis will be more willing to invest their savings in the markets if they believe the securities they trade are accurately priced. This, in turn, helps the capital market to perform its function of translating savings into productive projects. Finally, there are policy implications of evidence on market efficiency. If capital markets are efficient, then the government's role in capital markets should be very limited. If security prices do not accurately reflect fundamentals, however, there might be a case for regulating both the operation of the securities markets and the capital-allocation process itself.

A large amount of empirical research has been directed at answering the question as to whether capital markets are efficient. Most research has used stock price data, for two reasons. First, stock prices are easily available. Second, the stock market is likely to be less efficient than other securities markets (such as the bond market) because cash flows paid to stockholders are relatively uncertain, and there is no terminal payoff as in a bond. Therefore, stocks are relatively difficult to value, and evidence of stock market efficiency would be compelling evidence of efficiency in securities markets in general.

An overwhelming amount of empirical evidence shows that stock prices react quickly, in the expected direction, to the release of information. Stock prices react within 10 minutes to an earnings announcement, for example. This evidence is consistent with weak and semi-strong efficiency. Such evidence, however, does not show that the amount of price reaction accurately reflects fundamentals or, by extension, that security prices accurately reflect the fundamental value of the securities. Other evidence shows that corporate insiders have earned excess profits trading on inside information. This evidence means that capital markets are not strong-form efficient.

There are major differences between a portfolio which can invest in the global universe of stocks and an investment portfolio constrained Islamically. An Islamic investment portfolio is not allowed to invest in a variety of prohibited sectors. This is discussed further in *Chapter 4*.

Capital markets and the economy

Capital markets and institutions play two critical roles in an economy: allocation of risk capital through saving mobilisation and risk-pooling, and promotion of responsible governance and control through providing outside investors a variety of mechanisms for monitoring inside decision makers.

In its allocation function, the financial system helps transfer resources from individual savers to agents with managerial and entrepreneurial talents with investment opportunities and provides firms and investors risk-pooling and sharing facilities.

In its governance function the financial system provides monitoring and information production services by which it helps mitigate the various agency problems, described below, resulting in better project evaluation and selection. It is to these agency problems that we now turn.

Principal-agent problem

In political science and economics, the problem of motivating one party to act on behalf of another is known as 'the principal-agent problem'. The principal-agent problem arises when a principal compensates an agent for performing certain acts that are useful to the principal and where there are elements of the performance that are costly to observe. This is the case to some extent for all contracts that are written in a world of information asymmetry, uncertainty and risk.

Here, principals do not know enough about whether (or to what extent) a contract has been satisfied. The solution to this information problem – closely related to the moral hazard problem, defined below – is to ensure the provision of appropriate incentives so agents act in the way principals wish. In terms of game theory it involves changing the rules of the game so that the self-interested rational choices of the agent coincide with what the principal desires. Figure 3.5. illustrates the principal-agent problem.

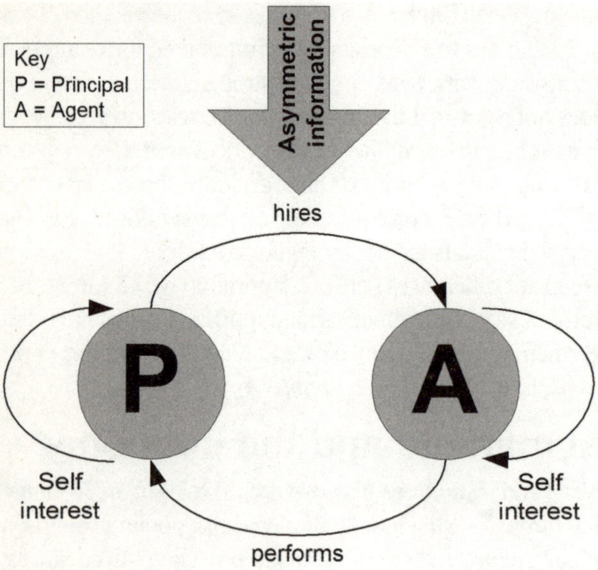

Figure 3.5. The principal-agent problem

Moral hazard is the prospect that a party insulated from risk may behave differently from the way it would behave if it were fully exposed to that risk. Moral hazard arises where an individual or institution does not bear the full consequences of its actions, and therefore has a tendency to act less carefully than it otherwise would, leaving another party to bear some responsibility for the consequences of those actions. For example, an individual with insurance against car theft may be less vigilant about locking his car, because the negative consequences of car theft are (partially) borne by the insurance company.

Moral hazard is related to asymmetric information, a situation in which one party in a transaction has more information than another. The party that is insulated from risk generally has more information about its actions and intentions than the party paying for the negative consequences of the risk. More broadly, moral hazard occurs when the party with more information about its actions or intentions has a tendency, or incentive, to behave inappropriately from the perspective of the party with less information.

A special case of moral hazard is called a principal-agent problem, mentioned above, where one party, called an agent, acts on behalf of another party, called the principal. The agent usually has more information about his actions or intentions than the principal does, because the principal usually cannot perfectly monitor the agent. The agent may have an incentive to act inappropriately (from the point of view of the principal) if the interests of the agent and the principal are not aligned.

Stockholders versus creditors: agency conflicts

Agency conflicts can occur between creditors and stockholders. **Creditors** have the primary claim on part of the firm's earnings in the form of interest and principal payments on the debt as well as a claim on the firm's assets in the event of bankruptcy. The **stockholders**, however, maintain control of the operating decisions (through the firm's managers) that affect the firm's cash flows and their corresponding risks.

Creditors lend capital to the firm at rates that are based on the riskiness of the firm's existing assets and on the firm's existing capital structure of debt and equity financing, as well as on expectations concerning changes in the riskiness of these two variables.

The shareholders, acting through the management, have an incentive to induce the firm to take on new projects that have a greater risk than was anticipated by the firm's creditors. The increased risk will raise the required rate of return on the firm's debt, which in turn will cause the value of the outstanding bonds to fall.

If the risky capital investment project is successful, all benefits will go to the firm's stockholders, because the bondholders' returns are fixed at the original low-risk rate. If the project fails, however, the bondholders are forced to share in the losses.

On the other hand, shareholders may be reluctant to finance beneficial investment projects. Shareholders of firms undergoing financial distress are unwilling to raise additional funds to finance positive net present value projects because these actions will benefit bondholders more than shareholders by providing additional security for the creditors' claims.

Managers can also increase the firm's level of debt, without altering its assets, in an effort to leverage up stockholders' return on equity. If the old debt is not senior to the newly issued debt, its value will decrease, because a larger number of creditors will have claims against the firm's cash flows and assets. Both the riskier assets and the increased leverage transactions have the effect of transferring wealth from the firm's bondholders to the stockholders.

Shareholder-creditor agency conflicts can result in situations in which a firm's total value declines but its stock price rises. This occurs if the value of the firm's outstanding debt falls by more than the increase in the value of the firm's common stock. If stockholders attempt to expropriate wealth from the firm's creditors, bondholders will protect themselves by placing restrictive covenants in future debt agreements.

Furthermore, if creditors believe that a firm's managers are trying to take advantage of them, they will either refuse to provide additional funds to the firm or will charge an above-market interest rate to compensate for the risk of possible expropriation of their claims. Thus, firms which deal with creditors in an inequitable manner either lose access to the debt markets or face high interest rates and restrictive covenants, both of which are detrimental to shareholders.

Principal-agent problems as applied to banking

An evolving literature has attempted to identify the optimal form of the financial contract between lender (bank) and entrepreneur, and between depositor and bank. The choice is usually posed in terms of 'debt versus equity'. Under a debt contract contractual payments are fixed, in the form of contracts that promise providers of finance a specified return in 'normal', non-default situations and first claim to the issuer's assets in default situations.

With an equity contract the repayments are contingent on output or profit performance, as with equity-type claims that give holders a claim on an issuer's residual income (that is, its profit) and ultimate control over its assets, provided the issuer does not default.

One of the most important results that has emerged from the contract design literature is that debt contracts are often optimal transacting vehicles because they minimise the costs associated with asymmetric information or unobserved actions.

This has major implications for an Islamic bank, which cannot use conventional debt contracts, but can instead use profit-and-loss share contracts. Three circumstances have been the subjects of examination: costly verification, moral hazard and adverse selection.

1. Costly verification

Costly verification and/or monitoring points to the optimality of the standard debt contract. The borrower pays the lender a fixed payment for good outcomes, when no verification or monitoring takes place, but must hand over the whole proceeds in the event of a bad outcome, when the fixed repayment cannot be met and bankruptcy occurs.

2. Moral hazard

Hidden actions or moral hazard also point to the optimality of the debt contract. A requirement to make debt payments independently of the state of the world may be a check against moral hazard. As mentioned the principal-agent literature is concerned with how one individual, the principal (say an employer), can design a compensation system (a contract) which motivates another individual, his agent (say the employee), to act in the principal's interests. A principal-agent problem arises when there is imperfect information, concerning what action the agent has undertaken or should undertake. Obviously, in many situations, the actions are not easily observable. Should there be the possibility that output depends on the agent's hidden actions, which the principal finds costly to monitor, then there is a moral hazard problem.

The hidden action usually referred to is the agent's choice of endeavour, i.e. whether they will work in the interest of the principal. The moral hazard problem, in this context, relates to the tendency of the agent to reduce effort on the grounds that some (perhaps most) of any extra effort would accrue to the principal, and not to the agent.

Verification costs and moral hazard both tend to encourage the parties involved to make debt contracts. Debt contracts are preferable because they reduce the impact of hidden information (since it will often not matter *ex post* that the investor does not directly see the output) and also of moral hazard (since debt gives the entrepreneur a strong incentive to work hard and capture the residual returns). Thus the possibility that the entrepreneur uses the funds by consuming perquisites (e.g. an expensive car) which may not benefit the principal, are reduced with debt contracts.

3. Adverse selection

Debt contracts may also be optimal, in certain circumstances, when there is the problem of adverse project selection. This is the problem when some important feature of the investor's project (or choice of project) is not observed by the investor. One such situation is where the investor does not observe the (appropriately defined) 'quality' of the project. In this case, debt contracts are still optimal over a wide range of circumstances. The reason for this debt optimality is that the entrepreneurs with better quality projects would prefer debt contracts to maximise their residual profits, while the entrepreneurs with poor quality projects would need to imitate them so as to avoid revealing themselves.

Collateral and screening

In a similar vein, the extent and quality of collateral also acts as a screening device aimed at selecting the honest entrepreneur (profitable project) from the dishonest one. The entrepreneur who is convinced that the project is profitable will be prepared to offer collateral as security. Otherwise he will not risk his personal wealth. Collateral thus has the potential of reducing the adverse selection problem in the credit markets. By choosing the size of the amount of collateral, a bank will be able to screen the riskiness of the entrepreneur, who is obliged to identify his/her risk attributes from the extent and amount of collateral offered.

The optimality of debt and the Islamic banking implications

As discussed above there are a large number of circumstances in which debt contracts appear to be optimal. In addition, particular features of real-world debt contracts, among them the use of collateral and credit rationing, covenant restrictions of various kinds, the on-going monitoring, and potential workout gain theoretical support as being incentive-compatible.

Many economists take comfort from the fact that debt contracts are defensible in theory given that they figure so prominently in real-world financial arrangements and have done so for a very long time in conventional banking markets.

This is rather less than reassuring from the viewpoint of the theory of Islamic banking. The standard debt *(riba)* contract, collateral requirements, loan covenants and enforced workouts – measures designed to ameliorate adverse selection and moral hazard – are all prohibited in Islamic financing.

At the same time Islamic banks go beyond pure financial intermediation of the traditional sort, and have direct participation in business and investments with profit-and-loss sharing along equity lines. To appreciate the nature of the problem let us examine one of the purer modes of Islamic financing, the *Mudaraba* contract.

Characteristics of *Mudaraba*

Unlike a conventional bank, which is basically a borrower of funds on the one hand and a lender of those funds on the other, an Islamic bank is essentially a partner with its depositors except in the case of current accounts and non-funded banking services, on one side, and also a partner with its clients on the other side as a manager of depositors' funds. It solicits funds from the community through a *mudaraba* contract which can be limited by time, or purpose or both. The bank thus becomes a managing partner for the duration of the contract.

Once the Islamic bank enters into the *Mudaraba* contract with the 'depositor', it then employs those funds through the various *Sharia'a*-accepted nominate contracts: *Mudaraba, Musharaka, Murabaha, Ijara* and so on.

In the case of a *Mudaraba* contract, the following conditions apply:

1) The bank provides the entire capital needed for carrying out a project.
2) The entrepreneur offers only his labour and effort. His capital contribution is effectively zero. He does not offer any collateral, except in the event that he transgresses the *Sharia'a* rulings regarding acceptable business behaviour.
3) The contract between the bank and the entrepreneur is usually an exclusive one, that is, the entrepreneur is not allowed to engage in other activities.
4) The compensation paid to the entrepreneur is a share of the net profit of the project, although he can be paid a market wage. This share is fixed in advance.
5) In the event of negative returns, the bank loses some or all of its capital, and the entrepreneur does not receive any profit share remuneration for his work.
6) As soon as the contract is accepted by both parties, the bank cannot monitor or enforce the entrepreneur by legal devices to undertake any additional actions.
7) Finally, the contract will be automatically cancelled in case of death, insanity, or apostasy from Islam of either party.

Incentive issues with Mudaraba

These characteristics of the *Mudaraba* contract *vis-à-vis* the standard interest-based loan create, at least potentially, three incentive problems on both sides of the bank's balance sheet. It can be interpreted in terms of a principal-agent problem in that the bank cannot monitor perfectly the actions of those to whom it advances funds, nor can bank depositors monitor the actions of the bank. Yet in both cases the action of one has an effect on the other. Furthermore agency theory tells us that there are reasons for believing that conflicts of interest could easily arise between the parties involved.

Consider, to begin with, the bank's investment of funds involving a *Mudaraba*-type contract. Potential incentive problems exist in three aspects.

1) First, the absence of a collateral requirement will aggravate the adverse selection problem in an Islamic banking system. According to the theory of Islamic banking, funds provided on a profit sharing basis have to be offered without any collateral. The lack of collateral requirement will likely attract entrepreneurs with a limited amount of wealth. In particular, the profit-and-loss share (PLS) contract will encourage new entrepreneurs who do not possess any assets except their effort and skills. Without collateral these

entrepreneurs would be considered to be high risk. In order to overcome the adverse selection problem, and discriminate between a high-risk project and a low-risk project, the lack of collateral may oblige an Islamic bank to ration the supply of funds to this Islamic financing mode.

2) Second, a *Mudaraba* contract will accentuate the moral hazard problem, because the bank cannot force the entrepreneur to apply the required level of effort the bank would prefer. According to the *Mudaraba* contract, the compensation to entrepreneurs takes the form of a predetermined share in the outcome of investment. This payment does not necessarily produce the 'right' incentive for the entrepreneur to provide the level of effort needed for the maximisation of outcome. In addition, the bank cannot *ex ante* constrain the activity of the entrepreneur by determining the intensity of his effort, for example by specifying in detail his budget expenses. The entrepreneur is guaranteed full freedom, more or less, in managing the project.

3) Third, as the expenditures on the venture are borne entirely by the bank, the *Mudaraba* contract provides an incentive to the entrepreneur to expand expenditures beyond the level needed for profit maximisation. In particular, a *Mudaraba* contract gives the entrepreneur an incentive to increase consumption of non-pecuniary benefits (say buying an expensive car) at the expense of a pecuniary return. This is due to the fact that the increased consumption is partly borne by the bank, while the benefits are entirely consumed by the entrepreneur.

An entrepreneur has access to a number of on-the-job spending opportunities and perquisites, which have a positive value for him, such as hiring staff, large office space, executive services, and so on. The expansion of staffing may enhance the entrepreneur's power, and status.

Moreover, the *Mudaraba* PLS contract cannot include subject matters expected to occur in the future. Such a contract is considered as illicit according to *Sharia'a* law. In this sense, the bank cannot insist on a contract where the share of the entrepreneur in the outcome will be altered, if a high level of expenditure (or a lower level of effort) has been observed.

Many of the same issues surface on the liabilities side, but in this case the bank is the agent *(Mudarib)* and the depositor is the principal. Under the trustee arrangement for investment accounts depositors act as financiers by providing funds and the bank acts as an entrepreneur by accepting them. Neither the nominal capital value nor a predetermined rate of return on deposits can be guaranteed. Depositors under *Mudaraba* effectively become shareholders.

If the bank makes profits then the shareholder-depositor would be entitled to receive a certain proportion of these profits. On the other hand, if the bank incurs losses the depositor is expected to share in these as well, and will receive a negative rate of return. Accordingly, from the depositor's perspective, dealing with an Islamic bank is in many respects similar to investing in a mutual fund or investment trust.

Islamic banks and corporate governance

As will now be evident Islamic banking represents a radical departure from conventional banking. This is also true from the viewpoint of corporate governance. Islamic banking embodies a number of different features since equity participation, risk and profit-and-loss sharing arrangements form the basis of Islamic financing. Because of the prohibition of interest *(riba),* an Islamic bank cannot charge any fixed return in advance, but rather participates in the yield resulting from the use of funds. The depositors also share in the profits according to a predetermined ratio, and are rewarded with profit returns for assuming risk.

Unlike a conventional bank, which is basically a borrower and lender of funds, an Islamic bank is essentially a partner with its depositors on the one side, and also a partner with entrepreneurs, on the other side, when employing depositors' funds in productive direct investment.

These financial arrangements imply quite different stockholder relationships, and, by corollary, governance structures from the conventional model since depositors have a direct financial stake in the bank's investment and equity participation.

In addition an Islamic bank is subject to an additional layer of governance since the suitability of its investment and financing must be in strict conformity with Islamic law and the expectations of the Muslim community. For this purpose, Islamic banks employ an individual *Sharia'a* Advisory Board, discussed in detail in *Chapter 2*.

Stakeholders in an Islamic bank

Governance structure are quite different from those under conventional banks as Islamic banks must obey a different set of rules viz those of the *Qur'an,* and meet the expectations of the Muslim community by providing Islamically-acceptable financing modes. These profit-and-loss sharing methods, in turn, imply different relationships than under interest-based borrowing and lending.

Figure 3.6 sets out the key stockholders in an Islamic bank. There are two major differences from the conventional banking framework.

First, and foremost, an Islamic organisation must serve Allah (God.) It must develop a distinctive corporate culture, the main purpose of which is to create a collective morality and spirituality which, when combined with the production of goods and services, sustains the growth and advancement of the Islamic way of life.

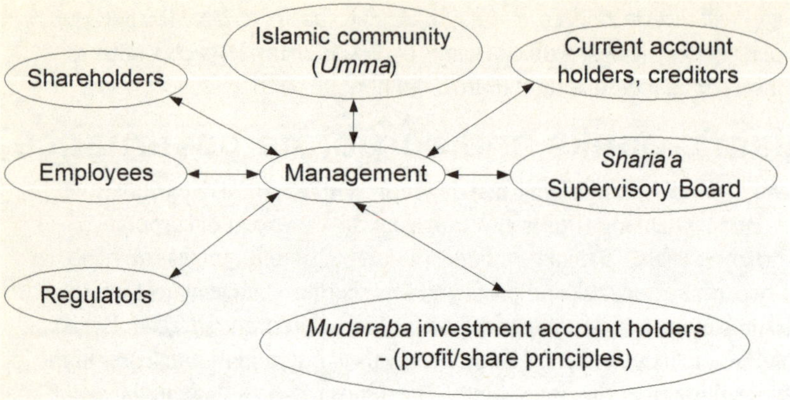

Figure 3.6. Stakeholders in an Islamic bank

To quote **Janachi** (1995):

> 'Islamic banks have a major responsibility to shoulder ... all the staff of such banks and customers dealing with them must be reformed Islamically and act within the framework of an Islamic formula, so that any person approaching an Islamic bank should be given the impression that he is entering a sacred place to perform a religious ritual, that is the use and employment of capital for what is acceptable and satisfactory to God.' (1)

There are equivalent obligations upon employees:

> 'The staff in an Islamic bank should, throughout their lives, be behaving in an Islamic way, whether at work or at leisure.' (1)

Further, obligations also extend to the Islamic community:

> 'Muslims who truly believe in their religion have a duty to prove, through their efforts in backing and supporting Islamic banks and financial institutions, that the Islamic economic system is an integral part of Islam and is indeed for all times ... through making legitimate and Halal profits.' (2.p.29).

Secondly, Islamic banking is based on the Islamic legal concepts of *shirkah* (partnership) and *Mudaraba* (profit sharing). An Islamic bank is conceived as financial intermediary mobilising savings from the public on a *Mudaraba* basis and advancing capital to entrepreneurs on the same basis.

Mudaraba and corporate governance

A two-tiered profit-and-loss sharing arrangement operates under the following rules:

1) The bank receives funds from the public on the basis of Unrestricted *Mudaraba*. There are no restrictions imposed on the bank concerning the kind of activity, duration, and location of the enterprise, but the funds cannot be applied to activities which are forbidden by Islam.

2) The bank has the right to aggregate and pool the profit from different investments, and share the net profit (after deducting administrative costs, capital depreciation and *zakat* (Islamic tax) with depositors according to a specified formula. In the event of losses, the depositors lose a proportional share or the entire amount of their funds. The return to the financier has to be strictly maintained as a share of profits.
3) The bank applies the restricted form of *Mudaraba* when funds are provided to entrepreneurs. The bank has the right to determine the kind of activities, the duration, and location of the projects and monitor the investments. However, these restrictions may not be formulated in a way which harms the performance of the entrepreneur, and the bank cannot interfere with the management of the investment.
4) The bank cannot require any guarantee such as security and collateral from the entrepreneur in order to insure its capital against the possibility of an eventual loss.
5) The liability of the financier is limited to the capital provided. On the other hand, the liability of the entrepreneur is also restricted, but in this case solely to labour and effort employed. Nevertheless, if negligence or mismanagement can be proven, the entrepreneur may be liable for the financial loss and be obliged to remunerate the financier accordingly.
6) The entrepreneur shares the profit with the bank according to a previously agreed division. Until the investment yields a profit, the bank is able to pay a salary to the entrepreneur based on the ruling market salary.

Many of the same restrictions apply to M*usharaka* financing, except that in this instance the losses are borne proportionately to the capital amounts contributed.

Thus under these two Islamic modes of financing, the project is managed by the client and not by the bank, even though the bank shares the risk. Certain major decisions such as changes in the existing lines of business and the disposition of profits may be subject to the bank's consent. The bank, as a partner, has the right to full access to the financial accounts, and can exercise monitoring and follow-up supervision. Nevertheless, the directors and management of the company retain independence in conducting the affairs of the company.

These conditions give the Islamic financing modes many of the characteristics of non-voting equity capital. From the viewpoint of the entrepreneur, there are no fixed annual payments needed to service the debt as compared with interest financing, while the financing does not increase the firm's risk in the way that other borrowings do through increased leverage. Conversely, from the bank's viewpoint, the returns come from profits – much like dividends – and the bank cannot take action to foreclose on the debt should profits not eventuate.

Governance structures

These structures are depicted in figure 3.7 which sketches the conceptual framework of corporate governance for an Islamic bank. Central to such a framework is the *Sharia'a* Supervisory Board (SSB) and the internal controls which support it. This is discussed further in *Chapter 2*.

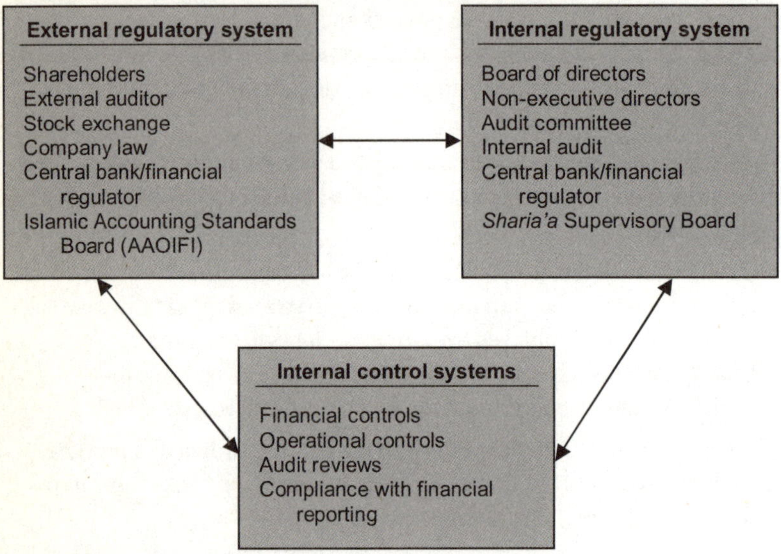

Figure 3.7. Corporate governance in an Islamic bank

The SSB is vital for two reasons. Firstly, those who deal with an Islamic bank require assurance that it is complying with *Sharia'a* law. Should the SSB report that the management of the bank has violated the *Sharia'a*, it would quickly lose the confidence of the majority of its investors and clients. This is known as reputational risk and is a major concern for Islamic banks.

Second, some Islamic scholars argue that strict adherence to Islamic religious principles will act as a counter to the incentive problems outlined above. The argument is that the Islamic moral code will prevent Muslims from behaving in ways which are ethically unsound, so minimising the transaction costs arising from incentive issues. In effect, it is argued, Islamic religious ideology acts as its own incentive mechanism to reduce the inefficiency that arises from elements of asymmetric information and moral hazard. This is not a line of thinking conventional bankers would apply!

References

Janachi, A.L., 1995. *Islamic Banking, Concept, Practice and Future*, 2nd edition, Manama: Bahrain Islamic Bank.
This treatise, first published in 1990, is distributed by the Bahrain Islamic Bank

Chapter 4

Islamic capital markets and Islamic securitisation

A capital market is typically a place where capital is traded between those having surplus capital and those requiring funds for their investment needs. Modern capital markets, particularly in a capitalist, monetised economy have, over a century or so, developed a very efficient system in order to facilitate the following demands:

- those with surplus capital would have the opportunity to select the best forms of investments not only in terms of yields or returns but also in terms of a good mix of short, medium and long-term investments to spread their risks;
- those who have the opportunities and expertise to innovate and manage investment concerns but lack the funds to finance their activities can get access to surplus funds from others;
- there are also those who need to vary their investment mix from time to time and wish to do so with ease and rapidity at very little cost;
- there are obvious needs to develop a mechanism that will ensure the generation of investment and financing activities which are operational, cost-effective and generally fair to all parties concerned;

The growing awareness of, and demand for, investing in accordance to Islamic principles on a global scale has created a flourishing Islamic capital market, a trend enhanced by the increasing wealth in the hands of Muslims worldwide who are actively involved in corporate and business activities.

A glance at the relevant statistics paints the picture:

- The Muslim population of the world today is estimated at about 1.7 billion, representing a sizeable 24% of the total world population of around 6.3 billion.
- The size of funds already invested Islamically is said to be at US$1.3 trillion while the Islamic financial market is estimated to be US$600-800 billion in size, with an annual growth rate of 20% to 25%.
- There are over 700 Islamic financial institutions currently operating in about 75 countries worldwide, with more than 100 Islamic equity funds managing assets in excess of US$19.0 billion.

Indeed, the pace of development in the Islamic financial market has gathered momentum with the formation and growth of various international Islamic organisations to provide the appropriate infrastructure, see figure 4.1.

These organisations include:

- The Accounting and Auditing Organisation for Islamic Financial Institutions (AAOIFI), based in Bahrain.
- The Islamic Financial Services Board (IFSB), based in Malaysia.
- The International Islamic Financial Market (IIFM), based in Bahrain.

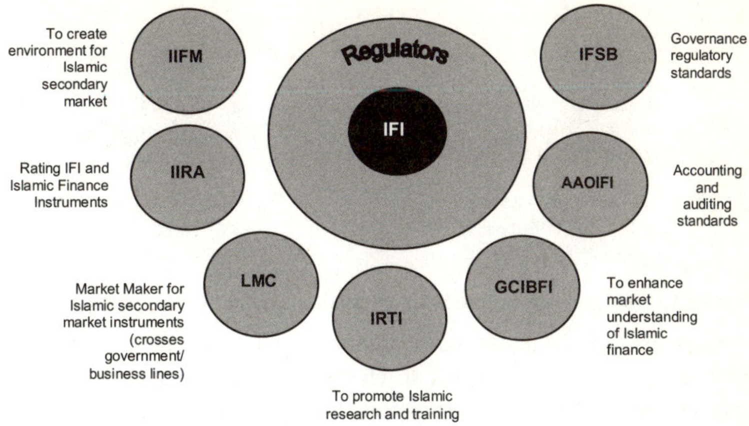

Key

IFI	Islamic financial institutions
Regulators	Central Banks, Monetary Authorities, Securities Commissions etc
IIFM	International Islamic Financial Market
IIRA	International Islamic Rating Agency
LMC	Liquidity Management Centre
IFSB	Islamic Financial Services Board
AAOIFI	Accounting and Auditing Organisation for Islamic Financial Institutions
GCIBFI	General Council for Islamic Banks and Financial Institutions
IRTI	Islamic Research and Training Institute

Figure 4.1. Islamic financial infrastructure

Today, the Islamic capital market operates in parallel to the conventional capital market and provides investors with an investment philosophy based on religion. It is rapidly gaining worldwide acceptance. It should be stressed that the fact that the Islamic capital market does not prohibit participation from non-Muslims creates unlimited upside to the depth and breadth of this market.

What are Islamic capital markets?

The differences between Western conventional finance and Islamic finance can be as stark as the two cultures. The respective cultures have, quite naturally, developed investment strategies reflective of their different regions. While Western investments often take on high risk and are structured to generate maximum returns, Islamic investments are based on *Sharia'a* law, which forbids the payment and receipt of interest and requires risks and profits to be shared amongst investors. Figure 4.2 illustrates the two main components of an Islamic capital market.

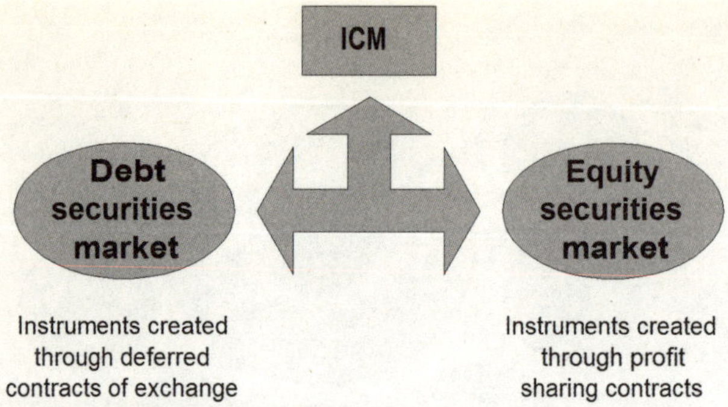

Figure 4.2. Two main components of an Islamic capital market (ICM)

The role of capital markets in promoting an efficient financial system cannot be over-emphasised. Given that a developed financial system can make positive contributions to economic development, the existence of vibrant capital markets becomes a necessity for any economy. As discussed in *Chapter 3* capital markets facilitate long-term financing for businesses and entrepreneurs by attracting savings from a large pool of investors. These markets provide long-term capital to entrepreneurs through a series of short-term securities with investors who may enter and exit the market at will.

An efficient capital market is expected to perform the following functions:

- to provide a resource mobilisation mechanism leading to an efficient allocation of financial resources in the economy;
- to provide liquidity in the market at the cheapest price, i.e. the lowest transaction cost or low bid-ask spread on the securities being traded in the market;
- to ensure transparency in the pricing of securities by determining the risk premia, reflecting the riskiness of the security;
- to provide opportunities for constructing well-diversified portfolios and to reduce the level of risk through diversification across geographic regions and across time.

Capital markets consist of primary and secondary markets. Whereas primary markets are important for raising new capital and depend on the supply of funds, secondary markets make a significant contribution by facilitating the trading of existing securities. In some ways, secondary markets play an equally critical role by ensuring liquidity and fair pricing in the market and by giving valuable signals about the security. In other words, secondary markets not only provide liquidity and low transaction costs, they also determine the prices of the securities and their associated risk on a continuous basis, incorporating relevant new information as it arrives.

Just as capital markets play a critical role in the conventional financial system, their role in the Islamic financial system is also equally important. Whereas conventional capital markets have an established and long-running track record, Islamic capital markets are at an early stage of their development.

Conventional capital markets have two main streams: the securities markets for debt trading and the stock markets for equity trading. Raising capital through conventional debt is not possible in the Islamic system due to the prohibition of interest. Although borrowing and lending on the basis of debt is a common practice in modern conventional markets, Muslims cannot participate in conventional debt markets.

It should be stressed that the concept of stock markets is most certainly in consonance with the *Sharia'a* principles of profit-and-loss sharing. However not every business listed on the stock market is fully compliant with the *Sharia'a*. These issues pose challenges for the development of Islamic capital markets.

An Islamic capital market refers to the market where the activities are carried out in ways that do not conflict with the conscience of Muslims and the religion of Islam. In other words, the Islamic capital market represents an assertion of religious law in capital market transactions where the market should be free from the involvement of prohibited activities by Islam, as well as free from elements such as usury (*riba*), gambling (*maisir*) and ambiguity (*gharar*). Figure 4.3 illustrates the parties to an Islamic capital market.

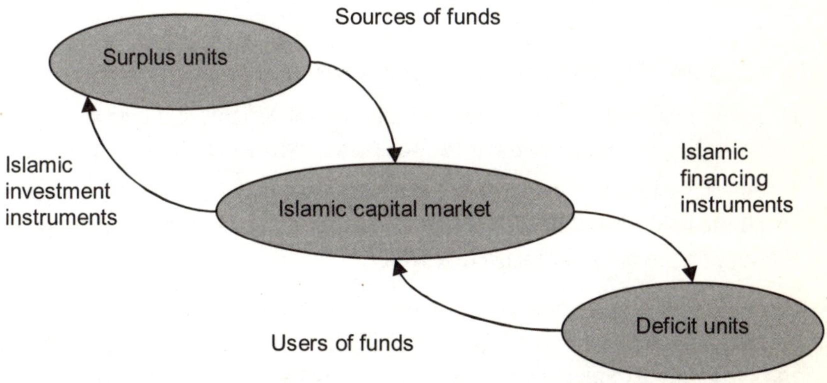

Figure 4.3. Parties to an Islamic capital market

Functions of an Islamic capital market

An Islamic capital market should ideally perform all the above listed functions of conventional capital markets but with the added Islamic concerns of justice and equitable distribution of benefits. The *Qur'an* and the *ahadith* have given clear guidance on moral rules and obligations, prohibition of interest, and the prohibition of obtaining others' property by wrongful means. Based on these and other guidelines, an Islamic capital market should function without interest and also without some of the other issues which, in the eyes of Muslims, adversely affect conventional markets viz *gharar* etc.

Another aspect of Islam is that it prescribes the compulsory financial obligation of *zakat*. The *Qur'an* prescribed that the purpose of *zakat* is to ensure that the wealth does not circulate only among your rich folk' (Al-Hashar 59:7). In this sense, if the capital market is not growing to allow for the overall increase in wealth and economic growth or if the growth results in the concentration of wealth to few groups of individuals, this indicates, in the eyes of Muslims, that there exists some weaknesses in the system and corrective measures need to be implemented by the appropriate authorities. This is also an area where capital markets fit within Islam.

As mentioned in *Chapter 3* in the conventional financial system, an ideal effective and efficient regulatory structure is said to promote financial markets that are:

1) liquid and efficient, where there exists a free flow of capital and where it is allocated efficiently given the underlying risks and expected returns;
2) transparent and fair where information must be reliable and relevant and must flow in a timely and fair-handed manner to all market participants; and
3) ethical and sound where market participants should act with integrity and in accordance with principles of unimpeachable conduct as they make capital transactions and other related activities.

The success of regulators is seen in terms of the extent to which they can build investor confidence in the integrity and fairness of transactions in capital market and the extent to which they are able to develop the markets in the direction of better transparency, greater competition and hence greater efficiency.

Objectives of an Islamic capital market

In principle, the objectives of an Islamic capital market are based on the *Sharia'a* which in essence should be treated as the necessary framework vehicle to transfer funds from surplus to deficit units. This is to ensure the equitable allocation of capital to sectors which would yield the best returns to the owners of capital and hence contribute towards the overall growth and expansion of the economy. The objective of the Islamic capital market is also to ensure that a means of attracting surplus funds for worthwhile investments exists in accordance with the owners' preferences in terms of the extent of risk involvement, rate of return as well as the period of investment preferred. Without a capital market, the fund owners would not find sufficient opportunities to invest for the short-term. Most investments have gestation lags and are long-term in character. Emergency needs may arise from time to time which cannot be easily met.

It is also un-Islamic to hoard wealth. It is therefore necessary for wealth owners to invest their funds in order to allow their funds not to be unnecessarily eroded by the obligatory *zakat* (Islamic tax). An Islamic stock market is ideally characterised by the absence of, interest-based transactions, derivative-based transactions and stocks of companies dealing in unlawful activities or items. It should also be free from any form of unethical or immoral transactions, such as market manipulations, insider trading and short selling.

Islamic capital market portfolio choices

Conditions for investment in shares [1]

In the light of the foregoing discussion, dealing in equity shares can be acceptable in *Sharia'a* subject to the following conditions:

1) The main business of the company is not in violation of the *Sharia'a*. This means that it is not permissible to acquire the shares of companies providing financial services associated with interest, such as conventional banks, insurance companies etc. Companies involved in some other business not approved by the *Sharia'a*, such as companies manufacturing, selling or offering alcohol, pork, *haram* meat, or involved in gambling, night club activities, pornography etc, are forbidden.
2) If the main business of the companies is *halal*, such as computers, cars, oil refining etc but the companies involved deposit their surplus earnings in an interest-bearing account or borrow money on interest, the shareholders, some scholars suggest, should express their disapproval against such dealings. Preferably they should do this by raising their voice against such activities in the Annual General Meeting of the company.
3) If some income from interest-bearing accounts is included in the income of the company, the proportion of such income in the dividend paid to the shareholder must be given to charity, and must not be retained by the investor. For example if 5% of the total income of a company has been earned from interest-bearing deposits, then 5% of the dividend earnings must be given to charity.

   This means that where profits are earned through dividends, a certain proportion of the dividend, which corresponds to the proportion of interest earned by the company, must be given to charity. Islamic Scholars have termed this process as 'purification'.

Sharia'a Scholars have different views about whether the 'purification' is necessary where the profits are made through capital gains (i.e. by purchasing the shares at a lower price and selling them at a higher price). Some scholars are of the view that, even in the case of capital gains, the process of 'purification' is necessary.

Other *Sharia'a* Scholars take the view that that no 'purification' is required if the share is sold, even if this results in a capital gain.

4) The shares of a company are negotiable (freely investible in) only if the company owns some non-liquid assets. If all the assets of a company are in liquid form, i.e. in the form of money that cannot be purchased or sold, except at par value, then these shares cannot be purchased. In this case the share represents money only and the *Sharia'a* principle states that 'money cannot be traded for money except at par'.

   What should be the exact proportion of non-liquid assets of a company enabling the negotiability of its shares? Contemporary scholars have different views about this question. Some scholars are of the view that the ratio of non-liquid assets must be 51% at the very least. They argue that if such assets are less than 50%, then most of the assets are in liquid form, and therefore, all its assets should be treated as liquid, on the basis of the juristic principle: 'The majority deserves to be treated as the whole of a thing.'

   Some other scholars, however, have opined that even if the non-liquid assets of a company are 33%, its shares can be treated as negotiable.

Islamic framework of financial regulation

In contrast to the conventional system the Islamic framework of finance consists of three institutions, namely *ukhuwah* (brotherhood), *adl* (justice) and *ihsan* (benevolence).

Ukhuwah

Under the institutions of *ukhuwah* or brotherhood, Islam unites all individuals in the bond of universal brotherhood whereby all individuals are regarded as members of a single family but each of them is entitled to equal social status. This implies that co-operation and mutual help is the backbone of this brotherhood institution. From this perspective and applying this concept to modern finance, we can infer that Islam views financiers and clients as members of one brotherhood and rules out any relationship in which the financier acts from a position of power and strength and the client acts from the position of being socially weak. This motivation should affect the forces of demand and supply in the financial market in a complementary manner whereby both parties understand each other's interest and, through fair dealing, focus on favourable synergies which facilitate greater use of risk-sharing modes of financing.

Adl

The institution of *adl* (justice) plays a key role in realising the goals of social balance because it provides legally enforceable measures specified in the contract. The fulfilment of a contract removes any injustice and exploitation. Islamic *fiqh* has developed a comprehensive code for making contracts which regulate the role of both parties and emphasises that all contracts should be honoured in accordance with the terms stipulated. Hence, adherence to the principles relating to financial contracts minimises the possibility of fraud and deception.

Ihsan

The institution of *ihsan* essentially means foregoing one's rights for the sake of others. This is an act which is considered to be a virtue of higher order and consistent with the Islamic concept of rationality. The individual displaying benevolence understands that Allah will compensate him for his sacrifices. Islamic teachings call upon both the financier and the client to be kind, honest, accommodating and generous. In fact, *ihsan* contains a set of values that give rise to professionalism, high ethical conduct and the concept of trust, the by-product of which is good governance. In Islam, elements of good governance that is trust, accountability and ethical conduct are a way of life.

Evolution of Islamic capital markets

The need for Islamic capital markets was realised at the early stages of development of the Islamic financial industry During the 1980s and 1990s, Islamic Financial Institutions (IFIs) mobilised funds successfully through attracting deposits, which were invested in a few financial instruments, mostly dominated by commodities or trade-financing. Due to the limited investment opportunities, lack of liquid assets and other constraints, the composition of IFIs' assets side remained fairly static and heavily focused on short-term instruments.

The main areas of concern were the lack of portfolio and risk management tools and the absence of derivative instruments. With continuing demand for *Sharia'a* compliant financing, there was a pressing need to develop capital markets to facilitate long-term, *Sharia'a* compliant financing, for businesses and to create portfolio diversification opportunities for investors and financial intermediaries.

One of the impediments to growth was the fast changing landscape of modern financial markets as well as the intricacies of rules demanded by the *Sharia'a*. The task was further complicated by the different schools of Islamic thought in various parts of the globe.

Nevertheless, by the late 1990s, Islamic financial institutions had realised that the development of capital markets was essential for their survival and further growth. Meanwhile, deregulation and liberalisation of capital movements in several countries led to close co-operation between Islamic financial institutions and conventional financial institutions in order to find solutions for liquidity and portfolio management.

The result was two distinct developments, both of which are on-going, the introduction of equity funds which were compliant with the *Sharia'a* and the launch of Islamic asset-backed securities (ABS), more commonly known as *sukuk*.

Whereas Islamic equity funds became popular with investors who had a risk appetite for equity investment, Islamic financial institutions, driven by the nature of their intermediation role, kept demanding securities which would behave like conventional fixed-income debt securities but also comply with the *Sharia'a*.

In addition, Islamic financial institutions wanted to extend the maturity structure of their assets beyond the typical short-term maturities provided by trade-finance instruments. This led to the creation of *Sharia'a* compliant ABS, *sukuk*, which have risk and return characteristics similar to conventional debt securities. The result is that within the short span of just a few years, the market for *sukuk* has reached an impressive size. *Chapter 9* discusses *sukuk* further. Figure 4.4 illustrates the range of *Sharia'a* compliant investment choices.

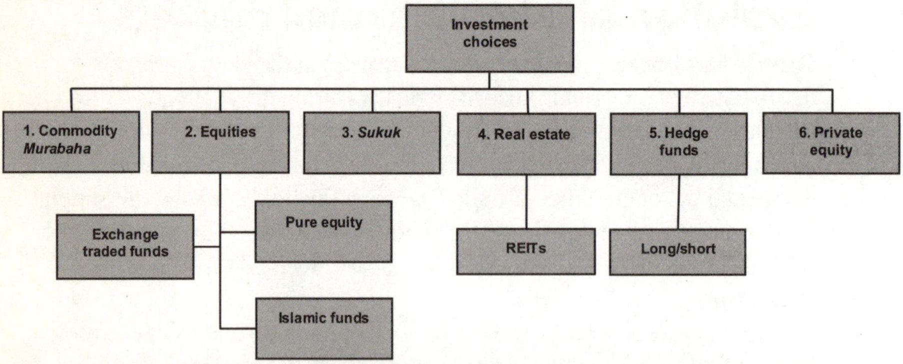

Figure 4.4. Range of *Sharia'a* compliant investment choices

An Islamic capital market should ideally provide a stable and viable source of long-term funds for financing large investments and development projects as well as for capital and business expansion. The Islamic capital market should also ensure greater diversification of risks emanating from asset and liability mismatches facing Islamic financial institutions. The market has a pivotal role in ensuring the overall stability of the Islamic financial system through its contribution to the enhancement of a resilient and robust Islamic financial system in withstanding financial shocks.

At present, a wide selection of Islamic capital market products and services are available in the market to meet the needs of those who seek to invest in accordance with *Sharia'a* principles, see figure 4.4. These include *Sharia'a* compliant stocks, Islamic bonds (*sukuk*), Islamic funds and Islamic risk management products. Nonetheless, the strong growth for Islamic finance products is not only driven by increasing demand from those who want to invest in instruments that are *Sharia'a* compliant, in order that they are able to meet their religious obligations but also by non-Muslims. The latter find some of the risk-return features attractive as do those investors who subscribe to ethical investment philosophies.

Current market environment

Islamic capital markets are now gaining the momentum to grow into a vibrant marketplace, especially for emerging market borrowers in the regions of the Middle East, South-East Asia and North Africa. On the supply side, the volume of Islamic investors, those with a preference for *Sharia'a* compliant investment instruments, has grown to form a critical mass that can support a well-functioning and efficient capital market. It is evolving into a truly international market. Not only highly rated borrowers such as the Multilateral Development Banks (for example, the World Bank), but also developing country borrowers with lower credit ratings, such as Pakistan, have successfully raised a considerable volume of funds in this market.

On the demand side, countries in the developing world, especially the middle-income countries, will require a significant volume of investments in infrastructure over the next decade. To illustrate, for Indonesia alone, additional infrastructure investments of US$5bn (2% of GDP) are required annually, to reach a 6% medium-term growth target, as estimated by the World Bank, as at 2007. Because the domestic capital markets of these borrowers are often not deep enough to satisfy their large investment needs, they are anxious to access external sources of financing.

Furthermore, Muslim stakeholders in middle-income countries are increasingly expressing their preference for *Sharia'a* compliant financing. Borrowers, especially public-sector institutions, are starting to reflect their stakeholders' voices in the implementation of financial operations. In turn, financial intermediaries, including private-sector commercial and investment banks, as well as development finance institutions, are paying more attention to such 'non-financial' needs of their clients – in addition to satisfying these borrowers' funding needs, in order to stay successful in the marketplace.

For the Multilateral Development Banks (MDBs), such as the World Bank, the development of Islamic capital markets continues to be a highly relevant topic for various reasons. Firstly, MDBs are deeply involved in infrastructure finance in their borrowing member countries and would therefore naturally be interested in the emerging Islamic capital market as a new and alternative source of financing. Secondly, by channelling the funds available in Islamic financial markets, which are mostly based in the countries with high savings such as the GCC countries and Malaysia, to finance investments in developing countries, MDBs can create a new model for international development co-operation while responding to the stakeholders' voices on both sides. Thirdly, MDBs can promote financial stability by encouraging the development of Islamic capital markets to enhance liquidity, and enabling Islamic financial institutions to have more diversified portfolios and sound risk management. Furthermore, this could also provide the momentum to integrate the Islamic financial markets within the framework of the international financial system.

Development of Islamic capital market products

As outlined earlier, the development of an Islamic capital market was the result of the pressing need to address liquidity management of Islamic financial institutions. During the 1980s and 1990s, Islamic financial institutions were able to mobilise their deposits by investing in a handful of financial instruments which were dominated by trade financing. Activities on the asset side of these institutions included cost-plus-sale, Islamic leasing, trust financing and equity participation. However, the asset composition of Islamic financial institutions remained fairly static and was heavily focused on short-term instruments, mainly commodity financing, due mostly to the lack of liquid assets. Hence the management of balance sheet liquidity became a major challenge facing the Islamic financial institutions owing to the scarcity of Islamic capital market instruments. This gave rise to the demand for the introduction of new Islamic financial instruments and to the promotion of Islamic financial engineering.

The development of the Islamic capital market can be seen through the development of a wide range of Islamic capital products that are becoming widely available such as *Sharia'a* compliant stocks, Islamic funds, Islamic bonds and Islamic stock broking services. To date, investors are able to place their savings in a wide range of *Sharia'a* compliant funds with real estate and private equity investment being the primary choice. The Islamic capital market is also seeing an increasingly wide offering of more innovative *Sharia'a* products, including exchangeable or convertible *sukuk*, commodity linked certificates, equity linked notes and structured foreign-exchange linked-products. In the capital markets, the introduction of the global sovereign *sukuk* more than a decade ago was an important innovation that has since gained significant ground.

By 2009 the global market for *sukuk* exceeded US$100 billion. Commodity *Murabaha* Investments, discussed in detail in *Chapter 6*, have also grown to be increasingly common, with such investments forming about 70% of Islamic short and medium-term money market transactions in the Islamic finance industry. The size of commodity *Murabaha* transactions is also around $100 billion

In terms of Islamic product innovation, Malaysia remains at the forefront particularly in *sukuk* issuance. The launch of *sukuk* by Malaysian companies has demonstrated the ability of local intermediaries in structuring products and offering services that are acceptable to financial investors. *Sukuk* originating from Malaysia, by 2009, accounted for nearly 70% of all *sukuk* issued globally. The Malaysian Islamic financial markets has also successfully introduced a variety of Islamic financial hedging Instruments such as the Islamic profit rate swap, the Islamic cross-currency swap and the Islamic forward rate agreement.

With the introduction of the Commodity Murabaha Programme (CMP) by Bank Negara (the Central Bank of Malaysia) the Malaysian government hopes to further spur the infrastructure development of the Islamic financial system and to diversify the policy instruments to manage short-term liquidity in the Malaysian Islamic capital market. The CMP is the first commodity transaction that utilises crude palm oil-based contracts as the underlying assets. With wider usage of commodity *Murabaha* transactions globally, it is intended that this will add breadth and depth to the Malaysian Islamic money market as it facilitates a more efficient distribution of money-market type liquidity and expands the range of instruments that market participants can actively transact in.

It must be said that many of the Malaysian Islamic financial products do not conform to the GCC concept of *Sharia'a* compliance although Malaysia is taking extensive steps to move towards the GCC model.

Islamic securitisation and Islamic capital markets

Islamic teachings emphasise that the whole of business and financial institutions activities should be pursued in a way that complies with *Sharia'a* principles. The major ruling aspects are the prohibition of interest-based transactions, adhering to lawful activities *(Halal)* and sinful activities (*Haram*) rules. In addition the whole business should be implemented with some degree of risk. The risk-free type of investment is not found within the Islamic investment environment. The reward system under Islamic philosophy is based upon risk taking considerations, allowing no room for gaining profits without exposure to some sort of business risk.

As Islamic jurisdiction prohibit dealings through interest-based transactions, so all financial and credit dealings, under Islamic principles, tend to relate finance to assets. Asset backed securitisation becomes Islamically possible as long as these assets can be structured and conveyed according to Islamic principles. The use of securitisation brings in much needed liquidity to Islamic institutions by enabling them to free up part of their capital which is tied up with these illiquid assets. These can be securitised into partnerships based on non-predetermined rate of return instruments.

Islamic capital markets are generally underdeveloped. Religious constraints on permissible investment rule out conventional forms of interest-bearing debt finance. In the absence of tradable debt and valuation problems of financing contracts, Islamic finance has proven conceptually difficult especially for money management. Banks operating under *Sharia'a* law are predisposed to adopt buy-and-hold investment strategies and carry excess short-term reserves given the lack of sufficient long-term reinvestment opportunities. This has inhibited efficient financial intermediation and capital market deepening within the Islamic capital market. Nonetheless, financial institutions have been able to develop various forms of Islamic finance instruments that are virtually identical to their conventional counterparts, at least in substance.

How does Islamic securitisation fit with the notion of Islamic finance? Since most Islamic financial products are based on the concept of asset backing, the economic concept of asset securitisation is particularly amenable to the basic tenets of Islamic finance. Asset securitisation describes the process and the result of issuing certificates of ownership as pledge against existing or future cash flows from a diversified pool of assets (reference portfolio) to investors.

Islamic securitisation transforms bilateral risk-sharing between borrowers and lenders in Islamic finance into the market-based refinancing of one or more underlying Islamic finance transactions. In its basic concept, originators would sell existing or future revenues from lease receivables (asset based), 'sale-back profit' (debt based) or private equity from a portfolio of Islamically acceptable assets to a special purpose vehicle (SPV), which refinances itself by issuing securities to market investors, who are the 'capital market corollary' to a singular lender in Islamic finance. They assume the role of a 'collective financier' whose entrepreneurial investment does not involve guaranteed, interest-based earnings.

Islamic framework for securitisation: the basics

Given the above mentioned constraints that bound the working of Islamic entities, there are several elements to the Islamic securitisation process which differ from their conventional counterparts.

1. Type of assets to be securitised

As securitisation has evolved in the non-Islamic world, the conventional ABS do not necessarily conform to Islamic principles particularly given the existence of interest-bearing elements and receivables etc. According to prescribed guidance, the assets to be securitised Islamically might include leasing contracts, equity ownership, *Murabaha* and other sales contracts. This is in addition to current tangible assets that generate systematic cash flows, which would be acceptable for trading by Islamic investors.

2. Securitisation structure

The structure of securitisation applying Islamic features does not differ greatly from that of the conventional type. The major players consist of the originator, trustee, Servicer, SPV, investment bankers, Credit Enhancer and rating agency. It is necessary to describe how these roles differ when applying Islamic investment principles:

1) The securities issued by the SPV are claims on assets held by the issuer SPV. This must be done in a way such that claims are closely attached to the ownership of such assets.
2) ABS cannot guarantee a predetermined rate of return but a variable one alongside with the performance of the assets under securitisation.
3) The credit enhancer provides the required credit enhancement (if needed). This could be either part of the fund generated from asset cash flows, or collateral pledged to support assets, or guarantees in order to obtain sound credit rating.
4) The pass-through securitisation structure can be visualised as the closest arrangement that satisfies Islamic principles.
5) The transfer of assets from an originator to an SPV should ideally be on a True Sale basis. In some securitisation cases the originator has a right to compete in the repurchasing of the underlying assets after selling them to an SPV, when the securitisation deal is finalised. This is nearly always done in securitising government productive assets where the public interest dictates the retention of Government ownership of specific strategic assets.

Islamic securitisation – building on the basic principles [(2)]

The implementation of Islamic securitisation requires a two-stage 'fundamental' verification process, which assesses the *Sharia'a* compliance of:

1) the *type of assets* in the underlying reference portfolio and the generation of investment returns, and
2) the *transaction structure*, which includes the configuration of credit enhancement (and other forms of credit and liquidity support) and the form of ownership conveyance.

Securitisation under *Sharia'a* law forbids interest income and must be structured in a way that rewards investors for their direct exposure to business risk, i.e. investors receive a share of profits commensurate to the risk they take in lieu of predetermined interest. All the asset types of Islamic finance are principally eligible for Islamic securitisation. However there are unresolved issues largely revolving around restrictions on debt trading, a particular issue with *Murabaha* and *Salam* contracts.

Characteristics of conventional securitisation only apply if they convey a sufficient element of ownership to investors as entrepreneurial investment in real economic activity within an interest-free structural arrangement. In addition administrative issues, such as underwriting standards, issue placement and the procurement of ratings, are subject to religious scrutiny. Any capital generated from securitised issuance under *Sharia'a* law is to be used exclusively for the repayment of initial funding.

Conventional securitisation, which originated in non-Islamic economies, invariably involves interest-bearing debt. Bond holders would typically hold (secured) contingent claims on the performance of securitised assets, which entitle them to receive both predetermined interest and the repayment of the principal amount. However, the issuance of interest-bearing debt securities with a secured redemption amount cannot be reconciled with Islamic financing principles given the prohibition of profit from debt and speculation. Financial relationships under *Sharia'a* law are not governed by interest but by shared business risk (and returns) from investment in religiously acceptable services, trade or products, with clear and transparent rights and obligations to investors.

In particular any gains from Islamic fixed-income securities are related to the purpose for which the funding is used. Such purpose under *Sharia'a* law must involve the funding or the production of real assets rather than the purchase of financial securities, which would amount to second-order financing akin to lending for derivatives type trading, with the subsequent gearing being speculative.

Islamic securitisation must confer upon investors' clearly identifiable rights and obligations in securitised assets in order to ensure direct participation in the distribution of risk and reward between lenders and borrowers with limited risk mitigation and/or indemnification through credit enhancement. Hence, from a procedural and substantive perspective, Islamic securitisation would need to involve the conversion of uncertain, business-related proceeds of direct investment in religiously-sanctioned real economic activity.

Hence, adapting the basic principles of conventional securitisation for Islamic purposes requires compliance with the following conditions:

1) there should be a *real* purpose behind raising funds via securitisation, and the type of collateral assets realising the securitised revenues must be clearly identified (or be capable of identification) and cannot be consumed;

2) each transaction participant should share in both the risk and return, and the investor should receive a positive payoff from profitable ventures only;

3) collateral assets must not be debt, cash or prohibited as *haram* (sinful activity) and must not be associated in any way with unethical or exploitative operations or with speculation and uncertainty (*gharar*) from non-productive investment;
4) the structure should provide investor compensation for business risk from direct participation in securitised assets and should not imply an exchange of debt for interest-generating investment return (unless those securitised assets are interest-free and sold at face value);
5) investors should hold an unconditional and unsecured payment obligation and *not* a guaranteed promissory note;
6) a sufficient element of ownership must be conveyed to investors;
7) the contribution from investors, in the form of proceeds from issued notes (and any returns generated by the issuing agent from managing collateral assets), cannot be reinvested in short-term cash instruments or interest-bearing debt;
8) the underlying assets and securitised obligations must not be employed for speculative purposes;
9) because conventional insurance violates *Sharia'a* provisions, Islamic insurance, based on co-operation and mutual help (*Takaful*) should be employed instead; and
10) any form of credit enhancement and/or liquidity support and limitations of prepayment risk must be in a permissible form.

Pass-through structure

The conventional *pass-through* payment structure (i.e. equity participation) of traditional securitisation seems to be closest to the strict interpretation of Islamic principles, which require the *transfer of a minimum level of ownership* to ensure direct investor participation in the business risk associated with the performance of a dedicated collateral pool of securitised assets.

An *asset-backed bond* (ABB) is a debt obligation collateralised by a reference portfolio of on-balance-sheet assets of the originator. ABBs can be over-collateralised as a form of credit enhancement, i.e. the value of securitised assets exceeds the notional value of issued debt obligations. As opposed to *pass-through* transactions, the cash flows from the reference portfolio are not dedicated to investors, who have no direct ownership rights to them.

Frequently, the underlying reference portfolio is reconfigured, with a residual claim held by the issuer or originator.

A *pass-through* payment structure conveys direct ownership of investors in a reference portfolio of off-balance sheet assets, which are similar in maturity and quality. The originator services the portfolio, makes the collections and passes them on, less servicing fee, to investors – without reconfiguration of the cash flows.

Pay-through structure

A *pay-through* payment structure combines security features of both a pass-through and an ABB.

True sale structure

If the pass-through transaction removes the securitised assets from the originator's balance sheet (off-balance sheet), ownership conveyance through a *true sale* payment structure implicitly satisfies three further criteria:

1) the exclusive dedication of cash flows from the underlying asset to establish the linkage of ownership interest to identifiable economic activity,
2) the irrevocable, but unconditional and unsecured repayment from the underlying assets, and
3) a transaction structure that does not involve interest payments.

For instance, pay-through bonds collateralised by on-balance sheet assets, whose asset proceeds are dedicated but conveyed through interest-bearing debt, would not qualify as suitable securities under these criteria.

However, *Sharia'a* compliant conveyance of legal title in pass-throughs can also be designed to represent a simple collection of ownership attributes, such as an assignment of a portion of ownership rights and obligations, which allow investors to exercise control over securitised assets, take over operations or even sell securitised assets to realise the redemption value of their investment claims. In cases of complex tax and legal issues as well as prevailing restrictions on foreign ownership of locally domiciled assets (such as in many Islamic countries), partial assignment is sometimes the only possibility of implementing securitisation with direct ownership rights under *Sharia'a* law.

Also *pay-through* structures (i.e. debt-type issuance) with dedicated collateral assets that fund unsecured, interest-free obligations with direct ownership rights, such as trust-based private equity funds, would theoretically meet *Sharia'a* requirements.

However, the conveyance of direct ownership through promissory notes, mortgages or security instruments to establish *Sharia'a* compliance may entail legal uncertainty if *Sharia'a* principles govern the transaction as a matter of form and negate the enforceability of investor interests under commercial law *vis-à-vis* the originator of securitised assets.

Subordination and Islamic finance

In principle, the flexible security design of conventional securitisation allows issuers to devise various mechanisms of risk-sharing, which includes subordination as one form of credit enhancement to improve the quality of issued securities. Issuers commonly subordinate investor claims into a three-tier transaction structure of junior, mezzanine, and senior tranches, which concentrates expected losses in a small junior tranche ('first loss position').

While capital market investors receive the mezzanine and senior tranches as subordinated debt-like notes, the issuer commonly bears most of the asset exposure and shifts most unexpected risk to larger, more senior tranches by retaining the junior tranche as a residual equity-like class to avert *ex ante* moral hazard and possible adverse selection.

Alternatively, issuers (or servicers) of transactions could set aside some of the cash flow generated by securitised assets to fund a 'reserve account' or 'first loss pool' as a form of self insurance. Other types of credit enhancement also involve over collateralisation, spread counts, standby letters of credit to the securitisation conduit (or by a sponsoring bank), pool insurance or monoline insurance.

Sharia'a law does not rule out the use of credit enhancement as long as it is optional for investors and does not change the overall character of the transaction. For instance tranche subordination of conventional securitisation can be replicated by a lease-buyback *(Ijara)* transaction under *Sharia'a* law. The issuer would assign partial ownership rights of the underlying asset portfolio to investors according to the riskiness of their investment and lease back the entire portfolio in return for fixed rental payments conditional on the option (or obligation) to repurchase the reference portfolio at a predetermined sales price at some future date. However this structure has come under *Sharia'a* scrutiny, an issue discussed further in *Chapter 9*.

Challenges for the Islamic capital markets

In the wake of the current wave and volatility of oil revenues and increasing demand for *Sharia'a* compliant products, Islamic capital markets are emerging at a quickening pace and stakeholders are starting to realise the potential. Development of institutional infrastructure in the international fora, such as the establishment of accounting standards and regulatory bodies, are all steps in the right direction. However, for the market to grow further, it also needs strong leadership and constructive policy actions of host governments, to enable market participants to originate Islamic finance transactions.

Well-developed Islamic capital markets will not only be beneficial for borrowers and institutional investors, they can also further enhance the stability of Islamic financial institutions, providing them with improved portfolio, liquidity and risk management tools. Ultimately, all these developments will contribute to integrating Islamic financial markets, as well as the players who form these markets, into the framework of the broader conventional international financial system.

The introduction of new Islamic capital market instruments will continue to be an uphill task if reviews are not made to the existing framework and structures governing the issuance of global *Sharia'a* compliant products. Fervent structural changes as well as judicial consciousness are imperative for the Islamic industry to survive the currents of globalisation and change as the current Islamic capital market products are segmented across countries. High transaction costs are still regarded as an issue and this stems from the differences in the regulatory and listing requirements, different trading platforms and trading rules, lack of support institutions for cross-border transactions and a range of *Sharia'a* compliant criteria.

Even if a robust regulatory structure is in place, the challenge that lays ahead remains one of as to how to bring convergence on regulatory structures across national borders. As discussed earlier, the Islamic capital market needs to be opened and accessible to all investors be it Muslims or non-Muslims. But in order to continue to attract big players into the market, it is essential to understand what global institutions look for when exploring the world's capital markets. Above all, they seek familiarity with the financial systems and regulations as well as certainty that justice will be upheld by the rule of law. Hence, this creates the challenge of developing homogeneity in the Islamic capital market.

Another issue facing the development of the Islamic capital market is the lack of convergence of *Sharia'a* interpretations. Different Muslim countries have adopted different practices in relation to various Islamic capital market products and services. This is a result of the varying interpretation on various *Sharia'a* issues across jurisdictions due to the differing schools of thought amongst *Sharia'a* Scholars. In fact there has evolved a clear schism in the industry between the Malaysian model and the GCC model. This may have implications for cross-border flows in relation to investment and trading of international Islamic instruments. Convergence of *Sharia'a* interpretations would facilitate a higher level of issuance of globally accepted Islamic capital market products and services in the international marketplace.

Arguably, the harmonisation of *Sharia'a* interpretations could lead to the creation of more homogeneous Islamic capital products and services. That in turn will increase investor's demand and enhance the overall growth of the Islamic capital market. Furthermore, standardised practices among market players in the market should result in a reduction in transaction costs as well as risks. Differing *Sharia'a* transactions may also affect the enforceability of a transaction, as differences in interpretation would affect the recognition of legal rights and liabilities of parties to a transaction, particularly in a cross-border transactions and listings. In order to expand the market for Islamic products and make them available at global level, efforts have been underway, for some time, to cross-list *Sharia'a* compliant products across markets.

Product Innovation is crucial in the process of deepening and broadening the Islamic financial industry and thus a critical factor in the development of the Islamic capital market and finance. For Islamic capital markets to remain competitive, attractive and innovative indigenous Islamic financial products must be introduced to meet the risk-reward profiles of investors and issuers, fulfilling all the tenets of the *Sharia'a* while remaining sufficiently cost-effective and competitive *vis-à-vis* conventional products.

Finally, Islamic financial products must be competitive investments in their own right. Islamic banks can no longer rely solely on the religious fervour of their clients as a stimulant for demand. As more non-Muslim investors (especially from Europe and the US) show more interest in Islamic products, banks must structure instruments so that they offer equivalent or better investment returns than their conventional rivals.

As globalisation increasingly brings the conventional and Islamic investment philosophies and peoples into contact with each other, new questions and opportunities will arise about how investments and culture can collaborate in a mutually-beneficial manner.

References

1. Usmani. T.U. *An Introduction to Islamic Finance*. Idaratul Ma'arif. Karachi, Pakistan 1999.

2. The author acknowledges drawing on 'The Economics of Islamic Finance and Securitisation' by Andreas Jobst, IMF Working Paper WP/07/117, with permission, for this section.

Chapter 5

Islamic investment principles

Why Islamic investing?

Muslims see Allah (God) as having appointed humans as His agents on earth. Each Muslim has been given stewardship of a small portion of His wealth, it is believed, which Muslims call their own during their short time on earth. Muslims, in turn, are each obligated to discharge this responsibility with justice, mercy, and attention to avoiding harm to themselves, fellow humans, and the rest of creation. Islamic investing is the mechanism whereby Muslims meet this individual responsibility whilst simultaneously growing their wealth and promoting a robust, efficient and fair economic system. To appreciate some of the principles of Islamic investing it is necessary to start with the guidance provided by the *Qur'an* and the *ahadith*.

What is Islamic investing?

Islamic investing is investing with a commitment to the *Sharia'a*, the Divine guiding principles revealed by God to humankind in the *Qur'an* and demonstrated by the Prophet Muhammad. Most of these principles are common to most religions and morality systems, including the three Abrahamic religions – Islam, Christianity and Judaism. The Islamic investor considering owning stock in a company must consider the level of *Sharia'a* compliance in the company's business practices. As a stockholder he becomes a minority owner of the company and shares some ethical responsibility for the company's activities.

Islamic business practices encourage co-operation in producing and distributing goods and services that enhance human prosperity and dignity. The *Sharia'a* prohibits all business activities that produce significant harm or undignified moral behaviour. Business activities involving gambling, pornography, alcohol, money-lending, harmful substances and pork are prohibited in Islam. The *Sharia'a* also requires avoidance of revenues derived from any direct or intentional support of such activities. It clearly calls for avoiding the payment or receipt of interest on money-lending (*riba* in Arabic), avoiding hazardous or excessive ambiguity in transactions (*gharar* in Arabic), and obeying the laws of the land.

The *Qur'an* prohibits *riba* (interest). *Riba* is considered to not only refer to usury. Any loan in which the lender specifies a return in excess of the capital amount loaned is *riba*, irrespective of whether such an amount is moderate or excessive. The prohibited forms of *riba* are not restricted to an excess over capital that is extended as a loan.

In the case of foreign exchange transactions, the failure to provide full reciprocal value in another currency, at the instance of the contract, is considered as a form of *riba*. This is because it allows the party that has received payment/or the currency without providing the reciprocal exchange currency to unjustifiably benefit from the money in the time period prior to providing the reciprocal payment.

Hadith on eating interest

> Ibn Mas'ud R.A. reported that Allah's Messenger S.A.W. cursed the eater of interest, him who fed it (to others), its two witnesses and him who recorded it.
>
> Narrated by Tirmidhi

Words in *Qur'anic* literature and the prophetic traditions (*ahadith*) often have figurative meanings and care should be taken against misinterpreting these as to having a strict literal meaning or, in some cases, to adopt a figurative meaning when a strictly literal meaning is intended. Thus interest earned on money is not actually eaten but it is used for a variety of financial requirements. In these narrations, the noun 'eating' is adopted instead of usage. Most likely, any form of usage is equated, in the *ahadith* to physical eating since, although other forms of using interest may be external, the religious harm or Divine punishment remains.

Capital owners are instructed to either directly trade or invest their capital in Islamically permitted formats of investment and partnerships. Islam refutes the notion that capital providers can justify interest on the grounds that time has value. Although money has a time value, it cannot be necessarily claimed that the passing of time always results in a profit to the providers of capital. The Islamic prohibition against interest is so stringent that it warns that even those who witness an interest transaction, or record it, are sinful. Although the *hadith* literally mentions two witnesses, the number of witnesses is not limited. Therefore, even if a hundred or more persons witness an interest transaction, they would all be committing sin. Islam declares, quite unequivocally, that acts of worship to Allah are unacceptable to Him if income is derived from prohibited sources.

Additional Islamic business principles include respect for the environment and human welfare, fair and transparent dealing, and fair and just employment and R&D policies. Adherence to these principles is usually required as part of the laws of the land in accordance with local standards. The political views, religion, race, gender or nationality of company managers, employees, or other stockholders are **not** criteria directly relevant to Islamic investing.

Is investing in the stock market allowed under the *Sharia'a*?(1)

Equity investing is strongly encouraged in Islam. Most Islamic scholars agree that owning common stock in modern corporations is allowed, within certain guidelines, and is analogous to the equity partnerships practised by the Prophet

Muhammad and encouraged in his traditions (the *Sunnah*). It is also covered by the overall principle of co-operation stated by God in the *Qur'an* (5:2). In fact, buying stocks can be one of the most *Sharia'a* conscious investments that are available to many individual Muslims today but only if certain guidelines are met.

Equity investing in modern companies has to be viewed in light of the common alternative options available to the average Islamic investor. These alternatives are:

1) buying bonds or certificates of deposit;
2) hoarding cash or precious metals 'under the mattress' or in a safe deposit box;
3) saving money in a conventional bank;
4) saving money in an Islamic bank;
5) buying real estate;
6) giving all of one's spare money away to charity every month; or
7) not saving at all and spending all one's income on consumption.

Are these Islamically acceptable alternatives?

Option #1 is engaging directly in 100% *riba*. These are financial instruments which pay the forbidden *riba*.

Option #2 is condemned in the *Qur'an* and *Sunnah*, and does nothing for the *Umma* (the Islamic community).

Option #3 is allowable, according to many scholars, as long as the money is held in a non-interest-bearing account or any interest generated is given to charity. However it is questionable Islamically how much better it is to deposit money with a bank engaged primarily in forbidden *riba* activities than to invest in a company primarily engaged in allowable (*halal*) activities, provided earnings from the prohibited activities are given to charity by the Islamic investor.

Option #4 is perfectly acceptable but this option is not available to most Islamic investors today outside of a few countries that have Islamic banks. However this situation is changing quickly.

Option #5 is allowed, as long as no *riba* loan or mortgage is involved. However, real estate is a very illiquid form of investment that must be supplemented by other alternatives to handle short-term investment needs.

Option #6 is taking a commendable activity (charitable giving) to an extreme that is actually discouraged in the *Qur'an* '… so that you become blameworthy and destitute' (*Qur'an* 17:29). It is deemed desirable for Muslims to not keep themselves without any financial reserves because one's first charitable responsibility is to try to reasonably ensure one does not require charity oneself, thereby becoming a burden on relatives or others. Furthermore, this behaviour would obviously prevent one from saving to pay for necessary items, children's education, unexpected medical costs, pilgrimage to Mecca etc.

Finally option #7 may involve an extravagance that is prohibited in Islam: 'Do not be wasteful and extravagant, for God does not love wasteful and extravagant people' (*Qur'an* 6:141).

These considerations lead many Islamic scholars to believe that buying and owning stock of companies, with a minority of the stocks activities being in prohibited activities as being allowable based on the *Sharia'a* rule of allowing that which is inescapable or necessary to avoid undue hardship. This route is only valid provided the following general guidelines are met:

1) The main line of business must be allowable (*halal*).
2) *Riba* and other prohibited activities must not generate more than a small percentage of the company's income.
3) Financial assets (liquidity in banks and account receivables) that may generate interest must not be too large a percentage of company value.
4) Leverage or dependence on borrowing must not be high.
5) The company must have honest and transparent business practices and not be involved in cheating, fraud etc.
6) The Islamic investor must estimate the percentage of her or his profits that may have income from *riba* and other prohibited activities and donate it to general charitable causes so that their investment and profit remain pure.

The effect of these investment constraints are summarised in figure 5.1.

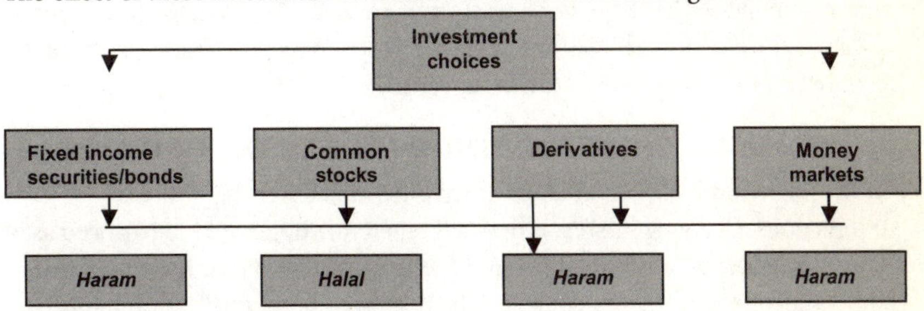

Figure 5.1. Islamic investment constraints

What is *riba*?

It can be stated that *riba* is one of the most important Islamic prohibitions when it comes to building an investment portfolio. But what is *riba* and why is it forbidden?

Riba is an Arabic word meaning increment or increase. In the context of business, it means an unearned increase in an exchange contract without offering anything in return that is recognisable under the *Sharia'a*. Interest on money-lending, or usury (under its classical definition), is the most common kind of *riba*. It is strongly condemned in the *Qur'an* in several verses. Examples of *riba* (usury) include interest paid on bank loans and credit cards, gains from trading bonds or other debts, and interest earned on saving and other deposit accounts.

On the other hand, charging rent for the use of a physical asset, such as a car, a machine or a house, is permissible and is certainly not *riba*. Therefore leases in which the lessor retains ownership and responsibility for the usability of the asset ('operating leases') do not involve *riba*. Trading on credit, where a higher-than-spot price is charged in deferred payment for goods or services, is also allowed and again is not *riba*. Gains from trading ownership shares in physical assets or business enterprises are not *riba*. And gains from the growth in the value of equity or other assets resulting from human effort or market conditions is certainly not *riba*. All of these allowable forms of earning a return on capital are encouraged in Islam: '... God has permitted trade, and forbidden *riba*.' (*Qur'an* 2:275).

What is the rationale for the Islamic prohibition of *riba*?[(2)]

It is important to understand the rationale of Divine commands even though Muslims' obligation to obey them is not contingent on such an understanding. This understanding makes *Sharia'a* compliance easier, helps Muslims apply it to specific situations, and improves Muslims' ability to secure the benefits God intended for Muslims when He revealed it. In the case of the prohibition of interest on money-lending, which was common to all three Abrahamic religions (Islam, Christianity, and Judaism), both micro-economic, or fairness, and macro-economic or social rationales can be discerned.

Micro-economic rationale for the ban on riba

At the micro level, the prohibition of *riba* aims at maintaining justice in transactions. Charging interest is deemed inherently unjust and unbalanced as it gives the lender an assured and secured return and puts all the burden of risk, and an unknown future outcome, on the borrower. Additionally, by limiting lending to a zero-return benevolent practice, the avoidance of *riba* places a healthy, natural limit on the amount of debt that a person, business or society can accumulate.

As with alcohol and gambling, it is often hard to demonstrate the harm involved in a small amount of interest on money-lending. But like gambling and alcohol, dealing in even a small amount of *riba* potentially puts a person on a slippery slope Muslims would reason, that can end in disaster. God, from an

Islamic perspective, in His infinite wisdom, sought to protect Muslims from bringing such disaster on themselves by prohibiting these vices.

In Islam, a loan is a benevolent act, and has little place in business or commerce. A person may loan someone their car, $100, or a cup of sugar, but they cannot take interest on the loan and can only demand return of the item loaned (or its like-kind equivalent in the case of money or consumables). However they may take and hold something as security for repayment of the loan. In commerce on the other hand, individuals engage not in benevolent acts but in commutative contracts, i.e. agreements where two parties trade things of value with the hope of financial gain. Therefore loans are deemed generally unsuitable for the realm of commerce within Islam.

However, it is perfectly allowable Islamically to buy, sell and rent goods, assets and services. Payment may be on the spot, advanced or deferred. A higher price may be charged for an item if payment is deferred. Similarly, a lower than spot price may be associated with advanced payment. Profit in trade, whether in sale for cash or credit, accrues only once and is based on the price as agreed upon at the time of sale. Debts may be created, but they can only be created in exchange for a real good or service of equal value. Debts, Islamically, do not grow merely with the passage of time. This puts a limit on the amount of debt a party can accumulate, equal to the value of goods or services they have purchased.

For example, a person may rent a refrigerator or buy it on extended payment terms, but if he does not make the scheduled payments, the seller may take back the refrigerator and/or refuse to offer future credit to the buyer. However this person cannot add to his debt Islamically other than to cover the cost caused by delinquency. On the other hand, *riba* borrowing may involve getting funds for vague or non-specific uses, such as a cash advance on a credit card. This can encourage wasteful spending and growing debts, Muslims believe.

Therefore, by prohibiting interest-bearing loans but allowing trade, God, Muslims believe, has allowed commerce to flourish while naturally limiting the amount and duration of debt each person or business can accumulate. Without *riba*, this accumulation is limited to the value of real products or services useful to the debtor, which are normally available to secure the corresponding debts. The potential for general bankruptcy, it is argued, is greatly reduced. Creditors' claims are straightforward and normally secured by the financed assets. Families and businesses avoid the temptation to borrow money to buy things they don't really need or can't afford. And because each debt is normally secured, primarily by the acquired asset, each creditor has a strong incentive to ensure the asset he is offering is affordable and will substantively improve the debtor's life or business. This whole system is deemed, by Muslims, to be fairer to both debtor and creditor.

Macro-economic rationale for the ban on riba

There is also an Islamic macro-economic rationale for the prohibition of *riba*. In a *riba*-free financial system, capital providers and capital users, it is argued, are brought closer together psychologically. Whether providing equity capital or *riba*-free debt capital (trade credit or leasing), capital providers must remain engaged to some extent with the business and share commercial risk with the users of their capital. This, Muslims believe, tends to improve capital allocation, smooth economic cycles and soothe the tension between social classes by tying the fortunes of capital and labour more closely together. The overall economy can become more stable and self-regulating and less dependent on the economic pronouncements and predictions, often of a speculative nature, associated with changing economic news.

The economy may also become more efficient because it allocates capital primarily on the basis of profit-making potential, rather than primarily on the basis of the creditworthiness of the borrower. Furthermore, by encouraging equity-based finance, a *riba*-free system may encourage more innovation and result in higher economic growth rates. Finally, the system, it is argued, is more just because profit sharing finance rules out a net transfer of pre-existing wealth from those without capital to those who already have it, thereby potentially avoiding antagonism between classes and the associated social and political problems.

As summarised below, Dr Mohammad Nejatullah Siddiqi describes four mechanisms in which a *riba*-free economy should function better than the conventional alternative. These mechanisms involve considerations of:

1) Stability,
2) Efficiency,
3) Growth and development, and
4) Justice.

These ideas are elaborated in more detail below.

(1) Stability

A *riba*-free financial system should arguably be more stable than a system based on interest-bearing deposits and loans because the payment obligations and cash collections of *riba*-free banks are more integrated and synchronised. Its depositors are not guaranteed a fixed return, only a fair share in the gains made by the bank with their deposits, similar to a mutual fund. Therefore, it is argued, there is no threat of bank insolvency.

Banks in a *riba*-free system are more like investment management firms providing some extra services (ATM cards etc). An additional stabilising effect of a *riba*-free system is that, as in conventional equity (stock) markets, the cost of capital automatically adjusts itself in response to supply and demand.

Furthermore, there is no ability for entrepreneurs or investors to speculate during good times by borrowing money to finance their equity positions in ventures that appear promising but may not support their debt obligations when times get bad. Probably all of the financial crises of recent memory would have been less painful or avoided altogether in an Islamic financial system. This includes the US Savings and Loan crisis of the 1980s, the Mexican debt crises of 1982 and 1994, the Russian debt crisis of 1998, the Asian financial crisis of 1997-1999, the LTCM hedge-fund 'crisis' of 1998, the Enron scandal of 2002 and the sub-prime crisis of 2007-2009.

(2) Efficiency

A *riba*-free financial system is arguably more efficient than a system involving contractually fixed interest payments because it allocates capital primarily on the basis of profit-making potential, rather than primarily on the basis of a predetermined fixed interest rate and the creditworthiness of the borrower. The allocation of a society's resources it is argued, departs from being optimal every time capital is allocated to a borrower simply because he has a track record of paying back loans, without exposing the proposed use of the funds to the 'marketplace of ideas'.

(3) Growth and development

A *riba*-free financial system would arguably promote economic growth and development far more so than the current system, Muslims believe, because it is more equity-based. In the conventional system, historical average returns on equity securities (stocks) have exceeded returns on debt, over long periods. These higher returns for equity have only been affordable because equity financing has generated greater rates of economic growth and wealth creation than has debt financing. Eliminating *riba* would potentially increase the level of equity investment across all industries, encourage more innovation and result in higher economic growth rates.

(4) Justice

A *riba*-free financial system would arguably be more than just the conventional system because equity-based or profit sharing finance does not permit an automatic net transfer of pre-existing wealth from entrepreneurs to their financiers. The financier can lay claim only to the value created by his investment, and cannot dig into the pre-existing wealth of anyone else. By potentially continuously digging into the pre-existing wealth of those without capital to lend, the institution of *riba* constantly worsens inequality between classes, with potentially severe social, psychological, and political consequences.

Moving on from *riba* another key element in Islamic finance is the concept of *gharar*.

What is *gharar*?

Gharar refers to ambiguity in transactions. The Prophet Muhammad prohibited *gharar* at levels large enough to be hazardous. An example would be selling anything that is indefinable such as the 'fish catch of tomorrow', or selling anything without actually owning it first (such as short selling of stock, where the cost of acquiring stock to meet future obligations is unknowable).

Gharar is not fraud or deception. Fraud and deception are prohibited under *Sharia'a* and the laws of the land, but *gharar* is more subtle. Deception is selling a car without telling the buyer it has a major engine problem. *Gharar* is both parties agreeing to the purchase knowing there is a major engine problem but without first having it assessed by a mechanic to determine its approximate cost of repair. Any transaction agreed to by the parties without describing its major defining specifications generally involves an unacceptable level of *gharar*.

However, a small amount of *gharar* is allowable and unavoidable in most transactions. For example, if the above problem involved a tear in the seat upholstery, the sale could occur without the parties determining its cost of repair. A general rule of thumb for avoiding a prohibited level of *gharar* is to avoid any transactions where, due to absence of knowledge or uncertainty of delivery, one or more parties risk the majority of their consideration (even if they agree to it).

Islamic investing and purification

What is purification?

Purification is donating to charity any Islamically illicit gains that are mixed with gains from allowable business activities. In the context of investing in stocks, this means determining the portion of investment gains that result from prohibited activities of the companies issuing the stock (such as company profits from alcohol sales or interest income), and donating this amount to charity.

Major prohibitions in Islam

Prohibitions within Islam are designed to protect Muslims and humanity from danger and evil. Through these injunctions Islam, Muslims believe, protects man's psyche, body and soul within the individual sphere and safeguards other human relations and community life within society, from the risks of subversion, perversion and decadence. Ideologically, Islam makes unbelief and distrust in God *haram* (prohibited). Also, attributing injustice, incarnation and the like, to God is *haram*.

Islam also makes *haram* superstition, charlatanism, blind imitation and anything that enslaves the mind's inquisitive and creative activity. In fact anything that prevents a good understanding of life and existence is haram. The relationship between man and God remains firm and binding, as it is the source of all human conduct and orientation, and it is the stimulus that moves Muslims on the right path.

With regard to man's self, Islam makes *haram* anything that may lead to pollute man's inner life, kill his conscience and moral intuition, and that which may change his life to one of total misery and helplessness. Thus Islam makes malevolence, hatred, despondency, mistrust etc *haram*. This is in order to uplift the human soul to the highest level of perfection and cleanliness, and to protect and purify it from unhealthy traits.

With respect to man's body, Islam makes *haram* all the activities, practices and actions that are detrimental to health. Therefore, wine-drinking, adultery, eating the flesh of swine (pork), dogs and many other animals, or for that matter animals killed by strangulation, carrion and blood are all *haram*.

When Islam protects man's psyche and his body on the one hand, it pays due attention to protect the community from crime and harmful practices in the domains of politics, economics, the judiciary, education and so on. Accordingly, Islam makes *haram*, oppression, usury, monopoly, cheating, theft, telling lies, backbiting, false witness, cursing, bribery, homicide, gambling, teaching and spreading harmful ideologies and ideas such as those made popular through pornographic literature, films and pictures. By so doing, Islam is designed to secure the health of both the individual and the society. Islam rules that carnal sins which constitute the gravest danger to man and environment are *haram*.

It is useful to cite these prohibited activities which Islam warns Muslims not to commit, given that painfully severe punishment is in store for them should they commit such acts. These acts which, if committed, may endanger life and social order. Some of these are relevant to Islamic investing and some take a broader moral viewpoint. It is still useful, however, to appreciate how Muslims perceive the major prohibitions.

Qaradawi has set out the major prohibitions (3). The following are the main haram items for Muslims:

1) Polytheism.
2) Desperation and despondency about one's fate and the idea that God will never have mercy on one.
3) The belief that God will never punish oneself.
4) Lack of diligence towards one's parents.
5) Homicide.
6) Falsely accusing a married woman of committing adultery.

7) Taking away an orphan's possessions and money unjustly.
8) Fleeing the battlefield of *jihad*.
9) Usury.
10) Adultery.
11) Sodomy.
12) Witchcraft.
13) Perjury.
14) Bearing false witness.
15) Concealing testimony (about something one knows which can help establish justice by providing information).
16) Drinking wine.
17) Breaking pledges.
18) Cutting off relations with one's next of kin.
19) Emigration from the Muslim homeland to a place where one's faith becomes at risk.
20) Theft.
21) Telling lies about God, His Apostle, Imams and common people or attributing to them something which they did not say.
22) Cannibalism.
23) Drinking blood.
24) Eating swine or flesh of animals that are slaughtered without being Islamically blessed.
25) Ill-gotten money earned by selling wine, or gained through prostitution, dancing, as well as money gained through bribery.
26) Giving short measure and weight.
27) Supporting oppression.
28) Pride.
29) Extravagance.
30) Squandering money.
31) Fighting the faithful and callers to Islam.
32) Backbiting.
33) False accusation.
34) Cursing the faithful, insulting and humiliating them.
35) Tale bearing.
36) Pandering or acting as pimps.

37) Cheating.

38) Sanctimoniousness.

39) Hypocrisy.

40) Ignoring or belittling one's sins and transgressions.

Appendix 5. 1 provides a case study of the issues involved in Islamic investing.

Zakat and Islamic prohibitions

Zakat is the Islamic concept of tithing and alms. It is an obligation on Muslims to pay 2.5% of their wealth to specified categories in society, when their annual wealth exceeds a minimum level (known as *nisab*). *Zakat* is one of the Five Pillars of Islam.

Who can receive *zakat*?

There are eight categories of people who may receive the collected *zakat*:

1) Poor people (if they do not have enough income to cover their basic needs);
2) The Destitute (those with no property or income at all);
3) The *zakat* collectors;
4) People whose hearts are to be reconciled (normally new Muslims or those close to becoming Muslim. Even non-Muslims could be included);
5) Freeing slaves;
6) Debtors (to help those heavily in debt to pay their debts);
7) Activities in the Way of Allah (running Islamic Schools, Hospitals, Mosques and many other charity works);
8) Travellers (who find themselves in difficult circumstances).

What has *zakat* got to do with Islamic prohibitions?

This issue here is whether impure income can be purified by donating it as *zakat*. And, if it can, to whom would be the appropriate recipients? Are the only appropriate recipients the same as the *zakat* eight categories? Most scholars would not accept *zakat* obligations to be alternatives to purifying impure income received from various *haram* activities.

Appendix 5.1 Islamic investment prohibitions: a case study

> I heard Allah's Messenger say 'The Halāl (permissible) is clear and the Harām (forbidden)' is clear. Between these are matters that are doubtful. Most people do not know whether these are from the Halāl or from the Harām. So, he who leaves it (such matters) to guard his religion (against adulteration) and his integrity has indeed saved himself. He who engages (to any degree) into any of these (doubtful matters) would soon engage in the Harām just as he who grazes (animals) around (another's) territory is likely to enter into it. Be cautious! Each king has a territory. Be cautious! And the (prohibited) territory of Allah is His prohibitions.
>
> *Hadith* narrated by an bin Bashir R.A.

Conventional banking is secular in its orientation. In contrast, in the Islamic system, all economic agents have to work within the moral value system of Islam. Islamic banks are no exception. As such, they cannot finance any project which conflicts with the moral value system of Islam. For example Islamic banks are not allowed to finance a distillery, a casino, a night club or any other activity which is prohibited by Islam or is *known* to be harmful to society.

The prohibitions, set out in *Sharia'a* law, severely constrain the choices open to investors seeking to invest Islamically. All Islamic financial institutions or institutions, providing Islamic financial services, are obliged to have a *Sharia'a* Board, to ensure these prohibitions are enforced. The prohibitions often do not involve simple *haram* or *halal* decisions. Many products involve combinations of *haram* or *halal* elements. This case examines these prohibitions and highlights the complexities of dealing with the issues.

Although the hadith cited above has many applications, in various areas of the *Sharia'a*, its application in finance is crucial since the earnings to be derived from an Islamic investment are required to be strictly *halal*. Any products intended for sale to the Islamic community (*Ummah*) must adhere to the Islamic prohibitions on a variety of goods. So any products sold and/or invested in by Muslims must ensure that the products are not prohibited (*haram*) under the *Sharia'a*.

To take an example, gelatine is produced from particular products of cattle and pigs. See box 5.1 for details of some of the widespread uses of gelatine. If particular cattle are not slaughtered in conformity with the *Sharia'a*, not only the slaughtered cattle would be classified as *haram* but also any products derived from its meat, bones and fat would also be impermissible for Muslim consumption. Thus, gelatine produced from such cattle would be *haram*.

Box 5.1. Is gelatine prohibited if it comes from cattle?

> Gelatine is produced from particular products of cattle and pigs. If particular cattle are not slaughtered in conformity to the *Sharia'a*, not only the slaughtered cattle would be classified as *haram* but also any products derived from its meat, bones and fat would also be impermissible for Muslim consumption. Thus, gelatine produced from such cattle would be *haram*. This implies that any other products containing such gelatine would also be *haram*. Therefore, if a particular sweet company has used such gelatine in various sweet products, then all such products would also become impermissible for Muslims.
>
> Gelatine did not exist in the Prophetic period. Therefore, contemporary jurists differ whether gelatine manufactured from non-*halal* bovine products and from pigs would be *halal* or *haram*.
>
> The cautionary route to be adopted by an Islamic financing institution would be to abstain from financing any sweets or other products which contain gelatine that is not strictly produced from slaughtered animals that are classified as *halal*. Thus, in the case when there is doubt regarding whether Islam sanctions a specified product, it would be judicious to abstain from purchasing it. Or should the cautionary route be followed when business conditions dictate otherwise?

Case study questions

Muslims all over the world, despite all their commitment to Islamic values, face the problems brought before them by unwanted interest income generated in their name through channels they do not control. This happens, in spite of taking care to avoid interest-bearing or *haram* activity. In this case they would be investing in shares of a company which involved products indirectly involved with haram activities

In the event that interest income does come into their accounts, no matter how unwanted, is there a valid way under the *Sharia'a* through which the identified amount can be disposed of?

You are asked to prepare briefs covering the questions below. It is not necessary to come up with definitive answers but some guidance is essential.

1) Would it be acceptable to finance food products whose ingredients are unknown?

2) Would it be the duty of a bank financing food production to keep a list of reputable and reliable institutions which are qualified to classify food products as *halal*?

3) What happens in the case of a Muslim who contends that the religious school to which he subscribes allows him to purchase, consume and sell products containing gelatine produced from non-*halal* sources? The argument here being that the religious school is of the opinion that the original material used to produce the gelatine is totally transformed within the production process.

4) Since the *Qur'an* prohibits assisting others in sin and evil, would an Islamic bank be allowed to finance:
   - equipment used to produce wine which is also used to make non-alcoholic drinks?
   - catering equipment for a company that primarily produces *haram* food products which are to be sold to non-Muslims?

5) Can an Islamic Bank finance an importer who wishes to purchase shoes that have interior pigskin lining which are to be sold to non-Muslims?

6) Is it permissible to invest in a holding company when the Islamic status of the subsidiary company's income is unknown?

7) What should be done in regard to interest earned on bank accounts in cases where money had to be held in bank accounts, due to business or safety reasons?

8) Can interest income be used to pay taxes in non-Muslim states?

9) Can interest income be used by the account holder or person who received it to pay other interest payments that are due, e.g. interest on a mortgage or other loan?

10) Can interest income be used by poor Muslims who have no other sources of income?

11) Should interest earned or received be returned to the very same institution that provided the interest?

12) What happens in the case of persons who are compelled to pay interest on loans, taken out to fulfil normal economic necessities, which are absolutely essential for economic reasons or survival, e.g. buying a car or house on interest?

13) Would it be justified to buy a house on an interest basis when you can rent premises? What would the ruling be if renting the premises is not economically viable and the exorbitant rentals would prevent one from gaining the capacity to eventually purchase the property or other premises?

14) Can Muslims charge non-Muslims interest or are Muslims prohibited from charging everyone interest irrespective of race or religion?

15) Is interest only prohibited on loans for consumption or is the prohibition also applicable for loans financing business and investment?

16) What are the religious implications for Muslim accountants, lawyers and others who have to witness and record interest transactions?

17) Can a Muslim investment consultant advise non-Muslim clients to invest in avenues where their income would generate interest?

18) Can Muslims buy assets, through interest financing mechanisms, purely to evade taxation?

19) Can interest earned on bank accounts be offset against bank charges?

20) Why should interest remain prohibited when it is well known that inflation eats into the purchasing power of money?

21) Are any earnings acquired through the use of money borrowed on an interest basis, say through owning equities with debt in their balance sheet, also be classified as prohibited in Islam?

22) Can a Muslim trade with another Muslim or non-Muslim whose earnings are from interest or other Islamically prohibited avenues?

23) What should a convert to Islam do in respect of previous earnings from interest?

24) Assume a Muslim had earned interest from particular investments. He was ignorant of the fact that investing in particular portfolios also implied the earning of interest through specific financial instruments. What should he do subsequent to gaining awareness in this regard?

25) Can any interest income be given to non-Muslim charities such as blood banks, Heart Associations, Community Service groups, Welfare Committees for the aged, sick, disabled and similar other disadvantaged groups?

26) Are beggars on the street entitled to be given this interest income?

Chapter 6

Sharia'a compliant wholesale markets

In the wholesale markets, Islamic investment alternatives can be broadly divided into commodity *Murabaha*; equities; property investment; *Takaful* or Islamic compliant insurance; foreign exchange, including *Sharia'a* compliant currency swaps; Islamic bonds or *sukuk* and structured finance. This chapter concentrates on commodity *Murabaha*, one of the most important *Sharia'a* compliant asset classes.

With an estimated value of more than $100 billion, commodity *Murabaha* currently is the most widely used Islamic money market product in the GCC and other jurisdictions for liquidity management purposes.

What is commodity *Murabaha*?

Commodity *Murabaha* is the sale of certain specified commodities, through a metal exchange, on a cost-plus-profit basis. Commodity *Murabaha* replicates, in terms of returns, short-term money market deposits, usually taken out for fixed terms between one week and one year. A commodity *Murabaha* is a contract between a bank and its client for the sale of goods at a price plus an agreed profit margin for the bank. As the bank is making profits rather than earning interest, this is considered *Sharia'a* compliant. Profits are allowed, indeed they are encouraged, under *Sharia'a* law.

The instrument is called a commodity *Murabaha* because the profits are made on the buying and selling of a commodity, usually metals, such as copper, aluminium, lead or other precious metals. The transactions take place under a *Murabaha* transaction. Gold and silver cannot be used in commodity *Murabaha* as they are deemed to be money. Gold and silver were used as money at the time of the Prophet. Money can only be traded, Islamically, for money at par value in order to avoid *riba* related considerations.

One bank will buy the metal at the spot price, or the current price. This bank will then sell the metal to another bank on a deferred payment basis, say for three months, at the spot price plus a mark-up or profit for doing so. The second bank will then immediately sell the metal to a broker or another institution for the spot price. The first bank has made a profit from the mark-up, while the second bank has raised funds for its investors. Figure 6.1 illustrates the flow of funds

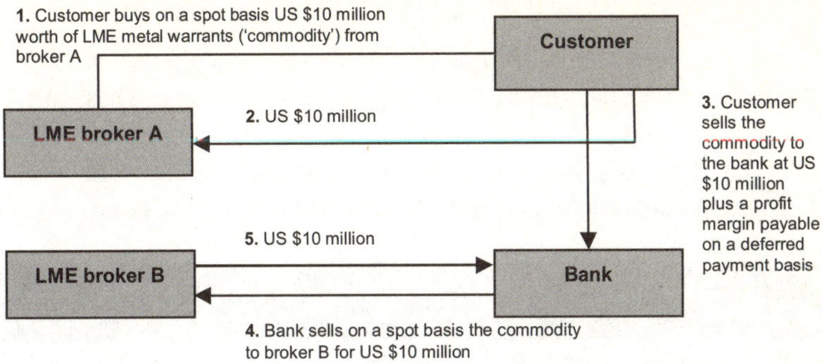

Figure 6.1. The flow of funds in a commodity *Murabaha*

Why is commodity *Murabaha Sharia'a* compliant?

Given the nature of the fixed returns one should ask how this can be Islamically acceptable given that fixed returns are not allowable Islamically. The reason these transactions are deemed Islamically acceptable is that a trading transaction, and not a fixed lending transaction, is taking place. Any increase generated is deemed to be a trading profit and not a *riba* related return. The bank buys for the client at five and sells for the client at 10, so to speak. Box 6.1 illustrates the key parties to a commodity *Murabaha*.

Box 6.1. Key parties to a commodity *Murabaha*

What is commodity *Murabaha?*

1) Definition: an exchange contract trade between an investor (seller) and financial institution (buyer), where the subject matter are metals listed on the major commodity exchanges (such as the London Metal Exchange);

2) Structure: it is structured in such a way that it leads to the subject matter being exchanged on the spot. In other words, there must not be any involvement of a forward contract, where the subject matter is delivered and the price that is to be settled, is to be determined at the deferred date in future;

3) It is structured in such a way that it is essentially similar to a loan granted by the seller to the buyer;

4) It has a risk-return profile broadly equivalent to a money market deposit;

5) It has a buy and sell arrangement that is done simultaneously and therefore, does not expose the investor/fund to the price risk of the underlying commodity;

Indicative money-market profit rates

The extent to which commodity *Murabaha* can be expressed in money-market terms can be seen in the rates given in tables (6.1) and (6.2) below. These rates are for investors seeking to invest in compliance with *Sharia'a* principles.

Tables 6.1 and 6.2 show annualised indicative profit rates available to investors entering into a commodity *Murabaha* investment for the given amounts or periods.

Amount (USD)	1 month	3 months	6 months	1 year	2 years	3 years
250k – 499k	4.37%	4.68%	4.60%	4.30%	4.08%	4.17%
500k – 749k	4.57%	4.88%	4.85%	4.50%	4.28%	4.35%
750k – 999k	4.62%	4.98%	4.85%	4.50%	4.28%	4.40%
1m – 2m	4.65%	4.98%	4.85%	4.50%	4.38%	4.50%
> 2m	Individually priced					

Source: European Islamic Investment Bank (EIIB)

Table 6.1. Commodity *Murabaha* indicative rates (US Dollar)

Amount (EUR)	1 month	3 months	6 months	1 year	2 years	3 years
200k – 299k	3.61%	4.24%	4.26%	4.29%	4.18%	4.19%
300k – 499k	3.76%	4.32%	4.36%	4.39%	4.28%	4.26%
500k – 749k	3.96%	4.62%	4.61%	4.59%	4.43%	4.44%
750k – 999k	4.01%	4.62%	4.61%	4.59%	4.48%	4.49%
1m – 2m	4.04%	4.62%	4.61%	4.59%	4.58%	4.59%
> 2m	Individually priced					

Source: European Islamic Investment Bank (EIIB)

Table 6.2. Commodity *Murabaha* indicative rates (€)

EIIB *amanah* commodity *Murabaha*

EIIB *amanah* commodity *Murabaha* provides a short-to-medium-term financing solution for working capital and liquidity needs. The structure is *Sharia'a* compliant involving trading in a commodity (typically a metal) on a cost-plus-profit basis.

With *amanah* commodity *Murabaha* EIIB aim to cover the following areas of financing for clients: payment for services, IPO financing, bridge financing – for purchasing equipment and general purpose finance. See box 6.2.

Box 6.2. Main features of the EIIB *amanah* commodity *Murabaha*

Pricing competitive with the market
1-6 months tenor (longer tenors will be financed under revolving structure)
Various payment schemes
Simple documentation and quick turn-around time
Product structure
Based on the amount of financing the client needs, the bank will purchase commodities at a specified cost price from the international market and will sell it to the client on deferred payment at a sale price (cost-plus-profit). The cost, profit amount and deferred payment date have to be determined at the outset. The client then sells the commodities to the broker on immediate payment and delivery basis through their agent (a subsidiary of the bank).

Commodity *Murabaha* – what are the principles?

- The purpose of this trading scheme is to enable private clients to place funds with the 'Principal', usually a large bank and receive a return approximately equal to the money market deposit interest rate.
- Investors want to be subject to the same risk they faced had they placed the funds in deposits with this same large bank.
- The trades can be undertaken in all forms of base and precious metals excluding gold and silver.

Figure 6.2 gives a detailed description of the different parties involved.

Given the need to ensure *Sharia'a* compliance it is essential for the documentation to be correct. Indeed a *Sharia'a* Scholar, when undertaking an audit, will insist on seeing this document. Box 6.3 illustrates the appropriate documentation needed.

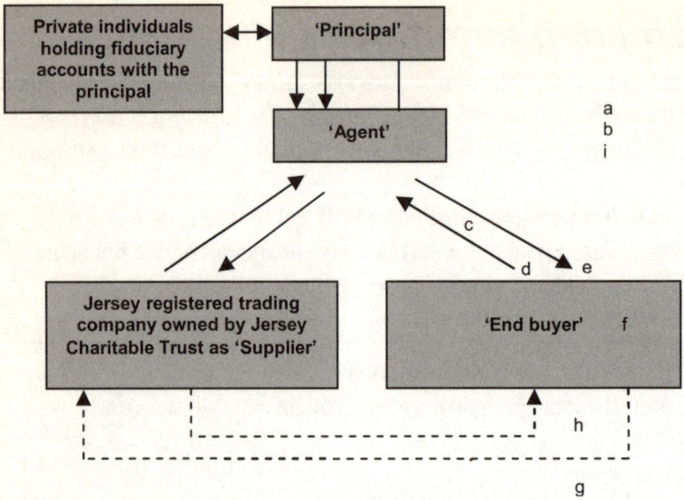

Key

- **a** Agency agreement between the 'Principal' and the 'Agent'. The agent undertakes all matters on behalf of the principal in relation to the trade.
- **b** Principal and agent agree to terms and conditions of trade and remittance of funds by principal.
- **c** Agent purchases platinum from the 'Supplier'.
- **d** Agent credits agreed amount to account of supplier in its books.
- **e** Agent immediately sells same ounces of platinum to the 'End buyer' for a higher price per ounce. The higher price reflects the interest rate embedded in the deal. Delivery of platinum is immediate with settlement deferred until the future date.
- **f** The 'End buyer' pays purchase price on deferred date agreed with the principal by the agent.
- **g** The 'End buyer' immediately sells platinum to the supplier for immediate delivery.
- **h** Supplier pays the 'End buyer' the settlement price instructing the agent to debit their account and credit the 'End buyer'.
- **i** On the deferred payment date, the 'End buyer' pays funds to the agent for onward payment to the principal.

***Source*: Deutsche Bank**

Figure 6.2. The parties to a commodity *Murabaha*

Box 6.3. Commodity *Murabaha* – the documentation

THE AGENT'S CONFIRMATION

To: XYZ Private Bank (Guernsey) Limited
From: XYZ Financial Services (Middle East) Ltd

This is to confirm the details of the transactions which we propose to enter on your behalf as your agent pursuant to the agreement.

	Purchase Transaction	
a)	Buyer:	XYZ Private Bank (Guernsey) Ltd acting for XYZ Financial Services (Middle East) Ltd
b)	Seller:	ABC Ltd
c)	Type and Grade of Metal:	Copper
d)	Location:	
e)	Value Date:	April 4, 2007
f)	Unit Price:	£3,488.45
g)	Quantity:	Ton 1,470.69
h)	Total Price:	£5,130,421.55 To be paid to ABC Ltd
i)	Agency Fee	£53.11
	Sale Transaction	
j)	Buyer:	XYZ Bank plc
k)	Seller:	XYZ Private Bank (Guernsey) Ltd acting for XYZ Financial Services (Middle East) Ltd
l)	Type and Grade of Metal:	Copper
m)	Location:	
n)	Value Date:	April 4, 2007
o)	Unit Price:	£3,491.88
p)	Quantity	Ton 1,470.69
q)	Total Price:	£5,135,469.04 To be paid in accordance with standard settlement instructions

***Source*: HSBC**

Singapore Central Provider Fund: commodity Murabaha scheme

An interesting example of the application of commodity *Murabaha* is provided by the Singapore-based Central Provident Fund (CPF). This is a comprehensive social security savings plan which has provided many working Singaporeans with a sense of security and confidence in their old age. The overall scope and benefits of the CPF encompass the following: retirement, healthcare, home ownership, family protection and asset enhancement.

Working Singaporeans and their employers make monthly contributions to the CPF. In addition the CPF scheme provides a commodity *Murabaha* alternative for Muslims seeking a *Sharia'a* compliant investment. The guidelines, set out below, demonstrate the basic commodity *Murabaha* principles.

CPF: Guidelines on Commodity *Murabaha*

Commodity *Murabaha* was approved with effect from 1 July 2004 under the CPF Investment Scheme (CPFIS) as a *Sharia'a* compliant treasury product. Funds offered under CPFIS can invest in Commodity *Murabaha* provided that the following conditions are met:

1) It is a commodity *Murabaha*, defined as an exchange contract trade between an investor (seller) and financial institution (buyer), where the subject matter are base metals listed on the major commodity exchanges (such as the London Metal Exchange);
2) It is structured in such a way that it leads to the subject matter being exchanged on the spot. In other words, there must not be any involvement of a forward contract, where the subject matter is delivered and the price that is to be settled, is to be determined at the deferred date in future;
3) It is structured in such a way that it is essentially similar to a loan granted by the seller to the buyer;
4) It has a risk-return profile broadly equivalent to a money market deposit;
5) It has a buy and sell arrangement that is done simultaneously and therefore, does not expose the fund to the price risk of the underlying commodity;
6) The financial institution which the collective investment schemes (CIS) included under CPFIS enters the arrangement with, must have individual/financial strength ratings of above C by Fitch Inc or Moody's;
7) It has to meet all other guidelines as listed under CPFIS, such as exposure to single party limit; and
8) There should be a clear and adequate disclosure of the structure and the risks of the product to the consumer.

Source: CPF

IIFM and the standardised commodity Murabaha programme

The IIFM are actively involved in a variety of product development initiatives designed to promote innovation within the industry. Some of these are discussed below.

Islamic hedging and commodity *Murabaha*

At present, the retail portfolio that is carried by most Islamic financial institutions consists of fixed-rate assets (structured on a *Murabaha* basis), whereas corporate customers use facilities based on floating and fixed benchmarks. Also, corporates and Islamic financial institutions are exposed to potential risks related to currency or exchange rate fluctuations as a result of their business operations in multiple currencies. There are a variety of hedging issues here.

As retail products such as Islamic housing finance and car finance increase their market share the need increases for Islamic financial institutions to be able to offer competitive fixed-price solutions. Equally, corporate customers need project-specific as well as overall balance sheet hedging solutions in order to conduct their entire financial needs in a *Sharia'a* compliant manner.

There are several other benefits from providing hedging solutions. Publicly listed corporate customers who become *Sharia'a* compliant will be able to attract incremental capital from Islamic investors and Islamic equity fund managers, and Islamic financial institutions will gain the capability to compete effectively in the market. The availability of basic hedging instruments will open additional avenues for both investors and customers on a variety of fronts such as debt capital markets, structured trade finance, project finance and overall balance sheet management for Islamic financial institutions, including banks and *Takaful* companies.

Commodity *Murabaha* and Islamic FX hedging

The general view of *Sharia'a* Scholars is that conventional FX forward contracts, being driven by interest rate differentials, are not permissible Islamically. However, some scholars have permitted a few alternative solutions to this issue.

One alternative is to execute back-to-back interest-free loans of different currencies. These loans do not carry any interest rate costs and, as the agreements are separate, there is no link between the loans. The second mechanism quite common in the market is based on the commodity *Murabaha* mechanism, see figure 6.3.

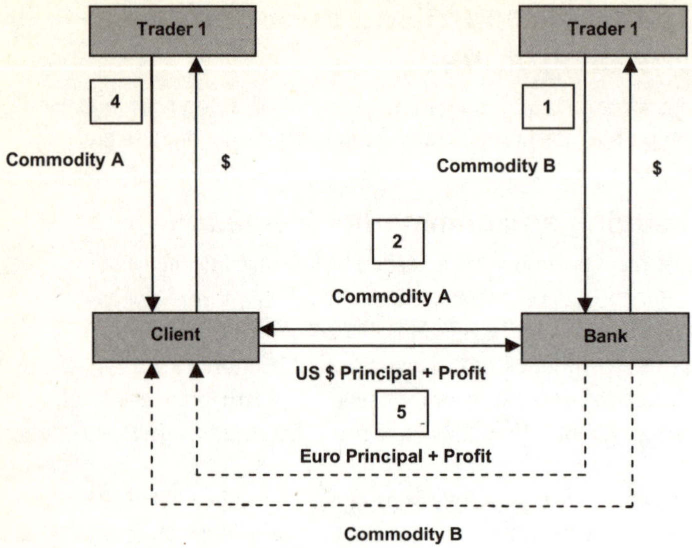

Figure 6.3. Commodity *Murabaha* mechanism

Under this arrangement, the customer and the bank enter into two separate *Murabaha* transactions to facilitate the FX forward contract. In such transactions, the customer will purchase a commodity for spot value and sell it to the bank for the purchase price plus profit (the basis point in the normal FX forward deal), payable on a deferred basis. In order to address the other side of the FX forward, the bank will purchase another commodity and sell it to the customer again for the purchase price and profit, payable on a deferred basis. Both deals facilitate the FX forward transaction. It should be noted that both the customer and bank will usually dispose of the metal back into the market to recover the initial investment.

Wa'd solution

Another hedging route is based on the promise (*Wa'd*) concept. The arrangement works as follows: party A, which is looking for hedging, would undertake to purchase a currency from party B in the future. The essential elements of the promise include the purchase price of the currency and the delivery date. The promise is not conditional on any event. The party that issues the promise (party A) is normally bound to fulfil its promise (made to party B). However, the receiving party (party B) of the promise is not under any obligation to act on the transaction when an offer to purchase is submitted.

Profit rate swaps

In addition to FX risk, Islamic institutions and corporates also need to manage the yield curve or rate volatility. There has been debate on this issue and various institutions have tried to offer solutions based mostly on the commodity

Murabaha model. Normally, for profit rate hedging, the product would work in a similar manner to that described above. However, in most cases, the related issues in both FX and profit rate swaps in the commodity structure make this inefficient from a capital allocation perspective.

In the case of FX swaps, there may be daily valuation requirements for the different currencies that may not be required for profit rate swap deals. However, there are complications in profit rate swaps on the mark to market (MTM) valuation if the metal transactions for the swap deals are not conducted. Such an event will not attract any penalty in the form of MTM recovery, as it would be against the *Sharia'a* principles to recover MTM. The only amount that may be permitted for recovery is that of the actual losses (if any) suffered by the affected party as a result of the deal not taking place. Many institutions have developed their own solutions to address this MTM issue.

Arboun

A number of institutions have tried to use different options structures to create viable hedging solutions. One structure involves providing a deposit against a right to purchase something in the future. The mechanism is commonly known as an *Arboun*, discussed further in *Chapter 8*, and resembles a conventional option with a premium. However, in an *Arboun*, the party receiving the deposit must have the asset and hold the asset for the life of the option. Some of the other structures that are being used in the market include both *Wa'd* and commodity *Murabaha* structures, as mentioned earlier.

All of the above structures have constraints attached to them that obviously put them at a slight disadvantage when compared with conventional counterparts. However, given the relative importance of such structures, a small disadvantage can be ignored, considering the overall benefit and need for the products.

What is *Tawarruq*?

Tawarruq is the reverse form of commodity *Murabaha*, where the bank sells commodities to the customer on deferred payment at cost-plus-profit. The customer then sells the commodities to a third party on a spot basis for instant cash.

Chapter 7

Islamic funds, equities, indices and ETFs

Sharia'a Islamic investment principles

Sharia'a Islamic investment principles were discussed in *Chapter 5* but it is useful to summarise the principles briefly here. We then turn to converting these principles into equity related investments. As mentioned in *Chapter 5* it is forbidden for any Islamic institution or investment fund to deal in the following goods:

- alcoholic drinks and related activities;
- pork, ham, bacon and related by-products;
- dead animals (i.e. those not slaughtered according to the rules of the *Sharia'a*);
- products associated with gambling such as casinos and gambling machines;
- tobacco, drugs etc;
- activities associated with pornography;
- gold and silver except for spot cash;
- armaments and destructive weapons.

According to the principles of Islamic jurisprudence the payment and receipt of interest is a grave sinful act, for which the participant is responsible in the Hereafter.

Since almost all of today's companies deal with some form of interest or otherwise prohibited activity, some *Sharia'a* Advisory Boards have determined an upper limit as to what percentage of a company's income can be earned through interest and/or such activities. It would be unacceptable to invest in a firm that exceeds these limits. These limits are evolving and, as a result, becoming more sophisticated and nuanced.

Companies that may have been excluded under simplistic models a few years ago (e.g. due to large cash holdings) may now be acceptable under newer models.

What is an Islamic fund?

Essentially Islamic funds apply the concept of a mutual fund. This concept is understood and well recognised from an Islamic perspective. The idea of a 'partnership' between the financial institution and the investors, whereby the institution will exercise control over and invest a pool of funds on behalf of such investors, is very acceptable Islamically.

The term 'Islamic investment fund' means a joint pool wherein the investors contribute their surplus money for the purpose of its investment to earn *halal* profits in strict conformity with the precepts of the *Sharia'a* (1). The subscribers to the fund may receive a document certifying their subscription and entitling them to the pro-rata profits actually accruing to the fund. These documents may be called 'certificates', 'units', 'shares' or may be given any other name, but their validity in terms of *Sharia'a* will always be subject to two basic conditions.

Firstly, instead of a fixed return related to their face value, they must carry a pro-rata profit actually earned by the fund. Therefore, neither the principal nor a rate of profit (tied up with the principal) can be guaranteed. The investors must enter into the fund with a clear understanding that the return on their subscription is tied up with the actual profit earned or loss suffered by the fund. If the fund earns huge profits, the return to the investors will increase by that proportion. However, in the event the fund suffers a loss, the investor will have to share it also. This is the basic principle underlying Islamic fund management. This profit-and-loss sharing principle applies unless any loss is caused by negligence or mismanagement, in which case the management, and not the fund, will be liable to compensate the investor.

Secondly, the amounts so pooled together must be invested in a business acceptable to *Sharia'a*. This means that not only the channels of investment, but also the terms agreed with the fund, must conform to Islamic principles.

Islamic mutual fund versus conventional mutual fund

A mutual fund is a company that pools money to invest in various companies and buys portfolios of securities. All securities are eligible to be included in a portfolio of conventional mutual funds. However, with an Islamic fund, screening must be done to ensure that the operations comply with the *Sharia'a*.

In a conventional mutual fund, investors will share the profits and losses earned from the investment. In an Islamic fund the profits are distributed based on the modes of investment agreed by the investors viz namely *Ijara* fund, equity fund, commodity fund, *Murabaha* fund, mixed fund etc.

Closed and open-ended funds

An open-ended unit trust will sell as many shares as investors will buy, and redeem those shares when the investor wants to sell. The price of the unit is the net asset value (NAV), calculated by the total asset value divided by the number of shares issued.

A closed-ended unit trust sells all its units at one moment in time. After the initial offering the fund takes in no additional money as the shares are traded, nor does it buy back shares investors want to sell. The prices of these units are not traded at the NAV, but are valued as the shares of the joint stock companies, i.e. the amount the purchaser is willing to pay for the shares viz the market price.

The most common form of closed-ended fund is a company which uses the funds provided by shareholders to 'invest' in the shares (stocks) of other companies. Shares in the investment company are simply bought or sold in the stock market. An example is the Faisal Fund for Egyptian Equities Ltd, organised under the laws of Jersey with participating shares listed on the Irish Stock Exchange. The Fund then invests mainly in listed Egyptian equities.

Because of the forces of supply and demand, the market price of closed-ended investment companies can differ from the market value of the underlying share portfolio. This cannot happen with open-ended funds, because the number of units or shares is not fixed or restricted like that of a closed-end fund (where, for example, participating shares may not exceed management shares by some specified ratio, for example 9:1), and thus the supply of shares or units, that is the capital, can be increased or decreased according to demand. Accordingly, the market price or value of units will vary directly with the market value of the securities represented by those units.

All mutual funds offer a number of features. First, they offer information services, in that participants acquire the services of professional investment management and administration of investments for a price, in the form of a management fee, expenses or profit share. Second, diversification is made possible by the size of the fund. Third, the funds offer liquidity, in that shares can be bought or sold before maturity or redeemed through the investment company at close to the current market value.

Sharia'a compliant fund market: historical overview

The first modern *Sharia'a* compliant investment funds can be traced back to Malaysia in the early 1960s where pioneering funds were established for local investors to save for their eventual *Hajj*. Throughout the 1960s and 1970s there are other examples of similar efforts. However the next significant developments in this field did not occur until the 1980s when new found oil wealth in the Arabian Gulf promoted a movement to develop funds that adhered to Islamic principles. The real growth in the Islamic funds industry did not take place until the mid 1990s.

It was in the midst of the 1990s prolonged bull-markets that high-net worth GCC-based investors began to push for more industry development. Concurrent efforts in Malaysia were also underway and by the end of the decade there existed a clear consensus that Islamically acceptable, if not fully compliant, funds were a viable investment alternative for pious Muslims.

As figure 7.1 below demonstrates, consistent growth began in 1994 and tapers off in the year 2000, largely in response to the 'tech bubble' that was particularly hard felt in the *Sharia'a* sector. Many early funds were 'tech heavy' owing to a preference for equity capital structures offered by technology firms.

Sharia'a compliant funds are prohibited from investing in highly leveraged firms.

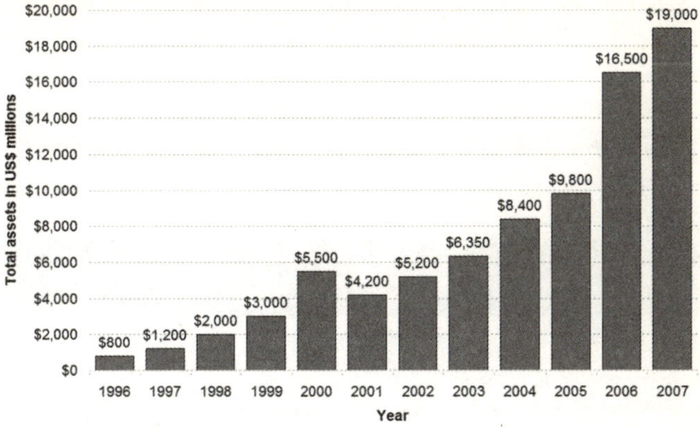

Source: **Failaka Advisors**

Figure 7.1. Total assets in Islamic equity and equity-related funds at year-end.

In the early 1990s there were only a few funds scattered across the globe. By 2008 there were over 320 Islamic equity funds managed by some of the world's top fund management companies, such as Citi, Deutsche Bank, HSBC and UBS.

Before the tech bubble of 2000, the preceding tech boom helped facilitate mass acceptance of equity funds as an investment solution. This helped the Islamic investment industry (which tends to favour less debt-ridden tech firms) grow rapidly from just $800 million in total equity assets in 1996 to over $15 billion in 2005. One key reason for the second big lift in Islamic fund assets was the rapid growth of GCC (Gulf Cooperation Council member countries: Bahrain, Kuwait, Oman, Qatar, Saudi Arabia and the United Arab Emirates) stock markets, which in recent years had been fuelled by a spate of widely popular IPOs, a heavy dose of speculative fever, and a general volatility in real estate prices.

The Saudi market in particular has experienced tremendous growth as a result of continued high liquidity. Naturally the prolonged rise in commodity prices, which has since fallen back, greatly enhanced GCC liquidity and helped spur regional growth and investment. Increasingly local investors are becoming more aware and comfortable with the principles of *Sharia'a* compliant investing with a significant percentage expressing a preference for Islamic investments.

As with any industry, however, not all players have succeeded. With many new Islamic funds on the market, it is easy to forget about those that did not make it (see table 7.1). A number of fund managers have lost interest in the Islamic market over the years. Very often, it is product distribution that is cited as the greatest obstacle. Just as in the conventional fund business, finding that right mix of basic success factors remains a challenge. Devising a new and demand-driven product, finding the right managers, obtaining *Sharia'a* approval, securing adequate distribution and achieving noteworthy results are challenges that must always be met. Simply branding a fund 'Islamic' is by no means a guarantee of future success.

At one time Flemings was considered a pioneer in the industry for having launched their Oasis International Equity Fund. The Oasis fund, however, was closed and its assets liquidated in 2000, as a result of a lack of interest and poor distribution. At its highest point, the fund had approximately $35 million in assets under management.

Fund	Sponsor	Year Closed
Ibn Khaldoun International Equity	PFM	1999
Islamic Multi-Investment Fund	American Express Bank and Faisal Finance	1999
Oasis International Equity	Flemings	2000
Egyptian Equity Fund	Faisal Finance	2000
AlKawthar Global Equity Fund	GAM	2001
Ibn Majid Emerging Markets	The International Investor	2002
Global Equity 2000 Sub-Fund	First Investment Company	2002

***Source*: Failaka Advisors**

Table 7.1 Islamic equity funds that closed down

PFM, a small London-based asset manager, was also one of the first to launch an Islamic global equity fund back in 1996 called the Ibn Khaldoun International Equity Fund. The fund never managed to attract more than $20 million in assets and closed down a few years later

Geographic focus

The earliest Islamic funds were broad in their focus. Funds offered in the Middle East tended to be global equity funds, US, or European equity funds. Early funds also tended to stick with the shares listed in either New York or London. Today we see a universe of funds dealing in virtually every major and emerging market. Increasingly, we have seen renewed interest in local Arab markets as well as a pronounced shift in emphasis towards the East, including China and emerging Asia. At present there are *Sharia'a* compliant specific sector funds (telecommunications and technology); country-specific funds (Saudi Arabia, Malaysia, United States); as well as a host of regional and global equity offerings.

Islamic indices

Arguably the biggest boost to fund managers came when Dow Jones launched their Islamic indices in 1999. This development not only gave credibility to the industry by having their global brand affiliated with Islamic finance, but it also spawned a new and viable investment category – Islamic index funds. Though others had come before, the Dow Jones basic rules formed what the industry and wider-world began to recognise as the standard for establishing *Sharia'a* index funds. The Dow Jones Islamic Indices are discussed further in *Appendix 7.1*.

What is *Sharia'a* compliance?

As Islam is a faith without a central authority it is often debated as to what is and what is not *Sharia'a* compliant. It is generally felt that terms like *Sharia'a* 'permissible' or 'acceptable' are more accurate than 'compliant'. Compliant implies a level of adherence not yet practised given that some leverage is indeed tolerated, even though all *riba* or interest is disallowed, strictly speaking.

In current practice, most fund managers engage a *Sharia'a* Board to assure compliance with issues related to Islamic investing. A *Sharia'a* Board composed of prominent scholars lend a fund a high degree of credibility with respect to Islamic legitimacy. *Sharia'a* Boards are discussed in *Chapter 2*. It is also common practice to engage a *Sharia'a* Board composed of members from different geographical regions within the Islamic world. Not only does such a practice assist the marketability of the fund but, perhaps more fundamentally, it assures the inclusion of a variety of Islamic schools of jurisprudence into the fund's Islamic credentials. There is a general consensus that scholars from the GCC, Sub-continent and Asia agree on 95% of the issues and disagree only on fine points, but nonetheless having a regionally diverse *Sharia'a* Board is now standard practice among global fund managers.

While a number of successful funds do not have their own boards, it is generally felt that having a board consisting of recognised experts can improve a new funds chances of success.

In 2008, Failaka Advisors, a leading provider of information on Islamic funds, published the world's first publication to profile the scholars who serve on these boards. In their publication, the *Sharia'a Report 2008*, profiles of the leading scholars are presented along with a listing of their *Sharia'a* Board affiliations. It is notable that often scholars serve on the boards of multiple *Sharia'a* Boards.

The cost of a *Sharia'a* Board can vary widely depending on the complexity of the transaction but generally, Failaka believes, the annual retainer will cost between $75,000-$200,000 plus travel expenses. This additional cost, if passed on to investors in the form of higher fees, can result in a slight premium being attached to the pricing of Islamic funds. This is a controversial notion within the industry. With many practitioners of the opinion that Islamic products must provide similar returns to conventional products in order to be competitive, the additional costs of *Sharia'a* Boards presents a strategic challenge for fund managers.

	Name	Nationality
1	Dr Abdul Sattar Kareem Abu Ghuddah	Syrian
2	Sheikh Abdullah bin Sulaiman Al-Manea	Saudi Arabian
3	Dr Ajeel Jassem Al-Nashmi	Kuwaiti
4	Sheikh Dr Ali Muhyealdin Al-Quradaghi	Qatari
5	Dr Mohammad Daud Bakar	Malaysian
6	Sheikh Yusuf Talal DeLorenzo	American
7	Dr Mohammed Ali El-Gari	Saudi Arabian
8	Dr Hussain Hamid Hassan	Egyptian
9	Justice Muhammad Taqi Usmani	Pakistani
10	Sheikh Nizam Yaquby	Bahraini

***Source*: Failaka Advisors**

Table 7.2. Top 10 Islamic finance scholars

In 2008, there existed roughly 260 *Sharia'a* Scholars actively working with banks on financial matters. In order to be included on the Failaka list the scholar must serve on at least one board. Additionally, Malaysian-based scholars must be certified by the Securities Commission in Malaysia before being able to serve as a scholar on a board. Table 7.2 provides details of the top 10 scholars and figure 7.2 gives a breakdown of their nationality. Table 7.3 provides details of the top 10 universities for studying the *Sharia'a*.

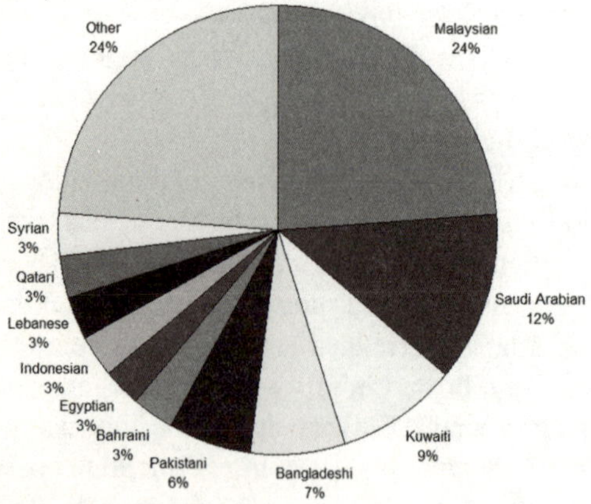

***Source*: Failaka Advisors**

Figure 7.2. *Sharia'a* Scholars by nationality

	Institution	Country
1	Al-Azhar University	Egypt
2	Damascus University	Syria
3	Darul Uloom University	Pakistan
4	Imam Mohammed ibn Saud Islamic University	Saudi Arabia
5	International Islamic University Malaysia	Malaysia
6	Islamic University at Al-Madinah Al-Munawwarah	Saudi Arabia
7	Kuwait University	Kuwait
8	Umm Al-Qura University	Saudi Arabia
9	University of Jordan	Jordan
10	University of Malaya	Malaysia

Source: Failaka Advisors

Table 7.3. Top 10 universities for studying _Sharia'a_

Islamic fund statistics

At the time this book went to print there was roughly $19 billion invested globally in *Sharia'a* compliant equity funds. The number is naturally much larger when bank deposits, *Murabaha* funds and closed-end (real estate and private equity) funds are added to the mix.

There are roughly 320 individual funds spread across the globe with over one third based in Malaysia. The remainder are predominately in the GCC with a smattering of others spread across Europe, North America and other parts of Asia. See figure 7.3 for a breakdown.

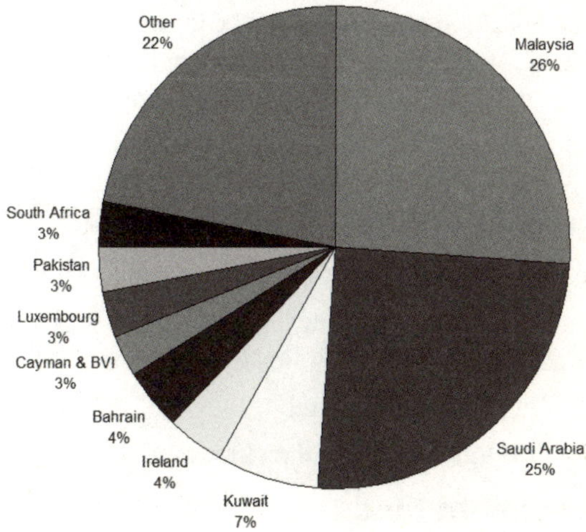

Source: Failaka Advisors

Figure 7.3. Domicile of Islamic equity and equity-related funds

Keeping the *Sharia'a* constraints in mind, Islamic funds may accommodate a variety of modes of investment. These are discussed below.

Types of Islamic funds

1. Equity fund

In an equity fund the capital is invested in the shares of joint stock companies. The profits are mainly achieved through capital gains achieved by purchasing the shares and selling them when their prices have increased. Profits are also achieved from the dividends distributed by the relevant companies. If the main business of a company is not lawful in terms of the *Sharia'a*, it is not allowable for an Islamic fund to purchase, hold or sell its shares, because it will entail the direct involvement of the shareholder in that prohibited business.

Similarly the contemporary *Sharia'a* Scholars are almost unanimous on the point that if all the transactions of a company are in full conformity with *Sharia'a*, which includes that the company neither borrows money on interest nor keeps its surplus in an interest-bearing account, its shares can be purchased, held and sold without any hindrance from the *Sharia'a* side. But such companies are very rare in the contemporary stock markets. Almost all the companies quoted in the present stock market or are some way involved in an activity which violates the injunctions of *Sharia'a*. Dealing in equities can be acceptable to the *Sharia'a* subject to the *Sharia'a* investment principles listed above.

Types of Islamic equity funds

The types of equity funds include:

- Global funds (Al-Rajhi Global Equity, NCB Global Trading Equity, Wellington Hegira, Al Sawfa, Al Baraka, Al Fanar Investment Holdings, Al-Dar World Equities, Riyad Equity Fund, Oasis International Equity),
- Regional funds (Mendaki Growth, Al Rajhi Middle East, TII Ibn Majid, Al-Nukhba),
- Sector funds (TII Small-Capital, Amana Income, Hi Tech Fund),
- European funds (Al-Dar European Equities, European Trading Equity Fund),
- Country funds (Saudi Trading Equity, Al Rajhi Egypt, most Malaysian funds, US equity funds),
- Hedge funds (TII Alkhawarizmi Fund),
- Index funds (Dow Jones Islamic Market Index Fund).

Islamic investment funds

Islamic investment funds are relatively large and varied in number but in terms of funds under management they are very modest compared to the conventional fund industry. The single largest Islamic equity fund is the Al-Ahli Global Trading Equity Fund of National Commercial Bank of Saudi Arabia with funds under management of about US$600m. With the exception of one or two others, most of the Islamic mutual funds have funds under management of between US$10m to US$75m, which makes the Islamic fund industry marginal in the wider picture of the Islamic banking market.

Investment funds include equities, real estate funds, currency funds, *sukuk* fund of funds, commodity funds, leasing funds, and private equity funds. Perhaps the most developed are the real estate and commodity funds. Traditional equities as an investment asset class vie with real estate and government bonds. But investors from the GCC are traditionally more at home with real estate investment because of the 'bricks and mortar' mentality. The government bond market in the GCC region is virtually non-existent and in any case there is a dearth of *Sharia'a* compliant Treasuries worldwide, with the exception of Malaysia.

Malaysia and Saudi Arabia are by far the two largest markets for Islamic mutual funds. This can be seen from figure 7.3. Malaysia has over 90 such funds and two institutions in Saudi Arabia – AlRajhi Bank and National Commercial Bank by far dominate the industry in the GCC with the two largest families of *Sharia'a* compliant funds.

The emergence of Islamic equity indices such as the Dow Jones and FTSE has opened up new areas for innovation in this respect especially index-linked funds and other more exotic products such as Exchange Traded Funds (ETFs).

There is also huge potential for private equity funds and for *Takaful* (Islamic insurance) funds. Although the sector has seen a proliferation of single private equity transactions, there are only a handful of Islamic private equity funds in the market. *Takaful* premiums have to be invested in Islamic instruments. Most are currently invested in commodity *Murabaha* transactions on the London Metals Exchange or the Commodity *Murabaha* Programme led by Bank Negara Malaysia. Structuring Islamic equity products is well established even amongst Western fund managers. Structuring value-added Islamic equity funds is the real challenge!

Islamic market indices

Ascertaining the detailed *Sharia'a* screened universe of available stocks would be costly for an individual fund, but has been made less so by the creation, in February 1999, of the Dow Jones Islamic Market Index (DJIM), launched in Bahrain, and in November, 1999 of the *Financial Times* Stock Exchange Global Islamic Index Series (GIIS).

Both indices are aimed at investors who follow Islamic investment guidelines, and classify quoted companies according to a number of screens. After removing companies with unacceptable core business activities, the remaining list is tested by a financial ratio 'filter', the purpose of which is to remove companies with an unacceptable debt ratio.

Both indices use a debt or asset ratio of less than one-third, while the DJIM uses two additional filters. Accounts receivable or total assets must be less than 49% and interest income or operating income must be less than 10%. Both series report a dividend cleansing or impure income figure. Here 'tainted dividend' receipts relate to the portion, if any, of a dividend paid by a constituent company that has been determined to be attributable to activities that are not in accordance with *Sharia'a* principles and therefore should be donated to charity. However, such cleansing cannot be counted as part of *zakat* obligations.

In this and other matters, both index compilers are advised by *Sharia'a* Scholars. In the case of the DJIM this forms part of the Dow Jones Global Index (DJGI) of nearly 3,000 companies from 33 countries, covering 10 economic sectors and 122 industry groupings. After the *Sharia'a* screening only about 600 companies from 30 countries remained. Details of the DJIM can be found in *Appendix 7.1*.

2. *Ijara* fund

Another type of Islamic fund is an *Ijara* fund. *Ijara* means leasing. In this fund the subscription amounts are used to purchase assets like real estate, motor vehicles or other equipment for the purpose of leasing them out to their ultimate users. The ownership of these assets remains with the fund and the rentals are charged to the users. These rentals are the source of income for the fund which is distributed pro-rata to the subscribers.

However, it should always be kept in mind that the leasing contracts must conform to the principles of *Sharia'a*. These Islamic leases differ substantially from the terms and conditions used in the agreements of conventional financial leases. Some basic principles are summarised below (1):

1) The leased assets must have some usufruct, and the rental must be charged only from that point in time when the usufruct is handed over to the lessee.
2) The leased assets must be of a nature that their *halal* (permissible) use is possible.
3) The lessor must undertake all the responsibilities consequent to the ownership of the assets.
4) The rental must be fixed and known to the parties at the beginning of the contract. In this type of fund the management should act as an agent of the subscribers and should be paid a fee for his services. The management fee may be a fixed amount or a proportion of the rentals received.

   Most of the Muslim jurists are of the view that such a fund cannot be created on the basis of *Murabaha*, because *Murabaha*, according to them, is restricted to the sale of commodities and does not extend to the business of services and leases. *Murabaha* funds are, however, permissible in Malaysia.

3. Commodity fund

Another type of Islamic fund is a commodity fund. In a commodity fund the subscription amounts are used for purchasing different commodities for the purpose of resale. The profits generated by the sale are the income of the fund which is distributed pro-rata among the subscribers. In order to make this fund acceptable to the *Sharia'a*, it is necessary that all the rules governing the transactions be fully complied with. These *Sharia'a* rules are:

1) The commodity must be owned by the seller at the time of sale. Therefore, short sales where a person sells a commodity before he owns it are not allowed in *Sharia'a*.
2) Forward sales are not allowed except in the case of *Salam* and *Istisna'a*.
3) The commodities must be *halal*. Therefore, it is not allowable to deal in alcohol, pork, or other prohibited items.
4) The seller must have physical or constructive possession of the commodity he wants to sell.
5) The price of the commodity must be fixed and known to the parties. Any price which is uncertain or is tied up with an uncertain event renders the sale invalid.

In view of the above and similar other conditions, it should be readily understood that the transactions prevalent in the contemporary commodity markets, especially in the futures commodity markets do not comply with these conditions. Therefore, an Islamic commodity fund cannot enter into such transactions. However, if there are genuine commodity transactions observing all the requirements of *Sharia'a*, including the above conditions, a commodity fund may be established.

4. Murabaha fund

Murabaha is a specific kind of sale where the commodities are sold on a cost-plus basis. Commodity *Murabaha*, as an Islamic asset class, was discussed in *Chapter 6*. This kind of sale has been adopted by contemporary Islamic banks and financial institutions as a mode of financing. The banks purchase the commodity for the benefit of their clients, and then sell it to them on the basis of deferred payment at an agreed margin of profit added to the cost. If a fund is created to undertake this kind of sale, it should be a closed-ended fund and its units cannot be negotiable in the secondary market.

The reason for this non-negotiability is that in the case of *Murabaha*, as undertaken by the present financial institutions, the commodities are sold to the clients immediately after their purchase from the original supplier, while the price being on deferred payment basis becomes a debt payable by the client. Therefore, the *Murabaha* portfolio does not own any tangible assets; rather it comprises either cash or the debt receivables. Both of these items are not negotiable Islamically. If they are exchanged for money it must be at par value.

See box 7.1 for an example of a commodity *Murabaha* fund.

Box 7.1. Commodity *Murabaha* fund

Islamic US Dollar *Murabaha* Fund

Fund objective and strategy

The investment objective of the fund is to provide stable returns in accordance with the *Sharia'a*. The investment seeks competitive money market like returns and capital preservation through participation in Al-Ahli Diversified US Dollar Trade Fund, which engages in *Murabaha* trade-based instruments and Islamic bonds (*sukuk)*, while offering weekly liquidity.

Fund facts

Fund structure:	**An open-ended fund.**
Currency:	**US Dollar.**
Inception date:	**31 October 2004.**
Liquidity:	**Weekly.**
Minimum investment:	**Initial subscription must be at least US$50,000. Subsequent subscriptions must be in minimum increments of at least US$5,000.**
Management fee:	**0.30% per annum.**
Manager:	**The National Commercial Bank, Saudi Arabia (Investment Services Division).**
Auditor:	**Whinney Murray & Company, Jeddah.**
***Sharia'a* Advisor:**	**National Management Consultancy Center, *Sharia'a* Advisor to NCB, headed by Dr. Mohamed Bin Ali Al-Garri, Associate Professor of Islamic Economics, King Abdul Aziz University, Saudi Arabia.**
Reporting:	**Weekly unit prices, quarterly performance reports and semi-annual customer statements.**

5. Mixed Islamic fund

Another type of Islamic fund is one where the subscription amounts are employed in different types of investments, such as equities, leasing, commodities etc. This is called a Mixed Islamic Fund. In this case if the tangible assets of the fund are more than 51% while the liquidity and debts are less than 50% the units of the fund may be negotiable. However, if the proportion of liquidity and debts exceeds 50%, its units cannot be traded according to the majority of the contemporary scholars. In this case the fund must be a closed-ended fund.

Recent innovations with Islamic funds

In recent years, the Islamic banking industry has launched a series of *Sharia'a* compliant investment funds – ranging from the relatively straightforward long-only equity funds to the more Islamically challenging private equity, venture capital and short-only funds. The general intention of most fund promoters appears to be to mirror structures familiar to Western bankers and investors. This is true with respect to both the form the product takes and the underlying substantive investment objectives sought to be achieved for the investor. The investment managers, *Wakils* or *Mudarib's*, as the case may be, usually adhere to pre-defined investment guidelines that set out the industries in which the fund may invest and the financial ratios it must maintain.

Real estate funds

Although real estate is hardly a new Islamic asset class, it is only recently that financial institutions have been able to package real estate in the form of investment funds for offer to retail investors in the Gulf Co-operation Council countries. This is quite an achievement given the fact that traditionally these funds were restricted to prime real estate in Europe and the US and were offered only to institutional and high net worth investors.

Another interesting proposition are leasing funds in which the underlying assets are equipment such as computers, cash machines and machinery. Investment funds which invest in this asset class have to deal with a mixture of legal and *Sharia'a* considerations that pertain to the jurisdiction of the assets, the jurisdiction of the offering, scope of due diligence, role of investment managers, fixed and floating-rates of return, credit enhancements, residual value, and taxation, among other issues.

Capital protected funds

A widely accepted, if somewhat controversial, Islamic alternative to conventional capital guaranteed funds are Islamic capital protected instruments. Most *Sharia'a* compliant capital protected funds and instruments use two investment mechanisms to achieve the required investment objective. The first mechanism is a *Murabaha* instrument which involves the investment of the bulk of the monies raised from investors in a fixed-term commodity trade transaction or a series of such transactions. See *Chapter 6* for details of commodity *Murabaha*. The second mechanism is an *Arboun* (a *Sharia'a* alternative to call options) transaction in which the fund invests a small percentage (for example 10%) of the monies raised from the investors to purchase an option over a basket or portfolio of *Sharia'a* compliant shares or commodities.

The *Murabaha* transactions, customarily viewed as low-risk transactions, are structured to generate the required capital protection, while the *Arboun* transaction(s) are intended to increase returns. If the basket of shares subject to the *Arboun* depreciates, the fund manager will not exercise the option and the payment price for the option will have been lost. The underlying *Murabaha* transactions, however, are structured to compensate for the lost option payment thereby protecting, but not guaranteeing, the capital.

The National Commercial Bank (NCB) spearheaded the process of developing an Islamic alternative to call options in the late 1990s following the encouraging results achieved by conventional capital guaranteed funds launched by NCB. A joint effort between NCB and Deutsche Bank, supplemented by an active and continuous dialogue with *Sharia'a* advisors and legal counsel representing both NCB and Deutsche Bank, led to the successful offering to retail investors in Saudi Arabia of the first Islamic capital protected fund. The fund appealed to investors who desired to benefit from any rise in the market while securing their principal from any downside. Evidence of the success of the fund included the high level of subscription in the first series, over US$275 million, which led NCB to issue a second series.

This product is one example of a highly successful investment product developed and offered successfully by a leading Middle Eastern bank. Also, the involvement of Deutsche Bank served to prove that financial institutions in the Middle East can benefit from collaboration with premier international financial institutions. Moreover, regional banks can benefit through entering into private labelling arrangements that strengthen inter-regional ties and allow the financial institution that developed the product to capitalise on its investment in 'research and development'.

Islamic capital protection is discussed in more detail in *Chapter 8* and *Appendix 8.3* provides a case study.

Innovative product development

Innovation in products and services is the engine of financial services. The Islamic banking sector is no exception. But given its relatively short contemporary history, product development and innovation is at best piecemeal. This is partly because research and development (R&D) is only just emerging in the sector.

The mainstay of the Islamic financial products suite has been the plain vanilla offerings of *Murabaha*, *Ijara*, *Istisna'a*, *Al Bai Bithaman Ajil*, Instalment Sale, and to a lesser extent *Musharaka* and *Mudaraba*. More recently, *sukuk* and securitisation have started to proliferate with structures such as *Salam Sukuk*, *Sukuk Al-Ijara*; *Musharaka Sukuk*; *Sukuk Al-Mudaraba*, *Sukuk Al-Intifaa*, *Murabaha Sukuk*, Islamic Private Debt Securities, Islamic Medium Term Notes etc. Another area of product innovations has been Islamic insurance (*Takaful*) based on the *Mudaraba*, *Wakala* and *Tabarru* concepts.

After three decades of Islamic finance development, investors and customers have now become much more sophisticated and demanding. Some continue to seek value-added returns especially in riskier asset classes such as Islamic derivatives, fixed-income, capital markets and private equity products.

On the other hand, plain vanilla offerings refined to suit specific market requirements, especially in consumer financing and trade finance, continue to prevail. Product development especially in the more exotic areas relating to options, repurchase agreements (repo's), hedge funds, swaps etc, is dictated by the quality of *Sharia'a* research and advisory, and the demand dynamics of investors and institutions. Product innovation, as with the conventional sector, is fast becoming the driver of the Islamic finance sector. Nevertheless, with a young demography, and huge liquidity, the mutual fund industry will certainly persist and perhaps flourish with the right product offerings and expertise in structuring, marketing, stock selection and portfolio and investment management.

Islamic private equity

The demand for *Sharia'a* compliant investments and financing sources as a whole grows ever more important and may well be on its way to becoming mainstream. As part of this development, *Sharia'a* compliant private equity funds are increasingly coming to the attention of private equity fund managers, keen to tap a market of investors not only from the booming Gulf States, but from the over one billion Muslims worldwide.

Those investors who prefer investing in a *Sharia'a* compliant fashion also seek an asset class that represents socially responsible investments and view fund investments much like conventional investors. Although the first Islamic equity fund was established as far back as 1986, it is only fairly recently that the sector has started to expand rapidly, as discussed earlier.

Traditionally, Islamic fund managers have directed their investment focus on the geographical area of the GCC, US and European equities as well as other asset classes such as real estate. Likewise, expansion into North Africa, the Indian Subcontinent and South-East Asia is also underway, with Malaysia for instance, proving an especially attractive, and to a large extent accommodating, jurisdiction. In 2007 alone, private equity firms in the GCC raised US$10 billion of capital, a figure which is expected to double each year over the coming years.

The key reason for the growing interest in *Sharia'a* compliant private equity is the sheer immensity of the current pool of available Islamic capital. Fuelled by high oil and gas prices and with production at almost maximum capacity, an ever-increasing amount of cash has been streaming into the Middle East, which — also a requirement under the *Sharia'a* — needs to be invested responsibly.

There is no reliable data on the size of funds available for investments, though estimates range from US$700 billion to several trillion US dollars. Regional high net worth individuals alone — most from Saudi Arabia, Kuwait and the United Arab Emirates — are said to control assets of over US$1.1 trillion. In addition, investors from the Gulf Region are putting their money into strategic investments to prepare for the future when oil and gas revenues decline, a trend which has already started.

Private equity funds are particularly attractive for Islamic investors because, as compared to other asset classes, they provide higher returns, diversification, relative price stability and a broad range of investment opportunities. As the industry matures and the track record of well managed Islamic equity funds evolves further, *Sharia'a* compliant private equity funds may well become an attractive asset class not only for Muslim but also for non-Muslim investors.

Exchange tradable funds (ETFs)

ETFs are similar to index mutual funds, but are traded more like stocks. As their name implies, ETFs represent a basket of securities that are traded on an exchange. So ETFs are securities certificates that state a legal right of ownership over part of a basket of individual stock certificates. As passively managed funds designed to track performance of an index, ETFs are similar to index mutual funds and are listed and traded on a stock exchange making them much cheaper to buy.

Several different kinds of financial firms are needed for ETFs to come into being. Laying all the groundwork is the fund manager. This is the main backer behind any ETF and the fund managers must submit a detailed plan for how the ETF will operate. Only then will they be given permission to proceed by the regulatory authorities.

In theory all that a fund manager needs to do is establish clear procedures and describe precisely the composition of the ETF (which changes infrequently) to the other firms involved in ETF creation and redemption. In practice, however, only the very biggest institutional money management firms with experience in indexing tend to play this role, such as The Vanguard Group and Barclays Global Investors. They direct pension funds with enormous baskets of stocks in markets all over the world to loan stocks necessary for the creation process. They also create demand by lining up customers, either institutional or retail, to buy a newly introduced ETF.

The creation of an ETF officially begins with an authorised participant, also referred to as a market maker or specialist. Highly scrutinized for their integrity and operational competence, these middlemen assemble the appropriate basket of stocks and send them to a specially designated custodial bank for safekeeping. These baskets are normally quite large, sufficient to purchase 10,000 to 50,000 shares of the ETF in question. The custodial bank double checks that the basket represents the requested ETF and forwards the ETF shares on to the authorised participant. This is a so-called *in-kind* trade of essentially equivalent items that does not trigger capital gains for investors.

The custodial bank holds the basket of stocks in the fund's account for the fund manager to monitor. There isn't too much activity in these accounts but some cash comes into them for dividends and there are a variety of oversight tasks to perform. Some managers have leeway to use derivatives to track an index. Once the authorised participant obtains the ETF from the custodial bank, it is free to sell it into the open market. From then on ETF shares are sold and resold freely among investors on the open market.

Redemption is simply the reverse. An authorised participant buys a large block of ETFs on the open market, sends it to the custodial bank and, in return receives back an equivalent basket of individual stocks which are then sold on the open market or typically returned to their loanees.

What motivates each player? The fund manager takes a small portion of the fund's annual assets as its fee. This is clearly stated in the prospectus. The investors who loan stocks to make up a basket earn a small interest fee for the favour. The custodial bank earns a small return likewise, usually paid for by the fund manager out of management fees. The authorised participant is primarily driven by profits from the difference in price between the basket of stocks and the ETF and on part of the bid-ask spread of the ETF itself. Whenever there is an opportunity to earn a little by buying one and selling the other, the authorised participant will jump in.

The process might seem cumbersome but it does allow for transparency and liquidity at modest cost. Everyone can see what goes into an ETF, investor fees are clearly laid out, investors can be confident that they can exit at any time, and even the authorised participant's fees are guaranteed to be modest. If ETF prices deviate from the underlying net asset value of the component stocks, arbitrageurs can step in and take profits on the difference. This competition tends to keep ETF prices very close to the underlying Net Asset Value (value of component stocks). Figure 7.4 provides a comparison of ETFs and other investment vehicles.

	Equity or bond ETF	Index fund	Individual equity	Individual bond
Pricing	Real-time, intra-day	End-of-day net asset value	Real-time, intra-day	Subject to availability and broker discretion
Accessibility	Any brokerage firm, any account	Fund manager or fund distributors	Any brokerage firm, any account	Most brokers, subject to inventory availability
Transparency	Portfolio daily disclosures and intra-day prices known to investors	Portfolio required to be reported semi-annually. Price known at the end of day	N/A	Prior to trade, actual cost of bond not always clear (may include broker mark-up)
Transaction Fee	Commission on trade through a broker. Intra-day bid/offer spread	Issuing commission fee depends on seller	Commission on trade through a broker. Intra-day bid/offer spread	Commission on trade through a broker. Intra-day bid/offer spread
Early Sales/ Redemption	N/A	Early sales/ redemption fee may be charged by some fund companies	N/A	N/A
Diversification	High, an entire index of assets	Depends. Some mutual index funds are likely to be more diversified than actively managed funds	No	No
Liquidity	Yes. Open-end fund structure	Yes. Open-end fund structure and end-of-day net asset value	Yes. Depends on market demand	Yes. Depends on market demand
Long or short selling	Long and short	Long only	Long and short	Long and short
Annual management fee	Yes. Includes management and administration fees	Yes. Includes management and administration fees	No	No

Figure 7.4. Comparison of ETFs and other investment vehicles

What are Islamic ETFs?

An Islamic ETF is a unit trust fund created by applying Islamic investment principles which is then traded on a stock exchange. It consists of securities designed to track the performance of an Islamic index. ETFs are open-ended funds with a unique creation and redemption mechanism, as mentioned earlier supported by a system of participating dealers and liquidity providers. The main difference between ETFs and unit trust funds is in the manner which the units are bought and sold. ETFs are designed to be a liquid, low cost financial instrument for investors seeking a performance generally similar to the benchmark index.

The first *Sharia'a* compliant ETF was launched in Malaysia on 22 January 2008. The fund, known as MyETF Dow Jones Islamic Market Malaysia Titan 25 (MyETFDJIM25), was listed on Bursa Malaysia Securities Bhd (Bursa Securities) on 31st January 2008. The exchange traded funds division of Barclays Global Investors, iShares, listed, in 2008, three new *Sharia'a* compliant listed products on the London Stock Exchange, aiming to capitalise on the transparency of ETFs.

To assist in the development and launch the three new *Sharia'a* compliant iShares funds, Barclays called upon a panel of distinguished *Sharia'a* Scholars: Dr Mohammed Elgari, Sheikh Nizam Yaquby and Dr Abu Ghuddah. The iShares team has devised methods of screening out non-compliant elements from the investment process. This process reduces exposure to financial services and also to certain media stocks. The Islamic ETFs allow a breakdown of dividends to be provided so that a differentiation between pure streams of return – those that are entirely *Sharia'a* compliant – can be differentiated from impure streams. The investor can then choose to donate this impure component of the return to charity.

The new iShares have a higher exposure to the energy, materials and technology sectors than the financial sector, due to the *Sharia'a* screens. For the initial tranche, iShares chose MSCI, the benchmarking group, to provide *Sharia'a* compliant indices to support the new products.

Appendix 7.1 Dow Jones Islamic Market Indices(2)

Nobody ever accused Wall Street of being too easygoing or charitable in its investment decision-making process. The fact is the Street operates to generate and circulate monies and revenues and profits. When it sees opportunities it grabs them. If they are too risky or unpopular, they whither.

Dow Jones Indexes has been a pioneer in indexing the Islamic markets. In 1999, it was the first company to create benchmarks for *Sharia'a* compliant stock portfolios. Others have since joined the fray, including top names in Western financial services.

Why did Dow Jones Indexes blaze a trail into this market? Why, after so many years on the scene, did the Islamic markets draw the gaze of one of the world's leading indexing bench markers?

The answer is simple: money. The meteoric expansion of *Sharia'a* compliant investing made Wall Street sit up and take notice. Just like all other financial trends, people only pay attention when the numbers make it sufficiently attractive. That is the case with Islamic investing. The combination of the rise in oil and gas incomes in the Middle East, the growth of the Islamic population worldwide and the idea of a brand of investing that avoided industries that some found objectionable, have focused world attention on this sector.

Currently, it is estimated that there are approximately $800 billion in some sort of *Sharia'a* approved investments or transactions globally, including $200 billion in assets under management with *Sharia'a* compliant banks. Some estimate the industry's growth rate at 15-20% annually, far outpacing many investment sectors.

Dow Jones Indexes had the foresight to see the opportunities and serve a niche (and growing) market. That is how the Dow Jones Islamic Market Indexes (DJIM) was born. Its creation was not for any cultural or social purpose. It was to make money for its clients by providing the very best data available on a strong and growing market. This is how they do it.

Benchmarking criteria

The DJIM has four main factors in selecting its portfolios for benchmarking:

- *Sharia'a* law compliance – all DJIM are monitored for strict adherence to Sharia'a law. Each index has a *Sharia'a* Board of experts that does periodic reviews to make sure that no forbidden industries are represented. A team of five scholars helped create the original DJIM.
- Liquidity – DJIM includes only stocks that are easily accessible (tradable) to investors. That means that the smallest, most thinly traded stocks are excluded from any index.
- Comprehensive coverage – DJIM's goal is to provide the broadest coverage. Its indexes cover countries, regions, market capitalisation ranges and

Sharia'a compliant industries. There are sub-indexes as well, covering even more specific markets and groups.

- Systematic methodology – All DJIM methodologies are systematic and transparent (published for investors and the markets to see). Each index's construction is based on a quantitative set of rules and guidelines. For inclusion in an index, stocks must pass consistently-applied industry and financial ratio screens.

In other words, DJIM components are held to the highest standards of *Sharia'a* law. At the same time, they are expected to adhere to the principles of the broader, secular financial services industry as well.

Sharia'a Boards serve as both a check and a conscience for all indices. DJIM has globally-known experts in *Sharia'a* law who are also well versed in today's markets. They marry the doctrines of *Sharia'a* law with the dynamic world of capital markets. Their job is to make sure that the companies that are components of the DJIM indexes conform to all the appropriate standards and that they are proper for the grouping (or sub-grouping) listed.

Sharia'a compliant industries

Sharia'a law prohibits involvement by Muslims in certain activities, as discussed earlier in this text. The essence of *Sharia'a* compliant investing is to absolutely avoid any companies that take part in these banned endeavours. The banned industries fall into the following categories:

- Alcohol,
- Tobacco,
- Pork-related products,
- Financial services (due to prohibitions on interest),
- Defence and weapons production,
- Entertainment (specifically pornography).

Sharia'a law also has specific prohibitions on how a company (any company in any industry) can operate. In particular, individuals and corporations are barred from having excessive cash or debt. Therefore, if a company has any of the factors listed below, it cannot be included in DJIM indexes:

- Total debt divided by trailing 12-month average market capitalisation of 33% or more.
- Cash plus interest-bearing securities divided by trailing 12-month average market capitalisation of 33% or more.
- Accounts receivable divided by 12-month average market capitalisation of 33% or more.

DJIM indexes are held to the same professional accounting standards as all the other Dow Jones indexes. That is why its indexes are weighted based on float-adjusted market capitalisation. And just like all its indexes, DJIM are reviewed quarterly for compliance and standards. The components undergo checks for bankruptcies, de-listings and mergers.

In fact, this issue greatly affects DJIM, as formerly permissible stocks can be subsumed by corporations that have forbidden operations. For instance, if Anheuser Busch, a company selling alcoholic products, decided to merge with agribusiness giant Archer Daniels Midland, the latter would have to be dropped from the index due to the formers impermissible main lines of business. Conversely, if Smithfield Foods, the largest pork producer in the US, decided to get out of the business and concentrate on chickens instead, it would then be considered a possible candidate for addition to an index.

Take a real life example: Loews Corp, the NYSE-traded conglomerate known for its hotels, also has pipelines, insurance and energy exploration. For 40 years, they also held Lorillard, which features some of the biggest names in tobacco, including Newport, Kent, True and Old Gold. In 2008, Loews spun off Lorillard.

Does that make Loews *Sharia'a* permissible? An investigation would be made to check if they offered 'adult' movies, a source of both revenues and controversy. A cursory check makes it appear as though they do not offer any such movies, but it would have to be checked for *Sharia'a* compliance. If found to be free of adult movies, Loews could be open to Islamic investment (and inclusion in DJIM and other indices).

Dodging falling boulders…

So, like any other type of investment, Islamic markets have built-in do's and don'ts. No surprise there. A Dow Jones European energy index would feature only gas and oil retailers; offshore explorers; importers and distributors; research and developers; utilities; and other companies directly related to that industry. It cannot include Nestlé, or any other company, just because it pays good dividends.

In the early years of the 21st century, to the outside observer, it seemed foolish that *Sharia'a* compliant investors could not get into the boom in financial services. There were enormous profits to be made on the booming real estate market and its ancillary (mortgages, lending) and derivative, asset-based cousins. This was to say nothing of the boom in credit, represented by the stratospheric rise in personal and business debt.

Mortgage companies like Countrywide could not keep up with demand from new home buyers, many of whom were given almost unbelievably easy access to credit. Among the terms being offered to many: no money down; interest-only; adjustable rate mortgages with favourable terms for the first five years. Some of these home buyers were under-qualified (no credit or bad credit; first time buyers with few assets), but thanks to the greatly expanding 'sub prime market', they too were able to grab a piece of the American dream.

Credit card companies – mainly banks and financial services companies such as Citigroup – were also taking in enormous profits thanks to a seemingly insatiable appetite for purchasing power among consumers. Credit cards could not be printed quickly enough to arrive in eager hands. And their colleagues in the university student loan business were having a grand time as well, with the combination of a wave of university-aged students graduating high school, dizzying university tuition fees and easy credit, making that market larger than it had ever been.

Securities companies like Bear Stearns (later to be taken over) were able to package these monies into securities that were sold and resold on the open markets to clients who were led to believe that they were as secure as any investment available. The profits were huge and steady. Mutual funds and pensions considered them prudent and safe. Brokers and their clients agreed in unison that they were both doing well thanks to housing and credit markets that could not say no.

And yet, *Sharia'a* prohibits the charging of interest. It also bans excess cash and credit. Therefore, Islamic markets (and DJIM, which was monitoring it) missed out on this boom, just as it missed out on its spectacular and devastating bust later in the decade. All the companies named above suffered almost unbelievable falls from grace. Their (and their clients') losses metastasized from millions to billions before stunned, disbelieving market eyes.

Some were able to weather the storm with perseverance, the strength of their enormous size and some bailouts (Citigroup); some found solace in the open arms of suitors (Countrywide, acquired by Bank of America); and still others stared oblivion straight in the eye before being rescued (Bear Stearns, subsumed by JP Morgan Chase). These same names that were once so mighty, have now become cautionary tales now, taught in business and ethics courses around the world in how to get lost in bubbles and illusions.

...But sitting out some opportunities, too

Of course, the sub-prime crisis is an easy target. Just as Enron would have been prohibited due to its gargantuan credit margins and thus, another disaster averted, Islamic markets could also be left out of strong, steady markets for the sake of faith.

Consider Altria, a global tobacco behemoth once known as Philip Morris. It is the producer of some of the biggest names in cigarettes: Marlboro, Parliament, Virginia Slims and dozens more around the world. Its products generate fierce loyalty from users (and fierce opposition from health advocates). It is also known for having one of the highest and most reliable returns on investment (ROI) of any business on the market. Its dividend makes it a valuable addition to mutual and pension funds. Even class action lawsuits, health advocates, media campaigns, shareholder activists and public settlements in the billions have not slowed the company's dividend payments. An ex-member of the prestigious Dow Jones Industrial Average (and current denizen of countless others), it is considered a solid, though controversial investment.

However, tobacco companies are banned from Islamic markets portfolios, including DJIM. So, looking at this solely from a markets and ROI point of view, not having Altria can be seen as a detriment.

Yet, since *Sharia'a* compliant investing by its very nature means that its practitioners are putting spiritual needs first, this is an acceptable price to pay. There is a greater global investment marketplace – one that is permissible for Islamic investors as well as their secular colleagues – that offers infinite possibilities for growth.

ROI compared with secular indexes

Islamic markets are treated just like any other markets by Dow Jones Indexes. DJIM has to compare itself against the broader markets to make sure that its component selections coincide (and that they are not falling behind). Customers rely on the data produced by Dow Jones Indexes to provide solid coverage. *Sharia'a* compliant investors are not just idealists. They expect returns that correspond to whichever market on which they focus.

Constituent indexes

Dow Jones Indexes realised soon after it started DJIM that it was filling a need in the investment world. They also realised that the need was huge and growing, and needed products to feed its appetite. Indexes and sub-indexes were made to keep up with client demand.

Today, in 2009, DJIM has more than 70 indices representing markets in 46 countries. Geographically, the indices range from the Western world of North America and Europe to Asia/Pacific to the Middle East. There are country, regional, sector and industry indices. There are indices covering emerging markets, European midcaps, Malaysia, consumer goods and Japan, to name a few. More are being created all the time. In fact, Dow Jones Indices has more than 130,000 indices worldwide with niches and specialisations that appeal to every type of investor (the Dow Jones Luxury, Dow Jones STOXX Grand Prix, Dow Jones Sri Lanka 20 Titans indices are examples). This shows an enormous (and growing) market.

Investors use indices for various reasons. It might be to benchmark a portfolio to prevent against market fluctuations; maybe licensing the Dow Jones name to give added weight to a new product; a fund manager might use the data to keep track of a portfolio. The list goes on.

Suffice it to say that as long as there is investing and the need to keep up with markets, indices will play a vital role. And so long as investors want *Sharia'a* compliant investments (and want to keep up with them as well), DJIM and other indices will track those investments, maintaining the same rigorous standards it applies to all its constituent components.

References

1. Usmani. T.U. *An Introduction to Islamic Finance*. Idaratul Ma'arif. Karachi, Pakistan 1999.
(2) The author would like to acknowledge the generous assistance of the DJIM for providing this Appendix.

Chapter 8

Derivatives and hedge funds in Islamic finance

Introduction

The ever-increasing innovation and application of the methodologies associated with derivative instruments have revolutionised the global financial industry over the past two decades, a trend not without its critics it must be said, given the gyrations associated with the 2008-2009 bank failures. Document standardisation in transacting derivative-based transactions has reached the point of uniform application in conventional markets and products, thus removing an immense amount of uncertainty and risk previously associated with these types of transactions. In this day and age, it can safely be said that derivatives have become *de rigueur* in the international financial arena. This is not to say that they are not without their critics, as mentioned!

What are conventional derivatives?

Conventional options, swaps and futures stem from debts and involve the sale and purchase of debts or liabilities. As a group, such instruments are called derivatives, i.e. they are derived from the expected future performance of the respective underlying assets such as securities or commodities. What does this definition mean?

Forward contracts

Let us take a basic example: a miller and grain farmer conclude an agreement today for the delivery of a specified quantity and quality of grain on an agreed future date, let's say six months ahead. The important element of this transaction is that the price to be paid for the grain is fixed on today's date. The primary reason for the immediate price determination is to remove the uncertainty for both parties of what the actual spot price for grain would be six months from now. Either party may stand to lose or gain a great deal from this uncertainty if the price movement is against them or in their favour but it does not bode well for financial planning. Since the parties face risk in the opposite directions of price movement, it will make financial sense for them to meet and agree on a price, which will suit both of them, to eliminate the price movement risk in the commodity (called 'hedging'). The grain farmer then knows what input costs he can safely invest into his harvest to still turn a profit. The miller, on the other hand, knows at what price he can sell flour into a competitive market six months into the future and can plan and market his product accordingly.

What has been explained above is a basic forward contract. The derivative element present in this simple set of facts is that, from the first day subsequent to this contract being concluded, the contract itself gains a value derived from the underlying price movements and future expectations of the spot price of grain on the agreed delivery date.

How does this work? The day the parties agreed the forward price of grain six months into the future was not a matter of mere guesswork. Both parties probably considered a plethora of elements and contingencies as to what was relevant in determining a fair price for grain six months into the future (e.g. market conditions, micro- and macro-economic indicators, price volatility, weather patterns, quality considerations etc). Every day thereafter, the input data on these elements and contingencies will vary constantly to the extent that, had the parties known about the changed conditions at the time they contracted on the price of the grain, they may well have come to a different conclusion.

This process of constantly monitoring the variations in the contingencies pertaining to the forecasted spot price of grain on the delivery date of the grain in this example (called 'marking to market') can give the contracting parties an indication whether the contract is in their favour ('in-the-money') or not in their favour ('out-of-the-money'). It is this mark-to-market value (i.e. derived from translating present market conditions into an expected future price of the commodity on a future date) that represents the derivative value of the contract in question. It should be clear by now that this represents value independent of the underlying commodity but at the same time it exists only because of changes in the variables determining the future price of the underlying commodity.

The forward contract is the most basic of derivative contracts. It may be of particular use in purchasing say foreign currency from authorised dealers in currency but in other areas it has certain obvious shortcomings. Firstly, it is not often parties have an exact match in (a) the opposite directions of price movement of the underlying instrument or commodity; and (b) the timing and the quantity of delivery (called the problem of 'double-coincidence'). Secondly, the risk of the counterparty defaulting (so-called 'counterparty risk') on his obligations is a higher than normal risk in these circumstances and can negate all good intentions when it comes to financial planning.

If one refers back to the example of the grain farmer and the miller, it will soon be obvious why possible default is higher than normal between the parties. If the miller saw a substantial dip in the spot grain price (far below his forward contract price, thus rendering his contract out-of-the-money) a few days before he was to take delivery of the grain in terms of the contract in the example, the attraction to default in terms of his forward contract with the farmer will be substantial. The same can be said of the farmer if there was a big increase in the spot price of grain way above the forward contract price a few days before delivery was due. Although the non-defaulting party will have recourse in law against the other, this can be a tedious and expensive exercise to bring to eventual fruition, which, once again, will undo all good intentions in respect of financial planning.

Futures and options contracts

Enter the next tool in the evolution of derivatives, futures contracts. Designed to take care of both problems of double coincidence and counterparty risk, a futures contract is a standardised forward contract with respect to size, maturity and quality interposing a futures exchange (in between the original buying and selling parties) as the buyer to each seller and the seller to each buyer. Each party can then buy the number of contracts that will suit its individual needs. Because a large number buyers and sellers deal via the exchange the problem of double coincidence is more easily overcome. Also, by doing daily marking to market and making margin calls from the party that is out-of-the-money, the futures exchange substantially reduces counterparty risk.

The final basic concept to consider under this heading is that of options. As was the case in the earlier story the inadequacies of futures contracts gave rise to the development of options. Futures contracts make the underlying assumption of actual delivery of the merchandise concerned at the initially agreed upon price. The only way of avoiding performance under the contract is to enter into an equal and opposite sale or purchase of the underlying merchandise on the exchange at the prevailing mark-to-market price for the goods. It is clear that this does not cater for contingent scenarios (where actual obligations are not certain) that might arise in a business on a daily basis. It also does not allow parties to take advantage of price movements in their favour.

To understand this properly, let us revert once again to the example of the grain farmer and the miller. Firstly, the grain farmer is not exactly sure how much grain he will produce or as to what quality it will be. Is it then sound financial planning to enter into a contract for the delivery of a specific amount and quality of grain in the early planting season? If he had taken out an option to sell the grain at a specific price to the miller (called a 'put option') and paid an upfront non-refundable minimal amount for such an option (called a 'premium'), he would have had the right (but not the obligation) to sell his goods at a specific price to the miller. If he couldn't deliver, due to contingencies beyond his control, he merely would not exercise his option and would only lose the minimal amount of the premium paid for the put option. At least he would not be caught in a situation where he would be obliged to deliver, as would be the case under the futures contract.

Secondly, if the farmer was capable of getting a far better spot price for his grain at the time, he also wouldn't exercise his put option but rather sell his grain onto the open market. Thus, by having taken a put option instead of a futures contract, he (a) covered the price risk on his goods; (b) catered for contingencies beyond his control regarding delivery of the goods; and (c) still had the opportunity to cash in on favourable movements in the spot price for grain, all in return for the premium. Conversely, the same reasoning applies for the miller. Instead of binding himself to one farmer, who may, or may not, be able to deliver, why not pay a premium for an option to purchase from more than one (called a 'call option')? This way he caters for contingencies on one farmer not being able to deliver and, if there is a favourable downturn in the spot price of grain, he need not take up any of the farmers on his call option.

Although the examples given above are oversimplified their basic elements are present in a great variety of business transactions worldwide on a daily basis. It should be clear by now that there is an acute need for these instruments in businesses that require sound financial planning to give them the edge in the competitive world of global markets. It should also be clear that once these basic principles are clearly understood, it doesn't take much to make the quantum leap to realise that derivative values can be realised in almost anything tradable in the open market. This includes equities, securities, currencies, interest rates, credit risk, any commodity imaginable, indices thereof and/or baskets of any combination of the above and can be utilised for a variety of purposes, notably those pertaining to hedging, arbitrage and speculation.

Derivatives have become an essential risk management tool in corporate finance because they serve to transfer a certain type of risk from one party that wishes to reduce its risk exposure to another party that receives monetary reward in exchange for bearing that risk. Some of the factors that have spurred the growth of derivatives as an important risk management tool are:

1) increased volatility in asset prices in the financial markets;
2) greater integration of the international financial markets;
3) advancement in ICT; and
4) development of more sophisticated risk management tools.

Derivative contracts – the Islamic story

The key issue here is the extent to which the principles underlying conventional derivatives can be applied to the creation of Islamic derivatives. This story is highly controversial Islamically *Appendix 8.1* provides the *Sharia'a* rationale for the prohibition of derivatives.

Issues involved in the creation of Islamic derivatives

In Islam a variety of injunctions influence the principles of investment or hedging activities. These are:

- ***riba*** – a form of usury,
- ***gharar*** – a form of deception in trade or trading of risk where an asymmetric information and risk profile exists in a contract,
- **maysir** – gambling.

Riba

Two forms of *riba* are defined in Islam. One form deals with trades in financial instruments (such as bonds and loans) and the other deals with trades in physical assets. *Riba* on financial instruments involves a fixed interest charge on a loan or debt due to the passage of time. It arises where a borrower enters into a contract to repay to the lender a fixed interest rate in addition to the principal that was borrowed. *Riba* on physical trades involves an exchange of unequal qualities or quantities of the same commodity simultaneously and is also considered as usury.

Riba is an issue within Islam. With regards to the acceptability of *riba* most non-Islamic countries are indifferent.

Gharar

Securities and investment laws in most countries do prohibit investment activities that might involve deception (insider information or asymmetric information flows to the contracting parties). Usually severe punishments are considered for this behaviour. With regards to the notion of gambling (which could be thought of as an extreme form of speculation) treatments are different. Some countries do promote this form of trading behaviour and some do not.

The literal meaning of the term *gharar*, according to some Islamic scholars is 'that which has a pleasant appearance and a hated essence'. The origin of the term is a three-letter (Arabic) past tense verb *gharra* meaning 'to deceive'. The type of uncertainty regarding future events which constitutes *gharar* may be one-sided or two-sided and it may be intentional or unintentional. However, in all definitions, one thing is common: the incorporation of risk.

It is claimed by some Islamic scholars that trading in certain amount of risk can be allowed as an exception if the risk is minor (*gharar yasir*) or if the economic needs for the contract embodying the risk is substantial (e.g. as in the *Salam* contract). This is where one sees differences in opinion among classical as well as contemporary jurists regarding which type of *gharar* are considered minor and which are considered major. Therefore one must be aware that minor *gharar* does not render a trade defective, since no trade can be entirely free of *gharar*.

There are four necessary conditions for the existence of *gharar* to make a contract invalid. These are:

- the *gharar* must be major;
- the *gharar* should involve a financial contract;
- the *gharar* must affect the principal components of the contract;
- no economic need is met by the contract containing *gharar* which cannot be met by an alternative mechanism.

A central tenet of Islamic finance is that, in general Islamic financial instruments should include sharing and participation features on the risk and return side on a fair and informationally symmetric basis. This means that investment situations where risk is asymmetrically distributed or shared without any compensation or reward will be questionable, from an Islamic point of view. The universe of Islamically unacceptable financial instruments is diverse. The categories include many types of stocks, bonds and derivative instruments with various features. These asset classes would usually satisfy conventional investor risk return profiles globally.

Forward contracts and Islamic finance

A forward contract is one that commits the user to buy or sell an asset, say gold or a given currency, at a specific price on a specific date in the future. This date is known as the maturity date. The price of the asset can be settled at the maturity date or it can be all paid at the initiation of the contract. In the first case, from an Islamic point of view, the contract will not be considered as a *Sharia'a* compliant contract, since no asset countervalue is transferred at the time of the contract initiation. In the second case the contract will be very much like the *Salam* contracts in Islam. Forward contracts are mostly used for private deals between two parties. The terms and conditions of these contracts are very flexible. These instruments are not traded on the exchanges.

Futures contracts and Islamic finance

A futures contract is very much like a forward contract except it is traded on an exchange. To make trading possible, the exchange specifies certain standardised features of the contract which makes the terms and conditions of the contracts structured and more easily regulated. These contracts could be Islamically valid since the payment and assets can be transferred or guaranteed to be transferred at the time of the contract origination through the exchanges.

Swap contracts and Islamic finance

A swap contract is one by which two parties exchange benefits (cash flows) resulting from a given asset or liability. For example, two firms, one with a loan on a fixed interest rate over 10 years and the other with a similar loan on a floating interest rate over the same period, may agree to take over each other's interest obligations, so that the first firm pays the floating-rate and the second the fixed rate. If one is careful regarding *riba* on physical trades, these contracts can be Islamically justified and could be used regularly in the commodities swap markets.

Option contracts and Islamic finance

An option contract gives the buyer the right, but not the obligation, to buy or sell a particular asset at a particular price, on or before a specific date. Whereas forwards, futures and swaps are binding commitments, an option is a form of insurance. A buyer is charged a premium, which is lost should the option not be used (exercised).

There are two basic types of options. A *call* option gives the holder the right to buy the underlying asset by a certain date for a certain price. A *put* option gives the holder the right to sell the underlying asset by a certain date for a certain price. The price in the contract is known as the strike price, the date in the contract is known as the maturity. It should be emphasised that an option gives the holder the **right** to do something not the **obligation** to do something.

Conventional options confer merely rights and not liabilities. An option has a nominal size, this being the amount of underlying asset that the option holder may buy or sell at the strike price – the price at which the holder may like to buy or sell the underlying asset upon exercise of the option. If the price moves favourably, the option is exercised and the commodity is bought or sold at the agreed price. If the price moves unfavourably, the buyer of the option simply abandons it.

This option pricing concept is against the principle of the *Sharia'a*, according to which delivery has to be given and taken pursuant to the sale contracts without regard to movement in prices. The buyer of the option pays a price (the premium) to the seller (the writer) of the option. Hence, the feature that an option contract confers the right but not the obligation to enter into an underlying contract of exchange at or before a specified future date (the expiry date) makes the contract *Sharia'a* non-compliant.

What are Islamic derivatives?

Sharia'a compliant derivative instruments are risk management techniques that are compliant with *Sharia'a* law. At present, there are only a handful of Islamic derivatives that are accepted by the *Sharia'a* Boards worldwide. Amongst the permitted and most commonly used contracts include *Salam*, *Arboun*, *Istisna'a*, *Istijrar* and *Murabaha.*

Salam contract

A *Salam* contract involves advance payment of the goods in full with the delivery of the goods made at a predetermined future date. Under a *Salam* contract, the goods have to be defined and the date of delivery has to be fixed.

Istisna'a contract

Under the *Istisna'a* contract, the price of the goods is paid to the manufacturer at a predetermined price to manufacture non-existent goods that are to be delivered at a future date. This also involves the buyer paying the seller in instalments as the work progresses in manufacturing the goods. Nonetheless in order to minimise *gharar*, an *Istisna'a* contract must provide specifications about the production of the goods to the manufacturer. A *Joa'la* contract is essentially an *Istisna'a* but is applicable for services.

Salam (forward purchase) and *Istisna'a* (contract of manufacture), both of which are contracts where one of the countervalues is absent at the time of contracting, are only allowed where an exact description of the absent countervalues is given.

Arboun contract

Arboun is a *Sharia'a* compliant alternative and is similar to a call option. In an *Arboun* contract, the buyer pays some money to the seller as part of payment of the price in advance with the understanding that the money will be forfeited if the buyer decides not to continue with the contract. The balance of the agreed price is paid only at the completion of the deal. The contract has embedded options that could be triggered if an underlying asset's price exceeds certain limits and hence, minimising *gharar*. By fixing the date of the price at a future date, *riba* is eliminated from the contract. *Arboun* is discussed in greater detail later in this chapter.

Murabaha contract

Currently, most *Sharia'a* compliant derivatives are based around the Islamic principle of *Murabaha*, where two parties agree to the sale of goods at a price that includes a profit margin. Islamic investors can execute a currency forward trade under the *Murabaha* principle where both parties agree to sell assets to each other for deferred payment.

Islamic swaps

Islamic swaps involve the swapping of the same amount of interest-free loans after the determined period has been contracted and thus, eliminating *riba* and *gharar*.

Derivatives and the role of promises in the *Sharia'a – Wa'd*

In Arabic the most common words used for the idea of a promise regarding some future event are *'ahd* and *Wa'd*. *'Ahd* has many meanings the most common of which are promise, covenant, pact, pledge, vow, oath, treaty, agreement. All these words convey the idea of commitment or obligation.

Wa'd also has a number of meanings but the most common ones are to promise, pledge or firmly intend. Both terms occur frequently in the *Qur'an*.

In *Sharia'a* law, a simple promise is different from a contract in that a contract is always effective in the present, while a simple promise usually involves the future. Nothing actual or tangible is fulfilled by the act of promising. Rather an obligation to do something arises on the part of the promisor at a purely moral level as there is no object in actual existence at the time of promising.

Sharia'a law does not recognise a contract which has as its object a future thing, or an agreement to agree, or the exchange of an obligation for an obligation *(bay'al'dayn bi al-Dayn)*. This creates problems when it comes to business arrangements concerning future events.

In fact the contract of hire (*Ijara),* in so far as it concerns an object which is fulfilled as and when it is used, was only admitted as an exception to this ruling. Similarly, *Salam* (forward purchase) and *Istisna'a* (contract of manufacture), both of which are contracts where one of the countervalues is absent at the time of contracting, are only allowed where an exact description of the absent countervalues is given.

This failure to give any legal weight to the promise in contracts is an inevitable result of the prohibitions on *riba* and *gharar.* The need to ensure that all transactions are free from these prohibitions means that it is necessary, whenever a transaction involves the exchange of two countervalues, to ensure:

1) that exchange, if it has to take place under conditions which could result in *riba al-nasi'a* (*riba* by way of deferment), should be concluded immediately, and
2) these countervalues must be in existence, in their essence at least, and also known to the contracting parties.

In relation to commercial dealings the Islamic Fiqh Academy, in Jeddah, resolved the matter of promises. After discussing the issue, they declared that the fulfilment of a promise made in commercial transactions is obligatory, not only in the eyes of God, but also in a court of law with the following conditions:

1) it should be a unilateral promise;
2) the promise must have caused the promisee to incur some liabilities;
3) if the promise is to purchase something, the actual sale must take place at the appointed time by the exchange of offer and acceptance. A mere promise itself should not be taken as the concluded sale;
4) if the promisor backs out of his promise, the court may force him either to purchase the commodity or pay actual damages to the seller.

There is no doubt that within an Islamic ethos promises are regarded as binding. It is generally accepted that a unilateral promise creates a moral obligation and it is advisable for the promisor to observe it. Its violation is reproachable Islamically.

The *Wa'd* is structured to conform to this resolution of the Islamic Fiqh Academy. They are also structured to be unilateral in nature as they are each given by one party only and they are each based on different conditions. The condition that the promise should be unilateral is imposed because bilateral promises are contracts, or like contracts, and would therefore be invalid under the *Sharia'a* unless they satisfy the conditions that are normally required for Islamic contracts. These conditions include knowledge of the price plus possession or ownership of the subject matter of the promises or contract.

Appendix 8.2 is a detailed analysis of the role played by *Wa'd* in some recent Islamic contracts. It is written by a distinguished *Sharia'a* Scholar Shaykh Yusuf Talal DeLorenzo. It must be said that this scholar's interpretation is very critical about the way a perfectly acceptable *Sharia'a* principle, *Wa'd*, has been applied in practice in recent years.

The Islamic scholars and derivatives

The acceptability of Islamic derivatives within the industry is widely, and it should be said hotly, debated. There are three different views on the use of derivatives in Islamic finance. Some Islamic scholars are of the view that derivatives contracts are much needed tools needed to mitigate risk in Islamic finance. They argue that the development and use of Islamic financial derivatives is the key to effective risk mitigation and optimum use of liquidity given that Islamic financial institutions are prone to long-term asset-liability mismatches. Thus, they argue, it is very important to develop an effective financial derivative market as a risk mitigating mechanism.

According to another group of scholars, derivatives are inherently against *Sharia'a* considerations because of the element of uncertainty (*gharar*) associated with these contracts. The third group, on the other hand, while not dismissing the need for derivatives in Islamic finance, are more vigilant in promoting their use.

Conventional derivatives are deemed as being non-permissible in *Sharia'a* law because *Sharia'a* compliance demands the need to eliminate elements of *riba* (interest), *gharar* (uncertainty) and *maisir* (gambling). Many, if not all, of these elements are present with conventional derivatives. *Sharia'a* prohibits the payment or receipt of interest because it can lead to inequitable distribution of wealth and can cause the exploitation of the poor and needy. Speculative activities are also forbidden because they are considered to be gambling and involve taking risks which are intentional, avoidable and significant. Furthermore, *Sharia'a* law clearly states that money cannot be traded for money and also that all transactions must be based on real assets.

Another feature of Islamic finance that makes conventional derivatives impermissible is the *Sharia'a* principle that you cannot sell something that you do not own. Hence, the short selling strategy, commonly used in the hedge fund industry, cannot easily be adopted under the *Sharia'a*. Forward and futures contracts are considered unlawful from a *Sharia'a* perspective for two main reasons:

1) both contracts involve the exchanges of unequivalence, and
2) there is a delay in the settlement of the payment and delivery of the goods.

Sharia'a principles clearly state that a purchase or sale cannot be effected for a future date, as mentioned earlier. In the case of options, these are considered as non-permissible because option contracts involve unnecessary risk which is equivalent to *gharar*. There is also the perceived lack of physical assets in the contract and the possibility of exploitation of the ignorant. Mufti Taqi Usmani observed that since options involve paying a commission for the promise to buy or sell a stock, options are not permissible because this promise cannot be the subject matter of a sale or purchase. Hence, the promisor cannot charge the promisee a fee for making such a promise(1).

Are *Sharia'a* Scholars' objections consistent?

The position of the scholars is however somewhat inconsistent. To take a few examples:

Futures

Mufti Taqi Usmani, then at the Fiqh Academy of Jeddah in an article answering a set of posed questions on the topic (*New Horizon*, June 1996, pp 10-11), argues that futures contracts are invalid because:

> 'Firstly, it is a well recognized principle of the *Sharia'a* that purchase or sale cannot be effected for a future date. Therefore all forward and futures contracts are invalid in *Sharia'a*. Secondly, they are invalid because in most futures transactions delivery of the commodities or their possession is not intended. In most cases the transactions end up with the settlement of the difference in price only, which is not allowed in the *Sharia'a*.'

From an opposite perspective Fahim Khan ('Islamic Futures and their Markets', Research Paper No.32, Islamic Research and Training Institute, Islamic Development Bank, Jeddah, Saudi Arabia, 1996, p.12) states that:

> 'we should realize that even in the modern degenerated form of futures trading, some of the underlying basic concepts as well as some of the conditions for such trading are exactly the same as were laid down by the Prophet for forward trading. For example, there are clear sayings of the Prophet that he who makes a *Salaf* (forward trade) should do that for a specific quantity, specific weight and for a specified period of time. This is something that contemporary futures trading pays particular attention to.'

Options and Arboun

A number of scholars have found option contracts objectionable (Ahmad Muhayyuddin Hasan, Abu Sayman and Taqi Usmani to mention a few notable ones). However, in perhaps the most comprehensive study of the subject

Hashim Kali (*Islamic Commercial Law: An Analysis of Options, 1995*) concluded that:

> 'there is nothing inherently objectionable in granting an option, exercising it over a period of time or charging a fee for it, and that options trading like other varieties of trade is permissible mubah and as such it is simply an extension of the basic liberty that the *Qur'an* has granted.'

Most scholars agree that, in principle, futures and option contracts may be compatible with *Sharia'a* principles. What makes them objectionable is the manner in which they have found application in the marketplace in certain instances, such as with speculation and exploitation of certain counterparties. The objections of the learned scholars differ in accordance with their individual interpretation of the *Sharia'a* and their understanding of the instruments.

As regards options relating to currencies, interest rates and stock indices, most scholars agree that these have no place in Islamic finance. Further, among the major schools of Islamic jurisprudence, only the Hanbali uphold the Arboun contract (discussed later in this chapter) with the condition imposed by some of them that a time period should be stipulated for the option. The OIC Fiqh Council has also endorsed the Arboun contract but again only if a time limit is specified. Even if the Arboun contract is accepted as a valid transaction, most of the derivatives currently in the market would still be unacceptable from the *Sharia'a* perspective due to the involvement of *gharar* and *riba*.

A call option can be considered to be similar to *Arboun* in the sense that the seller does not return the premium or advance payment to the buyer if the latter does not exercise the purchase option and the buyer loses the option premium even if the option is exercised and the contract is confirmed. In the case of *Arboun* is, however, not exactly the same as a call option as, with an *Arboun* contract, the option premium is adjusted into the sale price when the contract is confirmed.

Samuel L. Hayes, a distinguished US academic, after detailed discussion on derivatives, concluded:

> 'There are no effective derivates of Islamic debt contracts which replicate conventional risk-hedging and leveraging contracts such as swaps, futures and options. Similarly, in the equity security sector, there are no risk-hedging or leveraging contracts in Islamic finance truly comparable to available conventional derivatives. With respect to commodities and other goods, the *Salam* contract is an imperfect Islamic substitute for a conventional forward contract. The related *Istisna'a* contract for goods being manufactured for a buyer provides another partial Islamic proxy for a forward contract. It is also possible to construct an Islamic contract which partially replicates a conventional futures contract, via back-to-back *Salam* contracts.' (2)

The conventional institutions dealing in derivatives and hedge funds claim that the diversity of hedging products protects their clients against market volatility and provides a larger spectrum of risk management to the benefit of society. But some commentators believe that volatility is caused by their activities when they trade in derivatives, a view now widely held given the banking collapse of recent times. Derivatives may produce huge profits for financial institutions, but these profits are not necessarily indicative of productive efforts. Warren Buffet, Chairman of Berkshire Hathaway once commented:

> 'Derivatives are financial weapons of mass destruction, mainly due to opaque pricing and accounting policies in swaps, options and other complex products whose prices are not listed on exchanges. Credit derivatives and total return swaps that are agreements to guarantee counterparty against default or bankruptcy merit special concern.' (3)

These comments may well prove to have been one of the deepest insights provided in the history of finance given the ensuing global financial meltdown of 2007-2009. Given this discussion of derivatives let us now turn to the role of hedge funds in order to understand their role in Islamic finance. This is an industry currently going through some turmoil but it is still important to appreciate the underlying principles.

What are conventional hedge funds?

A conventional hedge fund is a private, limited investment partnership open only to accredited investors, meaning people with substantial assets. Beyond that restriction and certain disclosure and reporting requirements, hedge funds are largely unregulated by the regulatory authorities, so they are free to use virtually any kind of strategy a manager chooses. This position is changing.

Hedge funds come in many different flavours. They may be specialised, niche or sector players or make a handful of concentrated bets across many industries. They may be highly leveraged or use no leverage at all. In fact you can find almost as many hedge fund strategies as hedge fund managers. That's why one cannot generalise about hedge funds – either their returns or their risks. A hedge fund may be quite risky or very conservative or anywhere in between. It all depends on the strategy and how it is executed.

Traditional portfolio managers have a *relative return* orientation. They measure success by how well they perform relative to a benchmark such as the S&P 500. It is all about beating the market. Take an example where the market has gone down by 20%. The traditional manager can go to his client and legitimately boast, 'I've done a great job for you . . . your portfolio is down only 18%. Not only have I outperformed my benchmark, but I'm in the top quartile of my peer group!'

However, hedge fund managers look at things quite differently. Their goal is to avoid losing money, to achieve positive annual returns regardless of market direction. Hedge funds measure success the same way: by the level of absolute returns earned for investors. Hedge funds are considered 'alternative' investments since they employ an investment strategy that differs from conventional long only, money management. They encompass a greater variety of investment instruments (options and futures) and a greater variety of investment techniques (short selling, hedging, arbitrage etc) than conventional money managers.

Characteristics of hedge funds

The following key characteristics are common to most or all hedge funds.

1) **Free choice of asset classes:** hedge funds are not restricted to one specific asset class. Whereas some hedge funds managers may restrict their investment policy to one asset class (e.g. equity, currencies, commodities) they are not legally bound by any such restriction.
2) **Free choice of markets:** many hedge funds do not focus on one specific market but invest according to available opportunities in all kinds of geographic locations (US, Europe, Japan, Pakistan, emerging markets etc).
3) **Free choice of instruments:** the majority of hedge funds invest in both cash and derivative products. Instruments may be exchange or over-the-counter (OTC) traded, securitised, non-securitised etc.
4) **High minimum investment** levels are often required. Sometimes minimum of $1 million or more is required.
5) **Infrequent subscription and redemption possibilities** with long notification periods have become standard for the industry.
6) A common feature is the **performance oriented incentive fee**. Also, due to the nature of the business, high total fee and cost loads are charged.
7) Unlike traditional managers, who charge annual management fees based on the amount of assets they're handling, virtually all hedge fund managers charge performance-based fees – usually 20% of investment profits on top of a 1% or 2% asset based fee. Most funds have what is called a **high-water mark**, meaning that if they lose money in one year, they have to make up those losses before they can start earning the next year's performance fees.
8) **Managers of a hedge fund are expected to invest their own money** alongside the limited partners, thus ensuring that everyone's interests are aligned.
9) Hedge funds are marketed as being oriented towards absolute performance (performance above zero) instead of performance relative to a certain benchmark or reference index.
10) Most hedge funds are designed to show **low correlation to traditional markets**.

Although the above provides a list of hedge fund characteristics in practice most hedge funds use a combination of short selling and leverage to attempt to maximise risk free absolute returns. Hedge funds have become extremely volatile in recent years.

Many hedge funds use a short selling strategy. To appreciate the controversies surrounding Islamic derivatives it is important to understand the mechanics of short selling.

What is short selling?

To short a stock you sell shares which you do not own. How can you do this without exposing yourself to massive risk? You do this by borrowing them from a brokerage firm. To close out the short position you later buy shares on the open market and use them to replace the borrowed ones you've sold. If the stock has declined, as you hoped, then you gain the difference. But, if the position goes against you and the stock you shorted goes up in price, then you lose money when you close out the trade. So when you sell short, you do this with the hope the stocks will go down in price. See box 8.1 and figure 8.1 for examples of how this can work in your favour. Clearly it can also go against you.

Box 8.1. Profitable short selling

Mechanics of stock lending to cover a short position (profitable speculation):

1. Lender 'lends' stock at T1 – legal and beneficial ownership moves. Market value = £100.
2. Collateral provided by bank (gilts).
3. Stock lending fee paid.
4. Bank sells 'short' to buyer for £100.
5. Bank delivers shares borrowed at (1).
6. Bank buys shares borrowed at T90 with a market price of £50.
7. Bank returns 'borrowed' shares using shares bought at (6).
8. Stock lender returns gilts used as collateral.

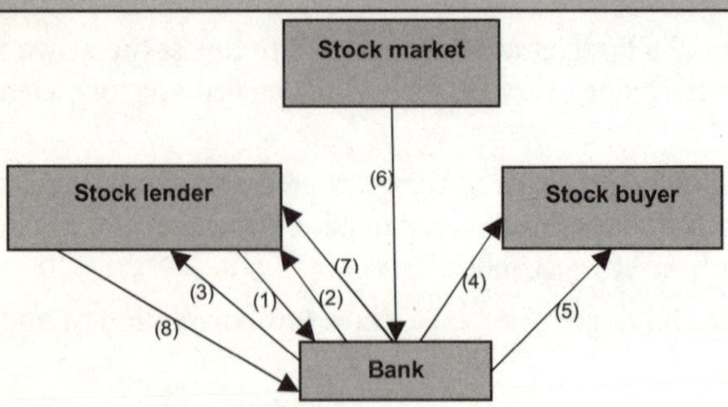

Figure 8.1. Example of short selling

The strategy can be risky if you do *only* short selling. Successful managers use short selling to hedge a long portfolio against a general market decline. Managers combine two speculative investment techniques – short selling and leveraging – to create a conservative investment approach designed to produce positive returns systematically in both up and down markets. As is discussed below the short selling strategy involves issues of major concern to Muslim investors.

What are Islamic hedge funds?

In order to be classified as a *Sharia'a* compliant hedge fund, the fund has to invest in eligible securities that will have been screened by certain qualitative criteria to ensure that the activities of the underlying company are *halal* (acceptable), and then by certain quantitative criteria to ensure that the underlying company is financed and trading in a *halal* manner. These are the hurdles that have to be overcome by a conventional non-*Sharia'a* compliant fund seeking to become Islamically acceptable.

With hedging comes additional hurdles: it is necessary to identify the nature of the hedging activity to be undertaken as there are many different strategies that have collectively been labelled as hedging, such as long or short, global macro, merger arbitrage, statistical arbitrage and event-driven. Some by their very nature will be *haram* (forbidden) as they focus on *riba* (interest) and other financial differentials.

The investment objective of hedge funds is a total return strategy, such that the fund maximises income and price appreciation with the preservation of investors' capital and prudent management of risk. In order to achieve this objective Islamically, it is necessary to produce a methodology that will allow the fund to 'short' a stock in a *Sharia'a* compliant manner.

Conventional shorting of a stock is *haram* under the *Sharia'a* for several reasons, but principally because, in a conventional short sale, there is the sale of a stock that has been borrowed and not owned (see box 8.1 and figure 8.1 to illustrate this). This would violate the general Islamic principle of 'do not sell what you do not own'. However, in traditional Islamic contractual law there are two forms of contract that have a similar economic outcome to a short sale, *Salam* and *Arboun*, as discussed earlier.

A *Salam* contract is in effect a sale at a current price with deferred delivery of the asset, whereas *Arboun* is a deferred sale with a down-payment where, should the buyer not complete the purchase, the down-payment is forfeited. Both forms of contract derive from a time when farmers needed to raise funds between harvests or similar such transactions, and in recent years there has been considerable debate within Islamic finance circles as to whether these forms of contract could be applied to transactions involving company shares.

While debate over this issue will certainly continue, *Sharia'a* Standard No. 21, issued by the Accounting and Auditing Organisation for Islamic Financial Institutions, Financial Papers (Shares and Bonds), has stated that shares 'cannot essentially be the subject matter of the contract of *Salam*' (see clause 3/11 and the accompanying bases of the *Sharia'a* ruling number 14). Therefore, Islamic hedge funds use the *Arboun* contract at the core of its substitute for short sale methodology, with other forms of Islamic contracts being used for other transactions between the various parties.

Devising a strategy that would replicate the economics of conventional shorting, whilst using traditional forms of Islamic contracts, is a major hurdle for Islamic hedge fund proponents and it is difficult to get the methodology accepted by the scholars.

Islamic hedge funds: *Sharia'a* issues

Conventional hedge funds tend to achieve high returns with the help of excessive leverage, an area of *Sharia'a* concern. A hedge fund manager has access to around 20 different strategies, including long or short, global macro, arbitrage, distressed securities, opportunistic and aggressive growth, to name a few. However, available statistics reveal that long or short funds represent the largest universe of current hedge funds (approximately 30%), and this is what Islamic hedge funds try to emulate in a *Sharia'a* compliant manner. The long or short (also known as market-neutral strategies) attempt to offer absolute positive returns to investors by typically combining a short strategy on over-valued assets with a long strategy on under-valued assets.

While going long poses no serious *Sharia'a* problems, shorting faces a number of restrictions in an Islamic framework. Islamic hedge funds replicate payoffs of a conventional short by using contracts of *Salam* and *Arboun*. The use of *Salam* for stocks or shares is not endorsed by most *Sharia'a* Scholars involved in the Islamic finance industry, as mentioned above. The use of *Arboun* is also problematic.

There are three *Sharia'a* concerns relating to the creation of an Islamic hedge fund:

1) hedging,
2) leverage, and
3) short selling.

Hedging was initially misunderstood by some *Sharia'a* Scholars to mean complete elimination of risk. The effect of this was that the early *Sharia'a* opinion was that hedging was not permissible, as it violated the principle that return should be proportional to the risk assumed (*al-Kharaj bi al-Daman*). In fact the idea of an 'absolute return strategy' targeting a return of certain basis points above a chosen benchmark made many scholars sceptical of the notion of an Islamic hedge fund.

However further scrutiny of such strategies, by *Sharia'a* Scholars, found them innocuous from a *Sharia'a* viewpoint which takes hedging as part of prudence and risk management. Indeed there has been a switch of focus in the hedge fund industry from performance (and consequent volatility of returns) to gathering and protecting assets. This also helped some *Sharia'a* Scholars to form an opinion in favour of Islamic hedge funds. Similarly *Sharia'a* does not have problems with leverage as long as it is achieved through Islamic debt. Leverage is not a *Sharia'a* concern; rather it is an economic issue. Having said that, it may actually be difficult to introduce leverage in an Islamic way, as conventional short selling is certainly not permissible in Islam.

Although some *Sharia'a* Scholars have endorsed the use of *Salam* and *Arboun* for short selling, such strategies have limited marketability as most *Sharia'a* Scholars do not favour the use of two contracts, in this context. The question arises why *Arboun* poses problems from a *Sharia'a* viewpoint. The reasons for non-suitability of *Arboun* for shorting are in fact the same as those for *Salam* because the way an *Arboun*-based shorting is executed is in fact more like *Salam* than *Arboun*. Figures 8.2 and 8.3 illustrate the structures of *Salam*- and *Arboun*-based shorting.

How does *Salam*-based shorting work?

Box 8.2. *Salam*-based shorting

1. A hedge fund manager identifies a basket of over-valued stocks, and advises a prime broker to sell it in the market for its market price.
2. The prime broker sells the basket of shares in the market.
3. The hedge fund, then, sells the same basket of shares to the prime broker on a Salam basis whereby the prime broker pays the price (from proceeds of the sale of the shares in the market) to receive the basket of shares on an agreed future date.
4. The hedge fund uses the money for leveraging.
5. On the future date, the hedge fund buys the basket of shares from the market and delivers the same to the prime broker.

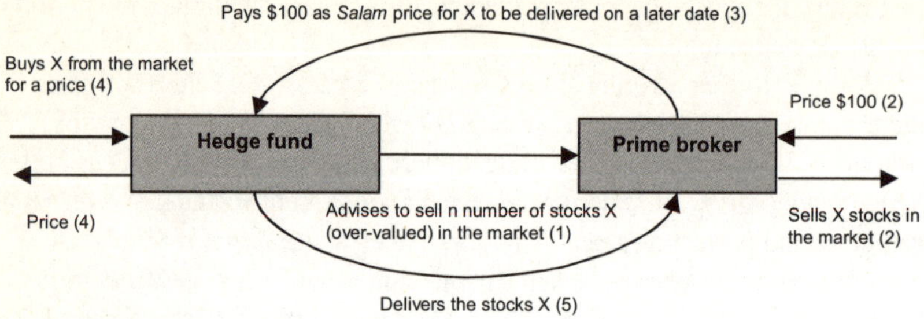

***Source*: Humayon Dar**

Figure 8.2. *Salam*-based shorting

The hedge fund enjoys the benefits of leveraging in addition to benefiting from the price differential of the basket (if price expectations are fulfilled). However, the hedge fund assumes the risk of loss on the *Salam* transaction in the event that the price movement goes against the forecast.

The use of *Arboun* for short selling is less convincing but it has been put into practice by almost all long-short Islamic hedge funds. Although the exact structure of an *Arboun*-based shorting may differ from fund to fund, it appears as if a large fraction of the price of the stocks to be sold is paid as advance payment (*Arboun*) to the seller up front. If so the *Arboun*-based structure is in effect closer to the spirit of a *Salam*-based sale. This may require the application of the principles of *Salam* to short selling rather than of *Arboun*, hence, rendering the use of *Arboun* not in compliance with *Sharia'a*, at least according to AAOIFI.

Given the controversy over *Salam* and *Arboun*, a hedge fund manager will, therefore, have to come up with a shorting method, which not only replicates the economic effect of a conventional short but also is acceptable to most *Sharia'a* Scholars.

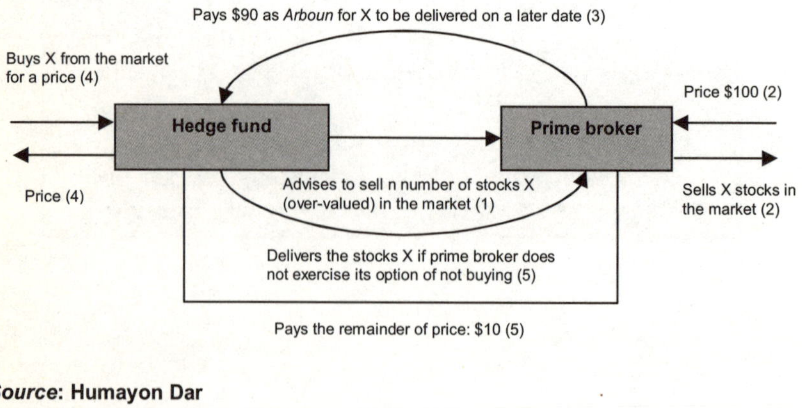

***Source*: Humayon Dar**

Figure 8.3. *Arboun*-based shorting

Arboun – some additional issues

An alternative to short selling is a down-payment with a revocable option (*Arboun*). This instrument is known classically in the Hanbali School of Fiqh but is not accepted among the other schools of Islamic jurisprudence. Beside the issue of whether part of the payment can be deferred until delivery if the down-payment remains with the seller in case of revocation, there is the issue of ownership of the stocks. The seller is supposed to hold the securities if he accepts the down-payment, as is generally required in any type of Islamic sales contract. If this is upheld, then *Arboun* could only work like an American option, letting the buyer benefit from prices rising, but neither side benefiting from falling prices.

However, if a down-payment with a revocable option is permitted without the seller being required to own the equities, then other types of benefits from falling prices can apply:

1) falling prices below the initial (high) down-payment force the buyer to execute the contract and pay the remaining price in order to minimise his losses, while the seller can buy more cheaply from the market to deliver, hence benefiting from the falling prices.
2) the client accepts a down-payment from his prime broker, who in the next step also makes a binding promise to purchase the equities from the client in case of being below the strike price of the down-payment.

The first method described is feasible; however, it does not fit into the framework of a prime broker, or the party with which the prospective Islamic hedge fund would execute its orders. As a *Salam* contract it could be negotiated, but it would not be as competitive an instrument, considering the costs of the transactions. The second method should be considered indicative at this point, as the precise *Arboun* method used by some funds is not disclosed to the wider public. It basically aims to replicate the economic effect of a conventional short sale, whereby the client may benefit from falling prices but can lose unlimitedly from rising prices. The actual restrictions imposed by regulation and legal documentation require a huge effort to realise such a concept.

Figures 8.4 and 8.5 provide examples of where an *Arboun* strategy makes and loses money for the investor. The term ACO refers to an *Arboun* Call Option and RM refers to Malaysian Ringgit.

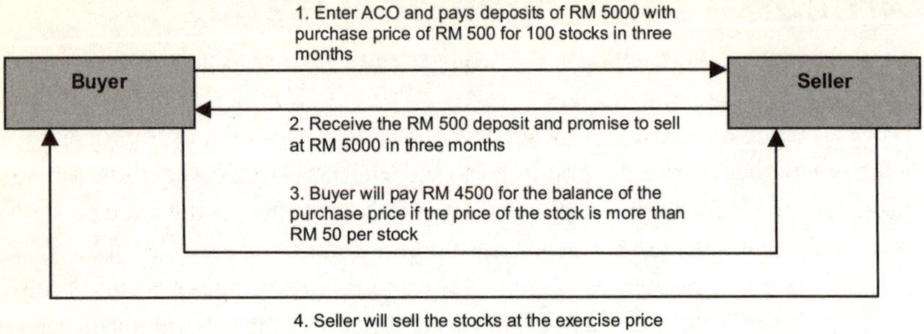

Figure 8.4. Example of an *Arboun* strategy where the market price is higher than the exercise price

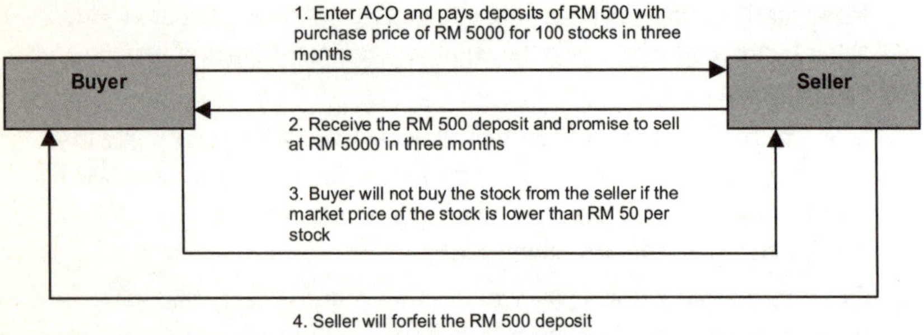

Figure 8.5. Example of an *Arboun* strategy where the market price is lower than the exercise price

Appendix 8.3 provides a case study illustrating capital protection within Islamic finance.

More issues with hedge funds

As mentioned earlier in this chapter there are a variety of *Sharia'a* issues with hedge funds, conventional and Islamic. *Sharia'a* issues apart there are however other issues of which all investors need to be aware. In their quest for positive alpha, viz the additional return investors gain as a reward for having taken a greater risk than merely following the market, all investors face issues with hedge funds.

As Chaudry and Lomonaco (4) point out, the first and sometimes most frustrating limitation for investors, when it comes to hedge funds are the large minimum investment amounts needed. This automatically narrows the target audience to high net worth individuals and institutional proprietary books. As a result, a sizeable retail market is left to choose its investments from an Islamic wealth management market that offers a limited choice of innovative, low-risk alpha strategies.

Second hedge funds, be they Islamic or conventional, very rarely offer capital protection. If the market turns against the fund, investors could lose a significant amount of the invested principal. In such an event, losses to investors can be compounded by the fact that hedge funds routinely limit or even ban redemptions when it suits them. In practice this means hedge funds restrict redemptions when they incur losses and investors would like to withdraw funds. In effect, liquidity in hedge funds is even more limited than assumed at the outset of the investment precisely at those times when investors may most want it.

This leads to a third issue: the level of risk taken by these vehicles. Whilst it used to be believed that hedge funds operate with strong risk controls in place, in practice it is impossible to tell exactly what the individual fund is doing. One has to trust on faith that the fund's managers have not decided to take on board excessive risk relative to their advertised mandate. At the end of the day this is left at the fund's discretion and investors have no way of ensuring or even demanding compliance. Recent developments in the industry have left unclear the extent to which hedge funds controlled risk.

This in turn leads us to the fourth issue: lack of regulation. It is because of this that Islamic hedge funds are able to operate as black boxes, making it difficult to follow their trading activities, which are often executed at high frequency. This also means that the level of protection that would otherwise be available legally to investors is lacking when they take up hedge fund investments.

The fifth issue is that despite all this, Islamic hedge funds charge high management fees, which can be as high as 10% upfront of the invested principal and up to 30% of the overall performance.

Finally, additional issues include an illiquid, or even complete lack of, secondary market, as well as short track records.

In an effort to address these concerns and provide Islamic investors with more accessible alpha ideas, Chaudry and Lomonaco recommend that the Islamic wealth management industry needs to encourage the development of what they call 'Islamic dynamic strategies'. Through whatever strategy the investor may believe is optimum, whether it be based on mean-reversion or momentum, a dynamic weightings adaptation of the efficient frontier or some other fundamental-based algorithm, it could be this breed of investing that will drive the Islamic wealth management industry over the next years. Chaudry and Lomonaco have designed one particular strategy which they label 'the Islamic navigator'.

The Islamic navigator

Under this technique the trend price for an asset is identified by comparing the prevailing spot price of the asset to its recent moving average. The length of the moving average may vary for each asset and can be optimised based on historical simulations. Should the algorithm detect a positive trend (i.e. when the spot price is above the moving average) for an asset, a fixed allocation is provided to that asset. In the event of a negative trend being detected, the allocation for the asset is directed to a commodity-based reserve asset. The shift in these weightings is conducted on a monthly basis. The initial result is a dynamic index linked to a number of underlying assets.

The strategy is then controlled through a volatility-stabilisation mechanism, which employs what Chaudry and Lomonaco call a 'dynamic participation' level based on the volatility of the initial index. Should the index observe high short-term volatility, the mechanism reduces exposure to the index, and vice versa. In effect, the strategy targets a certain standard deviation from the average daily returns by decreasing or increasing the exposure to the index. Hence, the volatility is ex ante defined and is measurable at the outset, which is unusual for Islamic strategies. The result, Chaudry and Lomonaco claim, should be a *Sharia'a* compliant low volatility strategy which provides stable returns.

References

1. Usmani. T.U. *An Introduction to Islamic Finance*. Idaratul Ma'arif. Karachi, Pakistan 1999.

2 For details see Vogel and Hayes, 1998, pp. 156-164, 220-232, 281, 282.

3 Buffet, Warren. 2003. Annual Letter to Berkshire Hathaway Shareholders.

4. These have been highlighted by Chaudry, A. and Lomonaco, R. *New Horizon*, October – December 2008.

Appendix 8.1

Why are derivatives forbidden (*haram*) under *Sharia'a* law?

Whether or not derivatives are permissible in Islamic finance has become the subject of heated debate between scholars, academics and banking practitioners. To appreciate the issues so hotly debated it is essential to go back to the primary sources of *Sharia'a* law.

The controversies revolve around gambling, the Arabic term for which is *maisir*.

Definition of *maisir*

Maisir means a game involving hazardous events – particularly a game of chance played by means of divining arrows, defined below. This was a popular game at the time of the Prophet Mohammed. *Maisir* comes in various categories. Some of these types of *maisir* are seeking omens or fortune telling by divining arrows, playing backgammon, chess, lotteries etc.

The word *maisir* (game of chance) is derived from the root:

1) *Yasara*: to become gentle, to draw lots by arrows;
2) *Yasara*: affluence because *maisir* brings about profit;
3) *Yusr*: convenience, ease. *Maisir* is so termed because it is a means of making money without toil and exertion;
4) *Yasr*: dividing a thing into a number of shares and distributing them among themselves. Gambling is called *maisir* because those who partake in the games of chance divide the meat of sacrificial animals amongst themselves.

All the above connotations are vividly found in the word *maisir*. Imam Malik, founder of the Maliki School of jurisprudence, said that gambling was of two categories: a game of chance that is partaken in with a view to sport (fun) and the game of chance which involves gambling. Gambling, in this sense, means all dealings in which people are required to make a bet. Every dealing which involves some aspect of gambling is *maisir*. So where does gambling fit within the *Qur'an*?

The *Qur'an* on the prohibition of gambling

> 'They ask thee (O' Prophet) about *Khamr* (intoxicants) and games of chance (gambling). Say: In both of them there is great harm although there is some advantage as well in them for men, but their harm is much greater than their advantages.'
>
> Sura 2: 219

> 'O' ye who believe, verily wine and games of chance, (ungodly) shrines, and divining devices are abomination of Satan's work. Avoid them, that ye may prosper. Only would Satan sow hatred and strife among you, by

> wine, and games of chance, and turn you aside from the remembrance of Allah, and from Prayer: Will you not, therefore, abstain from them?'
>
> Sura 5: 90, 91

From these Verses of the *Qur'an*, it is also made clear that games of chance (*maisir*) entail sin whilst promising petty benefits. In fact *maisir*, based on the above citations, is deemed by Muslims to be an abominable act of Satan. It is therefore imperative, for Muslims, to avoid gambling in order to achieving success and happiness. Satan, it is believed, through games of chance sows in the hearts of Muslims the seeds of enmity and hatred against one another and turns believers aside from the remembrance of Allah and His worship. The prohibition of gambling has, therefore, been declared obligatory.

Ahadith on the prohibition of gambling

> The Prophet said: 'Whosoever says to his Companion: Come let us place a game of haphazard, should give alms (as atonement).'
>
> (Bukhari and Muslim)
>
> It connotes that a mere invitation to gambling is such a serious sin as to warrant atonement thereof by charity. Then just imagine the position of a man who indulges in gambling. The Holy Prophet further said: 'Whosoever plays backgammon is as if he dyes his hands with the flesh of swine and its blood.'
>
> (Muslim)

Ibn Abi Al-Dunya has reported Yahya b Kathir as commenting on people playing backgammon, 'Their hearts are pre-occupied in sport, their hands are ill and (their) tongues make absurd utterances. Every game which involves gambling or mischief is a game of chance (*maisir*).'

There is no difference of opinion among the jurists that every sort of gambling is harmful, except betting for horse racing and archery. These have been declared lawful in order to encourage horsemanship archery and preparation for *Jihad*. This is because Allah says:

> 'Make ready for them all you can of (armed) force and of horses tethered, that thereby ye may dismay the enemy of Allah and your enemy.'
>
> Surah 8: 60

Stone altars, gambling and Jahiliya

Stone altars were erected round the Holy *Ka'ba* in the pre-Islamic period (known as Jahiliya, the period of ignorance). People used to slaughter their sacrificial animals beside these altars. Such altars were around 360 in number. Around the stone altars various forms of gambling took place.

On the advent of Islam, these altars were removed. This dismantlement of altars took place on the eve of the victory of Mecca when the Holy Prophet climbed on them with a staff in hand and demolished them one after the other and recited this *Qur'anic* Verse:

> 'And say: Truth hath come and falsehood hath vanished away. Lo, falsehood is ever bound to vanish.'
>
> Sura 17: 81

A brief history of the prohibition of gambling in Islam

The history of the unlawfulness of the games of chance viz, gambling in Islam, is as old as the history of the unlawfulness of wine because the prohibition of both was declared simultaneously in Sura al-Baqara (2 : 219) and Sura al-Ma'ida (5 : 90, 91), as already mentioned.

The first stage was the revelation of Verse 2: 219 in the month of Rabi-ul-Awwal, 4 AH (August 625 AD). Allah in this Verse mentioned the game of chance (*maisir*) as characteristic of great sin which has paltry benefits for mankind. This Verse is, therefore, a clear proof of the gradual prohibition of games of chance.

The second and the last stage is the revelation of Verses 5: 90, 91 in the month of Dhi-al-Qa'da, 6 AH (March, 627 AD). In these Verses, Allah totally declared gambling (*maisir*) unlawful leaving no room for relaxation.

Nature of gambling and the Arabs

In pre-Islamic times when famine broke out the Arabs brought sacrificial animals – camels and sheep – and slaughtered them. Then they divided them into 28 shares and placed 10 arrows near them, namely fadh, tawam, raqib, hils, nafis, musbil, mu'alli, manih, sanih and waghd.

One out of these 28 shares was earmarked for fadh, two for tawam, three for raqib, four for hils, five for nafis, six for musbil, seven for mu'alli. Mu'alli would receive a major share and from this a proverb came into vogue. Every one who would have a lion's share of anything was called 'Sahibu al-qidhil mu'alli. The last three arrows manih, sanih and waghd had no share at all. This process was completed among 10 persons, in effect drawing lots.

The Arabs then distributed these shares among the needy and they themselves did not eat anything out of them. They felt proud of that act and condemned those who did not participate in this ritual. The latter were nicknamed as '*baram*', i.e. a mean and niggardly man devoid of manly traits. Later on, they replaced the spirit of the ritual and made the arrows a means of business without any consideration of munificence and help to the needy. Later men began to gamble with all their property and as a result risked becoming destitute and penniless.

Divining arrows for seeking fortune

During pre-Islamic times, the Arabs used to make 10 arrows which were strips of wood without headpoints. They named them *aqlam* (pen-sticks), *qidah* (featherless arrows) and *azlam* (divinatory arrows), which were put in a *ribabah* or leather-bag. Divining arrows (*azlam*) are arrows cut off in thin slices of wood in the shape of arrows having no heads.

The gambling format involved paying the stake money and putting one's hand in the leather bag to bring out an arrow which would be in the name of a polytheist, and so on. If an arrow having some share was brought out for someone, he took the share specified for it and if an arrow having no share was brought out for someone he would not get anything and would lose his entire stake money.

There were two other kinds of seeking fortune and both of them involved securing some information about unseen events. The first case was one whereby the keeper of the Holy Ka'ba had three arrows. On one of these was written 'Do', on the second arrow was written 'Do not do', while on the third one nothing was written. According to another report of the same event on one arrow was written 'My Lord hath commanded me', on the second arrow was written 'My Lord hath forbidden me', while the third one carried no remarks whatsoever. Whenever anyone intended to go on some journey, make war, wanted to marry, make a business transaction or wanted to go out for some other reason, the custodian of the Ka'ba would cast divining arrows. If the arrow having the words 'My Lord hath commanded me' came out, the recipient would go out to whatever the recipient wanted to do. On the other hand if the arrow with the words 'My Lord hath forbidden me' was selected he would desist from going on his proposed endeavour. If the arrow which bore no words was drawn the above process was repeated.

The second category involving foreseeing future events and gambling using arrows. One of them was near the idol called Hubal placed inside the Holy Ka'ba. All the vicissitudes with which humanity comes across were inscribed on this arrow and the Arabs cast lots by means of it, in the manner already discussed. As can be seen *Qur'anic* citations on the perils of gambling are numerous.

Allah has forbidden all the gambling means of seeking fortune in the Verse:

> 'Forbidden it is that ye seek fortune by divining arrows. This is an abomination.'
>
> Sura 5: 3

Similarly other Verses have also been revealed in the *Qur'an*.

The rationale underlying the prohibition of seeking fortune by arrows is that it is seen as an absurd and superstitious action which is most certainly deemed un-Islamic. The act of seeking one's fortune by arrow heads leads, it is argued, is to claim knowledge of the unseen. This power, Muslims believe, exclusively vests in Allah. These omens of fortune were sought from the flight of birds, divination, augury, geomancy, sorcery, magic and astronomy. All these techniques, to succeed, involve prior knowledge of the future, the unseen.

All of these acts are unlawful in the sight of the *Sharia'a*. Allah, as the *Qur'an* says :

> 'Say (O' Prophet): None in the heavens and the earth knoweth the unseen save Allah.'
>
> Sura 27: 65

Again, the *Qur'an* says:

> 'And it is not (the purpose of) Allah to let you know the unseen.'
>
> Sura 3: 179

In conclusion derivatives, widely seen by Muslims as forms of gambling, are unequivocally condemned. Investment bankers are desperately attempting to structure Islamically acceptable forms of derivatives. They are fighting an up-hill struggle!

Appendix 8.2

Total returns swap and the '*Sharia'a* conversion technology' stratagem: a case study

By Yusuf Talal DeLorenzo
Sharia'a Scholar and member of the AAOIFI Sharia'a Board

Summary

This study will look at Islamic values in financial decision-making by considering whether or not *Sharia'a* Supervisory Boards will approve any financial product that is delivered by ostensibly *halal* means, even if what is delivered by those means, the end product, is derived from non-compliant investments. This may be characterised as a quasi-philosophical question about means and ends. Yet, it is one that carries a myriad of practical implications and far-reaching ramifications for the growing Islamic financial industry.

This is a case study, and not a theoretical study. The focus of the study is a particular means or process for the development of products sometimes called '*Sharia'a* Conversion Technology'. The reason for writing this paper is to draw the attention of scholars and industry experts to the importance of making a distinction between bringing returns from *Sharia'a* compliant investments and bringing returns from non-*Sharia'a* compliant investments. If care is not taken, this 'technology' represents a great danger to modern Islamic Finance. My own reaction to this threat, initially, was to suggest recourse to *sadd al-dhara'i*, the instrument in Islamic jurisprudence that blocks ostensibly legitimate means to illegitimate ends. On closer study, however, I have concluded that there is no need to resort to this instrument as the matter is simply one of distinguishing between what is truly lawful, *halal*, and what is truly unlawful, *haram*. In what follows, I will explain exactly what led me to this conclusion, and why I think it necessary to share my thoughts on the matter.

To date, I have shared this paper with only a handful of scholars and colleagues. In the coming months, however, Islamic banks and investment houses will look closely at products based on the '*Sharia'a* Conversion Technology' stratagem, and *Sharia'a* Boards will be asked to deliberate and opine on the compliance of such products with the rules of the *Sharia'a*. My intention in circulating this paper is to contribute to a wider and more comprehensive understanding of this particular stratagem. At a time when *Sharia'a* Scholars are increasingly being asked to opine on new and exotic products, I believe that due consideration must be given to not only the literal structure of products and processes, but also to their consequences for the future of Islamic Finance.[1] In other words, while up until now the *Sharia'a*

[1] In an article entitled 'The Black Box Syndrome' which I wrote for the April 2007 issue of *Islamic Finance*, I wrote: 'I would like to see more faith in what true and diligent *Sharia'a* compliance actually means to our industry. I am dismayed by quick fixes and shortcuts which in many cases circumvent the *Sharia'a*. The industry has proved time and again that adherence to the principles of *Sharia'a* can be profitable, and that such adherence does not spell hardship. We have no need of 'black boxes' and of arm's length transactions that

supervisory boards of modern Islamic financial institutions have focused almost exclusively on the rules for transacting in compliance with the *Sharia'a*, it is now time for them to focus as well on the higher purposes of Islamic law or the *Maqasid al-Sharia'a*.

Introduction

Recently, a financial stratagem known as '*Sharia'a* Conversion Technology' was developed, the purpose of which is to affect a total returns swap or to 'Wrap a non-*Sharia'a* compliant underlying into a *Sharia'a* compliant structure'.[2] In other words, the objective of the mechanism is to use non-compliant assets and their performance to bring returns into a so-called *Sharia'a* compliant investment or investment portfolio. This point is key to the entire transaction, and for that reason it needs repeating. What the product proposes to accomplish is to bring to the Islamic investor returns from investments that are not compliant with *Sharia'a* principles and precepts. The questions that such a product immediately brings to mind are: How can *Sharia'a* Boards approve such returns? Does the circumstance of direct or indirect delivery to the Islamic investor change the ruling? When the *Sharia'a* of Islam is understood to differ from other legal systems because it may be characterised as both positive law and morality[3], is it possible to ignore the moral aspect of a financial transaction like this?

The means of delivery, a *Wa'd* or promise, is widely seen to comply with *Sharia'a* norms. Since it is compliant, at least to the letter of the law,[4] some *Sharia'a* Scholars have approved products that use a *Wa'd* to deliver returns from non-compliant investments. By doing so, however, they have failed to consider the purpose of the transaction, they have failed to consider the movement of the cash and, most importantly, they have failed to consider the ramifications for the industry as a whole. At a very fundamental level, the reason for these failings is that they have not discerned the difference between the use

---

miraculously produce results by sacrificing the spirit of the *Sharia'a* to the letter of the law.'

[2] Quoted from a term sheet presented to the author by a multinational bank seeking approval for a structured product based on this stratagem. YTD.

[3] For a discussion of how the classical jurists of Islam assumed the role of 'moralists-cum-jurists' within Muslim society, see Bernard Weiss, *The Spirit of Islamic Law* (Athens and London: The University of Georgia Press, 1998) pp.165-166.

[4] '…for the jurists, letter and spirit can never be in genuine conflict if by 'letter' one means the clear, unambiguous pronouncements of the authoritative texts and if by 'spirit' one means a divinely ordained principle derivable from those same texts.' Weiss, op. cit., p.169.

of LIBOR as a benchmark for pricing and the use of non-*Sharia'a* compliant assets as a determinant for returns. In June of this year, 2007, a pioneering Islamic bank in the Gulf launched a principal protected note that was the first product using this '*Sharia'a* Conversion Technology' to be offered to the investing public. This was followed by another such product, also offered by a Gulf-based Islamic bank. Prior to this, the stratagem was used in structured products offered by multinational banks to institutional investors and the treasuries of Islamic banks and finance houses. All of these products have been approved and certified by *Sharia'a* Supervisory Boards. Not all of these products, however, bring to the Islamic investor returns from investments that are compliant with *Sharia'a*.

A few explanations

Before examining the '*Sharia'a* Conversion Technology' stratagem from an Islamic legal perspective, however, it may be helpful to make a few preliminary remarks.

1) There should be no reason to object to the use of a *Wa'd* on its own. The use of promises are a matter that the *Sharia'a* Boards of modern Islamic financial institutions have studied in detail.[5] Therefore, it will not be necessary to discuss the definition of a promise, its purpose, or its legal characterization (in terms of *wajib*, *makruh* etc.).
2) The financial instrument that the *Wa'd* structure seeks to facilitate is called a swap. Swaps are arrangements between counterparties to exchange cash flows over time, and they are very flexible. In conventional finance, the most popular forms of swaps are interest-rate swaps and currency swaps because these allow for the effective management of both balance sheets and risk profiles. In an interest rate swap, for example, no principal is exchanged between the counterparties; only interest is exchanged. The utility of a swap

[5] The modified form of the classical *murabaha* sale has been the mainstay of Islamic banking for the past twenty or more years, accounting for as much as 70% of all *Sharia'a* compliant transactions (until about five years ago). The modern version of the *murabaha* includes a promise on the part of the client ordering the purchase, *al-Amir bi'l-Shira'*, that it will repurchase the goods acquired by the bank on its behalf. From a modern business perspective, it is essential for the bank that such a promise be considered binding. Thus, while the notion that a promise is binding was a minority opinion in the classical jurisprudence, modern *Sharia'a* Boards have almost unanimously held the promise to be binding. Nicholas Dylan Ray, *Arab Islamic Banking and the Renewal of Islamic Law* (London: Graham & Trotman, 1995) pp. 51-54.

comes from the ease with which it is initiated and completed, as opposed to the numerous steps required to accomplish the same thing by other means.

3) The London Interbank Offered Rate (LIBOR) is the rate at which international banks charge one another for dollar denominated-loans in the London market and is therefore used widely as a reference for any floating-rate loan. Depending on the credit rating of the borrower, that rate may vary from LIBOR to LIBOR plus one or more points over LIBOR.

Before discussing the purpose of the '*Sharia'a* Conversion Technology' stratagem, the movement of the cash and, most importantly, the ramifications for the industry as a whole, it will be well to look at two points. (1) How the '*Sharia'a* Conversion Technology' stratagem is actually employed, and then (2) at the difference between the use of LIBOR as a benchmark for pricing and the use of non-*Sharia'a* compliant assets as a determinant for returns.

'*Sharia'a* Conversion Technology' Stratagem

The stratagem developed for the exchange of non-*Sharia'a* compliant returns for *Sharia'a* compliant returns generally begins with the purchase by the Islamic investor of *Sharia'a* compliant assets by means of a *Sharia'a* compliant contract such as a *Salam* sale or a *Murabaha*. In most cases, the subject of these transactions will be commodities or base metals. Through such contracts, the bank can offer apparent *Sharia'a* compliance and nominal fixed returns of, say, 4-5%. Then, to give the investor the ability to enhance the returns from the investment, the bank arranges to swap the returns from the *Sharia'a* compliant transaction with returns from another investment. The way it does this is by means of a promise, a *Wa'd*. Effectively, what the promise says is that at maturity, or at the end of a certain period of time (generally three to five years) the counterparties promise to swap their returns.[6] The bank can then take the further step of protecting the principal invested by the Islamic investor by one means or another.[7]

---

[6] The promise may also include a condition. For example, if the returns from the other basket of assets are greater than the returns from the *Salam* or the *murabaha*, then the parties promise to swap.

[7] Such principal protected products are similar in design to conventional capital guaranteed products with the obvious difference that to be *Sharia'a* compliant the capital must remain at risk. Using structured products, banks can 'protect' the capital without actually guaranteeing its return. Such products have been on the market for a number of years and have won the approval of many *Sharia'a* Boards. Generally speaking, principal protection employs either options or dynamic allocations among baskets of assets with varying degrees of risk.

The benefits to the Islamic investor are obvious; the principal is protected, the returns will almost certainly be at least 4-5% (from the *Sharia'a* compliant investment), and there is a strong likelihood that the assets in the other basket will outperform the *Sharia'a* compliant investment. The benefits to the bank may not be quite so obvious, but in fact they are far greater than the benefits to the Islamic investors as we shall see later in this paper when we 'follow the money'.

Most importantly, however, the Islamic investor is told that the investment is completely *Sharia'a* compliant. This is because the money invested has been used for nothing other than the purchase of *Sharia'a* compliant commodities by means of a *Sharia'a* compliant contract like a *Salam* sale. The return on the investment, if it comes from the *Salam* sale, is clearly compliant with *Sharia'a* principles and precepts. And if the return comes from the other investment, by means of the stratagem employing a promise to exchange returns, those returns, so says the bank, may be considered legitimate, *halal*, even if the investment is non-*Sharia'a* compliant. According to the *Sharia'a* Boards that have approved such exchanges, the non-*Sharia'a* compliant assets have been used to establish a price; and the promised exchange is for the value of the returns established by the performance of the non-*Sharia'a* compliant assets. This, they reason, is no different than using LIBOR, an interest rate,[8] to establish the price for a *Murabaha* or an *Ijara*. If the use of LIBOR has been nearly universally approved by *Sharia'a* Boards, then the swap achieved by a promise, the '*Sharia'a* Conversion Technology' stratagem should also be approved.

LIBOR and how returns are determined

Let us now consider the difference between the use of LIBOR as a benchmark for returns and the use of non-*Sharia'a* compliant assets as a determinant for returns. *Sharia'a* Boards have approved any number of less than ideal devices if they have been convinced that these will assist in promoting the industry in general. A good example is the use of LIBOR as a benchmark for pricing a *Murabaha* or an *Ijara* when floating-rates are to be preferred over fixed rates. In the absence of a viable and widely-published alternative, LIBOR has been used repeatedly; and will likely continue to be used until the industry can develop and then agree upon a benchmark, or a set of benchmarks, based on criteria of its own, i.e. *Sharia'a* compliant criteria. In the final analysis, a benchmark is no more than a standard, and therefore non-objectionable from a *Sharia'a* perspective. If it is used to determine the rate of repayment on a loan, then it is the interest-bearing loan that will be haram. LIBOR, as a mere benchmark, has

---

[8] LIBOR is the London Inter-Bank Offered Rate or the rate of interest at which banks in London offer to lend funds to other banks in London.

no direct effect on the actual transaction or, more specifically, with the creation of revenues.

In modern Islamic financial transactions, LIBOR has been used to facilitate the closing of literally hundreds, if not thousands, of *Sharia'a* compliant financings. It should be noted, however, that these do not involve interest. As explained above, LIBOR is merely a convenient and highly transparent measure of the financial markets. Most importantly, the use of LIBOR as a benchmark for pricing in no way means that interest has entered the transaction itself. This is because LIBOR is a notional rate. The bank loans that determine this rate will under no circumstances become a part of the *Sharia'a* compliant *Ijara* or *Murabaha* transaction that is benchmarked to LIBOR. Finally, the money paid into an Ijara investment using LIBOR will never pass through to the banks whose rates contribute to the setting of LIBOR, and will certainly never finance, directly or indirectly, assets whose performance or credit rating will set that rate.

When a Muslim investor invests in a product that uses a promise to swap returns from a non-*Sharia'a* compliant investment, however, the matter is quite different. For, while LIBOR is a benchmark used to set a price by marking value, the *Wa'd* is actually used to deliver that price, even if it does so synthetically. By means of the '*Sharia'a* Conversion Technology' stratagem, the unwitting Muslim investor actually participates in the non-*Sharia'a* compliant investment, however indirectly. This is because, when the investor agrees to exchange *Murabaha* returns for returns from another investment, the investor indicates *qubul* or approval of the other investment. If that investment includes non-compliant assets and instruments, like conventional bonds or treasury bills, then the investor is approving the same and the transaction must be considered unlawful. Finally, and perhaps most significantly, the money paid into an investment employing the '*Sharia'a* Conversion Technology' stratagem will most certainly be used to finance the other investment(s), however indirectly. Therefore, even if the Muslim investor is not directly financing non-*Sharia'a* compliant transactions, if the investment with the swap had not been made, those non-*Sharia'a* compliant transactions would not have taken place. This will be clarified later when we consider how the cash in such a transaction actually moves.

The attempt to draw a legal analogy, *Qiyas*, between the use of LIBOR for pricing and the use of the performance of non-*Sharia'a* compliant assets for pricing is both inaccurate and misleading. The only similarity is that both are used for pricing. Where LIBOR is used to indicate the return, however, the other is used to deliver the return or, as we shall see, the other is the return. Therefore, it is simply incorrect to justify the swap of returns from non-*Sharia'a* compliant assets by comparing the same to LIBOR and then saying that since the one is approved by *Sharia'a* Supervisory Boards, the other should also be approved.

The purpose of the transaction

The purpose of the transaction was clarified by a spokesperson for the bank offering the product to the public who explained that it was designed to allow Muslim investors access to funds that operate in a non-*Sharia'a* compliant manner by 'reflecting their performance'. The euphemistic description of what the product aims to achieve, like the simplistic explanation of how the money in the investment remains exclusively in compliance with *Sharia'a* rules, is in my opinion a manipulation and, ultimately, a misrepresentation of the truth. The term sheet for one such product states unequivocally that its purpose is to 'wrap a non-*Sharia'a* compliant underlying (asset) into a *Sharia'a* compliant structure'. Nothing could be clearer. When this is the purpose, how can a *Sharia'a* Board possibly approve? Does it matter if the structure and the transactional basis of these schemes are compliant with established *Sharia'a* rules if the end product is the result of prohibited investments? Does it really matter if that result is direct or indirect if the returns are from investments that do not discriminate between right and wrong, *halal* and *haram*, good and harmful? What the public is invited to invest in is a basket that will 'reflect' returns from anything from wineries, to pork futures, to casinos, to who knows what else? At the present time, the matter is in the hands of the investors, many of whom are institutional investors with their own *Sharia'a* Supervisory Boards; and it is still unclear as to how those boards will decide to view the matter. In my opinion, there can be only one response; and that is to reject the '*Sharia'a* Conversion Technology' stratagem and the investment products based on this stratagem.

The movement of the cash

Before the reader begins to suppose that this discussion is more about *taqwa* and less about *fatwa*, or morality rather than law, let us now consider the movement of the cash. The Islamic bank that offers this product insists that the Muslim investor's money is invested in a *Sharia'a* compliant product and that the returns are completely *halal*.[9] Their claim is that the investor's money is used to purchase a principal protected note, structured by a multinational bank, which invests in simple *Salam* or *Murabaha* contracts. The contract for the note

---

[9] It is interesting to see that the Prospectus for one such product clearly states the following: 'Security holders will have no individual or collective recourse to the Islamic Investment Account at any time.' It also states that, '... payments to Security holders in respect of the Securities (subject to and in accordance with the Product Conditions herein) will be made irrespective of the *Shari'a* compliance or otherwise of the Islamic Investment Account and the Securities at any time.'

includes an agreement, no more than a promise actually (sometimes termed 'a purchase undertaking'), that if the returns from the *Salam* are less than the returns from a particular index, or grouping of funds, then the structuring bank will pay the investor an amount equal to the returns from the index, or group of funds. To be more precise, if the non-*Sharia'a* compliant index or funds outperform the *Salam* investment, the investor will earn returns that are better than the *Salam* returns. Since the bank will pay investors with its own money,[10] the investors will not receive returns directly from the conventional index or group of funds (funds which may be using strategies that are non-*Sharia'a* compliant, investing in stocks that have never been screened, and selling securities that they borrowed but never owned, to say nothing of investing in interest-bearing bonds, futures, or any of a host of derivative instruments). In fact, the Islamic bank is happy to point out that it is not investing in any of these prohibited things! And, technically, the bank may be right. However, as we shall see, the matter is not this simple.

When the Islamic Bank takes in the investor's money, what actually happens? Let's imagine that the investor, say an Islamic pension fund, places $100 million in this product. The first thing that happens is that the Islamic Bank passes the money to the structuring bank. That bank will do two things. Firstly, it will invest 100 million, after deducting some fees for management, into *Salam* or *Murabaha* contracts. Then, using the *Salam* as collateral, it will make a loan to an asset managing bank, one with a prime brokerage of its own that works with hundreds of different fund managers. The asset managing bank will then allocate that money to a selected group of fund managers. In the absence of any mandate to transact in compliance with *Sharia'a*, the asset managing bank will choose managers and strategies solely on the basis of performance; and from a risk perspective, this means that the bank will seek to diversify its allocations. Of course, what this means is that some of the money allocated will certainly go to bonds, treasuries, debt instruments, and derivatives like futures, options, and swaps. Also, the loan made by the structuring bank to the asset managing bank will be made for interest at the same rate as the *Salam*. In this manner, the asset managing bank suffers no gap between the *Salam* swap rate and its borrowing costs. In the middle of the transaction, the structuring bank is fully secured for its loan because the rates for the *Salam* and the loan are matched. This means that the structuring bank, likewise, takes no risk. The structuring bank will also earn fees for the notes it has structured for the Islamic bank.

The investor's money, that of the client of the Islamic bank, is placed in a *Salam* investment. By means of a note provided by the structuring bank, the

[10] The Islamic bank's *Sharia'a* Board was careful to point out, quite correctly, that it is generally of no consequence to the Islamic investor where the bank's money comes from. This, however, is not the issue here.

investor's principal is protected as well. The client pays fees for both of these. Some fees go directly to the Islamic bank, others go to the structuring bank, to the asset managing bank, and to the managers of the various funds. In this transaction, the greater part of the returns are shared by the funds, the asset managing bank, and the structuring bank. The Islamic bank's earnings are significantly less than all these. The reason for detailing the money trail here is to point out how the investor's money, even though it remains in *Salam* contracts, is actually put to work in ways that are clearly not in compliance with *Sharia'a* rules.

It may be argued that this will happen anyway; that it happens whenever an Islamic bank or institution has dealings with a conventional bank. This may be so. Ultimately, what the conventional bank does with its money, when it becomes the bank's money, is its own business. But the transaction we are considering here has direct, predictable and immediate consequences. In other words, the Islamic client's investment in this product triggers a series of transactions, none of which is *Sharia'a* compliant. Moreover, these produce fees and earnings for other than the *Sharia'a* investor. Can the *Sharia'a* Board of the Islamic bank ignore all of this, and approve the entire transaction because the first link in the series is basically a *Salam* or a *Murabaha*? Or is the *Sharia'a* Board compelled to consider the transaction in its entirety?

Consider the parties to this series. There is an investor, an Islamic bank, a structuring bank, an asset managing bank, and a number of fund managers. Then consider how the money passes from one to the other, all the way to the fund managers. And then consider then how it passes all the way back. With each pass, more fees are added to the transaction. Consider also how the Islamic investor's money is the beginning point for the entire transaction. Without this initial investment, none of the rest will take place, no one will earn fees. It is this initial investment which ensures the participation of the structuring bank, the asset managing bank, and the fund managers because it is the initial transaction, the simple *Salam*, which effectively creates and guarantees the capital. The irony is that no one, other than perhaps the unwitting Islamic investor, considers this transaction to be only a principal-protected note with a *Murabaha* and a promise. On the contrary, this is a highly complex and profitable transaction involving several different parties at many different levels. In short, it is a golden opportunity for the banks because the money is virtually guaranteed and their risk is next to nothing. In short, the Muslim investor is assured that the investment product is *Sharia'a* compliant because the '*Sharia'a* Conversion Technology' stratagem, which involves a promise, apparently ensures that the Muslim investor's money never goes directly into anything prohibited. So, the Muslim investors' money may not be invested directly into the part of this transactional series that is actually performing and earning returns. Instead, a mechanism is required to bring the returns from that product to the Muslim investor indirectly. It is also clear, however, that an asset managing bank would not be allocating money to managers unless that money came from somewhere. Between the Muslim investor and the fund manager there may be an indirect link, but the cause and effect relationship is nonetheless present. In a very real sense, the promise to exchange the returns from the non-compliant funds establishes a direct link between those funds and the investor. It also identifies the series as a single transaction. As such, then, it cannot be ignored by the *Sharia'a* Board. The *Sharia'a* Board must consider every step in the transactional series; and when this is done, the *Sharia'a* Board must reject the product.

Ramifications for the Industry

When a *Sharia'a* Board gives consideration to only one part of the transactional series, it is only natural that it should fail to consider the consequences of the product for the industry as a whole. It is an unfortunate shortcoming on the part of the *Sharia'a Board* in this transaction that it has failed to consider the context of the offering. It is an even greater shortcoming when it fails to consider the consequences the product will have for the entire industry. When it is clear that a product cannot be offered in its own form or, in other words, when it cannot be offered directly, but must be offered by means of a stratagem that is basically a derivative like a swap, red warning flags should go up. In such situations, the *Sharia'a* Board must pay careful attention to the circumstances of the offering. If the circumstances can be found to justify such a product, then it may be possible to grant approval. If not, however, approval must be withheld. In the case of promised returns from a referenced basket of assets, the assets must be *Sharia'a* compliant in order for the returns to be *Sharia'a* compliant. It really cannot be otherwise.

If consideration is not given to the underlying assets, or to the assets referenced by the swap mechanism, it could spell the end of the need for authentic Islamic products, services and methodologies. Why should a bank bother to spend the extra time and money required to make a securitization into a *sukuk*? For less money and in less time, it can simply offer conventional bonds and then use the 'mechanism' to match performance, appear to sanitise the money, and satisfy the investor that the investment is *halal* and lawful. If such a mechanism is available at lower costs, then why license an Islamic index for *Sharia'a* compliant stocks? Why use mutual funds that follow guidelines laid down by *Sharia'a* Supervisory Boards? Why bother with all the complex structuring and documentation that go into *Sharia'a* compliant real estate deals? Or infrastructure projects? Or private equity? Or home finance? Why expend the resources required to develop new and innovative Islamic financial products and tools? The '*Sharia'a* Conversion Technology' stratagem makes all of that unnecessary. At a very fundamental level, however, this mechanism seeks to make the *haram halal*. This is the nature of the threat to our industry. The *fatwa* giving blanket approval for this misguided stratagem may well be referred to as the Doomsday *fatwa* for Islamic finance.

If the product described in this paper is successful, managers of all manner of funds, not just hedge funds, will never be motivated to do what is necessary to manage and invest in ways that comply with *Sharia'a*. But then why should they, if all they need to do is agree to swap returns? Asset managers can continue as before, buying and selling interest-bearing bonds, debt-based derivatives, pork futures, bank, casino and brewery stocks. They can trade these however they wish, even by borrowing stocks and then selling them into the market without ever owning them, or by leveraging them and incurring interest on the leverage! In other words, Islamic investors will not know what managers are doing because an Islamic bank and its *Sharia'a* Board have assured them that by means of a special 'technology' their money will remain separated and pure.

Sadd al-Dhara'i: blocking ostensibly legitimate means to illegitimate ends

When I first became acquainted with the details of the '*Sharia'a* Conversion Technology' stratagem (last year, when I was invited to approve it by a huge multinational bank), I had thought that the best way to combat it was to have resort to *sadd al-dhara'i*. This is the legal device from our classical jurisprudence that blocks ostensibly legitimate means when these are employed for illegitimate ends. In other words, in the same way that the digging of a well in the middle of a road may be declared unlawful for the reason that it may lead to great inconveniences and economic losses by those who travel the road. I thought that this mechanism might be declared unlawful by *Sharia'a* Boards for the reason that its use may lead to prohibited investments. So, while a promise to exchange returns may be lawful, if the returns promised have been earned by illegitimate means (by funds that invest in Treasury futures, for example), then that promise may be declared unlawful as it has become a means, an ostensibly legitimate means, for illegitimate ends.

I am now convinced, however, that this transaction is prohibited outright; and that the application of *sadd al-dhara'i* in this instance is unwarranted. This is because of a subtle point of law regarding the application of when it is possible to resort to *sadd al-dhara'i*. The classical jurists have stated that whatever leads to involvement in the unlawful will either lead to the unlawful as a certainty or lead to the unlawful as a possibility. This product includes investments, even though they are entered into indirectly, that are clearly unlawful. Moreover, there is no doubt whatsoever that the transactional series leads inevitably, and repeatedly, to what is unlawful. That being the case, that what leads to involvement in the unlawful does so as a certainty and not as a mere possibility, then *sadd al-dhara'i* is inapplicable. There is no need to resort to *sadd al-dhara'i* because the transaction is clearly unlawful.

I quote, in what follows, from *al-Bahr al-Muhit, Kitab al-Adillah al-Mukhtalif fiha* by Badr al-Din al-Zarkashi, on the subject of *Sadd al-Dhara'i*: Blocking Ostensibly Legitimate Means to Illegitimate Ends.

> Know that whatever leads to involvement in the unlawful will either lead to the unlawful as a certainty or lead to the unlawful as a possibility. The first of these two (that it will certainly lead to commission of the unlawful) is not to be discussed under this heading. Instead the proper place for its discussion is under the heading of 'That Which there is No Way to Escape the Unlawful Except by Avoiding It'. The commission of such an act (whatever will certainly lead to involvement in the unlawful) is unlawful for the reason that whatever is required to ensure the performance of a required act is itself required. (And here the required act is that one avoid what is unlawful; and what is required to ensure that it is avoided is avoidance of the act that will certainly lead to it.)[11]

To clarify this point, the stratagem we are discussing leads, without a doubt, to the unlawful. Obviously, if fund managers are given no guidelines to follow for *Sharia'a* compliance, they will surely make investments that are not *Sharia'a* compliant, they will surely manage their cash in ways that are not *Sharia'a* compliant, and they will surely transact in ways that are not *Sharia'a* compliant. The statements given to the press by the Islamic bank offering this product admits as much. This being the case, that the product leads surely to the unlawful, there is no need to resort to *sadd al-dhara'i* to prevent the proliferation of the product because the product is already unlawful, owing to its leading directly and without doubt to what is unlawful.

If there were some doubt about this, such that the product's leading to the unlawful was only a possibility, whether likely or unlikely, a strong possibility or a slight possibility, then recourse might be had by the jurists to the device known as *sadd al-dhara'i*. When the assets referenced by the '*Sharia'a* Conversion Technology' stratagem are known to be unlawful, however, the transaction is unlawful and there is no need for recourse to any legal device for its prohibition. This being the case, there is also no need to discuss the opinions of the various classical scholars in regard to *sadd al-dhara'i* and its use.

It is an established principle of Islamic Law that whatever is required to ensure the performance of a required act is itself required (ما لا يتم الواجب إلا به فهو واجب). When the avoidance of the unlawful is a requirement, if there is an act that will surely lead to the unlawful, then the avoidance of that act too is a

[11] The author continues, 'The second of these two, that it will possibly lead to commission of the unlawful, may be a likely possibility or an unlikely possibility, or a possibility in which both (likely and unlikely) are equal. Such a possibility may be termed "means", or *dhara'i*'.

requirement. It is for this reason that it is essential, *wajib*, to avoid or to reject, the stratagem and the product. This is because the stratagem is what allows the asset manager to deploy money gathered through this transaction, however indirectly, in funds that operate in ways that are non-compliant with *Sharia'a*, and that invest in businesses that are non-compliant with *Sharia'a*, ignoring all guidelines for Islamic investing that have been developed at great expense by businesses that respect the Muslim investor's need to transact and to invest only in ways that accord with the principles and precepts of the *Sharia'a*.

Conclusion

As jurists, *Sharia'a* Scholars are trained to look at texts and at classical models, especially in regard to transactions. If a question of law is not answered directly in the texts, jurists are trained to seek indirect answers, often by drawing parallels from the body of accumulated jurisprudence, or through recourse to legal maxims and principles. Then, while Islamic law may be characterised as both a moral and a legal system, the jurisprudence that has developed around modern trade and commerce relies almost exclusively on derived legal considerations; even if these may be characterised as legal means to moral ends.[12] Thus, it is difficult to suppose that jurists will make decisions on the basis of purely moral or *Maqasid*-related[13] considerations.

From a practical perspective, the best way to deal with this question may be to refer it to the *Sharia'a* Council of the Accounting and Auditing Organization of Islamic Financial Institutions (AAOIFI), the standard setting body for the entire industry. Since the stratagem that drives the product is based on a promise, or *Wa'd*, which has applications in many modern financial instruments including the modern *Murabaha*, AAOIFI might be requested to promulgate a standard dealing with every aspect of the *Wa'd* and its uses.

The cynical stratagem described above presents Muslim jurists with a real challenge. If investor confidence is to be maintained, the industry must demonstrate its ability to regulate itself and insist upon the Islamic authenticity of all that it does, or allows to be done in its name. In the past few years, modern Islamic finance has proved itself to be viable, innovative and profitable.

---

[12] Indeed, while the prohibition of *riba* may be characterized as a moral prohibition, the prohibition itself is a legal matter. Once the prohibition is incorporated into law, all *riba*-related issues become subject to legal classification and the element of morality is marginalized.

[13] What I mean by *Maqasid*-related are considerations having to do with the higher purposes of Islamic law, especially those related to the equitable distribution of wealth, the development of institutions, and the betterment of individuals and society. YTD.

The question it faces now is whether it can prove that it is moral and responsible.

والله تعالى أعلم، وهو ولي التوفيق والسداد...

Appendix 8.3

Capital protection and Islamic finance: a case study

What is the Meezan Capital Protected Fund-I?

Meezan Capital Protected Fund-I (MCPF-I) is Pakistan's first *Sharia'a* compliant capital protected fund, jointly developed by Al Meezan Investment Management Limited (Al Meezan Investments) Pakistan's largest *Sharia'a* compliant asset management company and Meezan Bank, Pakistan's first and largest Islamic Bank.

MCPF-I is an open end mutual fund with a maturity period of three years and six weeks from the first day of the IPO. MCPF-I provides an investment opportunity to investors who desire capital protection and are willing to invest for relatively longer periods and who want also to get the benefits of potentially higher returns of the stock market.

For capital protection a 70% to 80% portion of the fund will be placed through a *Murabaha* structure with Meezan Bank, which has a rating of A+ for long-term and A1 for short-term. The balance amount will be invested in *Sharia'a* compliant equities in order to generate healthy returns. Based on the backtracking exercise of the fund structure, MCPF-I is targeting returns higher than the returns being offered by debt or income funds and bank deposits.

MCPF-I will adhere to the *Sharia'a* guidelines laid by the *Sharia'a* Supervisory Board of Meezan Bank, chaired by Justice (Retired) Mufti Muhammad Taqi Usmani.

What are the salient features of MCPF-I?

- The first ever *Sharia'a* compliant capital protected fund of Pakistan.
- Capital protection upon maturity through Meezan Bank.
- Provides *halal* and *riba*-free returns under the supervision of Meezan Bank's *Sharia'a* Supervisory Board.
- Expected returns are higher than those offered by debt or income funds and bank deposits.
- The term of investment is three years and six weeks from the first day of the IPO.
- Provides tax rebate benefit up to Rs60, 000/- on investment up to Rs300, 000/- under applicable tax law.
- Minimum Investment Rs 5, 000/- with no cap on the maximum amount. Subsequent investment can be made during the open period with a minimum of Rs 1, 000/- only.

Investment objective, investment policy and investment restrictions

Investment objective

- MCPF-I is a capital protected fund with the objective to pay investors, with certain conditions, their Principal Investment over the term of its life in form of dividend, or return of capital on its termination, in a *Sharia'a* compliant manner.
- The capital protection will be secured by placing assets of the fund in a *Murabaha* placement with a Scheduled Islamic Bank having at least 'A' rating at the time of placement. This investment will be made through the Capital Protection Segment of the fund. The Management Company will allocate an appropriate amount to the Capital Protection Segment depending upon the returns available.
- The remaining assets of the fund will be allocated to the Investment Segment and may be invested in high risk assets that have the potential to give a high return to investors.
- The Management Company will allocate 76.97% of the initial fund size for Capital Protection Segment. Capital Protection Segment will be placed with Meezan Bank Limited under a *Murabaha* structure. The *Murabaha* structure will ensure that these funds grow to become at least 100% of the total initial investment at the time of maturity.

Capital protection

- Capital protection is provided through the investment structure of the Fund as detailed in the Offering Document and not through an undertaking or guarantee by the Management Company or the Trustee.
- Capital protection means that the Net Realisable Value of investment at the maturity of the fund should not fall below the Principal Investment if the investment is held for a minimum period as per the contractual terms laid down in the Offering Document.
- Capital protection will not be valid if units of the fund are redeemed before the minimum period and a back end load may be charged.
- The fund shall be closed from time to time and re-opened as and when determined by the Board of Directors of the Management Company, with prior approval of the Commission under intimation to the Trustee and by providing notice to investors in order to protect the interests of the Unit Holders of the fund. The Management Company shall comply with the terms of approval specified by the Commission, to protect the interest of Unit Holders.

- The capital of the fund is protected only in terms of the base currency, i.e. the Pakistani Rupee. In addition, the capital protection is only valid in terms of the current tax and legal environment of Pakistan and is subject to force majeure factors such as bankruptcy of an investment grade rated institution.

General investment policy

- After the registration of the Trust Deed of the Scheme, the Trustee may, on the recommendation of the Management Company, enter into contracts with relevant parties to purchase or enter into *Murabaha* placements or such investments for the Capital Protection Segment.
- All Investments of the fund would be as per the guidelines of the *Sharia'a* Advisor of the fund and will be in strict conformity with the rules of *Sharia'a*.
- The Management Company may invest the Fund Property in Authorised Investments as per the Investment Policy.

Investment policy for capital protection segment

- For the purpose of Capital Protection, the assets of the fund may be placed in a *Murabaha* placement with a Scheduled Islamic Bank having minimum investment grade rating such that it fulfils the requirement of capital protection, as outlined in the Deed and the Offering Document.
- In case of the maturity of the *Murabaha* placement prior to the termination of the fund, the Capital Protection Segment may again be placed in similar *Murabaha* structures or in bank accounts of Scheduled Islamic Banks or Islamic windows of Scheduled Commercial Banks only if such placement will, in the opinion of the Management Company, maintain the capital protection of the Fund.
- In case the rating of the financial institution with which *Murabaha* placement has been made is reduced from investment grade or the institution is placed on Watch list, the Management Company may at that time realise the investment at its discretion but only to reasonably protect the interest of the Unit Holders.
- If the investments in a Capital Protection Segment are realised on a date close to but before the termination of the fund, the funds so realised will be invested in short-term instruments such as bank account with a Scheduled Islamic Banks or Islamic windows of Scheduled Commercial Banks having minimum 'A' grade rating.

Investment policy of investment segment

- Investment Segment will generally invest in high return or high risk investments with the objective of providing Unit Holders a higher return than the minimum protection provided by the Capital Protection Segment.
- Investment avenues shall include fixed, floating and hybrid investment instruments. The fund would invest in the following instruments:
  - Shares of companies listed on the stock exchanges or for whose listing an application has been filed in the stock exchanges.
  - Certificates of Investment based on *Sharia'a* compliant structures.
  - Bank Deposits in licensed Islamic Banks and licensed Islamic Banking windows of conventional Banks.
  - Placement of funds under *Mudaraba*, *Murabaha* and *Musharaka* arrangements.
  - Placement of funds under *Istisna'a* and *Ijara* arrangements.
  - Spread Transactions as approved by the *Sharia'a* Advisor.
  - Secured and listed *Sharia'a* compliant securities including *sukuk* issued by Federal Government, Provincial Government, Local Government and Government Agencies.
  - Secured and unlisted *Sharia'a* compliant securities including *sukuk* issued by Federal Government, Provincial Government, Local Government and Government Agencies.
  - Secured and listed *Sharia'a* compliant securities including *sukuk* issued by public-sector entities.
  - Secured and unlisted *Sharia'a* compliant securities including *sukuk* issued by public-sector entities.
  - Secured and listed *Sharia'a* compliant securities including *sukuk* issued by private-sector entities and/or financial institutions.
  - Secured and unlisted *Sharia'a* compliant securities including *sukuk* issued by private-sector entities and/or financial institutions.
  - Unsecured and listed *Sharia'a* compliant securities including *sukuk* issued by Federal Government, Provincial Government, Local Government and Government Agencies.
  - Unsecured and unlisted *Sharia'a* compliant securities including *sukuk* issued by Federal Government, Provincial Government, Local Government and Government Agencies.
  - Unsecured and listed *Sharia'a* compliant securities including *sukuk* issued by public-sector entities.
  - Unsecured and unlisted *Sharia'a* compliant securities including *sukuk* issued by public-sector entities.
  - Unsecured and listed *Sharia'a* compliant securities including *sukuk* issued by private-sector entities and/or financial institutions.

- Unsecured and unlisted *Sharia'a* compliant securities including *sukuk* issued by private-sector entities and/or financial institutions.
- Any other *Sharia'a* compliant instrument that may be allowed by the Commission from time to time and is as per the guidelines of the Fund's *Sharia'a* Advisor.
- International investments in instruments based on the structures mentioned in sub clauses (a) to (i) subject to the conditions laid down by the State Bank of Pakistan from time to time for such investments and with prior approval of the Commission.

Investment restrictions

- The Management Company in managing the fund shall abide by all the provisions of this Deed, Rules and Regulations.
- The fund Property shall be subject to such exposure limits as are provided in this Deed, the Rules and the Regulations (subject to any exemptions that may be specifically given to the Fund by the Commission). In the event, the exposure limits exceeds due to the relative movement in the market prices of the investments or any corporate actions (including bonus shares or right shares) or through any disinvestments or decrease in Net Assets of the Scheme due to redemptions, the Management Company will have three (3) months to comply with the exposure limits in case such limits are exceeded.
- If and so long as the value of the holding in a particular security shall exceed the limit imposed by the Rules, the Management Company shall not purchase any further Investments in such security. However this restriction on purchase shall not apply to any offer of right shares or any other offering, if the Management Company is satisfied that accepting such offer is in the interest of the fund.
- The fund will not at any time:
    - Effect short sales in a security whether listed or unlisted.
    - Purchase any security in a forward contract.
    - Purchase any security on margin.
    - Apply any part of its asset to real estate, commodities or commodity contracts.
    - Acquire any security of which another asset management company managing a collective investment scheme is the issuer.
    - Issue at any time, without the prior approval of the Commission in writing, a senior security which is either stock or represents indebtedness.
    - Invest in any security of a company if any director or officer of the Management Company owns more than five per cent of the total amount

of securities issued, or, the directors and officers of the Management Company own more than 10% of those securities collectively.

- Lend, assume, guarantee, endorse or otherwise become directly or contingently liable for or in connection with any obligation or indebtedness of any person.
- Borrow except with the approval of the Trustee for meeting redemption request and such borrowing shall not exceed 15% of the total net asset value of the Fund at the time of borrowing and shall be repayable within a period of 90 days.

Exemptions to investment restrictions

- The Management Company, subject to the approval of the Commission, may invest the Capital Protection Segment in a single security or instrument that is sufficient to fulfil the capital protection provided in the Offering Document.
- The Management Company subject to the approval of the Commission may invest the Investment Segment in a single security or instrument internationally. This investment would be further subject to the conditions laid down by the State Bank of Pakistan for such investments.

Borrowing restrictions

- Subject to any statutory requirements for the time being in force, and to the terms and conditions herein contained, the Trustee may at any time at the request of the Management Company concur with the Management Company in making and varying arrangements with Banks or institutions, both financial and non financial, for borrowing by the Trustee for the account of the fund; provided that the borrowing shall not be resorted to, except for meeting the redemption requests.
- The charges payable to any Bank or institution against borrowings on account of the fund as permissible above shall not be higher than the normal prevailing bank charges or normal market rates for similar service and/or facility.
- The maximum borrowing for the account of the fund shall not exceed 15% of the total Net Asset Value of the Fund at the time of the borrowing or such other limit as may be provided in the Rules and Regulations.
- Neither the Trustee, nor the Management Company shall be required to issue any guarantee or provide security over their own assets for securing such borrowings from Banks and Financial Institutions. The Trustee or the Management Company shall not in any manner be liable in their personal capacities for repayment of such loans or advances.

- For the purposes of securing any such borrowing the Trustee may, upon instruction of the Management Company, mortgage, charge or pledge in any manner all or any part of the fund Property provided that the aggregate amount secured by such mortgage, charge or pledge shall not exceed the limits provided under the Rules.
- Neither the Trustee nor the Management Company shall incur any liability by reason of any loss to the Trust or any loss that a Unit Holder may suffer by reason of any depletion in the Net Asset Value that may result from any borrowing arrangement made hereunder.

Duration

The duration of MCPF-I is three years and six weeks from the first day of Initial Public Offering. MCPF-I shall stand automatically dissolved after the said period of three years and six weeks. However it can be wound up earlier by SECP or by the Management Company on the occurrence of certain events.

Open-end fund

MCPF-I is an open-end fund. It shall offer Units on a continuous basis during the Initial Offering Period. There is no upper or lower limit set on the number of Units to be issued to a single Unit Holder or on the total number of Units to be issued to the public. However, the Management Company may impose, from time to time, certain amounts of minimum monetary investment limits to facilitate economical and efficient management of investors' accounts. Fractional Units will be issued to enhance economical and efficient handling. Units may be redeemed for cash pursuant to the Redemption Procedures. Units are also transferable. Units will be issued in registered form and will be confirmed to investors by means of an account statement issued by the Registrar. Certificates, being the definitive certificate acknowledging the number of Units registered in the name of the Holder, shall be issued at the request of the Unit Holder subject to terms herein at a nominal charge.

Units

- All Units and fractions thereof represent an undivided share in the fund and rank *pari passu* as to their rights in the net assets, earnings, and the receipt of the dividends and distributions. Each Unit Holder has a beneficial interest in the fund, proportionate to the Units held by such Unit Holder.
- The Management Company may issue any of the following classes of Units:
  - Class A Units that shall be Capital Protected Units which may be charged with a Front-end Load, if any and also subject to Back-end Load.
  - Class B Units that shall be Capital Protected Units which may be charged with a Front-end Load that is less than Class A Units and also subject to

  Back-end Load. Class B Units will be offered for subscription if and when the Fund is reopened for subscription.
  - Class C Units are the Bonus Units that may be issued to the Unit Holders in case of stock dividends announced from time to time. Such units shall not have any capital protection and will also be subject to Back-end Load.
- Irrespective of the different classes of Units as set out in this Clause, all Units issued from time to time shall rank *pari passu inter se* and shall have such rights as are set out in the Deed and Offering Document, subject to the capital protection related characteristics mentioned.
- Core Units subscribed by the Core Investors shall be offered and issued at the Par Value. Rupees Fifty Million from that shall not be redeemable for a period of two years from the date of issue. However, for capital protection to hold Minimum Period requirement would apply for these Core Investors and a Back-end Load as per the Offering Document would be applicable in case of early redemption.

Risks

Investment process requires disciplined risk management. Al Meezan Investments would incorporate adequate safeguards for controlling risks in the portfolio construction process of MCPF-I. The risk control process involves reducing risks through optimal portfolio diversification. Al Meezan Investments believes that this diversification would help achieve the desired level of consistency in returns.

Al Meezan Investments' investment team aims to identify securities following proper credit evaluation of the securities proposed to be invested in. It will be guided by the ratings of Rating Agencies such as Pakistan Credit Rating Agency or JCR-VIS Credit Rating Company Limited or any other rating agencies that may be registered with SECP from time to time or any other reputed international credit rating agencies. In case a debt instrument is not rated, necessary clearance of the Investment Committee will be obtained for such an investment.

Performance risk

Performance risk is the uncertainty relating to the performance of the fund with respect to its ability to earn a return over and above Initial Investment as outlined in its investment objective. The NAV of the fund might go down.

Mitigant

Al Meezan Investments presently has four mutual funds and a voluntary pension scheme under its management. All four funds and the voluntary pension scheme have performed reasonably well when compared to their relevant benchmarks. The performance of these funds is evidence of the fund management and risk management abilities of Al Meezan Investments' team.

Equity risk

Companies issue equities, or stocks, to help finance their operations and future growth. The Company's performance outlook, market activity and the larger economic picture influence the price of a stock. Usually when the economy is expanding, the outlook for many companies is good and the stock prices may rise and vice versa.

Credit risk

Credit risk comprises Default Risk and Credit Spread Risk. Each can have negative impact on the value of the *Sharia'a* compliant income and money market instruments including *sukuk* etc:

- ***Default Risk*** – The risk that the issuer of the security will not be able to pay the obligation, either on time or at all;
- ***Credit Spread Risk*** – The risk that there may be an increase in the difference between the return or mark-up rate of any issuer's security and the return or mark-up rate of a risk free security. The difference between this return or mark-up rates is called a 'credit spread'. Credit spreads are based on macro-economic events in the domestic or global financial markets. An increase in credit spread will decrease the value of *Sharia'a* compliant income including money market instruments.

Capital protection risk

If the investment in the fund is not held to maturity, there is no capital protection. At maturity, the Capital Protection Level is 100% of the initial capital invested, through the investment structure.

Events risk

There may be adjustments to the performance of the fund due to events including but not limited to, natural calamities, market disruptions, mergers, nationalisation, insolvency and changes in tax law.

Interest rate risk

A rise in interest rates during the investment term may result in a reduced return in terms of opportunity cost.

Other risks

Government Regulation Risk – Government policies and the law regulate different sectors of the economy to a varying extent. Funds that invest in these sectors may be affected due to change in these regulations or policies, which directly or indirectly affect the earnings and/or the cash flows. Additionally, governmental or court orders may restrain payment of capital, principal or income.

Sharia'a governance and *Sharia'a* advisory services

Sharia'a governance

All activities of the fund shall be undertaken in accordance with the Islamic *Sharia'a* as per the guidelines given by *Sharia'a* Advisor.

Sharia'a Advisor

1) The Management Company shall appoint a *Sharia'a* Advisor from time to time to advise the Management Company regarding *Sharia'a*.
2) Meezan Bank Limited has been appointed the *Sharia'a* Advisor of the Fund. At present the *Sharia'a* Supervisory Board of Meezan Bank consists of Justice (Retired) Muhammad Taqi Usmani, Dr Abdul Sattar Abu Ghuddah, Sheikh Essam M Ishaq and Dr Muhammad Imran Ashraf Usmani.
3) The Management Company may, with prior notice to the Trustee, terminate its agreement with the *Sharia'a* Advisor(s) and appoint a new *Sharia'a* Advisor to the Fund with the approval of the Commission and under intimation to the Trustee.
4) The *Sharia'a* Advisor shall advise the Management Company on matters relating to *Sharia'a* compliance and recommend general investment guidelines consistent with *Sharia'a*. Any verdict issued by the *Sharia'a* Advisor in respect of any *Sharia'a* related matter would be final and acceptable to the Trustee, the Management Company, the Unit Holders and other parties related with the matter.
5) The *Sharia'a* Advisor shall provide technical guidance and support on various aspects of *Sharia'a*, so as to enable the Management Company to mould the Unit Trust into a *Sharia'a* Compliant Investment.
6) The *Sharia'a* Advisor via its letter, dated January 24 2008, has certified that the Trust Deed is compliant with the requirements of *Sharia'a*. However, in case there is a requirement for any amendment, based on future research for purposes of increasing the *Sharia'a* acceptability of the Trust Deed, permission for necessary amendments of the Deed may be sought from the Commission.
7) At the end of each Accounting Year, the *Sharia'a* Advisor shall issue a certificate to be included in the financial reports in respect of the *Sharia'a* compliance of the preceding year's operations of the fund. Cost of any

special investigations conducted by the *Sharia'a* Advisor would be borne by the Management Company.

Source: Meezan Bank MCPF-1 Prospectus

Case study questions

1) Outline the *Sharia'a* position on capital guarantees and capital protection.
2) Outline the mechanisms available to achieve capital protection for conventional investing.
3) Outline the mechanisms available to achieve capital protection for *Sharia'a* compliant investing.
4) Describe the key features of the MCPF-I.
5) What is the MCPF-I mechanism for achieving capital protection?
6) What is the MCPF-I investment policy?
7) Describe the investment constraints being applied by MCPF-I.
8) What are the risks faced by investors?
9) How can capital protection be offered given the risks listed in the prospectus?
10) Given that *Murabaha* is a mode of financing how can it be used for capital protection?
11) What *Sharia'a* mechanisms have been put in place?
12) To what extent what you consider the MCPF-I to be non-*Sharia'a* compliant?

Chapter 9

Sukuk (Islamic bonds)

What are *sukuk*?

The term *sukuk* is the Arabic plural of *sakk* which means a 'legal instrument, deed, cheque'. *Sukuk* are financial certificates but can be seen as the Islamic equivalent of a bond. However, fixed-income, interest-bearing bonds are not permissible in Islam, hence *sukuk* are securities that comply with *Sharia'a* law and its investment principles.

These principles prohibit the charging, or paying of interest. Financial assets that comply with *Sharia'a* law can be classified in accordance with their tradability and non-tradability in the secondary markets.

Some linguistics

While reading news about *sukuk*, on the web and even in major financial publications, readers may notice the use of the word '*sukuk*' as a singular and '*sukuk*s' as plural. This is incorrect usage from a linguistic perspective. *Sukuk* is the phonetic representation of the Arabic word for certificates or bonds, so it is fundamentally an Arabic word. At the same time, *sukuk* is a plural noun. The singular of *sukuk* is *sakk*. 'A *sukuk*' and '*sukuk*s' sound very strange and incomprehensible to an Arab's ear. They sound like 'A children is innocent' or 'Childrens are cheerful'.

Some history

In the classical period of Islam a *sakk*, which is cognate with the European root 'cheque' (which itself derives from Persian), meant any document representing a contract or conveyance of rights, obligations or monies employed in transactions which were in conformity with the *Sharia'a*. Historical evidence shows that *sukuk* were a product extensively used during medieval Islam for the transferring of financial obligations originating from trade and other commercial activities.

The essence of *sukuk*, in the modern Islamic perspective, lies in the concept of Islamic securitisation discussed in *Chapter 4*. The Arabic term for this process is *Taskeek*. The great potential for *Taskeek* is in transforming an asset's future cash flow into present cash flow. *Sukuk* may be issued on existing as well as specific assets that may become available at a future date. The differing *sukuk* format are discussed later in this chapter.

What do sukuk represent?

Sukuk represent an undivided proportionate ownership interest in an asset with the corresponding right to the Islamically acceptable income streams generated by the asset. *Sukuk* have economic characteristics similar to those of a conventional bond, but are structured so as to be compliant with *Sharia'a* law and can be sold to Islamic investors who are prohibited, by *Sharia'a* law, from investing in conventional debt securities. The *Sharia'a* is a body of Islamic law drawn from various sources, including the *Qur'an*, which includes a number of principles relating to financial transactions. *Sharia'a* law was discussed in more detail in *Chapter 2*.

The *Sharia'a* is not a codified body of law and is subject to development and sometimes conflicting interpretation. However, the major Islamic financial institutions have a *Sharia'a* Supervisory Board on which Islamic scholars sit and, in practice, these boards determine whether a proposed transaction being arranged by the institution is compliant with the *Sharia'a*.

Sukuk, sometimes referred to as Islamic bonds, are better described as Islamic investment certificates. This distinction is as crucial as it is important. The distinction is important as a bond is a contractual obligation whereby the issuer is obliged to pay bond holders, on certain specified dates, interest and principal. In comparison, under a ***sukuk*** structure, the ***sukuk*** holders each hold an undivided beneficial ownership in the underlying assets. Consequently, ***sukuk*** holders are entitled to share in the revenue generated by the ***sukuk*** assets as well as being entitled to share in the proceeds of the realisation of the ***sukuk*** assets.

Sukuk should not simply be regarded as a substitute for conventional interest-based securities. The aim is not simply to engineer financial products that mimic fixed-rate bonds and floating-rate notes as understood in conventional finance, but rather to develop innovative types of assets that comply with *Sharia'a* law. The essential underlying concepts of ***sukuk*** are:

- transparency and clarity of rights and obligations;
- income from the securities must be related to the purpose for which the funding is used, and not simply comprise interest; and
- securities should be backed by real underlying assets, rather than being simply paper derivatives.

Islamic fixed-income securities have emerged as a significant asset class and are as potentially important for the Muslim investor as conventional bonds are for investors generally. In addition, for non-Muslims who already own conventional bonds, the acquisition of ***sukuk*** introduces a new asset class into their portfolios, bringing further welcome diversity and possibly reducing risk.

Sukuk represent an undivided proportionate ownership interest in an asset with the corresponding right to the Islamically acceptable income streams generated by the asset. These current income streams are established and translated into tradable securities which are then issued in the capital markets for investors' participation. ***Sukuk*** allow investors to lock in either medium- to long-term fixed-income returns or variable rates of return, which are adjusted at periodic intervals and which, by virtue of being tradable, provide investors with the flexibility to exit the investment at any time prior to completion of the full investment holding period.

What is the underlying principle behind sukuk?

Sukuk must be structured alongside different Islamically acceptable nominate contracts. While a conventional bond is a promise to repay a loan, *sukuk* present partial ownership in a debt (*Murabaha sukuk*), asset (*Ijara sukuk*), project (*Istisna'a sukuk*) or business (*Musharaka sukuk*), or investment (*Istithmar sukuk*).

Most commonly *sukuk* structures replicate the cash flows of conventional bonds, being listed on exchanges and made tradable through conventional organisations like Euroclear or Clearstream. A key technique to achieve the capital protection,without this amounting to a loan, is a binding promise to repurchase certain assets by the issuer. This has been popular in the case of *Ijara sukuk*. In the meantime rent is being paid, which is often benchmarked to an interest rate benchmark, such as LIBOR.

Sukuk secondary market

From a *Sharia'a* perspective certificates of debt are not tradable while in Malaysia a different view is taken. Certain structuring elements for *Musharaka sukuk*, *Mudaraba sukuk* and *Istithmar sukuk* faced severe criticisms in late 2007 by Sheikh Taqi Usmani, followed by a recommendation of the Accounting and Auditing Organisation for Islamic financial institutions (AAOIFI). These criticisms are discussed in more detail below.

As the *Sharia'a* considers money to be a measuring tool for value and not an asset in itself, this requires that Muslims should not be able to receive income from money (or anything that has the genus of money) alone. This generation of money from money (simplistically interest) is '*Riba*', and is forbidden. The implications for Islamic financial institutions is that the trading and selling of debts, receivables (for anything other than par value), conventional lending and use of conventional credit cards are not permissible.

Sukuk investors tend to apply a 'buy-and-hold strategy', given the overwhelming demand for them and, as such, only few of them enter the secondary market (allowing them to be traded). The secondary market, whilst developing, remains a niche segment with virtually all trading done at the institutional level. The size of the secondary market remains unknown, although the Liquidity Management Centre (LMC) in Bahrain state they traded $55.5 million of *sukuk* in 2007. The European Islamic Investment Bank (EIIB), in an interview published on sukuk.net, stated 'Secondary market trading volume has contracted significantly in the first half of 2008 when compared to 2007 where *sukuk* with a nominal value of approximately $0.5bn was traded'.

Some controversies

Banks that issue *sukuk* are investing in real assets, not in financial assets. The return on such assets can take the form of rent, and be evenly spread over the rental period. The productivity of the asset forms the basis of the fixed-income stream and the return on investment. Given that there is an asset underlying the value of the certificate, there is more security for the investors involved, accounting for the additional appeal of *sukuk* as a form of investment.

Sukuk have sometimes been regarded as controversial. Conservative scholars claim that their perceived purpose of evading the restrictions on *Riba* is not effective, citing the fact that a *sakk* (Islamic bond) effectively requires payment for the time-value of money. This, some argue, can be regarded as the fundamental test of whether interest is being paid. *Sukuk* offer investors fixed return on their investments which is also similar in appearance to interest in that the investor's return is not necessarily dependent on the risks of that particular venture.

Characteristics of *sukuk*

Sukuk certificates serve to replicate the functions of tradable securities injecting liquidity into enterprises or government and in providing a stable income for investors. *Sukuk* bear the financial risk and they can be distinguished from conventional bonds and asset securitisations in several ways.

Investing in *sukuk* issuances involves the funding of trade or production of tangible assets. *Sukuk* are directly linked with real sector activities. Hence, it is hoped by some scholars, that they will not create the same short-term speculative movement of funds and potential financial crises associated with conventional bonds. *Sukuk* investors have an inherent right to information on the use of their investments, the nature of the underlying assets, and other particulars that would otherwise be considered redundant in conventional investments. It is hoped, by scholars, that this will help to introduce discipline into the financial markets. Other aspects of *sukuk* have led to their appeal to Islamic investors:

- They are tradable *Sharia'a* compliant capital market products providing medium- to long-term fixed or variable rates of return.
- The credit quality of *sukuk* instruments is assessed and rated by international rating agencies, which investors use as a guideline to assess risk or return parameters of *sukuk* issues.
- They are characterised by regular periodic income streams during the investment period with easy and efficient settlement and also provide the possibility of capital appreciation.

- The existence of a secondary market provides liquidity to the *sukuk* instruments.

Generally *sukuk* are asset-backed, stable income, tradable and *Sharia'a* compliant trust certificates. The primary condition of issuance of *sukuk* is the existence of assets on the balance sheet of the government, the monetary authority, the corporate body, the banking and financial institution or any other entity which wants to mobilise financial resources. The identification of suitable assets is the first, and arguably most integral, step in the process of issuing *sukuk* certificates. *Sharia'a* considerations dictate that the pool of assets should not solely be comprised of debts from Islamic financial contracts (e.g. *Murabaha*, *Istisna'a*).

Islamic legitimacy of *sukuk*

At the request of delegates from Jordan, Pakistan and Malaysia, the Fiqh Academy of the Organization of the Islamic Conference based in Saudi Arabia considered the question of Islamic investment certificates at their fourth annual plenary session, held in Jeddah, Saudi Arabia in February 1988.

The scholars noted that the *Sharia'a* encourages the documentation of contracts as stipulated in Surah 2:282 of the *Qur'an*:

> 'When ye deal with each other, in transactions involving future obligations in a fixed period of time, reduce them to writing ... It is more just in the sight of God, more suitable as evidence and more convenient to prevent doubts among yourselves.'

Subject to proper legal documentation, the Fiqh Academy, under decision number 5 of 1988 ruled that:

- any collection of assets can be represented in a written note or bond; and
- this bond or note can be sold at a market price provided that the composition of the group of assets, represented by the security, consists of a majority of physical assets and financial rights, with only a minority being cash and interpersonal debts.

Although there is no compulsion to comply with the rulings of the Fiqh Academy their rulings carry considerable weight with most Islamic financial institutions and with their *Sharia'a* committees and advisors.

Why have Islamic bonds?

Conventional bonds that yield interest, or *riba*, are prohibited under *Sharia'a* law, as mentioned. Furthermore, those who buy and sell conventional bonds are rarely interested in what is actually being financed through the bond issue. This could include activities and industries that are deemed *haram,* such as the production or sale of alcohol. Companies that are highly leveraged with bank debt may seek refinancing through issuing bonds, but such companies are not regarded as suitable investments for Muslim investors.

The aim of bond traders is usually to make capital gains as fixed-interest bond prices rise when variable market interest rates fall. Bond trading is therefore largely about exploiting interest rate movements and involves trading in paper that is usually unrelated to the value of any underlying asset. The major risk for holders of conventional bonds is of payments default, but this risk is usually assessed solely on the basis of credit ratings, with the ratings agency rather than the bond purchaser estimating the risk. Hence the bonds are regarded as mere pieces of paper with third parties estimating the risk and the purchaser, at best, only making a risk or return calculation without any reference to the business being financed.

A number of *Sharia'a* Scholars, most notably Muhammad Taqi Usmani, have stressed that one of the distinguishing features legitimising Islamic finance is that it must involve the funding of trade in, or the production of, real assets. Merely funding the purchase of financial securities would involve second-order financing akin to derivatives related activities, the subsequent gearing being speculative and increasing uncertainty or *gharar*.

As Islamic finance is by nature participatory, purchasers of *sukuk* securities have the right to be given information on the purposes for which their monies are to be allocated. In other words, the funding raised through *sukuk* issues should be hypothecated, or earmarked, rather than be used for general unspecified purposes, whether by a sovereign or corporate issuer. This implies that identifiable assets should back the *sukuk*.

Sukuk: a survey

Sukuk are securitised assets and therefore belong to the category of asset backed securities (ABS). Unlike conventional bond structures, *sukuk* need to have an underlying tangible asset transaction either in ownership or in a master lease agreement. Generally, *sukuk* are a form of commercial paper that provides an investor with ownership in an underlying asset. It is an asset-backed security that has a stable income and *Sharia'a* compliant trust certificates. The *Taskeek* model for *sukuk* securitisation is derived from the conventional securitisation process in which a special purpose vehicle (SPV) is set up to acquire assets and to issue financial claims on the assets. These financial asset claims represent a proportionate beneficial ownership to the *sukuk* holders.

Varieties of sukuk

Islamic capital markets offer different instruments to satisfy both providers and users of funds in a variety of ways. While the main types of Islamic financial instruments are conceptually simple, they become complicated in practice as some financial instruments combine aspects of two or more types of instruments. The proper classification of asset classes will determine the type of certificates to be issued. It is vital to note that these assets can be prepared and issued for the issuance in a number of ways conditional on the needs of the issuing entity. The most common types of *sukuk* are listed below:

Ijara sukuk

These are *sukuk* that are based on the *Ijara* mode of finance. They are one of the most common *sukuk* issuance types, especially for leasing and project finance. *Ijara sukuk* involves a leasing structure coupled with a right available to the lessee to purchase the asset at the end of the lease period (finance lease). The certificates are issued on stand-alone assets identified on the balance sheet.

The rental rates of return on those *sukuk* can be fixed or floating depending on the agreement. The cash flow from the lease including rental payments and principle repayments are passed through to investors in the form of coupon and principal payments. *Ijara sukuk* provide an efficient medium- to long-term mode of financing. These instruments have been used in a variety of cross-border applications for an increasing range of asset classes including ships, aircraft, telecommunications equipment and power station turbines.

Istisna'a sukuk

These are *sukuk* that are based on the *Istisna'a* mode of finance. *Istisna'a* is a mode of finance involving construction and manufacturing. This type of *sukuk* has been used for the advance funding of real estate development, major industrial projects or large items of equipment such as turbines, power plants, ships or aircraft. The Islamic financial institution funds the manufacturer or the contractor during the construction of the asset, acquires title to that asset and upon completion either immediately passes title to the developer on agreed deferred payment terms or, possibly, leases the asset to the developer under an *Ijara sukuk*. However, it should be noted that, if the *sukuk* are listed during the *Istisna'a* period, the *sukuk* can only be traded at par as the underlying asset does not yet exist. This is due to the *Sharia'a* ruling that debt cannot be traded, except at par value.

Salam sukuk

Salam sukuk are based on the *Salam* mode of finance. The main concept of *Salam sukuk* refers to a sale, whereby the seller undertakes to supply a specific commodity to the buyer at a future date in return for an advanced price paid in full on a spot basis. The price is in cash but the supply of the purchased good is deferred. As a form of financing, the purchaser is able to acquire the assets by advance payment at a discounted price and subsequently sells the assets upon delivery. *Salam sukuk* represents a type of a forward contract which is forbidden under *Sharia'a* law unless there are strict conditions attached that aim at the elimination of uncertainty.

The *Salam sukuk* differs from *Istisna'a sukuk* in that the purchase price for the assets under *Salam sukuk* must paid in full and the date of delivery must be fixed. *Appendix 9.1* illustrates how the Central Bank of Bahrain (CBB) issues *sukuk* based on the *Salam* mode of finance. *Appendix 9.2* provides the CBB Salam sukuk Term Sheet.

Mudaraba sukuk

These are *sukuk* that are based on the *Mudaraba* mode of finance. *Mudaraba* is an agreement made between one party, who provides the capital and another party (an entrepreneur), to enable the entrepreneur to carry out business projects, which will be on a profit sharing basis, according to predetermined ratios agreed on earlier (participation or trust financing). In the case of losses these are born by the provider of the funds.

Musharaka sukuk

These are *sukuk* that are based on the *Musharaka* mode of finance. *Musharaka* is very similar to the *Mudaraba* contract and it is widely used in equity financing. The structure of *Musharaka* requires both parties provide financing to the projects. In the case of losses, both parties will lose in proportion to the size of their investment.

Murabaha sukuk

Murabaha sukuk are based on the *Murabaha* mode of finance. The *Murabaha* technique (cost-plus financing) is one of the most widely used instruments for Islamic short-term financing. The structure of *Murabaha* is relatively straightforward and is based on declared mark-up integrated into the selling price with a deferred payment. The Islamic financial institution purchase and takes title of the necessary equipment or goods from a third party, the Islamic financial institution then sells the equipment or goods to its customer at cost plus a reasonable profit.

6. AAOIFI *sukuk* classifications

In response to the emergence of interest in issuances of Islamic asset-backed financial instruments, the Accounting and Auditing Organization for Islamic Financial Institutions (AAOIFI) released an exposure draft of its *Sharia'a standards concerning sukuk* in November 2002. According to the exposure draft: 'Investment *Sukuk* are certificates of equal value representing, after closing subscription, receipt of the value of the certificates and putting it to use as planned, common title to shares and rights in tangible assets, *usufructs*, and services, or equity of a given project or equity of a special investment activity.' *Exposure Draft of AAOIFI Sharia'a Standard No.18, p.4.*

AAOIFI issued Standards for 14 different types of ***sukuk***, where some of these ***sukuk*** are classified as tradable and others are classified as non-tradable, based on the type and characteristics of the issued ***sukuk***. The salient features of the different types of investment ***sukuk*** identified in the exposure draft are summarised in tables 9.1 to 9.6 below.

Types of investment *sukuk*	Description of investment *sukuk*	*Sharia'a* rulings and requirements
1. Certificates of ownership in leased assets	These are certificates that carry equal value and are issued either by the owner of a leased asset or an asset to be leased by promise, or by his financial agent, the aim of which is to sell the asset and recover its value from subscription, in which case the holders of the certificates become owners of the assets.	Issuer: sells a leased asset or an asset to be leased on a promise. Subscribers are: the buyers of the asset. Mobilised funds: Is the purchase price of the asset. Certificate holders: become the owners of the assets jointly with its benefits and its risks.

Adapted from *AAOIFI sukuk Exposure Draft*, November 2002

Table 9.1. Certificate of ownership on leased assets

Types of investment *sukuk*	Description of investment *sukuk*	*Sharia'a* rulings and requirements
2. Certificates of ownership of *usufructs*	These certificates have various types, including the following:	
(a) Certificates of ownership of *usufructs* of existing assets	These are documents of equal value that are issued either by the owner of usufruct of an existing asset or a financial intermediary acting on the owner's behalf, with the aim of leasing or subleasing this asset and receive rental from the revenue of subscription. In this case, the holders of the certificates become owners of the usufruct of the asset.	Issuer: sells usufruct of an existing asset. Subscribers are: buyers of the *usufructs*. Mobilised funds: are the purchase price of the *usufructs*. Certificate holders: become the owners of the *usufructs* jointly with its benefits and its risks.
(b) Certificates of ownership of *usufructs* to be made available in the future, as per description	These are documents of equal value issued for the sake of leasing assets that the lessor is liable to provide in the future whereby the rental is recovered from the subscription income, in which case the holders of the certificates become owners of the usufruct of these future assets.	Issuer: sells usufruct of an asset to be made available in the future as per the specification. Subscribers are: buyers of the *usufructs*. Mobilised funds: from subscription are the purchase price of the *usufructs*. Certificate holders: become the owners of the *usufructs* jointly with its benefits and its risks.

Table 9.2. Certificates of ownership in *usufructs*

Types of investment *sukuk*	Description of investment *sukuk*	*Sharia'a* rulings and requirements
3. Certificates of ownership of services of a specified supplier	These are documents of equal value issued for the sake of providing or selling services through a specified supplier (such as educational programmes in a nominated university) and obtaining the value in the form of subscription income, in which case the holders of the certificates becomes owners of the services.	Issuer: sells services. Subscribers are: buyers of the services. Mobilised funds: are the purchase price of the services. Certificate holders: are entitled to sell all types of *usufructs* in addition to the funds from reselling such *usufructs*.
4. Certificates of ownership of services to be made available in the future as per description	These are documents of equal value issued for the sake of providing or selling services through a non existing supplier with the description of the subject matter (such as educational programs of a specific quality, schedule, duration etc. without mentioning the educational institution) and obtaining the value in the form of subscription income, in which case the holders of the certificates become owners of the services.	

Table 9.3. Certificates of ownership of services of a specified supplier of services to be made available in the future

Types of investment *sukuk*	Description of investment *sukuk*	*Sharia'a* rulings and requirements
5. *Salam* certificates	These are documents of equal value issued for the sake of mobilising *Salam* capital and the items to be delivered on *Salam* basis are owned by the certificate holders.	Issuer: sells *Salam* commodity. Subscribers are: buyers of that commodity. Mobilised funds: are the purchase price of the commodity (S*alam* capital) Certificate holders: are entitled to the *Salam* commodity, the selling price or the price of selling them on a parallel *Salam* basis, if any.
6. *Istisna'a* certificates	These are documents that carry equal value and are issued with the aim of mobilising the funds required for producing a certain item and the items to be produced on *Istisna'a* basis are owned by the certificate holders.	Issuer: is the manufacturer (supplier). Subscribers are: the buyers of the item to be produced. Mobilised funds: are the cost of the item. Certificate holders: are entitled to the item or the selling price of the manufactured item.
7. *Murabaha* certificates	These are documents of equal value issued for the purpose of financing the *Murabaha* commodity and the certificate holders become the owners of the *Murabaha* commodity.	Issuer sells: *Murabaha* commodity. Subscribers are: the buyers of the commodity. Mobilised funds: are the purchasing cost of the commodity. Certificate holders: own the *Murabaha* commodity or the price of selling it.

Table 9.4. *Salam*, *Istisna'a* and *Murabaha* contracts

Types of investment *sukuk*	Description of investment *sukuk*	*Sharia'a* rulings and requirements
8. Participation certificates	These are documents of equal value issued with the aim of using the mobilised funds for establishing a new project or developing an existing one or financing a business activity on the basis of one of partnership contracts. The certificate holders become the owners of the project or the assets of the activity as per their respective shares. The participation certificates may be managed on the basis of *Musharaka* or *Mudaraba* or through an investment agent.	
(a) Participation certificates managed on the basis of *Musharaka* contract	These are documents representing projects or activities that are managed on the basis of *Musharaka* by appointing either one of the parties or any other party to manage the operation.	Issuer: is the inviter to a partnership in a specific project or activity. Subscribers are: the partners in the *Musharaka* contract. Mobilised funds: are the share contribution of the subscribers in the *Musharaka*h capital. Certificate holders: own the assets of partnership and are entitled to profit, if any.
(b) Participation certificates managed on the basis of *Mudaraba* contract	These are documents that represent projects or activities that are managed on the basis of *Mudaraba* by appointing *Mudarib* for management.	Issuer: is the *Mudarib*. Subscribers are: the capital owners. Mobilised funds: are the *Mudaraba* capital. Certificate holders: own the assets of *Mudaraba* operation and profit share as per the agreement. The certificate holders, being the capital providers, bear the loss, if any.
(c) Participation certificates managed on the basis of investment agency (*Wakala*)	These are documents that represent projects or activities that are managed on the basis of investment agency by appointing an agent to manage the operation on behalf of the certificate holders.	Issuer: is an investment agent. Subscribers are: the principals. Mobilised funds: are the subject-matter of investment. Certificate holders: own the assets represented by the certificates with its risks.

Table 9.5. Participation certificates

Types of investment *sukuk*	Description of investment *sukuk*	*Sharia'a* rulings and requirements
9. *Muzara'a* (sharecropping) certificates	These are documents of equal value issued for the sake of using the mobilised funds in financing a *Muzara'a* contract. The certificate holders become entitled to a share in the crop as per agreement.	Issuer: is the landlord. Subscribers are: farmers who invest on the basis of the *Muzara'a* contract. Mobilised funds: are the cultivation cost. Certificate holders: are entitled to a share of the produce of the land as per the agreement.
10. *Musaqa* (irrigation) certificates	These are documents of equal value issued on the basis of a *Musaqa* contract for the sake of using the mobilised funds for irrigating trees that produce fruit and meeting other expenses relating to maintenance of the trees. The certificate holders become entitled to a share in the crop as per agreement.	Issuer: is the owner of the land that consists of trees. Subscribers are: those who assume the irrigation process on the basis of *Musaqa* contract. Mobilised funds: stand as the maintenance cost of the trees. Certificate holders: are entitled to a share in the produce of the trees as per the agreement.
11. *Mugarasa* (agricultural) certificates	These are documents of equal value issued on the basis of a *Mugarasa* contract for the sake of using the mobilised funds for planting trees and meeting expenses of the work. The certificate holders become entitled to a share in the land and the plantation.	Issuer: is the owner of the land that is suitable for planting trees. Subscribers are: those who assume the agricultural or horticultural process on the basis of *Mugarasa* contract. Mobilised funds: stand as the cost of maintaining the plantation. Certificate holders: are entitled to a share in both the land and trees as per the agreement.
12. Concession certificates	These are documents of equal value that are issued for the sake of using the mobilised funds to finance execution of a concession offer in which case the certificate holders become entitled to rights associated with the concession.	

***Source:* Exposure Draft of AAOIFI Sharia'a Standard No.18, p.4.**

Table 9.6. Agricultural oriented and concession certificates

Are *sukuk* Islamic? The controversy

Sheikh Taqi Usmani, Chairman of the AAOIFI *Sharia'a* Board commented, in late 2007, that about 85% of Islamic bonds (*sukuk*) did not really comply with *Sharia'a* law. Usmani was in fact principally referring to equity-based *sukuk*, *Mudaraba* and *Musharaka*, rather than *Ijara* and the other *sukuk*. In practice he meant 85% of only the equity-based *sukuk*. The whole rationale for the creation of *sukuk* was to create an Islamically acceptable instrument that did not have the *Ribawi* (meaning linked to *riba*) elements associated with conventional bonds. Usmani's comments paralysed the industry.

Some 160 institutions from more than 30 countries are members of AAOIFI. The AAOIFI standards are mandatory in Bahrain, the Dubai International Financial Centre, Jordan, Qatar, Sudan and Syria, and are used as guidelines elsewhere. Note that AAOIFI standards are not mandatory in Malaysia. AAOIFI has a board of 20 *Sharia'a* Scholars, who are also members of the *Sharia'a* Boards of most of the world's largest financial institutions. Hence the industry-wide paralysis. What did Taqi Usmani say? His comments revolved around three issues:

Issue 1

> 'If *sukuk* are to be issued for existing businesses then the *sukuk* must ensure that *sukuk* holders have complete ownership in real assets.'

Reasoning behind Issue 1

What distinguishes *sukuk* from conventional bonds is that they represent ownership in assets that bring profits and/or leased assets that bring revenues. However many *sukuk*, he argued, have been issued in which there is doubt as to whether they really represent ownership.

Issue 2

> 'If there is to be an incentive for the *sukuk* manager it should be based on the profits expected from the enterprise and not on the basis of an interest rate. It is unlawful for a manager to lend money when actual profits are less than expected.'

Reasoning behind Issue 2

Many *sukuk* stipulate a return to the *sukuk* manager based on LIBOR under the assumption, some might say pretence, that this is an incentive for good management. However Usmani points out that any incentive should be based on the difference between expected profits and actual profits. The LIBOR link has nothing to do with measuring business efficiency and everything to do with the need to market the products. In addition Usmani points out that in the event of a shortfall if funds are paid to *sukuk* holders then effectively they are provided with a loan. Either way the returns to *sukuk* holders are not applying *Sharia'a* investment principles of risk and return with too many of them offering effectively fixed returns.

Issue 3

> 'It is unlawful for a manager to commit to repurchase assets at face value. Instead their resale must be undertaken on the basis of the net value of the assets, or at a price that is agreed at the time of purchase.'

Reasoning behind Issue 3

A promise to pay back capital, irrespective of the performance of the asset, violates the principle of risk- and profit sharing on which *sukuk* should be based. As Usmani said 'You must face the actual consequences of your investment. For current *sukuk*, risk is not shared and reward is not shared according to the actual venture proceeds. About 85% of *sukuk* are structured this way.'

Without a repurchase agreement at a set price, on maturity, the return on the *sukuk* would depend upon the performance of the underlying asset, which may deter issuers and investors looking for the steady predictable returns of bonds. Many of the *sukuk* investors have, in fact, been conventional investors seeking these fixed returns.

Following AAOIFI meetings in Medina, Mecca and Bahrain a press release was issued in late February 2008 designed to clarify the *Sharia'a* status of *sukuk*. There were five key issues in the press release:

1) 'All tradable *sukuk* should represent holdings of the *sukuk* holders with all their relevant rights and obligations in physical assets that may be legally and lawfully acquired whether in kind, usufruct or services in line with the *Sharia'a* Standards.'
   Implications: At face value this means that a True Sale (meaning ownership of the assets must legally move), with all the SPV implications, are now the only form of acceptable *sukuk*. If this is the case then it would have dramatic implications, particularly for sovereign *sukuk*. Most governments issuing *sukuk* use strategic assets, airports, hospitals etc to back the *sukuk*. They may now be reluctant to risk losing ownership of these assets.
2) 'The tradable *sukuk* should not normally represent either payables or revenues.'
   Implications: This is presumably to exclude *Murabaha* and *Salam sukuk* which are debt based and only being tradeable in the secondary market at face value. Hence the payables comment. However with revenues the returns payable to *sukuk* holders are based on revenues earned from the underlying asset and should be eminently acceptable under the *Sharia'a*.

3) '*Sukuk* managers are not allowed to commit to lend *sukuk* holders any deficits that may arise between expected and realised profits. A provision may be formed to make up such deficits as possible provided that such is stipulated in the prospectus.'
   Implications: This does not seem to deal with Usmani's criticisms. If there is a shortfall, Usmani would argue, that should be reflected in the payout to the *sukuk* holder in line with *Sharia'a* principles. A reserve is perfectly acceptable but where does the reserve come from? If it is from capital then investors should be told that a proportion of their investment will not go towards potential returns based on PLS. If it is based on returns then what if only losses have occurred?

4) 'The *Mudarib*, *Sharik* or investment agent should not undertake to buy the assets from the *sukuk* holders at face value at maturity date. However this undertaking may be based on the net asset value, market value, cash equivalent value or any price agreed upon at the time of purchase.'
   Implications: With regard to purchase undertakings if you have a clause which says 'for a price agreed at the time of purchase' is this not tantamount to a potential guarantee? In other words this ruling is unclear.

5) 'The *Sharia'a* Supervisory Board should verify all contracts and ensure that all stages are in compliance with *Sharia'a* Standards.'
   Implications: This seems to suggest that *Sharia'a* Board responsibilities are to become far more onerous regarding scrutiny than they have been in the past. This, of course, may be highly desirable from a *Sharia'a* perspective. However given the shortage of scholars this seems to potentially slow down the growth of the industry, possibly considerably.

Appendix 9.1 The Central Bank of Bahrain (CBB) *Salam* *sukuk* programme

The Kingdom of Bahrain hosts the largest concentration of banks and other financial institutions in the Middle East. Bahrain has emerged as the world's Islamic financial capital with 29 Islamic financial institutions and 15 Islamic insurance companies, as at January 2008.

The first *sukuk* issuance programme, and certainly the longest continuous one, is the Central Bank of Bahrain *Salam sukuk* programme. Originally launched by its predecessor, the Bahrain Monetary agency (BMA), it provides an early example of product innovation in an industry which has rapidly evolved ever since. An example of the details of the *sukuk* are given below.

CBB *sukuk al-salam* securities fully subscribed
28 April 2008 – The Central Bank of Bahrain (CBB) announces that the monthly issue of the *sukuk al-salam* Islamic bonds has been fully subscribed.
Subscriptions worth BD 6 million were received for the BD 6 million issue, which carries a maturity of 91 days.
The expected return on the issue, which begins on 30 April 2008 and matures on 30 July 2008, is 2.15%.
The *sukuk* are issued by the CBB on behalf of the Government of the Kingdom of Bahrain.
This is issue No. 84 of *Sukuk al-salam* bonds.
Source: *Gulf Daily News*

CBB: *al salam sukuk* (Islamic short-term securities)

The securities are based on the Islamic concept of '*al salam*' and accordingly referred to as '*al salam sukuk*' securities. The product has been structured in full compliance with Islamic Law (the *Sharia'a*).

The concept of al salam

Al salam is essentially a transaction where two parties agree to carry out a sale and purchase of an underlying asset at a future date but at a price determined and fully paid for today. The seller agrees to deliver the asset in the agreed quantity and quality to the buyer at a future date. This is similar to the conventional futures contract.

However, the big difference is that in an *al salam* sale the buyer pays the entire amount in full at the time the contract is initiated. The contract also stipulates that the payment should be in the form of cash. The idea behind such a prepayment requirement has traditionally to do with the fact that the objective in an *al salam* contract is to help businesses with working capital financing. The buyer in the contract therefore is often an Islamic financial institution. Since there is full prepayment an *al salam* sale is clearly beneficial to the seller.

An *al salam* contract is subject to several conditions. The most important ones are as follows:

- Full payment by the buyer at the time of effecting the sale.
- The underlying asset must be standardisable, easily quantifiable and of determinate quality.
- An *al salam* contract cannot be based on a uniquely identified underlying asset.
- The underlying asset should be something that is to be produced or purchased by the seller.
- Quantity, quality, the date, and place of delivery must be clearly enumerated in an *al salam* contract.

It should be noted that the exchange traded futures contract would conform to all these conditions with the exception of the first condition, which requires full advance payment, by the buyer. However, given the customised nature of *al salam*, it more closely resembles forward contracts rather than futures contracts. Thus some of the problems of forwards; namely, double coincidence; negotiated price and counterparty risk can exist in an *al salam* sale.

Counterparty risk however, would be one sided, in that, since the buyer has fully paid for the goods in advance it is only the buyer who faces the seller's default risk and not both ways, as in forwards. In order to overcome the potential for default on the part of the seller, the *Sharia'a* allows the buyer to require security. This may be in the form of a guarantee.

An example of *al salam* contract

An *al salam* contract can be constructed in such a way as to provide an alternative investment opportunity for Islamic banks. For example, a bank can buy 10,000 ingots of aluminium from a local manufacturer to be delivered after 3 months at, say $100 each, and pay fully in advance. At the same time, the bank can appoint an agent to market the promised quantity at the time of delivery at say $102 each. The difference between the purchase price and the sale price is the profit to the bank.

The CBB *sukuk* – structure

Aluminium has been designated as the underlying asset of the *al salam* contract. The Government of Bahrain will sell aluminium to the buyer. One bank, namely the Bahrain Islamic Bank (BIB), has been nominated to represent the other banks wishing to participate in the *al salam* contract. BIB has been delegated to sign the contracts and all other necessary documents on behalf of the other banks in the syndicate.

As consideration for this advance payment the Government of Bahrain will undertake to supply a specified amount of aluminium at a future date. At the same time, the buyer will appoint the Government of Bahrain as an agent to market the quantity at the time of delivery through its channels of distribution. The Government of Bahrain will provide an additional undertaking to the representative, Bahrain Islamic Bank (BIB), to market the aluminium at a price, which will provide a return to *al salam* security holder's equivalent to returns available through other conventional short-term money market instruments. This means that the securities have the characteristics of short-term government treasury bills.

The investors in *sukuk* will bear counterparty, as well as market risks. The counterparty risk would arise with regard to the possibility of the Government being unable to deliver the goods. The market risk would result from the Government being unable to market the aluminium at the time of the delivery. These risks are mitigated by the structure of the deal. It should be noted that the risk essentially translates into a sovereign risk on the Government of Bahrain.

Sukuk al-salam

Salam is the sale of a specific commodity, well defined in its quality and quantity which will be delivered to the purchaser on a fixed date in the future against an advanced full payment of price at spot. *Sukuk al-salam* are certificates of equal value issued for the purpose of mobilising *salam* capital so that the goods to be delivered on the basis of *salam* come to the ownership of the certificate holders.

The issuer of the certificates is a seller of the goods of *salam*, the subscribers are the buyers of the goods, while the funds realised from subscription are the purchase price (*salam* capital) of the goods. The holders of *salam* certificates are the owners of the *salam* goods and are entitled to the sale price of the certificates or the sale price of the *salam* goods sold through a parallel *salam*, if any.

Salam-based securities may be created and sold by an SPV under which the funds mobilised from investors are paid as an advance to the company SPV in return for a promise to deliver a commodity at a future date. SPV can also appoint an agent to market the promised quantity at the time of delivery perhaps at a higher price. The difference between the purchase price and the sale price is the profit to the SPV and hence to the holders of the *sukuk*.

All standard *Sharia'a* requirements that apply to *salam* also apply to *sukuk al-salam*, such as, full payment by the buyer at the time of effecting the sale, standardised nature of underlying asset, clear enumeration of quantity, quality, date and place of delivery of the asset and the like.

One of the *Sharia'a* conditions relating to *salam*, as well as for creation of *sukuk al-salam*, is the requirement that the purchased goods are not re-sold before actual possession at maturity. Such transactions amount to selling of debt. This constraint renders the *salam* instrument illiquid and hence somewhat less attractive to investors. Thus, an investor will buy a *salam* certificate if he expects prices of the underlying commodity to be higher on the maturity date. Figure 9A.1 illustrates the details of the transaction.

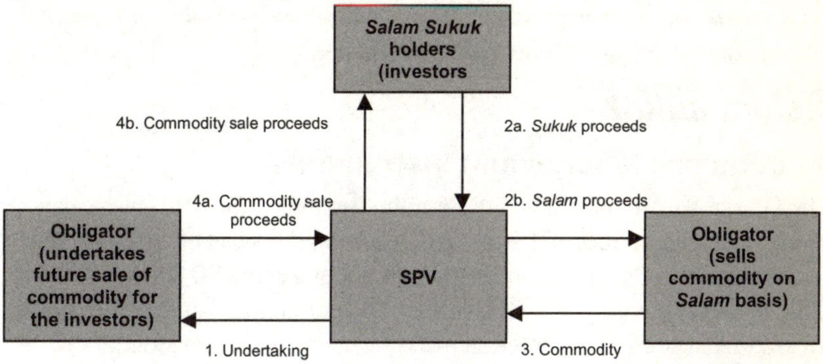

Figure 9A.1. *Sukuk al-salam* transaction structure

Steps involved in the transaction

1) SPV signs an undertaking with an obligator to source both commodities and buyers. The obligator contracts to buy, on behalf of the end-*sukuk* holders, the commodity and then to sell it for the profit of the *sukuk* holders.
2) Then:
   - *Salam* certificates are issued to investors and SPV receives *sukuk* proceeds.
   - The *salam* proceeds are passed onto the obligator who sells the commodity on a forward basis.
3) SPV receives the commodities from the obligator.
4) Then:
   - Obligator, on behalf of *sukuk* holders, sells the commodities for a profit.
   - *Sukuk* holders receive the commodity sale proceeds.

Sukuk al-salam in practice

As mentioned aluminium has been designated as the underlying asset of the Bahrain Government *al salam* contract, whereby it promises to sell aluminium to the buyer at a specified future date in return for a full price payment in advance.

One bank, namely the Bahrain Islamic Bank (BIB), has been nominated to represent the other banks wishing to participate in the *al salam* contract. BIB has been delegated to sign the contracts and all other necessary documents on behalf of the other banks in the syndicate. At the same time, the buyer appoints the Government of Bahrain as an agent to market the appropriate quantity, at the time of delivery, through its channels of distribution.

The Government of Bahrain provides an additional undertaking to the representative (BIB) to market the aluminium at a price, which will provide a return to *al salam* security holder's equivalent to those available through other conventional short-term money market instruments.

Salam sukuk

Auction procedures and instruments

The Central Bank of Bahrain (CBB) is authorised under the CBB law to issue money market securities and other debt securities on behalf of the Government of the Kingdom of Bahrain with an amount not exceeding BD 900 million. The CBB issues various government securities on a continuous basis. It also provides an array of facilities for commercial banks operating in the Kingdom.

Summarised below is a brief description of the CBB's operations with respect to issuance of government securities, ranges of facilities the CBB provides to commercial banks, and commercial banks reserve requirements and obligations.

Al salam Government *sukuk* (BD)

- Issued in accordance with *Sharia'a* standards.
- Issued on a monthly basis.
- Maturity period of 91 days.
- Issue amount of BD 6,000,000.
- Total outstanding al *salam sukuk* as of April 30 2007: BD 18 million.

CBB procedures

- Circulation of invitation letters that include details on the issue to all commercial banks and to both the Pension Fund Commission and the General Organisation for Social Insurance.
- Receive tenders.
- Tenders are then allotted according to quantity contribution.
- The CBB sends the individual results of the allotment to each participating institution.
- Settlement of *al salam sukuk* is processed within the CBB according to the allotment results.

Appendix 9.2
Salam sukuk: Term Sheet[1]

Government of Bahrain non-negotiable Government *salam* securities

Regulations and terms of issue

1) Nature and legality of *Salam* securities
   Salam government securities are an instrument representing assets (raw aluminium) and which are accounted as a liability sold against deferred delivery. The Government of Bahrain issues these securities to create a new avenue for the investment of surplus financing resources in society and to provide short-term financing for the expenditure and needs of various development projects. In issuing *Salam* securities, the Government of Bahrain undertakes to sell commodities to be delivered in the future to the investors for advance payment in the value of securities issued. The securities are kept until the delivery date. The investor may be authorised to receive the proceeds arising from sale of commodities to an independent party who is neither wholly nor partially owned by the seller, at a price exceeding the forward buying price. The Central Bank of Bahrain will perform the necessary arrangements and formalities of this issue.

2) Guarantee of Securities and expected return
   The Bahrain government, as an agent of the holders of the securities – via a delegation agreement which is separate from the *Salam* agreement, promised to sell the commodities of the *Salam* agreement to an independent party who is neither wholly or partially owned by it, at an expected profit margin of (--%).

3) Issue date, issue period and maturity date
   These securities shall be issued on -- or -- or ----. The date for the delivery for the commodities shall be -- or -- or ---- which is the date of these securities.

4) Issue price
   These securities shall be issued at their full nominal value.

5) Volume of issue
   The volume of issue shall total US$25 million.

6) Minimum subscription limit
   Minimum subscription limit shall be US$10,000.

7) Subscription in excess of the issue volume
   If the value of the subscription exceeds the value of the issue, the CBB shall allocate the securities to applicants according to percentage unless the agency of issue (Bahrain Government) decides to raise the issue volume by raising the quantity of the commodities scheduled to be sold by means of forward buying.

8) Issue records
   The security certificates allocated in the name of applicant shall be recorded in a special record established for this purpose with the CBB.

9) Submission of applications
   Applications must be delivered to the CBB during the subscription day, by latest at 10 o'clock in the morning on ----, -- or -- or ----. Applications may be sent by fax or telex.

10) Rejection of applications
    The CBB shall have the absolute right to reject any application fully or in part without providing the reason for rejection.

11) Payment of the value
    Payment shall be in US dollars by transferring the value of the allocated securities to the accounts of CBB.

12) Payment of the sale price
    The CBB shall pay the sale price in US dollars to the security holders by transferring the relevant amounts to their bank accounts on the due date.

13) Qualified investors
    All commercial banks and Islamic banking and financial institutions operating in Bahrain are entitled to invest in these securities.

14) Applicable law
    This issue and all documents pertaining thereto shall be subject to provisions of Islamic Law. The Bahraini Law Courts shall have jurisdiction to consider any dispute arising with respect to this issue.

15) Affirmation of the legality of the issue under Islamic law
    The legality of this issue and compatibility with the provisions and principles of Islamic law have been declared by Legal Opinion given on 28/2/1421 AH corresponding to 1/6/2000 by the *Sharia'a* Economic Committee appointed by the General Secretariat of the International Islamic Fiqh Assembly, Jeddah, and the Fatwa issued by the CBB appointed *Sharia'a* Committee, comprising:
    - Dr Abdul Satar Abu Qhuda,
    - Shaikh Abdulla bin Sulman Al Manie,
    - Shaikh Abdul Hussan Al Asfour,
    - Shaikh Mohamed Taqi Al Usmani.

16) Conformity with *Sharia'a* law
    The *Sharia'a* Committee of the Government *Salam* securities (listed above), who are appointed by the CBB, shall be responsible of following up the execution of this issue to ensure its conformity with the *Sharia'a* laws.

[1] This term sheet is modelled on the original BMA *Salam sukuk* term sheet and should not be taken as being fully representative of the current CBB *sukuk* programme.

Chapter 10

Islamic real estate investment trusts

What is a REIT?

A REIT is a company that owns and manages property on behalf of shareholders. A REIT can contain commercial and or residential property. REITs provide a mechanism for investors to invest in property related assets without having to buy property directly.

Combining real estate and unit trust funds

REITs are collective investment vehicles (typically in the form of unit trust funds) that pool money from investors to buy, manage and sell real estate. The objective is to obtain reasonable returns on investment. Returns are generated from rental income plus any capital appreciation that comes from holding the real estate assets over an investment period. Unit holders receive their returns in the form of dividends or distributions and capital gains for the holding period.

REITs, in general, combine the best features of real estate and trust funds, and sit between bonds and equities as an asset class. There are listed and non-listed REITs. Listed REITs may be bought and sold through a broker like listed stocks. Non-listed REITs may be bought from, and sold to, the management company or through other authorised agents. REITs, particularly the listed ones, are liquid assets and can be sold quickly to raise cash and take advantage of other investment opportunities.

By buying a REIT unit, the holder actually owns a fraction of a pool of real estate that generates income via renting, leasing and selling the said property. As an added bonus, REITs provide a platform for international investors to invest in real property without the hassle and responsibilities associated with direct ownership of such assets.

Real estate investment trusts (REITs)

A US REIT is a tax designation for a corporation investing in real estate that reduces or eliminates corporate income taxes. In return, REITs are required to distribute 90% of their income, which may be taxable, back to the investors. The REIT structure was designed to provide a similar structure for investment in real estate as mutual funds provide for investment in stocks.

In the UK REITs can apply for 'UK-REIT' status which exempts the company from corporate tax. Attaining UK-REIT status removes the potential for 'double taxation' at both the corporate and the investor level and is intended to help align returns from property held within REIT structures with property held directly. Like other corporations, REITs can be publicly or privately held. Public REITs may be listed on public stock exchanges like shares of common stock in other firms.REITs can be classified as equity, mortgage or hybrid.

REITs have received close attention from property investors as they offer to cut out the risk and hassle inherent in actually buying and owning bricks and mortar. They also allow the average investor access to areas of the property market such as shopping centres and offices, normally reserved for extremely wealthy individuals. Essentially a REIT is a stock market for property with investors contributing to a pool of money managed by the trust. In turn, the trust invests the collected assets in a number of properties, either commercial or residential, across the world and investors share in the profits from rent, leasing and sales according to their level of investment. REITs are now the focus of Islamic investors with an alternative Islamic asset class now evolving.

Features of REITs*

REITs are special purpose business trusts or corporations that purchase, own and manage income generating real estate assets. Essentially they can be seen as 'Pass-through' entities that distribute the majority of their net income to their unit or shareholders. Table 10.1 illustrates the characteristics of REITs showing a typical REIT structure: REIT rules and regulations vary across countries.

What is a REIT?	A passive investment vehicle (corporate or business trust) managed by a professional fund manager
What does a REIT invest in?	Typically acquires stable income generating real estate assets
How is income distributed?	After tax income from assets is consolidated into the REIT and distributed to unit holders. A REIT must distribute all or most of its income to unit or shareholders
How does a REIT increase in value?	By increasing returns, acquiring properties and through asset enhancement
How is a REIT governed?	Subject to a 'REIT Code' equivalent, which typically enforces strict corporate governance, transparency, conservative gearing levels, investment restrictions and minimum distribution levels
Unit holders level of control	Independent Trustee and often an external REIT manager. High corporate governance with regards to investment decisions and income distribution
Reasons for establishing a REIT	Access funding for financing real estate or efficient and attractive financing option or means of transferring assets off balance sheet

* Typical REIT structure. REIT rules and regulations vary across countries.

***Source*: HSBC**

Table 10.1 Characteristics of REITs

REITs versus alternative real estate investments*

REITs generally give investors access to the yield and potential capital gain returns of a portfolio of property assets, plus the liquidity generally associated with investing directly in a listed property company. Table 10.2 illustrates how REITs compare with alternative property related investment vehicles.

	REITs	Direct property ownership	Real estate company equity	Corporate property bonds
Type of investment	Unit is a listed trust or share of corporation owning rental properties	Investment in physical real estate	Shares of a listed company owning real estate and other businesses	Debt issued by the underlying real estate company
Payout	Majority of taxable income paid to unit holders	Majority of income paid to owner	Discretionary dividends to shareholders	Fixed payout
Investment strategy	Focused activity	Focused activity	Investment choices determined by the company board	Investment choices determined by the company board
Liquidity	Liquid investment	Illiquid investment	Liquid investment	Liquid investment
Diversification	Diversified portfolio	Concentration risk	Diversified portfolio	Concentration risk
Risk	Perceived low risk	Perceived high risk	Perceived high risk	Perceived low risk
Gearing	Gearing is limited to approx 35%	High gearing between 80-100%	Moderate gearing level	Moderate gearing level

Indicative of typical REITs. Structures may vary depending on country specific regulations

Source: HSBC

Table 10.2. REITs versus alternative forms of property investing

Figure 10.1 illustrates the structure of a typical REIT.

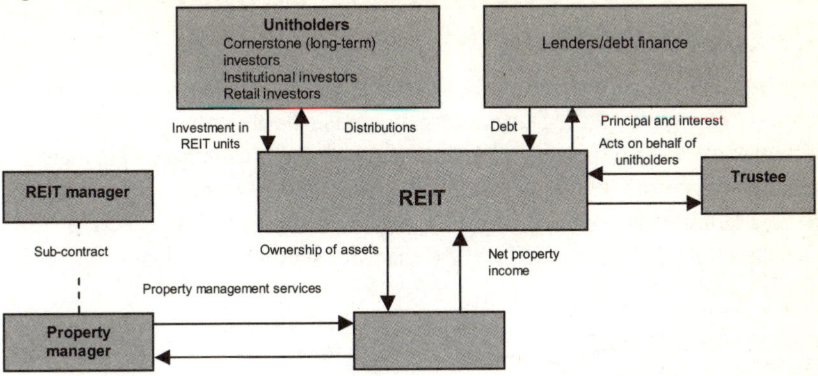

Figure 10.1. Typical REIT structure

What are Sharia'a compliant REITs?

In the context of *Sharia'a* compliant funds, REITs are becoming increasingly popular fund structures that can be offered in accordance with the *Sharia'a*. *Sharia'a* compliant REITs are essentially listed collective investment schemes where funds from investors are pooled and invested in a portfolio of *Sharia'a* compliant real estate assets, or real estate related assets. These assets are usually leased out to a third party (commonly under an *Ijara* structure) and rentals from the leased assets form the income of the REIT which can then be distributed to unit holders.

Recent *Sharia'a* compliant REIT structures have used *Ijara* as the basis of the investment. The typical *Ijara* REIT structure is set out in figure 10.2 below.

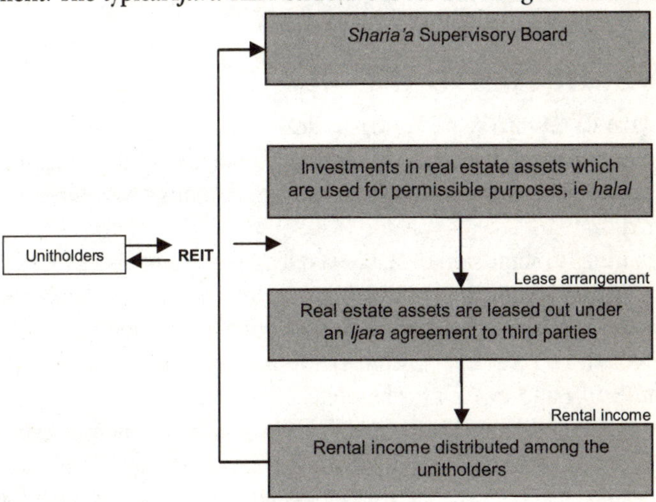

Figure 10.2. Summary of an *Ijara*-based REIT

Sharia'a compliant REITs under the DFSA regulatory regime

The Dubai Financial Services Authority (DFSA) permits REITs to be established and offered in or from the Dubai International Financial Centre (DIFC). Although there is no specific DFSA module for *Sharia'a* compliant REITs, the regime does permit REIT structures, and also permits *Sharia'a* compliant funds to be established and offered in or from the DIFC. An example of a REIT established in the DIFC could have the characteristics set out in figure 10.3 below.

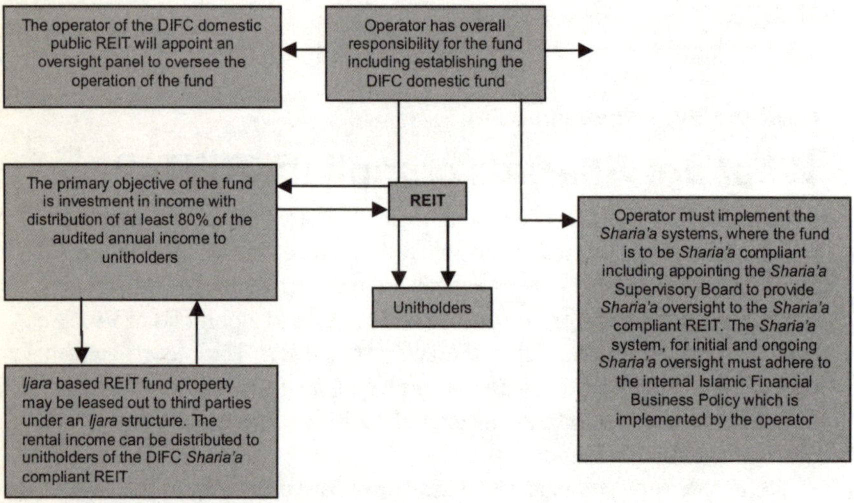

***Source*: Praesidium LLP**

Figure 10.3. An example of a DFSA REIT structure

Malaysian REITs (M-REITs)

REITs in Malaysia (M-REITs) are known as Real Estate Property Trusts. They are regulated under Securities Commission's (SC) guidelines released in January 2005, which superseded the earlier guidelines on Property Trust Funds issued in November 2002.

The Securities Commission of Malaysia released the Guidelines for Islamic Real Estate Trusts (Islamic REITs Guidelines) in November 2005, making the country the first jurisdiction to introduce such guidelines in the global Islamic finance sector and set a global benchmark for the development of Islamic REITs. See *Appendix 10.1* and *10.2* for further details.

The thrust of the Islamic REITs Guidelines is to provide a new investment opportunity for those who wish to invest in real estate through *Sharia'a* compliant capital market instruments. The guidelines facilitate the creation of a new asset class for investors and allow fund managers to diversify their investment sources and portfolios further. Figure 10.4 illustrates the permissible investments for Malaysian REITs.

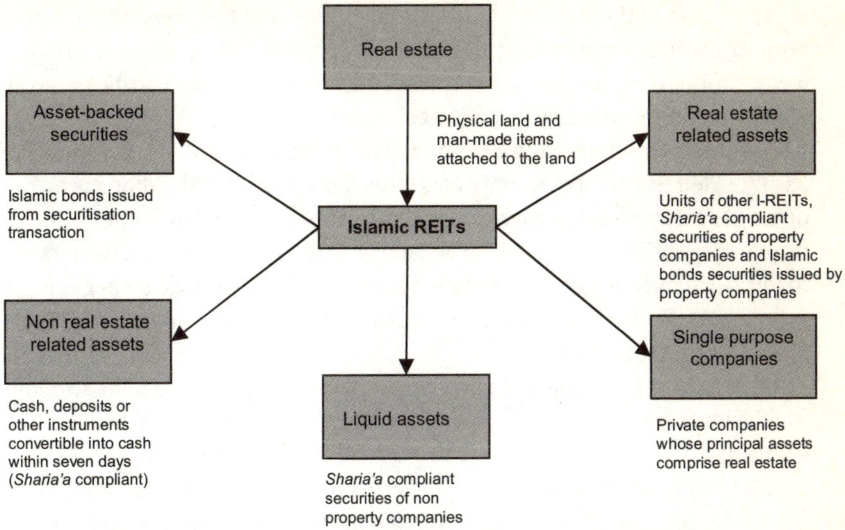

Figure 10.4. Malaysian *Sharia'a* permissible investments for I-REITs

Following the issuance of the Islamic REITs Guidelines, KPJ Healthcare became the first Malaysian company to establish and launch Islamic REITs. KPJ Healthcare identified seven hospitals within the group as its main asset class for the establishment of the REITs. In February 2007, Al-Hadharah Boustead REIT became the second Islamic REIT listed on Bursa Malaysia and the first Islamic plantation REIT to provide an opportunity for investors to participate in plantation ownership.

The Islamic REITs Guidelines complement existing guidelines on REITs, with the latter providing general rules on all aspects of investments in REITs and the former acting as a guide on *Sharia'a* compliance in structuring and managing Islamic REITs.

As required under the Islamic REITs Guidelines, market players must appoint a *Sharia'a* committee or advisor to review, monitor and approve investments by Islamic REITs. The main criteria covered include rental of real estate for business purposes, investment, deposit and financing, *Takaful* schemes and forward sales or purchases of currency for risk management.

Rental of real estate is permissible, except where the property is used for non-permissible activities such as financial services based on interest *(riba)*, gambling or gaming, conventional insurance, entertainment activities that are forbidden by *Sharia'a* law, manufacturing or sale of tobacco-based products or related products, stock-broking or share trading in non-*Sharia'a* compliant securities, and hotels and resorts.

Apart from the activities listed above, the *Sharia'a* committee advisor can apply *Ijtihad* (the process of making a legal decision by independent interpretation of the sources of the law, the *Qur'an* and the *Sunna*) for other non-permissible activities to be included as a criterion in assessing the rental income for Islamic REITs. The benchmark for non-permissible activities is set at 20% of total turnover of the Islamic REIT.

To promote Malaysia further as an Islamic financial centre, the government has provided several tax incentives for foreign investors. Withholding tax on dividends received was reduced from 20% to 10% and a REIT is fully exempted from paying income tax on taxable income if it distributes at least 90% of income to investors. Encouraged by this development, foreign investors are beginning to actively seek *Sharia'a* compliant structures as an opportunity to invest in Malaysia's property market.

As an added attraction, the government proposed, in Budget 2008, to allow foreign investors to increase their equity ownership in a REIT management company up to 70% (previously 49%). With this measure, the Malaysian REIT industry, including Islamic REITs, is expected to benefit through the transfer of knowledge and expertise, as higher foreign ownership will enhance the level of REIT management expertise. Over time, such a move should benefit the Malaysian REIT industry, not only through the injection of fresh capital and innovative methods, but also through the development of the industry's broad skills base and the introduction of new technology.

It is anticipated that the emergence of greater competition through enhanced foreign participation will bolster activity and efficiency within the industry. Higher foreign ownership will allow foreign corporations with REIT management expertise to set up operations in Malaysia.

Saudi Arabian REITs

Geneva-based Encore, an independent Swiss asset management company, together with Saudi partner Sumou Holding, in October 2008, launched the first Saudi *Sharia'a* compliant Real Estate Investment Trust. Sumou is the operational manager, while Encore Fund Management of Bahrain is the fund manager of the trust. The size of the REIT was not explicitly defined but it is possible that it may reach more than SAR5 billion.

Appendix 10.1
Guidelines for Malaysian Islamic real estate investment trusts

1.Rental of real estate by an Islamic REIT for business purposes

1.1 Acquiring real estate with existing tenant(s)

- *Sharia'a* compliant assessments must be carried out by the appointed *Sharia'a* committee or *Sharia'a* advisor to assess any property to be acquired by an Islamic REIT. In general, an Islamic REIT is a collective investment scheme in real estate, in which the tenant(s) operates permissible activities according to the *Sharia'a*. However, in the event that the tenant(s) is found to operate non-permissible activities, the fund manager for the Islamic REIT must perform additional compliance assessments.
- The fund manager must obtain the rental from each non-permissible activity operating at the property to be acquired. Rental from each non-permissible activity must be added to obtain the total rental from non-permissible activities. The list of non-permissible activities, as decided by the *Sharia'a* Advisory Council (SAC) of the Securities Commission are detailed below.
- Subsequently, the total rental from non-permissible activities will be compared to the total turnover of the Islamic REIT (latest financial year) to obtain the percentage of rental from non-permissible activities. The percentage amount will be referred to the 20% benchmark as determined by the SAC for the criteria on rental from non-permissible activities.
- In the event that the percentage exceeds the benchmark, the *Sharia'a* committee or *Sharia'a* advisor shall advise the Islamic REIT fund manager not to invest in the said real estate.
- However, an Islamic REIT is not permitted to own real estate, for example, a building, in which all the tenants operate non-permissible activities, even if the percentage of rental from that building to the total turnover of the Islamic REIT is still below the benchmark (20%). This is to protect the image of the Islamic REIT.

1.2 Renting out real estate to a new tenant(s)

- The *Sharia'a* committee or *Sharia'a* advisor must advise the Islamic REIT fund manager not to accept a new tenant(s) whose activities are fully non-permissible.

1.3 The method for calculating the portion of rental of non-permissible activities from the total rental paid by a tenant(s) operating mixed activities (non-permissible and permissible activities) is as follows:

- Calculation of the rental of non-permissible activities from a tenant(s) operating mixed activities can be based on the ratio of area occupied for non-permissible activities to the total area occupied. The percentage will be used as the basis for determining the ratio of rental of non-permissible activities to total rental paid by the tenant(s).

- For activities that do not involve the usage of space, such as service-based activities, the calculation method will be based on the *Ijtihad* of the *Sharia'a* committee or *Sharia'a* advisor of the Islamic REIT. *Ijtihad* is the process of reasoning by Islamic jurist to obtain legal rulings from the sources of *Sharia'a*.

2.Investment, deposit and financing for an Islamic REIT

2.1 An Islamic REIT must ensure that all forms of investment, deposit and financing instruments comply with the *Sharia'a* principles.

3.Insurance

3.1 An Islamic REIT must use the *Takaful* schemes to insure its real estate. If the *Takaful* schemes are unable to provide the insurance coverage, then the Islamic REIT is permitted to use the conventional insurance schemes.

4.Forward sales or purchase of currency for risk management

4.1 An Islamic REIT is permitted to participate in forward sales or purchases of currency, and is encouraged to deal with Islamic financial institutions. If the Islamic REIT deals with Islamic financial institutions, then it will be bound by the concept of *Wa'd*. *Wa'd* means a promise whereby only one party is obligated to fulfil his promise or responsibility. The party that is bound is the party that initiates the promise.

However if the Islamic REIT deals with conventional financial institutions, it is permitted to participate in the conventional forward sales or purchases of currency.

Rental activities that are classified as non-permissible

- Financial services based on *riba* (interest).
- Gambling or gaming.
- Manufacture or sale of non-*halal* products or related products.
- Conventional insurance.
- Entertainment activities that are non-permissible according to the *Sharia'a*.
- Manufacture or sale of tobacco-based products or related products.

- Stock broking or share trading in *Sharia'a* non-compliant securities.
- Hotels and resorts.

Apart from the activities listed above, the *Sharia'a* committee or *Sharia'a* advisor can apply *Ijtihad* for other activities that may be deemed non-permissible to be included as a criterion in assessing the rental income for the Islamic REIT.

Date issued: 21 November 2005

Source: Malaysian Securities Commission

Appendix 10.2
Frequently asked questions about Malaysian Islamic real estate investment trusts

1. Is an Islamic real estate investment trust (Islamic REIT) permitted to own (purchase) real estate in which the tenant(s) operates mixed activities that are permissible and non-permissible according to the Sharia'a?

An Islamic REIT is permitted to own (purchase) real estate in which its tenant(s) operate mixed activities that are permissible and non-permissible, according to the *Sharia'a*.

However, the Islamic REIT fund manager must perform some additional compliance assessments before acquiring real estate that has a tenant(s) who operate mixed activities.

2. What are the additional compliance assessments?

An Islamic REIT must obtain the total rental from non-permissible activities from the property that it wants to acquire, and subsequently compare the total rental from non-permissible activities to the total turnover of the Islamic REIT (latest financial year). This is to obtain the percentage of rental from non-permissible activities. The percentage amount will be referred to the 20% benchmark as determined by the *Sharia'a* Advisory Council (SAC) of the Securities Commission for the criteria on rental from non-permissible activities. In the event that the percentage exceeds the benchmark, the *Sharia'a* committee or *Sharia'a* advisor shall advise the Islamic REIT fund manager not to invest in the said real estate.

For example, if the total rental from non-permissible activities is RM210, 000 and the total turnover of the Islamic REIT for that financial year is RM1, 000,000, then the percentage of rental from non-permissible activities is 21%, which exceeds the 20% benchmark that has been determined by the SAC. In this situation, the *Sharia'a* committee or *Sharia'a* advisor shall advise the Islamic REIT fund manager not to invest in the said real estate.

3. What are non-permissible activities?

Rental activities that are classified as non-permissible as decided by the SAC are:

1) financial services based on *riba* (interest);
2) gambling or gaming;
3) manufacture or sale of non-*halal* products or related products;
4) conventional insurance;
5) entertainment activities that are non-permissible according to the *Sharia'a;*
6) manufacture or sale of tobacco-based products or related products;
7) stock broking or share trading in *Sharia'a* non-compliant securities;
8) hotels and resorts.

Apart from the activities listed above, the *Sharia'a* committee or *Sharia'a* advisor can apply *Ijtihad,* the process of reasoning by Islamic jurists to obtain legal rulings from the sources of *Sharia'a,* for other activities that may be deemed non-permissible to be included as a criterion in assessing the rental income for the Islamic REIT.

4. Can an Islamic REIT own real estate in which all the tenants operate non-permissible activities?

No. An Islamic REIT is not permitted to own real estate, in which all the tenants operate non-permissible activities, for example a casino building in which all the tenants are operating non-permissible activities, even if the percentage of rental from that building to the total turnover of the Islamic REIT is still below the benchmark (20%).

5. What if an Islamic REIT owns real estate that is vacant and plans to rent it out to a new tenant(s)? Is it bound by the application of the 20% benchmark as mentioned in the answer to question 2 above?

For a new tenant(s) that plans to rent the real estate of the Islamic REIT, the decision made by the *Sharia'a* committee or *Sharia'a* advisor does not need to be based on the 20% benchmark because the rental contribution from non-permissible activities is still unknown. Therefore, in this case the *Sharia'a* committee or *Sharia'a* advisor shall advise the Islamic REIT fund manager not to accept a new tenant(s) that operates activities that are **fully** non-permissible such as a gambling operator.

6. What is the method of calculating the portion of rental of non-permissible activities from the total rental payment paid by a tenant(s) operating mixed activities? For example, say the Islamic REIT receives a rental of RM3, 000 a month from a supermarket. The supermarket sells halal goods and alcoholic beverages. How do you determine the rental that is considered as non-permissible from the total rental that is paid by the supermarket (RM3, 000)?

The calculation for the rental of non-permissible activities from a tenant(s) operating mixed activities can be based on the ratio of area occupied for non-permissible activities to the total area occupied. The percentage will be used as the basis for determining the ratio of rental of non-permissible activities to total rental paid by the tenant(s).

For example, in a supermarket, if the total area rented out is 1,000 square feet and the area allocated for the sale of alcoholic beverages is 100 square feet, then the ratio of area used for the sale of alcoholic beverages is 10%. Therefore, the rental from non-permissible activities (sale of alcoholic beverages) is 10% of the total rental paid by the supermarket, that is RM300 a month (10% x RM3, 000).

In addition, for activities that do not involve the usage of space, such as service-based activities, the calculation method will be based on the *Ijtihad* of the *Sharia'a* committee or *Sharia'a* advisor of the Islamic REIT. An example of a service-based activity is packaging that involves packaging of goods that are non-permissible.

7. Is an Islamic REIT required to use instruments that comply with the Sharia'a principles for purpose of investment, deposit and financing?

Yes. An Islamic REIT must ensure that all forms of investment, deposit and financing instruments comply with the *Sharia'a* principles.

8. Is an Islamic REIT required to use insurance schemes that comply with the Sharia'a principles?

Yes. An Islamic REIT must use *Takaful* schemes to insure its real estate. If *Takaful* schemes are unable to provide the insurance coverage, then the Islamic REIT is permitted to use conventional insurance schemes.

9. Is an Islamic REIT permitted to participate in the forward sales or purchases of currency for risk management?

Yes. An Islamic REIT is permitted to participate in forward sales or purchases of currency, and is encouraged to deal with Islamic financial institutions. If the Islamic REIT deals with Islamic financial institutions, then it will be bound by the concept of *Wa'd*. *Wa'd* means a promise whereby only one party is obligated to fulfil his promise or responsibility. The party that is bound is the party that initiates the promise. However, if the Islamic REIT deals with conventional financial institutions, it is permitted to participate in the conventional forward sales or purchase of currency.

10. Would the Islamic REIT guidelines supersede the Guidelines on Real Estate Investment Trusts issued in January 2005?

No. The Guidelines on Islamic REIT essentially provide *Sharia'a* guidance on the investment and business activities of Islamic REIT and complement the SC's Guidelines on Real Estate Investment Trusts. The issuance of an Islamic REIT must therefore comply with both guidelines.

Source: Malaysian Securities Commission

World's 100 largest Islamic banks*

** This Appendix is reproduced with the kind permission of the Asian Banker.*

(Largest banks 1-25)

			Assets		Islamic financing		Islamic deposits	
Rank 2007	Islamic bank	Country	$mn	% Change	$mn	% Change	$mn	% Change
1	Bank Melli Iran	Iran	39431.0	*11.1*	20631.9	*9.1*	22675.9	*33.8*
2	Al-Rajhi Bank	Saudi Arabia	28093.1	*10.7*	24107.5	*12.3*	21098.0	*4.2*
3	Bank Saderat Iran	Iran	27872.0	*31.3*	16080.2	*55.3*	8227.7	*-9.1*
4	Bank Mellat Iran	Iran	25985.3	*10.4*	13302.5	*17.7*	19067.1	*22.9*
5	Bank Tejarat Iran	Iran	22489.6	*16.6*	14120.9	*23.8*	14441.9	*20.2*
6	Kuwait Finance House	Kuwait	21836.5	*36.2*	11848.9	*27.8*	16635.2	*39.9*
7	Dubai Islamic Bank	U.A.E.	17545.0	*49.9*	13681.9	*47.9*	14263.4	*39.7*
8	Bank Keshavarzi Iran	Iran	13129.5	*31.0*	9178.1	*34.9*	7626.5	*28.2*
9	Bank Maskan Iran	Iran	9886.8	*38.3*	7240.8	*46.5*	8140.9	*38.6*
10	Abu Dhabi Islamic Bank	U.A.E.	9881.7	*63.5*	5564.8	*53.0*	7942.2	*47.8*
11	Bank Parsian	Iran	8853.2	*150.8*	5629.4	*135.1*	7207.2	*142.6*
12	Bank Kerjasama Rakyat Malaysia	Malaysia	7796.3	*14.6*	5392.1	*21.2*	6437.6	*16.1*
13	Albaraka Banking Group	Bahrain	7625.8	*20.9*	4505.1	*31.8*	6146.7	*15.3*
14	Maybank Islamic	Malaysia	7077.1	*3.5*	5193.5	*7.6*	4703.5	*19.6*
15	Bank Islam Malaysia	Malaysia	5533.9	*30.9*	2460.6	*-1.8*	5098.5	*22.0*
16	Bank Refah Kargaran	Iran	4937.4	*6.1*	3748.9	*8.8*	3968.0	*5.1*
17	Bank Al-Jazira	Saudi Arabia	4195.7	*10.9*	1674.5	*-9.3*	2961.5	*1.1*
18	Qatar Islamic Bank	Qatar	4090.3	*55.9*	1965.9	*19.8*	2714.3	*43.4*
19	Bank Muamalat Malaysia	Malaysia	3808.8	*40.2*	1457.8	*39.1*	3477.0	*36.8*
20	Arcapita Bank	Bahrain	3805.5	*104.0*	614.7	*3.6*	n/a	*n/a*
21	Faisal Islamic Bank of Egypt	Egypt	3363.3	*17.4*	2462.2	*22.7*	3074.5	*18.7*
22	Bank of Industry and Mine	Iran	3114.5	*47.5*	1565.4	*56.7*	749.6	*14.0*
23	AmIslamic Bank	Malaysia	3048.4	*12.0*	1853.1	*-1.6*	1474.7	*14.2*
24	Asya-Asya Katilim Bankasi	Turkey	3039.3	*54.7*	2153.0	*43.5*	2321.4	*45.9*
25	Bank Al-Bilad	Saudi Arabia	3012.4	*61.0*	2623.4	*88.5*	2098.3	*100.7*

(Largest banks 1-25 continued)

Rank 2007	Shareholders' equity $mn	Operating income $mn	Operating income % Change	Operating expenses $mn	Operating expenses % Change	Net profit after tax and zakat $mn	Net profit after tax and zakat % Change	ROA %	ROE %	Cost / income ratio %	Capital adequacy ratio %	Gross NPL ratio %
1	3990.8	2928.4	282.1	2506.1	n/a	289.1	-33.1	0.7	7.2	85.6	n/a	n/a
2	5388.4	2539.3	19.1	589.6	-6.0	1949.8	29.6	6.9	36.2	23.2	26.5	2.0
3	3325.7	1785.8	19.0	1264.2	35.5	453.2	-9.5	1.6	13.6	70.8	n/a	n/a
4	1808.4	1086.4	29.2	952.4	39.2	66.1	-45.4	0.3	3.7	87.7	n/a	n/a
5	1801.6	759.6	27.3	558.8	32.4	213.6	-5.0	0.9	11.9	73.6	n/a	n/a
6	2663.4	1281.4	43.5	601.1	36.1	668.2	51.0	3.1	25.1	46.9	n/a	3.3
7	2254.5	767.5	58.6	334.8	72.8	429.6	48.4	2.4	19.1	43.6	n/a	n/a
8	1000.9	777.2	51.3	740.7	110.8	46.8	-60.4	0.4	4.7	95.3	n/a	n/a
9	921.6	441.2	12.9	314.3	37.5	131.2	-12.1	1.3	14.2	71.2	n/a	n/a
10	686.1	275.3	38.5	119.6	14.0	155.8	66.0	1.6	22.7	43.4	n/a	0.9
11	633.5	339.8	67.8	113.0	91.8	199.0	55.9	2.2	31.4	33.2	11.3	n/a
12	1035.3	358.2	22.9	132.4	17.7	109.6	31.2	1.4	10.6	37.0	21.6	6.6
13	1205.2	334.8	11.6	200.0	6.1	123.7	20.2	1.6	10.3	59.7	n/a	7.8
14	568.3	248.2	-3.8	92.4	1238.6	55.1	-60.5	0.8	9.7	37.2	16.3	6.8
15	302.2	n/a	n/a	n/a	n/a	72.7	L-P	1.3	24.1	n/a	12.7	10.9
16	130.5	212.3	47.5	196.2	53.0	16.2	272.5	0.3	12.4	92.4	n/a	n/a
17	1134.9	69.4	-80.3	145.0	23.1	526.6	124.8	12.6	46.4	208.9	41.5	3.1
18	1176.4	357.4	80.7	72.5	40.6	285.3	90.4	7.0	24.3	20.3	21.1	4.3
19	202.9	98.7	15.0	69.6	-7.2	20.5	140.3	0.5	10.1	70.5	15.6	6.6
20	955.0	623.3	190.2	337.6	205.5	285.7	173.9	7.5	29.9	54.2	37.0	n/a
21	130.9	59.2	7.5	37.9	2.1	20.8	19.1	0.6	15.9	64.1	n/a	n/a
22	913.6	207.5	15.0	107.8	38.0	113.5	-16.4	3.6	12.4	52.0	28.2	n/a
23	380.5	148.0	1.4	46.5	22.5	38.4	-10.5	1.3	10.1	31.4	15.0	7.4
24	490.7	316.7	63.8	180.5	43.9	114.6	85.9	3.8	23.4	57.0	18.0	4.1
25	807.6	174.8	300.5	127.3	82.2	47.6	L-P	1.6	5.9	72.8	n/a	0.4

(Largest banks 26-50)

			Assets		Islamic financing		Islamic deposits	
Rank 2007	Islamic bank	Country	$mn	% Change	$mn	% Change	$mn	% Change
26	**Turkiye Finans Katilim Bankasi**	Turkey	**2917.8**	*30.2*	**2252.9**	*34.0*	**2498.7**	*26.9*
27	**Bank Islam Brunei Darussalam**	Brunei	**2910.0**	*n/a*	**1295.4**	*n/a*	**2293.2**	*n/a*
28	**Emirates Islamic Bank**	U.A.E.	**2852.0**	*n/a*	**1797.4**	*n/a*	**2478.4**	*n/a*
29	**Kuwait International Bank**	Kuwait	**2779.3**	*6.0*	**1671.9**	*0.2*	**2076.8**	*6.9*
30	**Qatar International Islamic Bank**	Qatar	**2307.1**	*n/a*	**1002.2**	*n/a*	**474.6**	*n/a*
31	**RHB Islamic Bank**	Malaysia	**2291.5**	*13.6*	**1174.5**	*30.6*	**2017.6**	*15.5*
32	**Islami Bank Bangladesh**	Bangladesh	**2175.5**	*17.2*	**1644.5**	*16.3*	**1904.4**	*17.8*
33	**Sharjah Islamic Bank**	U.A.E.	**2080.8**	*n/a*	**1233.9**	*n/a*	**1227.0**	*n/a*
34	**Faysal Bank**	Pakistan	**1894.9**	*2.3*	**1222.4**	*15.4*	**1463.6**	*-2.6*
35	**Omdurman National Bank**	Sudan	**1884.4**	*78.1*	**1453.6**	*89.8*	**702.1**	*73.3*
36	**Hong Leong Islamic Bank**	Malaysia	**1801.8**	*2.9*	**1063.3**	*-0.9*	**1541.7**	*-2.9*
37	**Boubyan Bank**	Kuwait	**1744.1**	*55.0*	**236.6**	*366.9*	**1299.7**	*90.3*
38	**Shamil Bank of Bahrain**	Bahrain	**1693.3**	*10.9*	**676.1**	*194.9*	**1251.0**	*14.5*
39	**Eghtesad Novin Bank**	Iran	**1591.6**	*108.4*	**1045.4**	*94.7*	**1405.2**	*111.8*
40	**Export Development Bank of Iran**	Iran	**1575.2**	*16.5*	**1054.9**	*21.9*	**857.2**	*21.7*
41	**Gulf Finance House**	Bahrain	**1500.9**	*36.5*	**786.7**	*12.1*	**696.8**	*5.7*
42	**Eoncap Islamic Bank**	Malaysia	**1454.1**	*n/a*	**1158.0**	*n/a*	**1106.1**	*n/a*
43	**Saman Bank**	Iran	**1427.4**	*113.8*	**952.4**	*100.0*	**1282.0**	*126.5*
44	**Karafarin Bank**	Iran	**1387.4**	*88.2*	**799.5**	*78.6*	**1245.4**	*88.8*
45	**CIMB Islamic Bank**	Malaysia	**1261.1**	*383.0*	**458.8**	*10083.5*	**688.1**	*336.8*
46	**Masraf Al Rayan**	Qatar	**1188.0**	*n/a*	**51.2**	*n/a*	**61.3**	*n/a*
47	**Bahrain Islamic Bank**	Bahrain	**1160.9**	*36.1*	**738.8**	*41.9*	**945.5**	*45.0*
48	**Affin Islamic Bank**	Malaysia	**1106.3**	*7.0*	**362.1**	*-14.6*	**768.2**	*33.0*
49	**Noor Islamic Bank** [P]	U.A.E.	**1090.0**	*n/a*	**n/a**	*n/a*	**n/a**	*n/a*
50	**Bank Syariah Mandiri**	Indonesia	**1059.3**	*25.9*	**792.8**	*36.2*	**916.3**	*25.4*

(Largest banks 26-50 continued)

Rank 2007	Shareholders' equity $mn	Operating income $mn	Operating income % Change	Operating expenses $mn	Operating expenses % Change	Net profit after tax and zakat $mn	Net profit after tax and zakat % Change	ROA %	ROE %	Cost / income ratio %	Capital adequacy ratio %	Gross NPL ratio %
26	**302.5**	**223.4**	*18.3*	**124.6**	*-1.6*	**102.1**	*78.3*	*3.5*	*33.8*	*55.8*	*n/a*	*3.1*
27	**509.8**	**92.7**	*n/a*	**39.5**	*n/a*	**37.2**	*n/a*	*1.3*	*7.3*	*42.6*	*n/a*	*n/a*
28	**263.0**	**n/a**	*n/a*	**n/a**	*n/a*	**n/a**	*n/a*	*n/a*	*n/a*	*n/a*	*n/a*	*n/a*
29	**492.8**	**126.9**	*13.0*	**92.3**	*19.3*	**32.9**	*-1.0*	*1.2*	*6.7*	*72.7*	*23.3*	*15.4*
30	**392.2**	**n/a**	*n/a*	**n/a**	*n/a*	**n/a**	*n/a*	*n/a*	*n/a*	*n/a*	*n/a*	*n/a*
31	**184.4**	**67.3**	*93.1*	**32.4**	*92.2*	**24.5**	*122.8*	*1.1*	*13.3*	*48.1*	*17.8*	*5.7*
32	**144.9**	**87.2**	*22.7*	**45.0**	*17.4*	**20.3**	*19.3*	*0.9*	*14.0*	*51.7*	*9.4*	*n/a*
33	**574.4**	**n/a**	*n/a*	**n/a**	*n/a*	**n/a**	*n/a*	*n/a*	*n/a*	*n/a*	*n/a*	*n/a*
34	**143.6**	**97.7**	*12.6*	**40.7**	*118.8*	**47.1**	*-11.4*	*2.5*	*32.8*	*41.6*	*n/a*	*4.6*
35	**77.8**	**69.1**	*16.2*	**38.1**	*-11.3*	**18.6**	*104.7*	*1.0*	*24.0*	*55.1*	*n/a*	*n/a*
36	**173.7**	**41.6**	*-8.4*	**18.9**	*-35.4*	**16.4**	*40.2*	*0.9*	*9.5*	*45.4*	*17.5*	*1.6*
37	**416.4**	**74.4**	*69.9*	**40.5**	*100.5*	**35.6**	*50.8*	*2.0*	*8.5*	*54.4*	*n/a*	*n/a*
38	**381.6**	**96.7**	*30.3*	**32.8**	*0.3*	**63.1**	*55.4*	*3.7*	*16.5*	*33.9*	*n/a*	*n/a*
39	**123.2**	**55.3**	*35.9*	**19.3**	*88.7*	**30.6**	*6.6*	*1.9*	*24.8*	*35.0*	*n/a*	*n/a*
40	**443.1**	**95.0**	*44.6*	**50.0**	*95.9*	**30.3**	*53.8*	*1.9*	*6.8*	*52.7*	*n/a*	*n/a*
41	**667.8**	**310.0**	*60.6*	**102.0**	*92.1*	**211.9**	*50.9*	*14.1*	*31.7*	*32.9*	*n/a*	*n/a*
42	**116.2**	**29.0**	*n/a*	**21.6**	*n/a*	**3.6**	*n/a*	*0.2*	*3.1*	*74.6*	*12.3*	*5.8*
43	**97.2**	**56.0**	*34.0*	**29.4**	*100.6*	**25.5**	*8.3*	*1.8*	*26.2*	*52.5*	*n/a*	*n/a*
44	**93.1**	**59.3**	*64.7*	**21.0**	*80.1*	**36.2**	*54.8*	*2.6*	*38.9*	*35.4*	*10.5*	*n/a*
45	**153.6**	**26.8**	*333.3*	**13.6**	*65.6*	**4.8**	*-428.5*	*0.4*	*3.1*	*50.8*	*14.6*	*10.0*
46	**1120.2**	**49.1**	*n/a*	**17.9**	*n/a*	**31.0**	*n/a*	*2.6*	*2.8*	*36.4*	*n/a*	*n/a*
47	**173.7**	**58.2**	*73.8*	**23.4**	*69.2*	**34.8**	*77.0*	*3.0*	*20.1*	*40.2*	*n/a*	*n/a*
48	**55.8**	**26.5**	*24.9*	**7.7**	*1184.8*	**10.4**	*n/a*	*0.9*	*18.6*	*29.0*	*15.4*	*2.8*
49	**1090.0**	**n/a**	*n/a*	**n/a**	*n/a*	**n/a**	*n/a*	*n/a*	*n/a*	*n/a*	*n/a*	*n/a*
50	**77.3**	**67.2**	*17.8*	**56.0**	*30.0*	**7.3**	*-14.8*	*0.7*	*9.4*	*83.4*	*12.6*	*7.0*

(Largest banks 51-75)

Rank 2007	Islamic bank	Country	Assets $mn	Assets % Change	Islamic financing $mn	Islamic financing % Change	Islamic deposits $mn	Islamic deposits % Change
51	**Tadhamon International Islamic Bank**	Yemen	**936.7**	*36.8*	**530.8**	*34.5*	**836.6**	*31.5*
52	**Bank Syariah Muamalat Indonesia**	Indonesia	**928.0**	*22.8*	**720.6**	*18.1*	**781.8**	*25.4*
53	**Tamweel**	U.A.E.	**888.3**	*105.0*	**703.5**	*98.3*	**335.1**	*22.5*
54	**ABC Islamic Bank**	Bahrain	**823.3**	*34.7*	**546.4**	*17.6*	**589.7**	*84.6*
55	**Meezan Bank**	Pakistan	**771.7**	*47.9*	**443.7**	*34.5*	**635.4**	*47.7*
56	**Bank of Khartoum**	Sudan	**676.7**	*67.3*	**378.1**	*48.7*	**405.1**	*46.0*
57	**Islamic International Arab Bank**	Jordan	**571.1**	*0.7*	**215.4**	*34.4*	**451.1**	*-3.7*
58	**Bank Pasargad**	Iran	**511.4**	*n/a*	**123.1**	*n/a*	**97.2**	*n/a*
59	**Al-Salam Bank-Bahrain**	Bahrain	**500.3**	*n/a*	**368.4**	*n/a*	**131.6**	*n/a*
60	**The Islamic Bank of Asia P**	Singapore	**500.0**	*n/a*	**n/a**	*n/a*	**n/a**	*n/a*
61	**European Islamic Investment Bank**	U.K.	**463.9**	*139.7*	**10.4**	*n/a*	**1.8**	*n/a*
62	**Tadamon Islamic Bank**	Sudan	**407.7**	*52.4*	**73.5**	*74.5*	**154.1**	*31.8*
63	**Sudanese French Bank**	Sudan	**395.7**	*26.9*	**78.2**	*82.2*	**297.6**	*24.1*
64	**Oriental Bank Bangladesh**	Bangladesh	**358.5**	*31.8*	**277.1**	*35.0*	**359.2**	*30.0*
65	**Faisal Islamic Bank of Sudan**	Sudan	**356.5**	*65.0*	**105.3**	*33.1*	**268.5**	*74.1*
66	**Bank Ettamouil Saoudi Tounsi**	Tunisia	**352.4**	*41.6*	**202.8**	*69.7*	**282.3**	*50.4*
67	**Bank of London and Middle East P**	U.K.	**349.5**	*n/a*	**n/a**	*n/a*	**n/a**	*n/a*
68	**First Finance Company**	Qatar	**331.3**	*66.4*	**269.4**	*53.9*	**n/a**	*n/a*
69	**Social Investment Bank**	Bangladesh	**309.4**	*33.6*	**252.3**	*45.6*	**240.0**	*39.3*
70	**Shahjalal Islami Bank**	Bangladesh	**309.0**	*41.6*	**224.7**	*40.5*	**278.9**	*40.4*
71	**Saba Islamic Bank**	Yemen	**307.9**	*36.0*	**123.0**	*85.8*	**256.2**	*26.7*
72	**Unicorn Investment Bank**	Bahrain	**293.3**	*96.3*	**27.9**	*n/a*	**n/a**	*n/a*
73	**Al-Arahah Islami Bank**	Bangladesh	**285.1**	*-7.3*	**221.7**	*-2.8*	**231.8**	*-8.1*
74	**Elnilein Industrial Development Bank Group**	Sudan	**281.3**	*59.1*	**143.0**	*84.8*	**152.2**	*58.1*
75	**Farmers Commercial Bank**	Sudan	**255.7**	*55.7*	**130.0**	*73.5*	**80.8**	*4.0*

(Largest banks 51-75 continued)

Rank 2007	Shareholders' equity $mn	Operating income $mn	Operating income % Change	Operating income $mn	Operating income % Change	Net profit after tax and zakat $mn	Net profit after tax and zakat % Change	ROA %	ROE %	Cost / income ratio %	Capital adequacy ratio %	Gross NPL ratio %
51	**77.3**	**23.8**	*65.9*	**10.0**	*28.0*	**9.8**	*110.9*	*1.0*	*12.6*	*42.1*	*n/a*	*2.3*
52	**87.2**	**63.4**	*29.4*	**44.0**	*34.2*	**12.0**	*10.7*	*1.3*	*13.8*	*69.4*	*14.2*	*5.8*
53	**495.4**	**56.4**	*166.3*	**14.8**	*53.1*	**231.9**	*1918.4*	*26.1*	*46.8*	*26.3*	*n/a*	*n/a*
54	**100.6**	**10.9**	*39.7*	**5.4**	*31.7*	**5.3**	*43.2*	*0.6*	*5.3*	*49.5*	*n/a*	*n/a*
55	**87.1**	**34.6**	*16.5*	**20.0**	*47.0*	**11.5**	*-4.0*	*1.5*	*13.3*	*57.7*	*14.0*	*1.5*
56	**97.7**	**52.5**	*82.6*	**31.7**	*68.8*	**12.1**	*67.8*	*1.8*	*12.3*	*60.5*	*n/a*	*n/a*
57	**76.3**	**17.1**	*83.3*	**8.2**	*38.1*	**5.4**	*153.3*	*0.9*	*7.0*	*47.9*	*n/a*	*n/a*
58	**387.1**	**28.7**	*n/a*	**10.7**	*n/a*	**18.0**	*n/a*	*3.5*	*4.6*	*37.4*	*n/a*	*n/a*
59	**362.8**	**54.3**	*n/a*	**10.6**	*n/a*	**43.6**	*n/a*	*8.7*	*12.0*	*19.6*	*n/a*	*n/a*
60	**500.0**	**n/a**	*n/a*	**n/a**	*n/a*	**n/a**	*n/a*	*n/a*	*n/a*	*n/a*	*n/a*	*n/a*
61	**364.5**	**15.3**	*135.4*	**11.8**	*242.3*	**2.4**	*5.3*	*0.5*	*0.6*	*77.0*	*190.0*	*0.0*
62	**48.3**	**36.2**	*41.2*	**16.8**	*45.8*	**18.9**	*35.9*	*4.6*	*39.2*	*46.4*	*n/a*	*n/a*
63	**36.6**	**32.3**	*19.3*	**20.2**	*33.9*	**10.1**	*5.4*	*2.6*	*27.6*	*62.6*	*n/a*	*n/a*
64	**-21.6**	**-1.4**	*-60.3*	**5.3**	*12.8*	**-6.7**	*L-L*	*-1.9*	*31.0*	*-369.4*	*n/a*	*22.8*
65	**45.6**	**33.5**	*76.2*	**18.1**	*45.9*	**14.2**	*119.2*	*4.0*	*31.2*	*54.0*	*n/a*	*n/a*
66	**63.9**	**17.5**	*118.8*	**9.5**	*137.5*	**8.0**	*100.0*	*2.3*	*12.5*	*54.3*	*n/a*	*n/a*
67	**349.5**	**n/a**	*n/a*	**n/a**	*n/a*	**n/a**	*n/a*	*n/a*	*n/a*	*n/a*	*n/a*	*n/a*
68	**128.4**	**29.6**	*94.8*	**8.4**	*80.6*	**22.2**	*92.8*	*6.7*	*17.3*	*28.5*	*n/a*	*2.4*
69	**24.5**	**17.9**	*41.9*	**7.2**	*12.5*	**6.8**	*71.4*	*2.2*	*27.8*	*40.2*	*10.7*	*3.2*
70	**17.4**	**15.5**	*52.0*	**4.1**	*29.8*	**6.7**	*73.8*	*2.2*	*38.4*	*26.5*	*10.4*	*n/a*
71	**15.1**	**9.6**	*45.0*	**6.7**	*42.8*	**2.0**	*35.1*	*0.7*	*13.3*	*69.5*	*n/a*	*n/a*
72	**231.8**	**66.9**	*27.2*	**36.8**	*26.9*	**30.1**	*27.5*	*10.3*	*13.0*	*55.0*	*n/a*	*n/a*
73	**14.2**	**9.2**	*16.1*	**7.4**	*4.9*	**0.8**	*297.1*	*0.3*	*5.9*	*81.0*	*7.2*	*n/a*
74	**13.1**	**16.6**	*31.1*	**13.6**	*30.9*	**2.2**	*23.8*	*0.8*	*16.8*	*82.0*	*n/a*	*n/a*
75	**22.2**	**17.7**	*47.9*	**14.4**	*51.3*	**1.9**	*79.6*	*0.8*	*8.7*	*81.3*	*n/a*	*n/a*

(Largest banks 76-100)

Rank 2007	Islamic bank	Country	Assets $mn	Assets % Change	Islamic financing $mn	Islamic financing % Change	Islamic deposits $mn	Islamic deposits % Change
76	**Islamic Bank of Britain**	U.K.	**231.6**	*50.6*	**15.9**	*109.9*	**165.1**	*101.0*
77	**Islamic Co-operative Development Bank**	Sudan	**217.7**	*30.8*	**127.9**	*23.1*	**163.1**	*40.2*
78	**Byblos Bank Africa Ltd**	Sudan	**198.4**	*32.5*	**14.2**	*179.9*	**128.2**	*44.6*
79	**Capivest**	Bahrain	**195.4**	*183.6*	**18.8**	*-24.5*	**37.8**	*43.2*
80	**Arab Islamic Bank**	Palestine	**187.0**	*29.1*	**91.8**	*31.3*	**157.0**	*27.2*
81	**Saudi Sudanese Bank**	Sudan	**181.6**	*58.5*	**87.5**	*88.9*	**104.0**	*43.6*
82	**Sudanese Islamic Bank**	Sudan	**154.0**	*53.3*	**20.1**	*46.9*	**81.9**	*34.6*
83	**Islamic Bank of Thailand**	Thailand	**149.2**	*158.1*	**93.3**	*456.2*	**134.0**	*216.0*
84	**Investors Bank**	Bahrain	**138.3**	*126.7*	**17.9**	*n/a*	**7.0**	*-62.0*
85	**Animal Resources Bank**	Sudan	**133.0**	*31.6*	**20.4**	*-10.4*	**28.4**	*41.2*
86	**Savings & Social Development Bank**	Sudan	**118.6**	*25.7*	**33.8**	*78.4*	**82.4**	*34.5*
87	**Islamic Bank of Yemen for Finance & Investment**	Yemen	**98.3**	*-12.0*	**39.6**	*-11.9*	**81.2**	*-14.8*
88	**Kurdistan International Bank for Investment and Development**	Iraq	**93.4**	*128.8*	**n/a**	*n/a*	**38.4**	*531.8*
89	**Banque Al Wava Mauritanienne Islamique**	Mauritania	**91.9**	*-2.0*	**42.1**	*-7.8*	**56.9**	*10.1*
90	**Bank Syariah Mega Indonesia**	Indonesia	**91.3**	*123.7*	**25.0**	*730.3*	**16.9**	*347.1*
91	**Al-Shamal Islamic Bank**	Sudan	**80.6**	*31.0*	**21.0**	*15.2*	**49.9**	*44.2*
92	**Arab Finance House Holding**	Lebanon	**74.3**	*n/a*	**35.5**	*n/a*	**10.6**	*n/a*
93	**BankIslami Pakistan**	Pakistan	**66.1**	*167.7*	**17.6**	*n/a*	**30.4**	*n/a*
94	**Blue Nile Mashreq Bank**	Sudan	**64.4**	*16.1*	**4.2**	*57.7*	**53.6**	*17.8*
95	**National Bank of Sudan**	Sudan	**58.5**	*20.1*	**18.6**	*-14.5*	**38.3**	*19.4*
96	**Export Development Bank**	Sudan	**52.6**	*48.4*	**19.5**	*-1.7*	**22.2**	*67.0*
97	**Real Estate Commercial Bank**	Sudan	**50.9**	*32.1*	**0.0**	*0.0*	**16.9**	*27.0*
98	**First Dawood Islamic Bank**	Pakistan	**44.3**	*na*	**0.2**	*n/a*	**n/a**	*n/a*
99	**Emirates Global Islamic Bank**	Pakistan	**40.2**	*n//a*	**0.5**	*n/a*	**0.7**	*n/a*
100	**Workers' National Bank**	Sudan	**32.9**	*74.5*	**3.6**	*110.7*	**23.8**	*71.8*

(Largest banks 76-100 continued)

Rank 2007	Shareholders' equity $mn	Operating income $mn	Operating income % Change	Operating expenses $mn	Operating expenses % Change	Net profit after tax and zakat $mn	Net profit after tax and zakat % Change	ROA %	ROE %	Cost / income ratio %	Capital adequacy ratio %	Gross NPL ratio %
76	**62.2**	**6.1**	*60.6*	**23.4**	*57.8*	**-17.3**	*L-L*	*-7.5*	*-27.8*	*383.9*	*84.6*	*n/a*
77	**18.0**	**21.2**	*22.5*	**16.3**	*36.8*	**3.3**	*-3.4*	*1.5*	*18.1*	*76.9*	*17.8*	*n/a*
78	**40.2**	**17.1**	*60.9*	**7.0**	*38.7*	**6.9**	*138.5*	*3.5*	*17.2*	*40.8*	*n/a*	*n/a*
79	**140.4**	**18.0**	*24.1*	**9.2**	*-8.9*	**10.2**	*75.9*	*5.2*	*7.3*	*51.1*	*n/a*	*n/a*
80	**23.7**	**9.6**	*65.5*	**5.3**	*10.4*	**3.6**	*414.3*	*1.9*	*15.2*	*55.2*	*n/a*	*n/a*
81	**14.3**	**18.6**	*28.1*	**13.2**	*18.1*	**2.8**	*27.9*	*1.5*	*19.4*	*71.0*	*n/a*	*n/a*
82	**26.1**	**14.7**	*52.1*	**11.9**	*43.9*	**1.9**	*115.6*	*1.2*	*7.2*	*81.1*	*n/a*	*n/a*
83	**11.2**	**2.1**	*1027.5*	**5.9**	*136.3*	**-3.9**	*L-L*	*-2.6*	*-34.5*	*287.8*	*n/a*	*6.7*
84	**131.0**	**58.5**	*557.3*	**5.6**	*93.1*	**52.9**	*781.7*	*38.3*	*40.4*	*9.6*	*n/a*	*n/a*
85	**8.7**	**7.2**	*5.0*	**6.7**	*9.9*	**0.5**	*-28.4*	*0.4*	*5.8*	*92.3*	*n/a*	*n/a*
86	**25.0**	**11.4**	*54.5*	**8.0**	*38.2*	**3.4**	*112.8*	*2.9*	*13.7*	*69.9*	*n/a*	*n/a*
87	**10.9**	**5.4**	*4.8*	**5.4**	*7.1*	**0.0**	*-100.0*	*0.0*	*0.0*	*100.0*	*n/a*	*n/a*
88	**38.1**	**2.7**	*1389.6*	**2.3**	*744.6*	**0.5**	*L-P*	*0.5*	*1.2*	*83.2*	*n/a*	*n/a*
89	**20.5**	**7.8**	*-6.4*	**6.0**	*-4.4*	**1.4**	*2.7*	*1.6*	*7.0*	*76.6*	*n/a*	*n/a*
90	**6.9**	**n/a**	*n/a*	**n/a**	*n/a*	**0.3**	*-61.1*	*0.4*	*4.7*	*n/a*	*n/a*	*n/a*
91	**7.6**	**2.6**	*57.9*	**6.9**	*59.9*	**-4.3**	*L-L*	*-5.4*	*-56.8*	*268.5*	*n/a*	*n/a*
92	**62.2**	**5.4**	*n/a*	**3.7**	*n/a*	**1.7**	*n/a*	*2.2*	*2.7*	*69.0*	*n/a*	*n/a*
93	**32.9**	**1.4**	*n/a*	**2.6**	*n/a*	**-0.1**	*n/a*	*-0.2*	*-0.4*	*187.6*	*62.0*	*n/a*
94	**6.7**	**3.7**	*46.3*	**2.3**	*23.3*	**1.2**	*424.5*	*1.9*	*18.5*	*63.2*	*n/a*	*n/a*
95	**1.0**	**5.4**	*10.0*	**4.9**	*32.4*	**0.3**	*-64.2*	*0.5*	*32.9*	*90.9*	*n/a*	*n/a*
96	**5.5**	**4.8**	*52.6*	**4.3**	*45.1*	**0.4**	*216.8*	*0.8*	*7.9*	*90.9*	*n/a*	*n/a*
97	**23.5**	**10.3**	*27.1*	**3.0**	*64.1*	**6.8**	*12.3*	*13.3*	*28.8*	*29.2*	*n/a*	*n/a*
98	**44.1**	**n/a**	*n/a*	**n/a**	*n/a*	**n/a**	*n/a*	*n/a*	*n/a*	*n/a*	*n/a*	*n/a*
99	**38.7**	**0.3**	*n/a*	**3.0**	*n/a*	**-1.8**	*n/a*	*-4.4*	*-4.6*	*1063.4*	*n/a*	*n/a*
100	**8.4**	**3.7**	*72.3*	**2.2**	*22.5*	**1.5**	*308.5*	*4.7*	*18.4*	*58.6*	*n/a*	*n/a*

Bank-specific notes

All banks listed in the above ranking are wholly *sharia'a* compliant independent Islamic banks. This ranking does not take into consideration banks that offer Islamic banking services via windows or other non-banking financial institutions that offer Islamic banking services without a banking licence. For Islamic banks operating as a subsidiary or an overseas branch of a wholly shariah-compliant independent Islamic banking parent institution, this ranking only takes into consideration the parent institution. Whenever possible, consolidated figures are used for compiling this ranking. **Change** indicates year-on-year growth in percentage. All values are quoted in **US$ million** and all % changes are calculated using local currencies. **Assets** are the sum of cash and bank balances, marketable securities and other short-term investments, long-term investments, net finances, fixed assets and other assets. **Islamic Financing** are commercial, consumer and other credits provided to non-bank customers (net of general and specific loan loss provisions), and are compliant with principles of Islamic law and Islamic economics. **Islamic Deposits** are demand, savings, time deposits received from non-bank customers, and are consistent with principles of Islamic law and Islamic economics. **Operating Income** is the summation of income derived from investment of depositors' funds and shareholders' equity, after deducting income attributable to depositors. **Operating Expense** is the summation of staff expenses, other administrative operating expenses, and impairment charges. **Operating Profit before Provisions, Impairment Charges,** is operating revenue less operating expense. **Net Profit After Tax and *Zakat*** is the profit recorded after taxation and zakat, and is attributable to shareholders. In the change in revenue and profit, **P-L** denotes profits from the previous FY deteriorating to losses; **L-P** denotes losses to profits; **L-L** denotes losses to losses. **n/a** – data not available. Data for rows with incomplete information was primarily complied from several media sources given that financials could not be sourced from the organisations. All data in this table is collected and updated to the best of our knowledge. **We provide this service with no warranty whatsoever as to the currency, accuracy, or applicability of the data for any purposes.** P: Noor Islamic Bank (U.A.E.), The Islamic Bank of Asia (Singapore) and Bank of London and Middle East were launched in recent months with only paid-in capital figure available, and we assume the latest size of their balance sheet will be equal to their respective paid-in capital.

Top 500 Islamic Financial Institutions*

* *Supplement to The Banker, November 28th, 2008.*

Ranking		Bank na	Country	Institution type	S / W	*Sharia'a* compliant assets		Total assets		Profits and returns			Result date
Current	Previous					Total US$m	% change	US$m	% *Sharia'a*	Profits US$m	% change	Asset returns %	
1	1	Bank Melli Iran, Tehran	Iran	Government owned Bank	S: Full Islamic	48469.9	0.21	48469.9	1	542.1	-0.167	0.012	20-Mar-07
2	7	Kuwait Finance House	Kuwait	Commercial Bank	S: Full Islamic	37177.9	0.281	37177.9	1	618.5	0.299	0.019	30-Jun-08
3	4	Al Rajhi Bank	Saudi Arabia	Commercial & Investment Bank	S: Full Islamic	33347.5	0.187	33347.5	1	1722.2	-0.117	0.056	31-Dec-07
4	2	Bank Saderat Iran, Tehran	Iran	Government owned Bank	S: Full Islamic	32610	0.169	32610	1	228	-0.568	0.008	20-Mar-07
5	5	Bank Mellat, Tehran	Iran	Government owned Bank	S: Full Islamic	32533.6	0.256	32533.6	1	162.2	-0.17	0.006	20-Mar-07
6	8	Bank Tejarat, Tehran	Iran	Government owned Bank	S: Full Islamic	26340	0.171	26340	1	0.02	-0.439	0.006	20-Mar-07
7	11	Bank Sepah, Tehran	Iran	Government owned Bank	S: Full Islamic	24142.4	0.399	24142.4	1	28.8	-0.864	0.001	20-Mar-07
8	9	Dubai Islamic Bank, Dubai	UAE	Commercial Bank	S: Full Islamic	22801.6	0.3	22801.6	1	512.3	0.188	0.025	31-Dec-07
9	21	Bank Keshavarzi (Agr. Bank), Tehran	Iran	Government owned Bank	S: Full Islamic	16298	0.241	16298	1	0	-0.491	0.002	20-Mar-07
10	14	HSBC Amanah	UK	Commercial & Retail Banking	S: Full Islamic	15194	0.562	0	0	0	0	0	30-Jun-08
11	12	Parsian Bank	Iran	Commercial Bank	S: Full Islamic	15117.4	0.442	15117.4	1	128.4	-0.505	0.01	20-Mar-07
12	222	Bank Maskan Iran, Tehran	Iran	Government owned Bank	S: Full Islamic	13075	0.323	13075	1	0	0	0	20-Mar-07
13	13	Abu Dhabi Islamic Bank	UAE	Commercial Bank	S: Full Islamic	12063.4	0.221	12063.4	1	66.6	0.475	0.006	31-Mar-08
14	17	Al Baraka Banking Group	Bahrain	Wholesale Bank	S: Full Islamic	11167.5	0.293	11167.5	1	139.3	-0.293	0.014	30-Jun-08
15	16	Bank Rakyat	Malaysia	Commercial Bank	S: Full Islamic	10397.1	0.269	10397.1	1	246.9	0.323	0.027	31-Dec-07
16	15	National Commercial Bank Ltd, Jeddah	Saudi Arabia	Commercial Bank	W: Islamic Windows	10358.3	0.129	55732.2	0.186	1612.2	-0.038	0.033	31-Dec-07
17	23	Riyad Bank	Saudi Arabia	Commercial & Retail Banking	W: Islamic Windows	9932.2	0.329	38487.1	0.258	426.4	0.063	0.013	30-Jun-08
18	19	Maybank Islamic Berhad	Malaysia	Commercial Bank	S: Full Islamic	7755.1	0	7755.1	1	24.1	0	0	31-Mar-08
19	22	Saudi British Bank	Saudi Arabia	Commercial Bank	W: Islamic Windows	7351.1	0.278	26225.1	0.28	696.1	-0.143	0.03	31-Dec-07
20	20	Samba Financial Group	Saudi Arabia	Commercial Bank	W: Islamic Windows	6885.4	0.165	41232	0.167	1283.7	-0.077	0.035	31-Dec-07
21	24	BIMB Holdings	Malaysia	Commercial Bank	S: Full Islamic	6595.5	0.159	6595.5	1	82.3	0.323	0.013	31-Mar-08
22	222	Pasargad Bank	Iran	Commercial Bank	S: Full Islamic	6169	1.581	6169	1	181.9	0.959	0.043	20-Mar-08
23	33	Asya Finans Kurumu A.S.	Turkey	Commercial Bank	S: Full Islamic	5872.6	0.552	5872.6	1	31.3	-0.124	0.006	31-Mar-08
24	29	Qatar Islamic Bank	Qatar	Commercial & Investment Bank	S: Full Islamic	5861.5	0.433	5861.5	1	457.6	0.322	0.092	31-Dec-07
25	25	Bank Refah	Iran	Government owned Bank	S: Full Islamic	5787.1	0.199	5787.1	1	12.6	-0.331	0.002	20-Mar-07
26	27	Bank Al Jazira	Saudi Arabia	Commercial Bank	S: Full Islamic	5758.1	0.372	5758.1	1	215	-0.592	0.043	31-Dec-07
27	18	Banque Saudi Fransi	Saudi Arabia	Commercial Bank	W: Islamic Windows	4710.5	0.684	26651	0.177	723.9	-0.098	0.03	31-Dec-07
28	35	Turkiye Finans Katilim Bankasi A	Turkey	Commercial Bank	S: Full Islamic	4703.4	0.357	4703.4	1	150.2	0.28	0.037	31-Dec-07
29	30	Investment Dar	Kuwait	Investment Bank	S: Full Islamic	4643.7	0.209	4643.7	1	464	0.357	0.109	31-Dec-07
30	38	Emirates Islamic Bank	UAE	Commercial Bank	S: Full Islamic	4616.4	0.619	4616.4	1	65	1.031	0.017	31-Dec-07
31	58	Eghtesad Novin Bank	Iran	Commercial Bank	S: Full Islamic	4500.5	1.855	4500.5	1	105.3	2.028	0.035	20-Mar-07
32	222	Bank Albilad	Saudi Arabia	Commercial Bank	S: Full Islamic	4442.1	0.475	4442.1	1	19.3	-0.593	0.005	31-Dec-07
33	31	Bank Muamalat Malaysia Berhad	Malaysia	Commercial Bank	S: Full Islamic	4115.5	0.026	4115.5	1	19.5	-0.374	0.005	31-Dec-07
34	36	Public Bank Berhad	Malaysia	Commercial Bank	W: Islamic Windows	4094.3	0.345	47210	0.087	849.3	0.168	0.019	31-Dec-07
35	34	Ithmaar Bank BSC	Bahrain	Investment Bank	S: Full Islamic	4078.8	0.229	4078.8	1	208.3	0.078	0.056	31-Dec-07
36	n/a	QNB Al Islami	Qatar	Commercial & Retail Banking	S: Full Islamic	3956	0	3956	1	11.4	0	0.021	30-Jun-08
37	37	Faisal Islamic Bank of Egypt, Cairo	Egypt	Commercial Bank	S: Full Islamic	3903	0.146	3903	1	0	0	0	31-Dec-07
38	40	Arcapita Bank	Bahrain	Investment Bank	S: Full Islamic	3805.5	0.405	3805.5	1	308.6	1.014	0.095	30-Jun-07
39	222	Bank Sanat Va Maadan	Iran	Government owned Bank	S: Full Islamic	3792	0.395	3792	1	0	0	0	20-Mar-07

Ranking		Bank na	Country	Institution type	S / W	*Sharia'a* compliant assets		Total assets		Profits and returns			Result date
Current	Previous					Total US$m	% change	US$m	% *Sharia'a*	Profits US$m	% change	Asset returns %	
40	n/a	AMMB Holdings	Malaysia	Commercial Bank	W: Islamic Windows	3671.9	0.118	25752.1	0.143	84.8	-0.183	0.003	30-Jun-08
41	56	Gulf Finance House	Bahrain	Investment Bank	S: Full Islamic	3507.8	0.925	3507.8	1	220.3	0.51	0.083	30-Jun-08
42	39	Kuwait International Bank	Kuwait	Commercial & Retail Banking	S: Full Islamic	3269.4	0	3432.7	0.952	65.1	0.895	0.021	31-Dec-07
43	52	Albarakah Tur	Turkey	Commercial Bank	S: Full Islamic	3112	0.481	3112	1	90.7	0.501	0.035	31-Dec-07
44	61	Dubai Bank	UAE	Commercial Bank	S: Full Islamic	2972.7	0.964	2972.7	1	29.6	0.093	0.013	31-Dec-07
45	6	AmIslamic Bank Berhad	Malaysia	Commercial Bank	S: Full Islamic	2832.6	0.018	2832.6	1	34.4	-0.046	0.012	31-Dec-07
46	64	Masraf Al Rayan	Qatar	Commercial & Investment Bank	S: Full Islamic	2799.9	1.357	2799.9	1	327.6	9.57	0.164	31-Dec-07
47	44	Islami Bank Bangladesh Limited	Bangladesh	Commercial Bank	S: Full Islamic	2788	0.274	2788	1	55.1	0.3	0.022	31-Dec-07
48	117	International Leasing and Investment Company	Kuwait	Credit & Finance	S: Full Islamic	2783.8	0.576	2783.8	1	264.9	-0.038	0.116	31-Dec-07
49	42	Qatar International Islamic Bank, Doha	Qatar	Commercial & Investment Bank	S: Full Islamic	2733.8	0.185	2733.8	1	131.9	0.203	0.052	31-Dec-07
50	n/a	Bank Islam Brunei Darussalam Berhad	Brunei	Commercial Bank	S: Full Islamic	2723.1	0	2723.1	1	68.7	0.353	0	31-Dec-07
51	43	Sharjah Islamic Bank	UAE	Commercial Bank	S: Full Islamic	2721.7	0.308	2721.7	1	46.8	0.197	0.019	30-Sep-07
52	53	Bank Boubyan	Kuwait	Commercial Bank	S: Full Islamic	2701.4	0.479	2701.4	1	67.5	0.806	0.03	31-Dec-07
53	83	CIMB Islamic Bank Berhad	Malaysia	Commercial & Retail Banking	S: Full Islamic	2677.9	0.874	2677.9	1	27.7	8.551	0.013	31-Dec-07
54	41	RHB ISLAMIC Bank Berhad	Malaysia	Commercial Bank	S: Full Islamic	2605.5	0.039	2605.5	1	50.3	0.332	0.02	31-Mar-08
55	75	Tamweel	UAE	Credit & Finance	S: Full Islamic	2318.2	1.61	2318.2	1	122.9	-0.47	0.077	31-Dec-07
56	51	Cagamas Berhad	Malaysia	Commercial Bank	W: Islamic Windows	2302.3	0.213	7365.8	0.313	49.5	0.288	0.007	31-Dec-07
57	46	Jordan Islamic Bank for Finance and Investment	Jordan	Commercial Bank	S: Full Islamic	2242.6	0.0871	2242.6	1	48.5	0.47	0.023	31-Dec-07
58	45	Kuwait Turket Evcaf Finance House	Turkey	Commercial Bank	S: Full Islamic	2094.7	0.25	2094.7	1	28.2	0.633	0.015	31-Dec-06
59	54	Shamil Bank	Bahrain	Commercial & Investment Bank	S: Full Islamic	2045.7	0.208	2045.7	1	85.6	0.341	0.046	31-Dec-07
60	62	Karafarin Bank	Iran	Commercial Bank	S: Full Islamic	2020.4	0.456	2020.4	1	58	0.513	0.034	20-Mar-07
61	55	Aayan Leasing and Investment Company	Kuwait	Investment Company	S: Full Islamic	2019.2	0.174	2019.2	1	89.1	0.479	0.048	31-Dec-07
62	222	Qatar National Bank	Qatar	Commercial Bank	W: Islamic Windows	1969.2	0.216	31417.8	0.063	693.8	0.259	0.027	31-Dec-07
63	69	Kuwait Finance House (Bahrain)	Bahrain	Commercial Bank	S: Full Islamic	1955.6	0.824	1955.6	1	86.9	0.573	0.057	31-Dec-07
64	49	Omdurman National Bank	Sudan	Commercial Bank	S: Full Islamic	1884.4	0.638	1884.4	1	15.1	0.752	0.01	31-Dec-05
65	77	Kuwait Finance House (Malaysia) Berhad	Malaysia	Commercial & Investment Bank	S: Full Islamic	1877.8	1.089	1877.8	1	9.1	3.673	0.007	31-Dec-07
66	57	Saudi Hollandi Bank	Saudi Arabia	Commercial Bank	W: Islamic Windows	1876.1	0.152	13461	0.139	117.1	-0.54	0.009	31-Dec-07
67	68	Affin Bank Berhad	Malaysia	Commercial Bank	W: Islamic Windows	1867	0.606	7815.2	0.239	74.8	0.15	0.01	31-Dec-07
68	67	EONCAP Islamic Bank Berhad	Malaysia	Commercial Bank	S: Full Islamic	1823.1	0.192	1823.1	1	14.3	0.849	0.009	31-Dec-07
69	50	Hong Leong Islamic Bank Berhad	Malaysia	Commercial Bank	S: Full Islamic	1815.5	-0.033	1815.5	1	23.7	0.302	0.013	30-Jun-07
70	85	Islamic Development Bank	Saudi Arabia	Development Financial Institutions	S: Full Islamic	1794	0.1	1794	1	43.7	0.324	0.025	09-Jan-08
71	66	Bahrain Islamic Bank Bsc.	Bahrain	Commercial Bank	S: Full Islamic	1752.6	0.51	1752.6	1	66.6	0.917	0.046	31-Dec-07
72	222	Bahrain Islamic Investment Co. Bsc. Closed	Bahrain	Investment Bank	S: Full Islamic	1752.6	0.51	1752.6	1	34.7	0.917	0.046	31-Dec-07
73	72	Egyptian Saudi Finance Bank, Cairo	Egypt	Commercial Bank	S: Full Islamic	1751.8	0.097	1751.8	1	0	0	0	31-Mar-08
74	63	National Investment Trust Ltd., Karachi	Pakistan	Investment Bank	S: Full Islamic	1724.7	0.398	1724.7	1	190.8	0.276	0.129	30-Jun-07
75	65	AREF Investment Group	Kuwait	Investment Company	S: Full Islamic	1706.3	0.381	1706.3	1	221.5	0.826	0.151	31-Dec-07
76	222	Export Development Bank of Iran	Iran	Government owned Bank	S: Full Islamic	1623	0	1623	1	0	0	0	20-Mar-06

Ranking		Bank na	Country	Institution type	S / W	*Sharia'a* compliant assets		Total assets		Profits and returns			Result date
Current	Previous					Total US$m	% change	US$m	% *Sharia'a*	Profits US$m	% change	Asset returns %	
77	98	Saudi Investment Bank	Saudi Arabia	Commercial Bank	W: Islamic Windows	1549.5	0.499	12427.7	0.125	219.5	-0.59	0.019	31-Dec-07
78	60	Iran Insurance Company	Iran	Insurance Company	S: Full Islamic	1516	0.13	1516	1	80.8	-0.024	0.057	20-Mar-06
79	59	HSBC Bank (M) Berhad	Malaysia	Commercial Bank	W: Islamic Windows	1496.3	-0.065	14340.7	0.104	307.3	0.087	0.023	31-Dec-07
80	90	Standard Chartered Bank Malaysia Berhad	Malaysia	Commercial Bank	W: Islamic Windows	1405.8	1.306	12486.8	0.113	221.9	0.183	0.018	31-Dec-07
81	32	ABC Islamic Bank	Bahrain	Wholesale Bank	S: Full Islamic	1364.9	0.673	1364.9	1	50.9	8.6	0.047	31-Dec-07
82	n/a	Habib Bank	Pakistan	Commercial Bank	W: Islamic Windows	1314.2	0.032	11161.2	0.118	15144.6	-0.196	1.46	31-Dec-07
83	70	Qatar Real Estate Investment Company	Qatar	Investment Company	S: Full Islamic	1214.4	0.222	1214.4	1	82.3	1.218	0.075	31-Dec-07
84	73	PT Bank Muamalat Indonesia, Jakarta	Indonesia	Commercial Bank	S: Full Islamic	1197.2	0.271	1197.2	1	0	0	0	31-Dec-07
85	222	Bank of London and the Middle East	UK	Commercial Bank	S: Full Islamic	1196.3	1.031	1196.3	1	3.4	4.219	0.004	30-Jun-08
86	86	Bank of Khartoum	Sudan	Commercial Bank	S: Full Islamic	1176.8	0.538	1176.8	1	22.5	0	0.023	31-Dec-07
87	138	Tadhamon International Islamic Bank	Yemen	Commercial Bank	S: Full Islamic	1163.8	0.247	1163.8	1	14.7	0.068	0.014	31-Dec-07
88	81	Meezan Bank Limited	Pakistan	Commercial Bank	S: Full Islamic	1102	0.447	1102	1	20.8	0.627	0.022	31-Dec-07
89	74	OCBC Bank (Malaysia) Berhad	Malaysia	Commercial Bank	W: Islamic Windows	1095.7	0.163	12568	0.087	213.8	0.19	0.018	31-Dec-07
90	95	Al Salam Bank	Bahrain	Investment Bank	S: Full Islamic	1057.9	1.115	1057.9	1	61.6	0.41	0.079	31-Dec-07
91	n/a	Al Baraka Islamic Bank (EC) BSC	Bahrain	Commercial Bank	S: Full Islamic	1045.4	0.057	1045.4	1	6.9	5.605	0.007	31-Dec-07
92	n/a	The Securities House Company	Kuwait	Investment Company	S: Full Islamic	1024.6	-0.039	1024.6	1	28.4	-0.55	0.027	31-Dec-07
93	71	PT Bank Shyariah Mandiri	Indonesia	Commercial Bank	S: Full Islamic	1020	0.282	1020	1	7.3	-0.501	0.008	30-Nov-06
94	79	Syarikat Takaful Malaysia Bhd	Malaysia	Insurance Company	S: Full Islamic	1015.5	0.1	1015.5	1	7.7	-0.404	0.008	30-Jun-07
95	222	BAMIS	Mauritius	Commercial Bank	S: Full Islamic	943.5	0.145	943.5	1	0.1	0	0.0001	31-Dec-07
96	n/a	Alliance Islamic Bank Berhad	Malaysia	Commercial Bank	S: Full Islamic	936.5	0	936.5	1	2.9	0	0	30-Jun-08
97	76	Alliance Bank Malaysia Berhad	Malaysia	Commercial Bank	W: Islamic Windows	918.8	-0.0006	8005.2	0.115	157.6	2.254	0.02	31-Mar-08
98	78	Alafco Aviation Lease and Finance Company	Kuwait	Credit & Finance	S: Full Islamic	887.5	0.008	887.5	1	33.1	0.11	0.037	30-Sep-07
99	100	Islamic International Arab Bank	Jordan	Commercial Bank	S: Full Islamic	866.4	0.034	866.4	1	15.5	0.373	0.018	31-Dec-07
100	91	Banque Al Baraka D`Algerie	Algeria	Investment Bank	S: Full Islamic	837.5	0.224	837.5	1	6.4	-0.228	0.008	31-Dec-07
101	80	DMI Trust	Switzerland	Commercial & Retail Banking	S: Full Islamic	830	0.02	830	1	50.1	-0.297	0.061	31-Dec-07
102	97	First Investment Company	Kuwait	Asset Management	S: Full Islamic	781	0.546	781	1	91.9	0.258	0.143	31-Dec-07
103	n/a	Al Rajhi Banking & Investment Corp. (Malaysia)	Malaysia	Commercial Bank	S: Full Islamic	757	7.721	757	1	-31.6	0.253	-0.075	31-Dec-07
104	131	Al Madina for Finance and Investment Company	Kuwait	Investment Company	S: Full Islamic	751.9	2.239	751.9	1	75.9	1.787	0.154	31-Dec-07
105	84	Export Import Bank of Bangladesh	Bangladesh	Specialized Bank	S: Full Islamic	750.4	0.232	750.4	1	23.6	0.35	0.035	31-Dec-07
106	82	The Company for Co-operative Insurance	Saudi Arabia	Insurance Company	S: Full Islamic	733.3	0.25	733.3	1	46.7	0.036	0.071	31-Dec-04
107	121	Khaleeji Commercial Bank	Bahrain	Commercial & Investment Bank	S: Full Islamic	716.8	1.8	716.8	1	55.4	1.609	0.114	31-Dec-07
108	130	Al Safat Investment Company	Kuwait	Investment Company	S: Full Islamic	687.9	1.936	687.9	1	89.7	2.101	0.195	31-Dec-07
109	93	The International Investor, Safat	Kuwait	Investment Bank	S: Full Islamic	685	0.19	685	1	46.1	0.035	0.073	31-Dec-07
110	105	Islamic Arab Insurance Company-Salama	UAE	Insurance Company	S: Full Islamic	683.8	0.167	683.8	1	43	-0.143	0.068	31-Dec-07
111	222	Doha Bank	Qatar	Commercial Bank	W: Islamic Windows	651.3	1.125	8266	0.079	254.6	0.245	0.036	31-Dec-07
112	99	European Islamic Investment Bank	UK	Investment Bank	S: Full Islamic	648.2	0.341	648.2	1	-5.1	-2.315	-0.009	31-Dec-07

Ranking		Bank na	Country	Institution type	S / W	*Sharia'a* compliant assets		Total assets		Profits and returns			Result date
Current	Previous					Total US$m	% change	US$m	% *Sharia'a*	Profits US$m	% change	Asset returns %	
113	222	Cham Bank	Syria	Commercial Bank	S: Full Islamic	641.4	0	641.4	1	-22.7	0	0	31-Dec-07
114	119	International Investment Group	Kuwait	Investment Bank	S: Full Islamic	628.3	0.125	628.3	1	76.6	-0.105	0.129	31-Dec-07
115	87	Al Madar Finance and Investment Company	Kuwait	Credit & Finance	S: Full Islamic	618.7	-0.052	618.7	1	32.7	0.249	0.052	31-Dec-07
116	222	Islamic Bank of Asia	Singapore	Commercial Bank	S: Full Islamic	618	0	618	1	3.8	0	0	31-Dec-07
117	n/a	KAF Investment Bank Berhad	Malaysia	Investment Bank	W: Islamic Windows	603.3	0.52	1749.1	0.345	38.1	0.395	0.02	31-Dec-07
118	89	Credit Institution for Development	Iran	Government owned Bank	S: Full Islamic	595.9	0.379	595.9	1	4.8	0.473	0.009	20-Mar-06
119	113	Bank Pembangunan Malaysia Berhad	Malaysia	Commercial Bank	W: Islamic Windows	576.9	0.604	6944.6	0.083	113.3	-0.312	0.017	31-Dec-07
120	92	Al Baraka Islamic Investment Bank	Bahrain	Commercial & Investment Bank	S: Full Islamic	559.7	0.095	559.7	1	0.7	-0.896	0.001	31-Dec-06
121	126	Malaysia Building Society	Malaysia	Building Society	W: Islamic Windows	513.9	1.044	2004.8	0.256	12.5	0.401	0.0071	31-Dec-07
122	96	Citibank Berhad	Malaysia	Commercial Bank	W: Islamic Windows	499.2	0.64	10835.6	0.046	208.2	0.007	0.02	31-Dec-06
123	125	Islamic Bank of Thailand	Thailand	Commercial Bank	S: Full Islamic	495.5	0.913	495.5	1	-8.4	0.061	-0.022	31-Dec-07
124	103	National Credit & Commercial Bank Ltd	Bangladesh	Commercial Bank	S: Full Islamic	473	0.249	473	1	8.4	0.721	0.02	31-Dec-06
125	222	Commercial Bank of Qatar	Qatar	Commercial Bank	S: Full Islamic	466.6	0.972	12471.8	0.037	382.1	0.612	0.037	31-Dec-07
126	222	Parsian Insurance Co	Iran	Insurance Company	S: Full Islamic	465.7	0.136	465.7	1	34.5	0.491	0.079	20-Mar-07
127	112	Unicorn Investment Bank BSC	Bahrain	Investment Bank	S: Full Islamic	446.7	0.523	446.7	1	49.6	0.645	0.134	31-Dec-07
128	n/a	Malaysian Industrial Development Fianance Berhad	Malaysia	Mortgage Provider	W: Islamic Windows	445.1	-0.246	2738.8	0.163	52.4	0.406	0.017	31-Dec-07
129	128	Al-Arafah Islami Bank Limited	Bangladesh	Commercial Bank	S: Full Islamic	439.7	0.412	439.7	1	11	-0.116	0.029	31-Dec-07
130	26	Bank Alfalah Ltd	Pakistan	Commercial Bank	W: Islamic Windows	436	0.131	5395.1	0.081	74.4	0.768	0.015	31-Dec-07
131	115	Bank Perusahaan Kecil & Sederhana Malaysia Berhad	Malaysia	Development Financial Institutions	W: Islamic Windows	428.7	0.255	1374.1	0.312	15.9	-1.174	0.012	31-Dec-07
132	108	First Finance Co.	Qatar	Credit & Finance	S: Full Islamic	420.7	0.27	420.7	1	7.7	0.857	0.021	31-Dec-07
133	111	Shahjalal Islami Bank Ltd	Bangladesh	Commercial Bank	S: Full Islamic	413	0.328	413	1	17.7	0.544	0.049	31-Dec-07
134	222	Al Dar Asset Management (ADAM)	Kuwait	Asset Management	S: Full Islamic	409.2	0	409.2	1	48.3	0	0	31-Dec-07
135	102	Tadamon Islamic Bank of Sudan	Sudan	Commercial Bank	S: Full Islamic	407.7	0.331	407.7	1	19.6	0.164	0.055	31-Dec-06
136	222	Muthanna Investment Company	Kuwait	Investment Company	S: Full Islamic	384.3	0.799	384.3	1	16.1	0.42	0.054	31-Dec-07
137	110	United International Bank	Bahrain	Investment Bank	S: Full Islamic	383.4	0	383.4	1	20.9	0	0	31-Dec-07
138	104	Gulf Investment House	Kuwait	Investment Bank	S: Full Islamic	373.9	0.088	373.9	1	53	-0.104	0.148	31-Dec-07
139	137	Asian Finance Bank Berhad	Malaysia	Commercial Bank	S: Full Islamic	373.2	2.462	373.2	1	-1.6	0.167	-0.007	31-Dec-07
140	123	Al Baraka Islamic Bank (EC) BSC-Pakistan	Pakistan	Commercial Bank	S: Full Islamic	362.1	0.17	362.1	1	5.2	0.846	0.015	31-Dec-07
141	n/a	Finance House PJSC	UAE	Mortgage Provider	S: Full Islamic	358.1	0.242	358.1	1	43.7	-0.157	0.135	31-Dec-06
142	116	Social Investment Bank Ltd	Bangladesh	Commercial Bank	S: Full Islamic	357.6	0.247	357.6	1	3.9	1.228	0.012	31-Dec-07
143	106	Faisal Islamic Bank (Sudan)	Sudan	Commercial & Private Banking	S: Full Islamic	356.1	0.65	356.1	1	15.4	1.331	0.054	31-Dec-06
144	n/a	Best Bank	Tunisia	Commercial & Investment Bank	S: Full Islamic	352.4	-1	352.4	1	8	1.022	0.027	31-Dec-06
145	134	Islamic Co-operative Development Bank	Sudan	Development Financial Institutions	S: Full Islamic	347	0.25	347	1	4.3	0.524	0.014	31-Dec-07
146	127	Islamic Bank of Britain	UK	Commercial & Private Banking	S: Full Islamic	337.4	0.398	337.4	1	-14.1	-0.217	-0.049	31-Dec-07
147	107	AmInvestment Group Berhad	Malaysia	Investment Bank	W: Islamic Windows	321	-0.154	5234.1	0.061	37.7	0.141	0.006	31-Mar-08
148	222	Ahli Bank	Qatar	Commercial Bank	W: Islamic Windows	320.5	0.168	4279.2	0.075	83.1	0.496	0.024	31-Dec-07

Ranking		Bank na	Country	Institution type	S / W	*Sharia'a* compliant assets		Total assets		Profits and returns			Result date
Current	Previous					Total US$m	% change	US$m	% *Sharia'a*	Profits US$m	% change	Asset returns %	
149	222	Mawarid Finance	UAE	Credit & Finance	S: Full Islamic	309.6	0.09	309.6	1	15.6	0.522	0.053	31-Dec-07
150	133	Arab Islamic Bank	Palestine	Commercial Bank	S: Full Islamic	301.6	0.376	301.6	1	6.2	0.323	0.024	31-Dec-07
151	114	Sokouk Holding Company	Kuwait	Investment Company	S: Full Islamic	299.5	0	299.5	1	34.3	-0.157	0.115	31-Dec-07
152	94	Khaleej Finance & Investment Company	Bahrain	Investment Bank	S: Full Islamic	283.3	0.45	283.3	1	13.8	0.495	0.058	30-Sep-07
153	222	CIMB Investment Bank Berhad	Malaysia	Investment Bank	W: Islamic Windows	280.6	1.568	1262.3	0.222	131	0.18	0.116	31-Dec-07
154	118	B.E.S.T. Retakaful	Tunisia	Insurance Company	S: Full Islamic	279.9	0.436	279.9	1	6.7	0.466	0.028	31-Dec-05
155	120	PT Bank Shyariah Mega Indonesia	Indonesia	Commercial Bank	S: Full Islamic	277.2	0.092	277.2	1	13.5	1.272	0.051	31-Dec-07
156	222	PT Bank Negara Indonesia	Indonesia	Commercial Bank	W: Islamic Windows	275.6	0.593	19697.3	0.014	159.8	-0.476	0.008	31-Dec-07
157	222	International Investment House	Bahrain	Investment Bank	S: Full Islamic	257.3	1.722	257.3	1	21.1	0.135	0.12	31-Dec-07
158	142	Al Aman Investment Co.	Kuwait	Asset Management	S: Full Islamic	256.1	0.334	256.1	1	32.6	2.585	0.145	31-Dec-07
159	141	Al Khaleej Insurance & Reinsurance Co	Qatar	Insurance Company	S: Full Islamic	255.9	0.351	255.9	1	29.4	2.251	0.132	30-Jun-08
160	n/a	The Oriental Bank	Bangladesh	Commercial Bank	S: Full Islamic	254.7	-0.069	254.7	1	8.9	-1.142	0.034	31-Dec-07
161	122	Al Salam Bank Sudan	Sudan	Commercial & Private Banking	S: Full Islamic	251.6	-0.04	251.6	1	0	0	0	31-Dec-06
162	135	Al Baraka South Africa	South Africa	Commercial & Private Banking	S: Full Islamic	249.8	0.147	249.8	1	4	0.732	0.017	31-Dec-07
163	124	Dubai Islamic Bank Pakistan Ltd	Pakistan	Commercial & Private Banking	S: Full Islamic	244	0	244	1	-5.5	0	0	30-Jun-07
164	160	Bank Islami Pakistan	Pakistan	Commercial Bank	S: Full Islamic	237	2.59	237	1	-1.6	1.921	-0.011	31-Dec-07
165	222	Global Banking Corporation	Bahrain	Investment Bank	S: Full Islamic	236.2	0	236.2	1	35.9	0	0	31-Dec-07
166	129	Solidarity Insurance Co.	Bahrain	Insurance Company	S: Full Islamic	227.1	0.635	227.1	1	4.3	-3.853	0.024	31-Dec-06
167	222	Osoul Leasing & Finance Co	Kuwait	Credit & Finance	S: Full Islamic	222.1	-0.107	222.11	1	28.6	-6.744	0.121	31-Dec-07
168	132	Liquidity Management Centre	Bahrain	Investment Bank	S: Full Islamic	220	0	220	1	6.1	0	0	31-Dec-08
169	136	Al Baraka Sudan	Sudan	Commercial Bank	S: Full Islamic	207.2	0.6	207.2	1	0	0	0	31-Dec-05
170	139	Animal Resource Bank	Sudan	Specialized Bank	S: Full Islamic	204.7	0.078	204.7	1	1.3	-0.094	0.006	31-Dec-06
171	152	Arab Finance House	Lebanon	Commercial & Investment Bank	S: Full Islamic	203	0.678	203	1	-0.2	2.497	0.012	31-Dec-07
172	n/a	United Capital Bank Sudan	Sudan	Investment Bank	S: Full Islamic	190.6	1.004	190.6	1	6.8	-6.199	0.048	31-Dec-07
173	140	Alborz Insurance Co	Iran	Insurance Company	S: Full Islamic	189.8	0.251	189.8	1	0	0	0	31-Dec-04
174	n/a	Orient Investment Co.	Kuwait	Investment Company	S: Full Islamic	173.1	0.307	173.1	1	38.9	3.029	0.254	31-Dec-07
175	145	Qatar Islamic Insurance Co.	Qatar	Insurance Company	S: Full Islamic	159.2	0.264	159.2	1	12.2	0.235	0.086	31-Dec-07
176	222	Dubai Islamic Insurance and Reinsurance Co.	UAE	Insurance Company	S: Full Islamic	156.8	0.394	156.8	1	11.3	-4.026	0.084	31-Dec-07
177	222	UM Financial	Canada	Credit & Finance	S: Full Islamic	149.3	0.5	149.3	1	0.5	0	0.004	18-Jul-08
178	167	Emirates Global Islamic Bank Ltd	Pakistan	Commercial Bank	S: Full Islamic	146.7	2.652	146.7	1	-1.4	-0.498	-0.015	31-Dec-07
179	143	Investors Bank EC	Bahrain	Investment Bank	S: Full Islamic	145	-0.021	145	1	1.4	-0.294	0.01	30-Sep-07
180	144	National Leasing Company	Qatar	Credit & Finance	S: Full Islamic	141.5	0.069	141.5	1	15.1	0.871	0.11	31-Dec-07
181	222	Al Ritaj Investment Co.	Kuwait	Investment Company	S: Full Islamic	138.3	0	138.3	1	14.1	0	0	31-Dec-07
182	222	FNB Islamic Finance	South Africa	Commercial & Retail Banking	W: Islamic Windows	137	0	0	0	10.6	0	0.063	01-Jun-07
183	222	PT Bank Bukopin	Indonesia	Commercial Bank	W: Islamic Windows	133.9	0.194	3458.3	0.039	50.4	0.226	0.016	31-Dec-06
184	n/a	Warba Investment Company	Kuwait	Investment Company	S: Full Islamic	131.7	0.098	131.7	1	82.6	34.175	0.656	31-Dec-07
185	n/a	CIMB Aviva Takaful Bhd	Malaysia	Insurance Company	S: Full Islamic	131.2	1.504	131.2	1	1.9	0.202	0.02	31-Dec-07
186	n/a	Dawood Islamic Bank Ltd	Pakistan	Commercial Bank	S: Full Islamic	127.3	0.138	127.3	1	0.4	0.811	0.003	31-Mar-08
187	n/a	Al Masar Leasing and Investment Co. KSC (Closed)	Kuwait	Investment Company	S: Full Islamic	124.9	0	124.9	1	7.6	0	0	31-Dec-06

Ranking		Bank na	Country	Institution type	S / W	*Sharia'a* compliant assets		Total assets		Profits and returns			Result date
Current	Previous					Total US$m	% change	US$m	% *Sharia'a*	Profits US$m	% change	Asset returns %	
188	n/a	MCB Bank Limited	Pakistan	Commercial Bank	W: Islamic Windows	123.3	0.735	6733.5	0.018	349.5	0.152	0.057	31-Dec-07
189	147	Prime Bank	Bangladesh	Commercial Bank	W: Islamic Windows	119.1	0.111	1159.6	0.103	34.2	0.35	0.033	31-Dec-07
190	222	PT Bank Rakyat Indonesia	Indonesia	Commercial Bank	W: Islamic Windows	118.1	0.067	22048	0.005	842	0.317	0.1	31-Dec-07
191	222	First Leasing Bank	Bahrain	Wholesale Bank	S: Full Islamic	116.2	0.136	116.2	1	1.2	-0.5685	0.011	30-Jun-08
192	146	Financial Investment Bank	Sudan	Investment Bank	S: Full Islamic	114.4	-0.364	114.4	1	10.7	0.333	0.073	31-Dec-06
193	222	PT Bank Niaga	Indonesia	Commercial Bank	W: Islamic Windows	109.7	0.905	5939.8	0.018	111.1	0.102	0.02	31-Dec-07
194	156	Habib Metropolitan Bank	Pakistan	Commercial Bank	W: Islamic Windows	109.2	0.45	2835.7	0.038	69	0.337	0.026	31-Dec-07
195	222	Aseambankers Malaysia Bd	Malaysia	Investment Bank	W: Islamic Windows	107.3	0	2680.4	0.04	62.7	1.083	0.031	30-Jun-07
196	148	Sheikan Insurance & Reinsurance Co. Ltd.	Sudan	Insurance Company	S: Full Islamic	105.7	0.684	105.7	1	11	0.248	0.131	31-Dec-04
197	149	Takaful Ikhlas Sdn Bhd	Malaysia	Insurance Company	S: Full Islamic	98.4	0.589	98.4	1	0.4	2.519	0.005	31-Mar-07
198	150	Commercial Bank	Bosnia and Herzegovina	Specialized Bank	U: Islamic Windows	19.4	0.97	100	0.0003	-101.5	0.0003	0	31-Dec-08
199	151	Beit Al Mal Saving and Investment for Housing	Jordan	Investment Company	S: Full Islamic	96.9	0.409	96.9	1	0	0	0	31-Dec-06
200	n/a	Kurdistan International Bank for Inv. and Dev.	Iraq	Development Financial Institutions	S: Full Islamic	96.8	0.001	96.8	1	5	8.842	0.051	31-Dec-07
201	n/a	European Finance House	UK	Asset Management	S: Full Islamic	94.1	0	94.1	1	0	0	0	30-Sep-08
202	153	Real Estate Finance Co.	Bahrain	Credit & Finance	S: Full Islamic	93.2	0	93.2	1	4	0	0	31-Dec-06
203	157	Venture Capital Bank	Bahrain	Venture Capital	S: Full Islamic	90.9	0.212	90.9	1	13.3	0	0.16	31-Dec-06
204	222	Faisal Private Bank	Switzerland	Commercial & Private Banking	S: Full Islamic	84.1	0.062	84.1	1	-2.9	-1.273	-0.035	31-Dec-06
205	222	PT Bank Danamon	Indonesia	Commercial Bank	W: Islamic Windows	82.9	0.567	9676.1	0.009	358.6	0.575	0.039	31-Dec-07
206	162	First Habib Bank Modaraba	Pakistan	Commercial Bank	S: Full Islamic	82	0.286	82	1	2.7	0.058	0.037	30-Jun-07
207	222	Wethaq Takaful Insurance Co.	Kuwait	Insurance Company	S: Full Islamic	79.6	0.086	79.6	1	2.1	2.086	0.027	31-Dec-07
208	155	Mayban Dicount Bd	Malaysia	Discount House	W: Islamic Windows	79	-0.268	1640.5	0.048	17.1	-0.179	0.01	31-Dec-06
209	154	Islamic Bank of Yemen for Fin. and Invest.	Yemen	Commercial Bank	S: Full Islamic	78.9	-0.184	78.9	1	0	0	0	31-Dec-06
210	174	The Bank of Khyber	Pakistan	Commercial Bank	W: Islamic Windows	78.3	1.132	487.8	0.161	1.5	-0.553	0.003	31-Dec-07
211	222	PT Bank Permata	Indonesia	Commercial Bank	W: Islamic Windows	78	1.273	4306.7	0.018	80.7	0.619	0.019	31-Dec-06
212	n/a	Alliance Investment Bank Berhad	Malaysia	Investment Bank	W: Islamic Windows	75.5	-0.258	719.4	0.105	2.6	-0.514	0.004	31-Mar-08
213	168	Shamil Bank of Yemen and Bahrain	Yemen	Commercial Bank	S: Full Islamic	75	0.295	75	1	1.4	65.402	0.021	31-Dec-05
214	192	Askari Bank Limited	Pakistan	Commercial Bank	W: Islamic Windows	74.7	6.005	2988.3	0.025	37.7	-0.313	0.013	31-Dec-07
215	170	Islamic Financial Securities	Qatar	Stock & Commodity Brokers	S: Full Islamic	71.6	0.384	71.6	1	2.9	1.603	0.047	31-Dec-07
216	161	Abu Dhabi National Takaful Co.	UAE	Insurance Company	S: Full Islamic	68.1	0.046	68.1	1	2.9	0.306	0.043	31-Dec-07
217	159	Saudi Arabian Insurance Co.	Saudi Arabia	Insurance Company	S: Full Islamic	67.8	-0.16	67.8	1	4.8	-0.164	0.064	31-Dec-04
218	163	Gulf Takaful Insurance Co. K.S.C.C	Kuwait	Insurance Company	S: Full Islamic	61	0	61	1	5.7	0	0	31-Dec-05
219	165	Bayt Al Mal Holding Co.	Kuwait	Investment Company	S: Full Islamic	60	0	60	1	0	0	0	31-Dec-05

Ranking		Bank na	Country	Institution type	S / W	*Sharia'a* compliant assets		Total assets		Profits and returns			Result date
Current	Previous					Total US$m	% change	US$m	% *Sharia'a*	Profits US$m	% change	Asset returns %	
220	169	First Takaful Insurance Co.	Kuwait	Insurance Company	S: Full Islamic	57.6	0.069	57.6	1	6.9	-0.041	0.124	31-Dec-07
221	222	PT Bank DKI	Indonesia	Commercial Bank	W: Islamic Windows	55.9	3.207	1260.1	0.044	8.2	0.059	0.007	31-Mar-08
222	222	Amin Reinsurance Co.	Iran	Insurance Company	S: Full Islamic	53	0.233	53	1	6.9	0.208	0.143	21-Sep-07
223	173	Takaful International Company	Bahrain	Insurance Company	S: Full Islamic	50.3	0.186	50.3	1	0.2	-1.302	0.004	31-Dec-07
224	n/a	Prudential BSN Takaful Berhad	Malaysia	Insurance Company	S: Full Islamic	49	0.327	49	1	-4	-0.001	-0.093	31-Dec-07
225	172	Standard Chartered Modaraba	Pakistan	Commercial Bank	S: Full Islamic	42	0.001	42	1	1.3	0.336	0.032	30-Jun-07
226	n/a	Bank Al Habib Lmt	Pakistan	Commercial Bank	W: Islamic Windows	41.7	1.238	2316.8	0.018	50.1	0.135	0.024	31-Dec-07
227	186	University Bank Islamic Financial Corp.	USA	Commercial Bank	S: Full Islamic	35.6	0.599	35.6	1	-0.4	2.273	-0.012	31-Dec-07
228	176	UBL Ameen	Pakistan	Commercial Bank	W: Islamic Windows	33.7	39.252	8969.5	0.004	226.3	-0.049	0.028	31-Dec-07
229	222	PT Bank International Indonesia	Indonesia	Commercial Bank	W: Islamic Windows	32.8	0.505	5968.3	0.005	40.8	-0.493	0.007	31-Dec-07
230	n/a	Hong Leong Tokio Marine Takaful Berhad	Malaysia	Insurance Company	S: Full Islamic	30.1	0	30.1	1	-0.8	0	0	30-Jun-07
231	185	Karafarin Insurance Co	Iran	Insurance Company	S: Full Islamic	28.9	0.396	28.9	1	4	0.282	0.161	20-Mar-07
232	182	Muslim Community Cooperative Australia Ltd	Australia	Co-operatives	S: Full Islamic	27.2	0.074	27.2	1	0.7	0.242	0.028	30-Jun-07
233	178	Islamic Corp. for the Insurance of Inv. & Export Credit	Saudi Arabia	Credit & Finance	S: Full Islamic	26.5	0.016	26.5	1	0.3	-0.492	0.012	19-Jan-07
234	180	Farest Islami Life Insurance	Bangladesh	Insurance Company	S: Full Islamic	25.8	0.566	25.8	1	0	0	0	31-Dec-05
235	181	Premier Bank Ltd	Bangladesh	Commercial Bank	W: Islamic Windows	25.3	0.607	393.4	0.064	13.6	0.048	0.038	31-Dec-06
236	164	Southeast Bank Ltd	Bangladesh	Commercial & Private Banking	W: Islamic Windows	25.2	0.316	937.8	0.027	37.8	0.585	0.044	31-Dec-07
237	222	Ahli United Bank	Bahrain	Commercial Bank	W: Islamic Windows	23.2	0	23049.9	0.001	372.2	0.426	0.017	31-Dec-07
238	183	Arabia ACE Insurance Company Ltd EC	Bahrain	Insurance Company	S: Full Islamic	21.6	0.19	21.6	1	2.5	-0.415	0.126	31-Dec-04
239	184	Al Amin for Investment	Jordan	Investment Company	S: Full Islamic	21	0	21	1	5.6	0	0	31-Dec-04
240	222	Omdurman National Bank	Sudan	Commercial Bank	W: Islamic Windows	20	0	25	0.8	0.2	0	0	31-Dec-07
241	189	Islamic Finance & Investment Limited	Bangladesh	Investment Company	S: Full Islamic	19.5	0.324	19.5	1	0.9	0.127	0.053	31-Dec-07
242	187	Arab Gambian Islamic Bank	The Gambia	Commercial & Retail Banking	S: Full Islamic	18.7	0.451	18.74	1	0.3	1.265	0.016	30-Jun-06
243	222	Soneri Bank Limited	Pakistan	Commercial Bank	W: Islamic Windows	17.9	0.196	1260.7	0.014	24.2	0.019	0.02	31-Dec-07
244	n/a	Gatehouse Bank	UK	Investment Bank	S: Full Islamic	15.2	0	15.2	1	-8.9	0	0	31-Dec-07
245	188	PT Asuransi Syari'a Mubarakah	Indonesia	Insurance Company	S: Full Islamic	14.9	-0.006	14.9	1	-0.2	-0.705	-0.011	31-Dec-04
246	190	Islamic Insurance Company Ltd.	Sudan	Insurance Company	S: Full Islamic	13.2	0.466	13.2	1	2.3	3.242	0.209	31-Dec-04
247	171	Tejoori	UAE	Investment Company	S: Full Islamic	12.2	0.045	12.2	1	1	-1.792	0.081	30-Jun-07
248	191	Allied Cooperative Insurance Group	Saudi Arabia	Insurance Company	S: Full Islamic	12	2.757	12	1	-1.5	-2.009	-0.193	31-Dec-05
249	n/a	Parsoli Corporation Ltd.	India	Specialized Bank	S: Full Islamic	11.7	1.152	11.7	1	1.4	0.343	0.157	31-Mar-07
250	195	The City Bank Ltd	Bangladesh	Commercial Bank	W: Islamic Windows	11.5	-0.347	710.3	0.016	11.8	0.238	0.017	31-Dec-07
251	193	Sosar Al Amane	Senegal	Insurance Company	S: Full Islamic	10.5	0.138	10.5	1	0	0	0	31-Dec-04
252	194	Al Baraka Takaful Insurance Company	Jordan	Insurance Company	S: Full Islamic	10.3	-0.037	10.3	1	0	0	0	31-Dec-06
253	208	RBS Pakistan	Pakistan	Commercial Bank	W: Islamic Windows	10.1	0.74	1764	0.006	-22.4	-1.383	-0.012	31-Dec-07

Ranking		Bank na	Country	Institution type	S / W	*Sharia'a* compliant assets		Total assets		Profits and returns			Result date
Current	Previous					Total US$m	% change	US$m	% *Sharia'a*	Profits US$m	% change	Asset returns %	
254	196	The National Reinsurance Company	Sudan	Insurance Company	S: Full Islamic	8.7	0.22	8.7	1	0.1	1.207	0.007	31-Dec-04
255	197	The Sudanese Insurance & Reinsurance Co. Ltd.	Sudan	Insurance Company	S: Full Islamic	8.4	0	8.4	1	0.1	0	0	31-Dec-04
256	203	Amana Takaful	Sri Lanka	Insurance Company	S: Full Islamic	8.3	0.488	8.3	1	-1.4	-14.287	-0.2	31-Dec-07
257	213	National Bank of Pakistan	Pakistan	Commercial Bank	W: Islamic Windows	7.9	3.662	12502.8	0.001	460.3	0.067	0.04	31-Dec-07
258	198	The United Insurance Co. (Sudan) Ltd	Sudan	Insurance Company	S: Full Islamic	7.8	0.194	7.8	1	1.3	22.174	0.187	31-Dec-04
259	199	Export & Investment Insurance Co	Iran	Insurance Company	S: Full Islamic	7.6	0.481	7.6	1	0.01	-0.987	0.001	20-Mar-05
260	200	Juba Insurance Company Ltd.	Sudan	Insurance Company	S: Full Islamic	7.5	0.196	7.5	1	0.4	-0.264	0.064	31-Dec-04
261	179	Asean Retakaful International	Malaysia	Insurance Company	S: Full Islamic	7.1	-0.01	7.1	1	0.5	-0.073	0.073	30-Jun-07
262	202	Egyptian Saudi Insurance House	Egypt	Insurance Company	S: Full Islamic	5.7	0.429	5.7	1	-0.2	-0.101	-0.045	31-Dec-04
263	204	Seyad Shariat Finance Ltd	India	Credit & Finance	S: Full Islamic	5.1	0.073	5.1	1	0.3	0.444	0.062	31-Mar-07
264	205	Neighborhood Development Center	USA	Non Profit Inst	S: Full Islamic	4.8	0	4.8	1	0	0	0	31-Dec-03
265	206	Prime Islami Life Insurance Ltd	Bangladesh	Insurance Company	S: Full Islamic	4.1	0.981	4.1	1	0	0	0	31-Dec-05
266	222	PT Bank IFI	Indonesia	Commercial Bank	W: Islamic Windows	3.8	-0.229	62.3	0.06	-0.9	-0.502	-0.014	30-Jun-08
267	222	PT BPD NTB	Indonesia	Commercial Bank	W: Islamic Windows	3.1	0.536	208.1	0.015	6.5	0.011	0.032	31-Dec-07
268	207	Al Baraka Insurance Co. (Sudan) Ltd.	Sudan	Insurance Company	S: Full Islamic	3	0.515	3	1	0.2	0.232	0.073	31-Dec-04
269	209	Watania Co-operative Insurance Co. Ltd.	Sudan	Insurance Company	S: Full Islamic	2.2	3.146	2.2	1	-0.3	-3.408	-0.201	31-Dec-04
270	210	Arabia ACE Insurance Company Ltd	Saudi Arabia	Insurance Company	S: Full Islamic	2.2	0.19	2.2	1	0.3	-0.415	0.126	31-Dec-04
271	211	Red Sea Insurance Company Limited	Sudan	Insurance Company	S: Full Islamic	2.1	0.035	2.1	1	0.2	-0.686	0.099	31-Dec-04
272	212	The Blue Nile Insurance Co. Ltd.	Sudan	Insurance Company	S: Full Islamic	1.9	0.216	1.9	1	0	0	0	31-Dec-04
273	214	Tokio Marine and Nichido Fire Insurance Co.	Saudi Arabia	Insurance Company	S: Full Islamic	1.3	0	1.3	1	-2	0	0	31-Dec-04
274	215	El Nilein Insurance Co. Ltd	Sudan	Insurance Company	S: Full Islamic	0.8	3.009	0.8	1	0.2	0.244	0.373	31-Dec-03
275	216	Savanna Insurance Co. Ltd.	Sudan	Insurance Company	S: Full Islamic	0.6	-0.052	0.6	1	0.01	0.332	0.007	31-Dec-04
276	217	Saba Islamic Bank	Yemen	Commercial Bank	S: Full Islamic	0.3	0.436	0.3	1	0	0	0	31-Dec-05
277	218	Yemen Islamic Insurance Company (Y.S.C)	Yemen	Insurance Company	S: Full Islamic	0.2	0.937	0.2	1	-0.01	-0.501	-0.065	31-Dec-04
278	219	PT Syarikat Takaful Indonesia	Indonesia	Insurance Company	S: Full Islamic	0.04	0.14	0.04	1	0	0	0.023	31-Dec-06
279	220	PT Ansuransi Takaful Keluarga	Indonesia	Insurance Company	S: Full Islamic	0.03	0.168	0.03	1	0	8.072	0.022	31-Dec-06
280	221	PT Ansuransi Takaful Umum	Indonesia	Insurance Company	S: Full Islamic	0.01	0.141	0.01	1	0	-0.48	0.014	31-Dec-06
281	222	Perbadanan Tabung Amanah Islam Brunei	Brunei	Commercial Bank	S: Full Islamic	0	0	0	0	0	0	0	31-Dec-08
281	222	PICIC Commercial Bank	Pakistan	Commercial Bank	W: Islamic Windows	0	0	0	0	0	0	0	31-Dec-07
281	222	Postbank of Iran	Iran	Commercial Bank	S: Full Islamic	0	0	0	0	0	0	0	31-Dec-08
281	222	PT Bank BTN	Indonesia	Credit & Finance	W: Islamic Windows	0	0	4	0	65.1	0.108	0.037	31-Dec-07
281	222	PT Bank Jawa Barat	Indonesia	Investment Bank	W: Islamic Windows	0	0	2360	0	64	0.13	0.031	31-Dec-06
281	222	NIB Bank Limited	Pakistan	Investment Bank	W: Islamic Windows	0	0	2897.8	0	-9.4	-27.067	-0.005	31-Dec-07
281	222	Noor Islamic Bank	UAE	Investment Bank	S: Full Islamic	0	0	0	0	0	0	0	31-Dec-07
281	222	Noriba Bank	Bahrain	Investment Company	S: Full Islamic	0	0	0	0	0	0	0	31-Dec-08
281	222	OCBC BANK	Singapore	Asset Management	W: Islamic Windows	0	0	105089.2	0	1774.6	0.153	0.018	31-Dec-07

Ranking		Bank na	Country	Institution type	S / W	*Sharia'a* compliant assets		Total assets		Profits and returns			Result date
Current	Previous					Total US$m	% change	US$m	% *Sharia'a*	Profits US$m	% change	Asset returns %	
281	222	Oman Arab Bank	Oman	Investment Bank	W: Islamic Windows	0	0	1692.4	0	57.2	0.325	0.037	31-Dec-07
281	222	Oman International Bank S.A.O.G.	Oman	Investment Bank	W: Islamic Windows	0	0	2798.1	0	44.6	0.155	0.016	30-Jun-08
281	222	Oman International Bank S.A.O.G. (Pakistan)	Pakistan	Commercial Bank	W: Islamic Windows	0	0	45.3	0	-1.1	0	0	30-Jun-07
281	222	Palestine Islamic Bank	Palestine	Commercial Bank	S: Full Islamic	0	0	0	0	0	0	0	31-Dec-08
281	222	National Bonds Corporation	UAE	Commercial Bank	S: Full Islamic	0	0	0	0	0	0	0	31-Dec-08
281	222	Millennium Finance Corporation	UAE	Credit & Finance	S: Full Islamic	0	0	0	0	0	0	0	31-Dec-08
281	222	Misr Exterior Bank SAE	Egypt	Investment Bank	W: Islamic Windows	0	0	0	0	0	0	0	31-Dec-08
281	222	Mullak Arabia	Saudi Arabia	Investment Company	S: Full Islamic	0	0	0	0	0	0	0	01-Dec-06
281	222	Murabahat Investment Co.	Kuwait	Investment Company	S: Full Islamic	0	0	0	0	0	0	0	31-Dec-08
281	222	Muslim Commercial Bank	Sri Lanka	Investment Bank	S: Full Islamic	0	0	0	0	0	0	0	31-Dec-08
281	222	Mybank LTD	Pakistan	Commercial Bank	W: Islamic Windows	0	0	666	0	3.7	-0.639	0.007	31-Dec-07
281	222	National Bank for Development, Cairo	Egypt	Investment Bank	W: Islamic Windows	0	0	1537.5	0	-26.3	0	-0.017	31-Dec-06
281	222	National Bank Islamic	Iraq	Commercial Bank	S: Full Islamic	0	0	0	0	0	0	0	31-Dec-08
281	222	National Bank of Abu Dhabi	UAE	Offshore Banking Units	W: Islamic Windows	0	0	37966.2	0	711	0.157	0.022	31-Dec-07
281	222	National Bank of Egypt	Egypt	Investment Bank	W: Islamic Windows	0	0	37453.7	0	82.3	0.056	0.002	30-Jun-07
281	222	National Bank of Kuwait	Kuwait	Commercial Bank	W: Islamic Windows	0	0	153077.3	0	4129.2	0.051	0.032	31-Dec-07
281	222	National Bank of Oman	Oman	Commercial Bank	W: Islamic Windows	0	0	3835.4	0	36.3	1.431	0.011	31-Dec-07
281	222	Maybank	Malaysia	Commercial Bank	W: Islamic Windows	0	0	67947.2	0	966.8	-0.199	0.014	30-Jun-08
281	222	Lloyds TSB	UK	Commercial Bank	W: Islamic Windows	0	0	727758.1	0	1185.3	-0.699	0.002	30-Jun-08
281	222	Makaseb Islamic Financial Services	UAE	Commercial Bank	S: Full Islamic	0	0	0	0	0	0	0	31-Dec-08
281	222	Masrafy	Bahrain	Investment Company	S: Full Islamic	0	0	0	0	0	0	0	31-Dec-06
281	222	Manafa`e Investment Company	Kuwait	Commercial Bank	S: Full Islamic	0	0	0	0	0	0	0	31-Dec-06
281	222	Mashreqbank, UAE	UAE	Commercial Bank	W: Islamic Windows	0	0	23860.4	0	580.6	0.293	0.03	31-Dec-07
281	222	Kuwait Turkish Evkaf Finance house Inc.	Bahrain	Credit & Finance	S: Full Islamic	0	0	0	0	0	0	0	31-Dec-08
281	222	Lebanese Islamic Bank	Lebanon	Commercial & Investment Bank	S: Full Islamic	0	0	0	0	0	0	0	31-Dec-08
281	222	Kuwait Investment Co	Kuwait	Commercial Bank	W: Islamic Windows	0	0	1349.7	0	165.8	0.67	0.13	31-Dec-07
281	222	Punjab Provincial Cooperative Bank	Pakistan	Commercial Bank	W: Islamic Windows	0	0	291.7	0	2.2	0	0	30-Jun-07
281	222	Qaiser Islamic Bank	Pakistan	Commercial Bank	S: Full Islamic	0	0	0	0	0	0	0	31-Dec-08
281	222	PT BPD Sumatera Selatan	Indonesia	Commercial Bank	W: Islamic Windows	0	0	761.5	0	8.4	0.579	0.013	31-Dec-06
281	222	PT BPD Sumatera Utara	Indonesia	Commercial Bank	W: Islamic Windows	0	0	455.5	0	14.4	-0.015	0.035	31-Dec-05

Ranking		Bank na	Country	Institution type	S / W	*Sharia'a* compliant assets		Total assets		Profits and returns			Result date
Current	Previous					Total US$m	% change	US$m	% *Sharia'a*	Profits US$m	% change	Asset returns %	
281	222	PT Bank Riau (Syariah)	Indonesia	Commercial Bank	W: Islamic Windows	0	0	1588.5	0	45	1.496	0.036	31-Dec-06
281	222	PT BPD Kalimantan Barat	Indonesia	Commercial Bank	W: Islamic Windows	0	0	193.4	0	4.8	0.054	0.028	31-Dec-05
281	222	PT BPD Kalimantan Selatan	Indonesia	Commercial & Investment Bank	W: Islamic Windows	0	0	345.7	0	8.7	0.847	0.031	31-Dec-06
281	222	Sabaek Leasing & Investment Company	Kuwait	Investment Bank	S: Full Islamic	0	0	0	0	0	0	0	31-Dec-06
281	222	Sakana Holistic Housing Solutions B.S.C.	Bahrain	Commercial Bank	S: Full Islamic	0	0	0	0	0	0	0	31-Dec-06
281	222	Saman Bank	Iran	Commercial & Investment Bank	S: Full Islamic	0	0	0	0	0	0	0	31-Dec-08
281	222	Royal Bank of Scotland	UK	Commercial Bank	W: Islamic Windows	0	0	3760700.7	0	19589.9	0.078	0.007	31-Dec-07
281	222	Royal Bank of Scotland Berhad	Malaysia	Commercial Bank	W: Islamic Windows	0	0	3232	0	7.6	-0.323	0.003	31-Dec-07
281	222	Rusd Group	Saudi Arabia	Commercial Bank	S: Full Islamic	0	0	0	0	0	0	0	31-Dec-08
281	222	Reba Free LLC	USA	Commercial Bank	S: Full Islamic	0	0	0	0	0	0	0	31-Dec-08
281	222	Sepah Investment Company	Iran	Commercial Bank	S: Full Islamic	0	0	0	0	0	0	0	31-Dec-08
281	222	Saudi National Commercial Bank	Bahrain	Commercial Bank	W: Islamic Windows	0	0	0	0	0	0	0	31-Dec-08
281	222	Saudi Pak Commercial Bank Limited	Pakistan	Commercial Bank	W: Islamic Windows	0	0	880.2	0	-54.5	7.119	-0.059	31-Dec-07
281	222	Sarmaye (Capital) Bank	Iran	Commercial Bank	S: Full Islamic	0	0	0	0	0	0	0	31-Dec-08
281	222	Saudi Economy and Development Company	Saudi Arabia	Commercial Bank	S: Full Islamic	0	0	0	0	0	0	0	31-Dec-08
281	222	Sorooh Investment Company	Kuwait	Government owned Bank	S: Full Islamic	0	0	0	0	0	0	0	31-Dec-06
281	222	Societe Generale	France	Commercial Bank	W: Islamic Windows	0	0	1553345.8	0	2733.5	-0.767	0.002	31-Dec-07
281	222	Sharjah Islamic Financial Services	UAE	Commercial Bank	S: Full Islamic	0	0	0	0	0	0	0	31-Dec-06
281	222	SHAPE Financial Corp.	USA	Investment Company	S: Full Islamic	0	0	0	0	0	0	0	31-Dec-08
281	222	Shariah Capital Inc.	USA	Commercial Bank	S: Full Islamic	0	0	0	0	0	0	0	31-Dec-08
281	222	Shuaa Capital	UAE	Development Financial Institutions	W: Islamic Windows	0	0	1575.6	0	108.1	0.513	0.086	31-Mar-08
281	222	Siraj Capital	Saudi Arabia	Commercial Bank	S: Full Islamic	0	0	0	0	0	0	0	31-Dec-08
281	222	SME Bank	Pakistan	Commercial Bank	W: Islamic Windows	0	0	108	0	2.5	-0.344	0.019	31-Dec-07
281	222	Zarai Taraqiati Bank Limited	Pakistan	Development Financial Institutions	W: Islamic Windows	0	0	1532.1	0	29.5	1.757	0.02	31-Dec-07
281	222	Yazi Investment Bank	Bahrain	Development Financial Institutions	S: Full Islamic	0	0	0	0	0	0	0	31-Dec-05
281	222	Wafra Investment Advisory Group, Inc.	USA	Credit & Finance	W: Islamic Windows	0	0	0	0	0	0	0	31-Dec-08
281	222	United Finance Company SAOG	Oman	Commercial Bank	W: Islamic Windows	0	0	289.8	0	11.3	1.557	0.049	31-Dec-07
281	222	United Gulf Bank	Bahrain	Commercial Bank	W: Islamic Windows	0	0	2847.7	0	38.1	-0.714	0.015	31-Mar-08
281	222	United National Bank	UK	Commercial Bank	W: Islamic Windows	0	0	0	0	0	0	0	31-Dec-08
281	222	Union Bank Ltd	Pakistan	Commercial Bank	W: Islamic Windows	0	0	0	0	0	0	0	31-Dec-08

Ranking		Bank na	Country	Institution type	S / W	*Sharia'a* compliant assets		Total assets		Profits and returns			Result date
Current	Previous					Total US$m	% change	US$m	% *Sharia'a*	Profits US$m	% change	Asset returns %	
281	222	United Bank Ltd	Qatar	Commercial Bank	W: Islamic Windows	0	0	0	0	0	0	0	31-Dec-08
281	222	United Bank of Egypt	Egypt	Commercial Bank	W: Islamic Windows	0	0	0	0	0	0	0	31-Dec-08
281	222	UBS Islamic Finance	UAE	Commercial Bank	S: Full Islamic	0	0	0	0	0	0	0	31-Dec-08
281	222	The Tigris and Euphrates Bank for Dev. & Inv.	Iraq	Investment Company	S: Full Islamic	0	0	0	0	0	0	0	31-Dec-08
281	222	The International Islamic Union Bank	Yemen	Commercial Bank	S: Full Islamic	0	0	0	0	0	0	0	31-Dec-08
281	222	The First Community Bank Limited	Kenya	Investment Company	S: Full Islamic	0	0	0	0	0	0	0	31-Dec-08
281	222	The First Investor	Qatar	Commercial Bank	S: Full Islamic	0	0	0	0	0	0	0	31-Dec-06
281	222	The Government Saving Bank	Thailand	Commercial Bank	W: Islamic Windows	0	0	19738.7	0	279.4	-0.184	0.014	31-Dec-06
281	222	Standard Chartered Saadiq	UK	Commercial Bank	W: Islamic Windows	0	0	0	0	0	0	0	31-Dec-08
281	222	Syrian International Islamic Bank	Syria	Investment Bank	S: Full Islamic	0	0	0	0	0	0	0	31-Dec-06
281	222	Tabarak	UAE	Investment Company	S: Full Islamic	0	0	0	0	0	0	0	31-Dec-08
281	222	TAIB Bank of Bahrain	Bahrain	Credit & Finance	W: Islamic Windows	0	0	473.6	0	17	-0.247	0.037	31-Dec-07
281	222	Ta`jeer Company	UAE	Investment Company	S: Full Islamic	0	0	0	0	0	0	0	31-Dec-08
281	222	The Bank of Punjab	Pakistan	Investment Company	W: Islamic Windows	0	0	3854.4	0	79.5	0.016	0.024	31-Dec-07
281	222	The Bank of Tokyo-Mitsubishi	Pakistan	Credit & Finance	W: Islamic Windows	0	0	95.9	0	0.9	0	0	30-Jun-07
281	222	Tayseer Bank	France	Investment Company	S: Full Islamic	0	0	0	0	0	0	0	31-Dec-08
281	222	Elaf Bank BSC	Bahrain	Commercial Bank	S: Full Islamic	0	0	0	0	0	0	0	31-Dec-08
281	222	Emirates and Sudan Bank	Sudan	Credit & Finance	S: Full Islamic	0	0	0	0	0	0	0	31-Dec-05
281	222	Emirates Bank International	UAE	Investment Company	W: Islamic Windows	0	0	39551.6	0	650.9	0.266	0.02	31-Dec-07
281	222	Emirates Financial Services	UAE	Investment Company	W: Islamic Windows	0	0	0	0	0	0	0	31-Dec-08
281	222	Europe Arab Bank (subsidiary of Arab Bank)	UK	Investment Company	W: Islamic Windows	0	0	8.4	0	0	0	0	31-Dec-07
281	222	El Nilein Industrial Developmetn Bank	Sudan	Investment Company	S: Full Islamic	0	0	0	0	0	0	0	31-Dec-06
281	222	Faysal Bank Ltd, Pakistan	Pakistan	Investment Company	W: Islamic Windows	0	0	2317.5	0	44.3	-0.303	0.021	31-Dec-07
281	222	Faysal Islamic Bank of Bahrain	Bahrain	Investment Company	S: Full Islamic	0	0	0	0	0	0	0	31-Dec-08
281	222	First National Bank of Botswana	Botswana	Investment Company	W: Islamic Windows	0	0	1802.4	0	69.5	0.228	0.045	30-Jun-08
281	222	First Finance Company -Jordan	Jordan	Investment Company	S: Full Islamic	0	0	0	0	0	0	0	31-Dec-08
281	222	Blom Development Bank	Lebanon	Investment Company	W: Islamic Windows	0	0	0	0	0	0	0	31-Dec-08
281	222	BNP Paribas	France	Investment Company	W: Islamic Windows	0	0	2455837.2	0	16026.78	0.046	0.007	31-Dec-07
281	222	BNP Paribas NAJMAH	Bahrain	Commercial & Investment Bank	W: Islamic Windows	0	0	0	0	0	0	0	31-Dec-08
281	222	BPD Aceh	Indonesia	Commercial Bank	W: Islamic Windows	0	0	1231.4	0	30	1.647	0.03	31-Dec-06

Ranking		Bank na	Country	Institution type	S / W	*Sharia'a* compliant assets		Total assets		Profits and returns			Result date
Current	Previous					Total US$m	% change	US$m	% *Sharia'a*	Profits US$m	% change	Asset returns %	
281	222	Bristol & West	UK	Commercial Bank	W: Islamic Windows	0	0	258.8	0	11.1	0	0.0003	31-Mar-08
281	222	CIMB Islamic Investment House B.S.C	Bahrain	Commercial Bank	S: Full Islamic	0	0	0	0	0	0	0	31-Dec-08
281	222	Citi Islamic Investment Bank	Bahrain	Offshore Banking Units	S: Full Islamic	0	0	0	0	0	0	0	31-Dec-08
281	222	Calyx Financial	USA	Commercial Bank	W: Islamic Windows	0	0	0	0	0	0	0	31-Dec-08
281	222	Capital Management House	Bahrain	Commercial Bank	S: Full Islamic	0	0	0	0	0	0	0	31-Dec-07
281	222	Capitas Group LLC	USA	Investment Bank	S: Full Islamic	0	0	0	0	0	0	0	31-Dec-08
281	222	Ceylinco Islamic Investment Corporation	Sri Lanka	Commercial Bank	S: Full Islamic	0	0	0	0	0	0	0	31-Dec-08
281	222	Commercial Bank	Sudan	Commercial Bank	U: Islamic Windows	0	0	0	0	0	0	0	31-Dec-08
281	222	Commercial Bank International	UAE	Commercial Bank	W: Islamic Windows	0	0	3027.4	0	87.3	36.04	0.035	31-Dec-07
281	222	Citibank, N.A.	Pakistan	Commercial Bank	W: Islamic Windows	0	0	1742.9	0	15.5	0	0	30-Jun-07
281	222	Credit Suisse	Switzerland	Mortgage Provider	W: Islamic Windows	0	0	1187796.3	0	7985.7	-0.148	0.007	31-Dec-07
281	222	Crescent Commercial Bank Limited	Pakistan	Commercial Bank	W: Islamic Windows	0	0	338.8	0	-22.5	0.618	-0.095	31-Dec-07
281	222	Daman Investments	UAE	Commercial Bank	W: Islamic Windows	0	0	0	0	0	0	0	31-Dec-07
281	222	Dawnay Day Global Investment	UK	Commercial Bank	W: Islamic Windows	0	0	0	0	0	0	0	31-Dec-08
281	222	Deutsche Bank AG	Germany	Commercial Bank	W: Islamic Windows	0	0	2928169.3	0	12680.3	0.049	0.005	31-Dec-07
281	222	Deutsche Bank AG (Pakistan)	Pakistan	Commercial Bank	W: Islamic Windows	0	0	153.3	0	7.1	0	0	30-Jun-07
281	222	Devon Bank	USA	Commercial Bank	W: Islamic Windows	0	0	0	0	0	0	0	31-Dec-08
281	222	Dhaka Bank	Bangladesh	Investment Bank	W: Islamic Windows	0	0	836.9	0	22.3	0.611	0.029	31-Dec-07
281	222	Dlala Islamic Brokerage Company	Qatar	Commercial Bank	S: Full Islamic	0	0	0	0	0	0	0	31-Dec-06
281	222	Commerical Bank of Kuwait	Kuwait	Commercial Bank	W: Islamic Windows	0	0	15533.7	0	452.1	0.204	0.035	31-Dec-07
281	222	CrÃ©dit Agricole Egypt	Egypt	Investment Bank	W: Islamic Windows	0	0	2791.5	0	4.1	-0.939	0.002	31-Dec-06
281	222	Dubai Bank	Kenya	Commercial Bank	W: Islamic Windows	0	0	15.6	0	0.4	-0.06	0.028	31-Dec-05
281	222	Kabul Bank	Afghanistan	Commercial Bank	W: Islamic Windows	0	0	398.9	0	0.6	11.477	0.015	31-Mar-08
281	222	JS Bank Limited	Pakistan	Commercial Bank	W: Islamic Windows	0	0	333.5	0	-1	152.254	-0.004	31-Dec-07
281	222	KASB Bank Limited	Pakistan	Commercial Bank	W: Islamic Windows	0	0	670.8	0	1.1	0.242	0.002	31-Dec-07
281	222	Kenanga Investment Bank Berhad	Malaysia	Commercial Bank	W: Islamic Windows	0	0	644.4	0	33.2	5.707	0.071	31-Dec-07

Ranking		Bank na	Country	Institution type	S / W	*Sharia'a* compliant assets		Total assets		Profits and returns			Result date
Current	Previous					Total US$m	% change	US$m	% *Sharia'a*	Profits US$m	% change	Asset returns %	
281	222	Kenya Commercial Bank	Kenya	Commercial Bank	W: Islamic Windows	0	0	1847.5	0	64.8	0.392	0.041	31-Dec-07
281	222	K-rep Bank	Kenya	Commercial Bank	W: Islamic Windows	0	0	73.5	0	2.1	1.879	0.034	31-Dec-06
281	222	Jaber Islamic Bank	Kuwait	Commercial Bank	S: Full Islamic	0	0	0	0	0	0	0	31-Dec-06
281	222	Jadwa Investment	Saudi Arabia	Commercial Bank	S: Full Islamic	0	0	0	0	0	0	0	31-Dec-08
281	222	Islamic Capital Partners	Pakistan	Commercial Bank	S: Full Islamic	0	0	0	0	0	0	0	31-Dec-08
281	222	Islamic Corp. for the Dev. of the Private Sector	Saudi Arabia	Commercial Bank	S: Full Islamic	0	0	0	0	0	0	0	31-Dec-08
281	222	First Women Bank Limited	Pakistan	Commercial Bank	W: Islamic Windows	0	0	147.4	0	3.9	-0.07	0.027	31-Dec-07
281	222	Global Investment House	Kuwait	Commercial Bank	W: Islamic Windows	0	0	3306.3	0	334	0.268	0.115	31-Dec-07
281	222	Guidance Financial Group	USA	Commercial Bank	S: Full Islamic	0	0	0	0	0	0	0	31-Dec-08
281	222	Gulf African Bank	Kenya	Commercial Bank	S: Full Islamic	0	0	0	0	0	0	0	31-Dec-08
281	222	Gulf Arab Investment Group Company k.s.c.c.	Kuwait	Commercial Bank	S: Full Islamic	0	0	0	0	0	0	0	31-Dec-08
281	222	Gulf Bank	Kuwait	Commercial Bank	W: Islamic Windows	0	0	18407.8	0	472.4	0.232	0.029	31-Dec-07
281	222	Halal Financial Services	UK	Investment Bank	S: Full Islamic	0	0	0	0	0	0	0	31-Dec-08
281	222	Halal Mortgages	UK	Stock & Commodity Brokers	S: Full Islamic	0	0	0	0	0	0	0	31-Dec-08
281	222	HBOS	UK	Credit & Finance	W: Islamic Windows	0	0	1364318.3	0	11197.7	-0.041	0.009	31-Dec-07
281	222	Gulf North Africa Holding Company	Kuwait	Commercial Bank	S: Full Islamic	0	0	0	0	0	0	0	31-Dec-05
281	222	Gulf One Investment Bank	Bahrain	Commercial Bank	S: Full Islamic	0	0	0	0	0	0	0	31-Dec-06
281	222	Gulf International Bank BSC	Bahrain	Credit & Finance	W: Islamic Windows	0	0	29954	0	201.2	-0.23	0.007	31-Dec-07
281	222	HSBC (Syariah)	Indonesia	Commercial Bank	W: Islamic Windows	0	0	2935.8	0	69.6	-0.243	0.025	31-Dec-06
281	222	HSBC Amanah Takaful (Malaysia) Sdn. Berhad	Malaysia	Credit & Finance	S: Full Islamic	0	0	0	0	0	0	0	31-Dec-08
281	222	HSBC Pakistan	Pakistan	Investment Bank	W: Islamic Windows	0	0	475	0	2.9	0	0	30-Jun-07
281	222	I&M Bank	Kenya	Investment Bank	W: Islamic Windows	0	0	451.2	0	19.8	0.382	0.05	31-Dec-07
281	222	IBJ International London (Industrial Bank of Japan)	UK	Investment Company	W: Islamic Windows	0	0	0	0	0	0	0	31-Dec-08
281	222	Ilaf Islamic Bank	Iraq	Investment Company	S: Full Islamic	0	0	0	0	0	0	0	31-Dec-08
281	222	Injazat Capital	UAE	Investment Company	S: Full Islamic	0	0	0	0	0	0	0	31-Dec-08
281	222	Iraqi Islamic Bank for Investment and Development	Iraq	Investment Company	S: Full Islamic	0	0	0	0	0	0	0	31-Dec-08
281	222	Investment Liquidity Management House Co. K.S.C.	Kuwait	Commercial Bank	S: Full Islamic	0	0	0	0	0	0	0	31-Dec-08
281	222	Ansar Finance Group	UK	Commercial Bank	S: Full Islamic	0	0	0	0	0	0	0	31-Dec-08
281	222	Aqsa islamic Bank	Palestine	Commercial Bank	S: Full Islamic	0	0	0	0	0	0	0	31-Dec-08
281	222	Arab Islamic Bank E.C	Bahrain	Commercial Bank	S: Full Islamic	0	0	0	0	0	0	0	31-Dec-08

Ranking		Bank na	Country	Institution type	S / W	*Sharia'a* compliant assets		Total assets		Profits and returns			Result date
Current	Previous					Total US$m	% change	US$m	% *Sharia'a*	Profits US$m	% change	Asset returns %	
281	222	Arab National Bank	Saudi Arabia	Commercial & Private Banking	W: Islamic Windows	0	0	25225	0	657.2	-0.017	0.029	31-Dec-07
281	222	Arab Union Investment Company of Egypt	Egypt	Commercial Bank	W: Islamic Windows	0	0	0	0	0	0	0	31-Dec-08
281	222	Arab Investment Bank	Egypt	Commercial Bank	W: Islamic Windows	0	0	0	0	0	0	0	31-Dec-08
281	222	Arab Investment Company S.A.A.	Bahrain	Commercial & Retail Banking	W: Islamic Windows	0	0	4373.4	0	0	0	0	31-Dec-07
281	222	Anchor Finance Group	USA	Commercial & Investment Bank	S: Full Islamic	0	0	0	0	0	0	0	31-Dec-08
281	222	Aseel Finance	UAE	Commercial Bank	S: Full Islamic	0	0	0	0	0	0	0	01-Dec-06
281	222	Arbah Capital	Saudi Arabia	Specialized Bank	S: Full Islamic	0	0	0	0	0	0	0	31-Dec-08
281	222	Arif Habib Rupai Bank Limited	Pakistan	Commercial & Private Banking	W: Islamic Windows	0	0	297.2	0	5.4	5.535	0.027	31-Dec-07
281	222	Badr Al-Islami Banking	UAE	Commercial Bank	S: Full Islamic	0	0	0	0	0	0	0	31-Dec-08
281	222	Badr-Forte Bank (closed)	Russia	Commercial Bank	S: Full Islamic	0	0	0	0	0	0	0	01-Oct-06
281	222	Balance Finance	Australia	Commercial Bank	S: Full Islamic	0	0	0	0	0	0	0	31-Dec-08
281	222	Athman Investment Company	Kuwait	Investment Company	S: Full Islamic	0	0	0	0	0	0	0	31-Dec-08
281	222	Atlas Bank Limited	Pakistan	Commercial Bank	W: Islamic Windows	0	0	377	0	-9	2.902	-0.027	31-Dec-07
281	222	Azizi Bank	Afghanistan	Credit & Finance	W: Islamic Windows	0	0	77.6	0	-3	0	0	31-Mar-07
281	222	Bank of Kuwait and the Middle East	Kuwait	Commercial Bank	W: Islamic Windows	0	0	8106.9	0	200.9	0.122	0.027	31-Dec-07
281	222	Bank of Bahrain & Kuwait	Bahrain	Commercial Bank	W: Islamic Windows	0	0	5565.2	0	79.6	-0.086	0.016	31-Dec-07
281	222	Bank of Beirut	Lebanon	Investment Company	W: Islamic Windows	0	0	5250.3	0	54.8	0.179	0.011	31-Dec-07
281	222	Bank of Regional Cooperation Islamic for Dev. & Inv.	Iraq	Stock & Commodity Brokers	S: Full Islamic	0	0	0	0	0	0	0	31-Dec-08
281	222	Bank Of Whittier	USA	Stock & Commodity Brokers	W: Islamic Windows	0	0	0	0	0	0	0	31-Dec-08
281	222	Banque Al Baraka Djibouti	Djibouti	Credit & Finance	S: Full Islamic	0	0	0	0	0	0	0	31-Dec-08
281	222	Banque Islamique du Senegal	Senegal	Commercial Bank	S: Full Islamic	0	0	0	0	0	0	0	31-Dec-08
281	222	Banque Misr	Egypt	Credit & Finance	W: Islamic Windows	0	0	18486.8	0	38.3	0.313	0.002	30-Jun-05
281	222	Barclays	UK	Commercial Bank	W: Islamic Windows	0	0	2510710.9	0	14474.8	-0.008	0.006	31-Dec-07
281	222	Barclays Bank of Kenya Ltd.	Kenya	Credit & Finance	W: Islamic Windows	0	0	2421.7	0	108.6	0.576	0.051	31-Dec-07
281	222	BankMuscat International	Bahrain	Credit & Finance	W: Islamic Windows	0	0	1356.8	0	13	-0.044	0.011	31-Dec-07
281	222	Al Baraka Investment and Development	Saudi Arabia	Commercial & Private Banking	S: Full Islamic	0	0	0	0	0	0	0	31-Dec-08
281	222	Al Aqeelah Finance Leasing and Investment Company	Kuwait	Commercial Bank	S: Full Islamic	0	0	0	0	0	0	0	31-Dec-06
281	222	Ajal Finance & Investment Company	Kuwait	Commercial & Investment Bank	S: Full Islamic	0	0	0	0	0	0	0	31-Dec-08
281	222	ABSA Group (ABSA Islamic Bank)	South Africa	Investment Bank	W: Islamic Windows	0	0	94776.2	0	2082.8	0.232	0.025	31-Dec-07

Ranking		Bank na	Country	Institution type	S / W	*Sharia'a* compliant assets		Total assets		Profits and returns			Result date
Current	Previous					Total US$m	% change	US$m	% *Sharia'a*	Profits US$m	% change	Asset returns %	
281	222	Abu Dhabi Commerical Bank	UAE	Investment Bank	W: Islamic Windows	0	0	28921.4	0	567.7	-0.029	0.022	31-Dec-07
281	222	ABC Investments (Baraka Islamic Financial Service)	Sri Lanka	Investment Company	W: Islamic Windows	0	0	0	0	0	0	0	31-Dec-08
281	222	Al Baraka Lebanon	Lebanon	Stock & Commodity Brokers	S: Full Islamic	0	0	0	0	0	0	0	31-Dec-08
281	222	Al Farabi Investment Company	Kuwait	Credit & Finance	S: Full Islamic	0	0	0	0	0	0	0	31-Dec-04
281	222	Al Faysal Investment Bank Ltd, Islamabad	Pakistan	Credit & Finance	S: Full Islamic	0	0	0	0	0	0	0	31-Dec-08
281	222	Al Hilal Bank	UAE	Investment Company	S: Full Islamic	0	0	0	0	0	0	0	31-Dec-07
281	222	Al Imtiaz Investment Company	Kuwait	Investment Company	S: Full Islamic	0	0	0	0	0	0	0	31-Dec-06
281	222	Al Jazeera Islamic Company	Qatar	Investment Bank	S: Full Islamic	0	0	0	0	0	0	0	31-Dec-08
281	222	Al Masref	Bahrain	Commercial Bank	S: Full Islamic	0	0	0	0	0	0	0	31-Dec-06
281	222	Al Manar Financing & Leasing Company	Kuwait	Credit & Finance	W: Islamic Windows	0	0	304	0	10.5	0.462	0.04	31-Dec-05
281	222	Al Khaleej Islamic Investment Bank	Bahrain	Stock & Commodity Brokers	S: Full Islamic	0	0	0	0	0	0	0	31-Dec-08
281	222	A`Ayan Capital Investment	Kuwait	Credit & Finance	S: Full Islamic	0	0	0	0	0	0	0	31-Dec-08
281	222	Amanah Capital	UAE	Commercial & Retail Banking	S: Full Islamic	0	0	0	0	0	0	0	31-Dec-08
281	222	Amar Finance and Leasing Company	Kuwait	Commercial & Retail Banking	S: Full Islamic	0	0	0	0	0	0	0	31-Dec-08
281	222	Ameen Housing Co-operative	USA	Commercial & Retail Banking	S: Full Islamic	0	0	0	0	0	0	0	31-Dec-08
281	222	American Finance House, La Riba	USA	Mortgage Provider	S: Full Islamic	0	0	0	0	0	0	0	31-Dec-08
281	222	Amlak Finance and Real Estate Investment	Egypt	Commercial & Retail Banking	S: Full Islamic	0	0	0	0	0	0	0	01-Jun-07
281	222	AMLAK Finance PJSC	UAE	Investment Company	W: Islamic Windows	0	0	2576.9	0	71.3	0.888	0.036	31-Dec-07
281	222	Amlak International for Real Estate Dev. & Finance Co.	Saudi Arabia	Commercial Bank	S: Full Islamic	0	0	0	0	0	0	0	01-Jun-07
281	222	Amlak Investments	UAE	Commercial & Retail Banking	S: Full Islamic	0	0	0	0	0	0	0	31-Dec-06
281	222	Alraya Investment Company	Kuwait	Commercial & Investment Bank	S: Full Islamic	0	0	0	0	0	0	0	31-Dec-08
281	222	AlRaya Investment Company KSCC	Kuwait	Credit & Finance	S: Full Islamic	0	0	0	0	0	0	0	31-Dec-08
281	222	Al-Tawfeek Company for Investment Funds Ltd	Cayman Islands	Mortgage Provider	S: Full Islamic	0	0	0	0	0	0	0	31-Dec-92
281	222	Alwatany Bank of Egypt, Cairo	Egypt	Mortgage Provider	W: Islamic Windows	0	0	1766.2	0	0	0	0	31-Dec-06
281	222	Allied Bank Limited	Pakistan	Commercial Bank	W: Islamic Windows	0	0	4924.9	0	97.7	-0.106	0.022	31-Dec-07
281	222	Al-Buraq Investment Company	Kuwait	Mortgage Provider	S: Full Islamic	0	0	0	0	0	0	0	31-Dec-08
281	222	Al-Hidayah Investment Bank	Malaysia	Commercial Bank	S: Full Islamic	0	0	0	0	0	0	0	31-Dec-08
281	222	Alinma Bank	Saudi Arabia	Mortgage Provider	S: Full Islamic	0	0	0	0	0	0	0	31-Dec-08
281	222	Albaraka Bank Syria	Syria	Mortgage Provider	S: Full Islamic	0	0	0	0	0	0	0	31-Dec-06
281	222	Albilad Islamic Bank	Iraq	Mortgage Provider	S: Full Islamic	0	0	0	0	0	0	0	31-Dec-06
281	222	Al Wifaq Finance Company	UAE	Mortgage Provider	S: Full Islamic	0	0	0	0	0	0	0	31-Dec-06
281	222	Al Salam Bank - Algeria	Algeria	Mortgage Provider	S: Full Islamic	0	0	0	0	0	0	0	31-Dec-08
281	222	Al Safwa Islamic Financial Services	UAE	Mortgage Provider	S: Full Islamic	0	0	0	0	0	0	0	31-Dec-06
281	222	Al Rayan Investment	UAE	Commercial & Investment Bank	S: Full Islamic	0	0	0	0	0	0	0	31-Dec-08

Glossary of Islamic capital market terminology

Arboun: A deposit or 'earnest money' which forms a part payment of the price of goods or services paid in advance, but will be forfeited in the event the transaction is cancelled. The forfeited money is considered as *hibah* (gift).

Bai' Bithaman Ajil (BBA): A contract that refers to the sale and purchase transaction for the financing of assets on deferred and instalment basis with a pre-agreed payment period. The sale price will include a profit margin.

Bai' al-'Inah: A contract, which involves the sale and buy back transaction of the assets by a seller. A seller will sell the asset to a buyer on a cash basis. The seller will later buy back the same asset on a deferred payment basis where the price is higher than the cash price. This can also be applied when a seller sells an asset to a buyer on a deferred basis. A seller will later buy back the same asset on a cash basis at a price lower than the deferred price.

Bai' al-Istijrar: A contract between the client and the supplier, whereby the supplier agrees to supply a particular product on an ongoing basis, for example monthly, at an agreed price and on the basis of an agreed mode of payment.

Bai' al-Dayn: A transaction that involves the sale and purchase of securities or debt certificates that conforms with the *Sharia'a*. Securities or debt certificates will be issued by a debtor to a creditor as evidence of indebtedness.

Bai' al-Muzayadah: An action by a person to sell his asset in the open market, which is accompanied by the process of bidding among potential buyers. The asset for sale will be awarded to the person who has offered the highest price. In other words a sale and purchase transaction based on an auction or tender.

Bai' al-Salam: A contract whereby the payment is made in cash at the time of contract but the delivery of the asset purchased will be deferred to a predetermined date.

Bai' al-Wafa': A contract with the condition that when the seller pays back the price of the goods sold and the buyer returns the goods to the seller.

Dhaman: A contract of guarantee whereby a guarantor will underwrite any claim and obligation that must be fulfilled by an owner of the asset. This concept is also applicable to a guarantee provided on a debt transaction in the event a debtor fails to fulfil his debt obligation.

Gharar: *Gharar* occurs when there is an element of deception either through ignorance of the goods, the price, or through faulty description of the goods, in which one or both parties stand to be deceived through ignorance of an essential element of the exchange. As an example, gambling is a form of *gharar* because the gambler is ignorant of the outcome of the gamble.

Gharar is divided into three types, namely *gharar fahish* (excessive), which vitiates the transaction, *ghara yasir* (minor), which is tolerated and *gharar mutawassit* (moderate), which falls between the other two categories. Any transaction can be classified as a forbidden activity because of excessive *gharar*.

Haq Maliy: *Haq maliy* are rights on financial assets. Examples of such rights are *haq dayn* (debt rights) and *haq tamalluk* (ownership rights).

Hibah: A gift awarded to a person.

Hawala: A contract that allows a debtor to transfer his debt obligation to a third party.

Ibra': Rebate. An act by a person to withdraw his rights, i.e. his rights to collect payment from a person who has the obligation to repay the amount borrowed from him.

Ijara: A *Manfa'a* (*usufruct*) type of contract whereby a lessor (owner) leases out an asset or equipment to its client at an agreed rental fee and predetermined lease period upon the *aqad* (contract). The ownership of the leased equipment remains in the hands of the lessor.

Ijara Thumma Bai': A contract which begins with an *Ijara* contract for the purpose of renting out or leasing the lessor's asset to the lessee. Consequently, at the end of the lease period, a lessee will purchase the asset at an agreed price from the lessor by executing a purchase (*Bai'*) contract.

Istisna': A purchase order contract of assets whereby a buyer will place an order to purchase an asset that will be delivered in the future. In other words a buyer will require a seller or a contract to deliver or construct the asset that will be completed in the future according to the specifications given in the sale and purchase contract. Both parties to the contract will decide on the sale and purchase prices as they wish and the settlement is based on the schedule of the work completed.

Ittifaq Dhimni: A sale and re-purchase of an underlying asset whereby the prices are agreed by the parties prior to the completion of the contract. This is an external agreement, which must be reached before the contract can be concluded to allow for the bidding process (*Bai' al-Muzayadah*) to take place.

***Wakala**:* A contract, which gives power to a person to nominate another person to act on his behalf, as long as he is alive, based on the agreed terms and conditions.

***Wadiah Yad Dhaman**:* Goods or deposits, which have been deposited with another person, who is not the owner, for safekeeping. As *wadiah* is a trust, the depository becomes the guarantor and therefore guarantees repayment of the whole amount of the deposits, or any part thereof, outstanding in the account of depositors, when demanded. The depositors are not entitled to any of the profits but the depository may provide returns to the depositors as a token of appreciation.

***Zakat**:* A tax, which is prescribed by Islam on all persons having wealth above a certain amount. According to the Islamic belief *Zakat* purifies wealth and souls. The objective of *zakat* is to take away a part of the wealth of the well-to-do and to distribute it among the eight needy categories stated in the *Qur'an*.

References and bibliography

The text has drawn on wide variety of references. In order to appreciate the central elements which lie at the heart of Islamic capital markets you are strongly urged to consult the following *Sura* from the *Qur'an.*

The key references to riba can be found in:

- Sura 2: 275-280
- Sura 3: 130
- Sura 4: 161
- Sura 30:39

Ahmad, Ausaf and Khan, Tariqullah (1997), *Islamic Financial Instruments for Public Sector Resource Mobilization,* Jeddah: IDB, IRTI

Ahmad, Ausaf and Khan, Tariqullah (eds.) (1998), *Islamic Financial Instruments for Public Sector Resource Mobilization*, Jeddah: IRTI

Ahmad, Khurshid (ed.) (1976), *Studies in Islamic Economics*, Leicester: The Islamic Foundation

Al-Harran, Saad Abdul Sattar (1993), *Islamic Finance: Partnership Financing*, Pelanduk Publications: Selangor, Malaysia

al-Harran, Saad Abdul Sattar (1995), *Leading Issues in Islamic Banking and Finance*, Pelanduk Publications: Selangor, Malaysia

Ali, Syed Ameer (1978), *The Spirit of Islam: A History of the Evolution and Ideals of Islam, with a Life of the Prophet*, London: Chatto & Windus

Ali, S. Nazim and Ali, Naseem N. (1994), *Information Sources on Islamic Banking and Economics, 1980-1990*, Kegan Paul International

al-Misri, Ahmad ibn Naqid (1988), *Reliance of the Traveller: A Classical Manual of Islamic Sacred Law*, Translation by Nuh Ha Mim Keller

Al-Omar, Fouad and Abdel Haq, Mohammed (1996), *Islamic Banking, Theory, Practice and Challenges*, London: Oxford University

al-Qaradawi, Yusuf (1985), *The Lawful and the Prohibited in Islam*, Islamic Book Trust: Kuala Lumpur, Malaysia

Archer, Simon and Rifaat Abdel Karim (2002), *Islamic Finance: Innovation and Growth*, London: Euromoney Books and AAOIFI

Ariff, Mohammad and Mannan, M.A. (1990), *Developing a System of Islamic Financial Instruments*, Jeddah: IDB, IRTI

Armstrong, Karen (2002), *Islam: A Short History*, New York: Modern Library (revised edn.)

Ayub, Mohammad (2008), *Understanding Islamic Finance*: John Wiley

Bowker, John (1999), *What Muslims Believe*, Oxford, UK: OneWorld

Burton, John (1990), *The Sources of Islamic Law: Islamic Theories of Abrogation*, Edinburgh: Edinburgh University Press

Burton, John (1994), *An Introduction to the Hadith*, Edinburgh: Edinburgh University Press

Chapra, M.U. (1985), *Towards a Just Monetary System*, Islamic Foundation

Chapra, M.U. (1992), *Islam and the Economic Challenge*, Islamic Foundation

Chapra, M.U. (2000), *The Future of Islamic Economics*, Islamic Foundation

Cook, Michael (2000), *The Koran: A Very Short Introduction*, Oxford, UK: Oxford University Press

Cooter, Robert and Thomas Ulen (2000), *Law and Economics*, 3rd Edition, Reading MA: Addison-Wesley

Coulson, N.J. (1994), *A History of Islamic Law*, Edinburgh University Press

De Lorenzo, Yusuf Talal (eds) (1997), *A Compendium of Legal Opinions on the Operations of Islamic Banks: Murabahah, Mudarabah and Musharakah*, Institute of Islamic Banking and Insurance: London, UK

El-Gamal, M.A. (2003), *A Basic Guide to Contemporary Islamic Banking and Finance*, elgamal@rice.edu http://www.ruf.rice.edu/~elgamal

El-Gamal, M.A. (2003), *Financial Transactions in Islamic Jurisprudence*, Vols 1 and 2, Translation of Book by Dr Al-Zuhayli

Esposito, John L. (1995), *The Oxford Encyclopedia of the Modern Islamic World*, 4 Vols., Oxford, UK: Oxford University Press

Farouqui, Mahmood (ed.) (1997), *Islamic Banking and Investment: Challenge and Opportunity*, Kegan Paul International

Garrett, R. and Graham, A. (eds) (1998), *Islamic Law and Finance*, Introduction by William Ballantyne, Graham & Trotman Limited, London

Hallaq, Wael B. (ed.) (2003), *The Formation of Islamic Law*, Aldershot: Ashgate

Haron, Sudin (1997), *Islamic Banking: Rules and Regulations*, Pelanduk Publications: Selangor, Malaysia

Haron, Sudin and Bala Shanmugam (1997), *Islamic Banking System: Concepts and Applications*, Pelanduk Publications: Selangor, Malaysia

Henry, C.M. and Rodney Wilson (eds) (2004), *Politics of Islamic Finance*, Edinburgh University Press

Homoud, Sami Hassan (1985*), Islamic Banking*, London: Arabian Information

Homoud, S. (1985), *Islamic Banking,* Graham & Trotman Publication

Institute of Islamic Banking and Insurance (1996), *Islamic Banking: An Overview*, Institute of Islamic Banking and Insurance: London, UK

Institute of Islamic Banking and Insurance (2000), *International Directory of Islamic Banks and Institutions*, Institute of Islamic Banking and Insurance: London, UK

International Association of Islamic Banks (1997), *Directory of Islamic Banks and Financial Institutions*, Jeddah: International Association of Islamic Banks

Iqbal, M. (ed.) (2002), *Islamic Banking and Finance*, The Islamic Foundation, Leicester, UK

Iqbal, M. and Khan, Tariqullah (2005), *Financial Engineering and Islamic Contracts*, Palgrave-Macmillan

Iqbal, M. and Philip Molyneux (2005), *Thirty Years of Islamic Banking: History and Performance*, Palgrave-Macmillan

Iqbal, Munawar and Llewellyn, David T. (2002), *Islamic Banking and Finance: New Perspectives in Profit Sharing and Risk*, London: Edward Elgar Publishers

Jaffer, S. (ed.) (June, 2004), Islamic Asset Management: Forming the Future for Sharia-Compliant Investment Strategies, *Euromoney*

Kahf, Monzer (1998), 'Asset Ijara Bonds', in Ausaf, Ahmad and Khan, Tariqullah eds, *Islamic Financial Instruments for Public Sector Resource Mobilization*, Jeddah: IRTI

Kahf, Monzer and Khan, Tariqullah (1992), *Principles of Islamic Financing*, Jeddah: IRTI

Kamali, H. (2003), *Islamic Commercial Law: An Analysis of Futures and Options*

Kamali, Mohammad Hashim (2000), *Principles of Islamic Jurisprudence*, Cambridge, UK: The Islamic Texts Society, revised edn

Kettell, B. (2008), *Introduction to Islamic Banking and Finance*. Published by the Author. Contact the author on brian.kettell@islamicbankingcourses.com or see his website on www.islamicbankingcourses.com

Kettell, B. (2006), *Islamic Sukuk: A Guide to Islamic Structured Finance*. Published by the Author. Contact the author on brian.kettell@islamicbankingcourses.com or see his website on www.islamicbankingcourses.com

Khan, M. Fahim (1996), *Islamic Futures and their Markets*, Jeddah: IRTI

Khan, Shahrukh Rafi (1988), *Profit and Loss Sharing: An Islamic Experiment in Finance and Banking,* Oxford University Press

Khan, W.M. (1985), *Towards an Interest-Free Islamic Economic System*, The Islamic Foundation, Leicester, UK

Lewis, Mervyn K. and Latifa M. Algaoud (2001), *Islamic Banking*, Edward Elgar: Cheltenham, UK

Mehdi, Rubya (1994), *The Islamization of the Law in Pakistan*, Richmond, Surrey: Curzon Press

Mills, Paul S. and John R. Presley (1999), *Islamic Finance: Theory and Practice*, London: Macmillan

Moore, Philip (1997), *Islamic Finance: A Partnership for Growth*, Euromoney Publications PLC: London, UK

Rahman, Dr Yahia Abdul (1994), *Interest Free Islamic Banking – Lariba Bank*, Al-Hilal Publishing, Kuala Lumpur

Rosly, S.A. (2005), *Critical Issues in Islamic Banking and Financial Markets*, Bloomington, Indiana

Roy, O. (2004), *Globalised Islam, The Search for a New Ummah*, Huot & Co. Publishers

Saeed, Abdullah (1997), *Islamic Banking and Interest: A Study of the Prohibition of Ribā and Its Contemporary Interpretation*, Leiden: E.J. Brill, 2nd edn

Saleh, Nabil A. (1992), *Unlawful Gain and Legitimate Profit in Islamic Law*, 2nd edn, London, UK: Graham and Trotman

Shirazi (1990), *Islamic Banking Contracts*, Butterworth-Heinemann Taleghani, Sayyid Mahmood

Siddiqi, M.N. (1983), *Issues in Islamic Banking*, The Islamic Foundation

Siddiqi, M.N. (1985), *Partnership and Profit Sharing*, The Islamic Foundation

Siddiqi, M.N. (1988), *Banking Without Interest*, The Islamic Foundation

Udovitch, Abraham L. (1970) *Partnership and Profit in Medieval Islam*, Princeton University Press, Princeton, NJ

Usmani, Muhammad Taqi (1998), *An Introduction to Islamic Finance*, Karachi; Idaratul Ma'arif

Usmani, M.T. (2000), *The Historic Judgment on Interest*, Idaratul-Ma'arif, Karachi

Vogal, Frank E. and Samuel L. Hayes (1988), *Islamic Law and Finance: Religion, Risk and Return*, The Hague: Kluwer Law International

Warde, I. (2000), *Islamic Finance in the Global Economy*, Edinburgh University Press

Zineldin, Mosad, *The Economics of Money and Banking: A Theoretical and Empirical Study of Islamic Interest-Free Banking*

AAOIFI publications

AAOIFI (1999), Statement on the Purpose and Calculation of the Capital Adequacy Ratio for Islamic Banks, The Accounting & Auditing Organization for Islamic Financial Institutions: Manama, Bahrain

AAOIFI (2008), Accounting, Auditing and Governance Standards, The Accounting & Auditing Organization for Islamic Financial Institutions: Manama, Bahrain

AAOIFI (2002), Investment Sukuk (Shari'ah Standard No.18), The Accounting & Auditing Organization for Islamic Financial Institutions: Manama, Bahrain

AAOIFI (2008), Shari'ah Standards, The Accounting & Auditing Organization for Islamic Financial Institutions: Manama, Bahrain

AAOIFI (2004), Guiding Principles of Risk Management for Institutions (Insurance companies offering only Islamic Financial Services)

AAOIFI (2004), Capital Adequacy Standard for Institutions (offering only Islamic Financial Services)

Articles

Abdallah, A. (1987), 'Islamic Banking', *Journal of Islamic Banking and Finance*, Jan-Mar, 4(1): 31-56

Abdul, Majid and Abdul, Rais (2003), 'Development of Liquidity Management Instruments: Challenges and Opportunities', paper presented to the International Conference on Islamic Banking: Risk Management, Regulation and Supervision, held in Jakarta, Indonesia, 30 September – 2 October 2003, organised by IRTI, Bank Indonesia and Ministry of Finance: Indonesia

Abdul-Rahman, Yahla and Abdulah, S. Tug (1999), 'Towards a LARIBA (Islamic) Mortgage in the United States: Providing an Alternative to the Traditional Mortgages', *International Journal of Islamic Financial Services*, Vol.1, No.2, Jul-Sep

Aftab, M. (1986), 'Pakistan moves to Islamic banking', *The Banker*, June: 57-60

Aggarwal, R.K. and Yousef, T. (2000), 'Islamic Banks and Investment Financing', *Journal of Money, Credit and Banking*, Vol.32, pp.93-120

Ahmad, Dr Abdel Rahman Yousri (2001), 'Riba, its Economic Rationale and Implications', *New Horizon*, No.109, May-June

Ahmad, Ziauddin (1995), 'Islamic Banking: State of the Art', IDB Prize Lecture, Jeddah: Islamic Research and Training Institute, Islamic Development Bank

Alam, M.A. (2000), 'Islamic Banking in Bangladesh: A Case Study of IBBL', *International Journal of Islamic Financial Services*, Vol.1, No.4, Jan-Mar

Al-Bashir, M. and Muhammed al-Amine (2001), 'The Islamic Bonds Market: Possibilities and Challenges', *International Journal of Islamic Financial Services*, Vol.3, No.1, Apr-Jun

Al-Jarhi, Mabid Ali and Iqbal, Munawar (2001), 'Islamic Banking: FAQs', Occasional Paper #4, Jeddah: Islamic Research and Training Institute

Al-Suwailem, Sami (2000), 'Decision Under Uncertainty, An Islamic Perspective', in Islamic Finance: Challenges and Opportunities in the Twenty-First Century (Conference Papers), Loughborough: Fourth International Conference on Islamic Economics and Banking

Anouar, H. (2002), 'Profitability of Islamic Banks', *International Journal of Islamic Financial Services*, Vol.4, No.2, Jul-Sep

Archer, S., Karim, R. Abdel, and Al-Deehani, T. (1998), 'Financial Contracting, Governance Structures and the Accounting Regulation of Islamic Banks: An Analysis in Terms of Agency Theory and Transaction Cost Economics', *Journal of Management and Governance*, Vol.2, pp.149-170

Ariff, M. (1982), 'Monetary Policy in an Interest-Free Islamic Economy – Nature and Scope' in Ariff, M. (ed.), Monetary and Fiscal Economics of Islam, International Centre for Research in *Islamic Economics: Jeddah*

Ariff, Mohammad and Mannan, M.A. (1990), Developing a System of Islamic Financial Instruments, Jeddah: Islamic Research and Training Institute

Ayub, Muhammad (1995), 'Meaning of Riba', *Journal of Islamic Banking and Finance*, 12(2)

Babikir, Osman Ahmed (2001), Islamic Financial Instruments to Manage Short-term Excess Liquidity, Research Paper No.41, 2nd edn, Jeddah: Islamic Research and Training Institute

Bacha, O.I. (1999), 'Financial Derivatives: Some Thoughts for Reconsideration', *International Journal of Islamic Financial Services*, Vol.1, No.1, Apr-Jun

Baldwin, K. (2002), 'Risk Management in Islamic Banks', in Karim, R. Abdel and Archer, S. (eds.), *Islamic Finance: Innovation and Growth*, Euromoney Books and AAOIFI, pp.176-197

Basel Committee on Banking Supervision (BCBS) (2003), Consultative Document – Overview of the New Basel Capital Accord, Bank for International Settlements, April

Bashir, A. (1996), 'Profit-sharing Contracts and Investment under Asymmetric Information', *Research in Middle East Economics*, Vol.1, pp.173-186

BenDjilali, Boualem and Khan, Tariqullah (1995), Economics of Diminishing Musharakah, Jeddah: IRTI

Buckmaster, Daphne (ed.) (1996), 'Central Bank Supervision: The Need for Unity', in *Islamic Banking: An Overview*, Institute of Islamic Banking and Insurance: London, pp.143-145

Buckmaster, Daphne, (ed.) (1996), 'Alternative Tools of Supervision by Central Banks', in *Islamic Banking: An Overview*, Institute of Islamic Banking and Insurance: London, pp.146-150

Chapra, M. Umer (2000), 'Why has Islam Prohibited Interest?: Rationale Behind the Prohibition of Interest', *Review of Islamic Economics*, No.9

Chapra, M. Umer and Habib Ahmed (2002), Corporate Governance in Islamic Financial Institutions, Occasional Paper #6, Jeddah: Islamic Research and Training Institute

Chapra, M. Umer and Tariqullah Khan (2000), Regulation and Supervision of Islamic Banks, Occasional Paper No.3, Jeddah: Islamic Development Bank – Islamic Research and Training Institute

Chapra, M. Umer (1982), 'Money and Banking in an Islamic Economy', in Ariff, M. (ed.)

Cunningham, A. (2001), Culture of Accounting: What are the Real Constraints for Islamic Finance in a Riba-Based Global Economy? Moody's Investor Services, London: UK

Dale, Richard (2000), 'Comparative Models of Banking Supervision', paper presented to the Conference on Islamic Banking Supervision, Bahrain: AAOIFI, February

Dar, H.A. and Presley, J.R. (1999), 'Islamic Finance: A Western Perspective', *International Journal of Islamic Financial Services*, Vol.1, No.1, Apr-June

Dar, H.A. and Presley, J.R. (2000), 'Lack of Profit Sharing in Islamic Banking: Management and Control Imbalances', *International Journal of Islamic Financial Services*, Vol.2, No.2, Jul-Sep

El-Din, A.K. (1986), 'Ten Years of Islamic Banking', *Journal of Islamic Banking and Finance*, Jul-Sep, 3(3): 49-66

El-Gamal, Mahmoud (2000), 'An Economic Explication of the Prohibition of Gharar in Classical Islamic Jurisprudence', in Islamic Finance: Challenges and Opportunities in the Twenty First Century (Conference Papers), Loughborough: Fourth International Conference on Islamic Economics and Banking

Elgari, M. Ali (1997), 'Short Term Financial Instruments Based on Salam Contracts', in Ausaf Ahmad and Tariqullah Khan (eds.), *Islamic Financial Instruments for Public Sector Resource Mobilization*, Jeddah: Islamic Research and Training Institute, pp.249-66

El-Karanshawy, Hatem (1998), 'CAMEL Ratings and their Relevance for Islamic Banks', paper presented to a Seminar on Islamic Banking Supervision, organised by the Arab Monetary Fund: Abu Dhabi

El Sheikkh, Fath El Rahman (2000), 'The Regulation of Islamic Banks by Central Banks', *The Journal of International Banking Regulation*, Fall (2000), pp.43-49

Errico, Luca, and Mitra Farahbaksh (1998), 'Islamic Banking: Issues in Prudential Regulations and Supervision', IMF Working Paper 98/30, Washington: International Monetary Fund

Fadeel, Mahmoud (2002), 'Legal Aspects of Islamic Finance', in Archer, Simon and Karim, Rifaat Abdel (eds.), *Islamic Finance: Growth and Innovation*, Euromoney Books, London: UK

Gafoor, A.L.M. Abdul (2001), 'Mudaraba-based Investment and Finance', *New Horizon*, No.110, July

Gafoor, A.L.M. Abdul (2001), 'Riba-free Commercial Banking', *New Horizon*, No.112, September

Grais, W. and Kantur, Z. (2003), 'The Changing Financial Landscape: Opportunities and Challenges for the Middle East and North Africa', World Bank Policy Research Working Paper 3050, May 2003

Haque, Nadeemul and Abbas Mirakhor (1999), 'The Design of Instruments for Government Finance in an Islamic Economy', *Islamic Economic Studies*, 6(2), pp.27-43

Haron, S. and Norafifah Ahmad (2000), 'The Effects of Conventional Interest Rates on Funds Deposited with Islamic Banking System in Malaysia', *International Journal of Islamic Financial Services*, Vol.1, No.4, Jan-Mar

Hassan, Sabir Mohammad (2000), 'Capital Adequacy and Basel Guidelines: On Risk Weights of Assets for Islamic Banks', paper presented at the Conference on the Regulation of Islamic Banks, in Bahrain, February

Hoque, M.Z. and Masdul Alam Choudhury (2003), 'Islamic Finance: A Western Perspective Revisited', *International Journal of Islamic Financial Services*, Vol.4, No.4, Apr-June

Ibrahim, Tag El-Din S. (1991), 'Risk Aversion, Moral Hazard and Financial Islamization Policy', *Review of Islamic Economics*, Vol.1, No.1

Iqbal, Zamir and Abbas Mirakhor (2002), 'Development of Islamic Financial Institutions and Challenges Ahead', in Archer, Simon and Karim, Rifaat Abdel (eds.) *Islamic Finance: Growth and Innovation*, Euromoney Books, London: UK

Iqbal, Zamir (1997), 'Islamic Financial Systems', *Finance and Development* (IMF), Vol.34, No.2, June

Iqbal, Z. (2001), 'Profit and Loss Sharing Ratios: A Holistic Approach to Corporate Finance', *International Journal of Islamic Financial Services*, Vol.3, No.2, Jul-Sep

Iqbal, Zubair and Abbas Mirakhor (1987), Islamic Banking, IMF Occasional Paper No.49, Washington: International Monetary Fund

Iqbal, Munawar et al. (1999), Challenges Facing Islamic Banking, Jeddah: IRTI, Occasional Paper #2

Islamic Fiqh Academy of the Organization of Islamic Conference (1989), Islamic Fiqh Academy Resolutions and Recommendations, Jeddah

Kahf, Monzer (1997), 'The Use of Assets Ijārah Bonds for Bridging the Budget Gap', in Ahmad, Ausaf and Khan, Tariqullah (eds.), Islamic Financial Instruments for Public Sector Resource Mobilization, Jeddah: Islamic Research and Training Institute, pp.265-316

Kahf, Monzer (1996), 'Distribution of Profits in Islamic Banks', *Studies in Islamic Economics*, Vol.4, No.1

Kahf, Monzer (1994), 'Time Value of Money and Discounting in Islamic Perspectives Revisited', *Review of Islamic Economics*, Vol.3, No.2

Kahf, Monzer and Khan, Tariqullah (1992), *Principles of Islamic Financing*, Jeddah: IRTI

Karim, Rifaat Ahmed Abdel (2001), 'International Accounting Harmonization, Banking Regulation and Islamic Banks', *The International Journal of Accounting*, Vol.36(2), pp.169-193

Karsten, I. (1982), 'Islam and Financial Intermediation', IMF Staff Papers, March, 29(1), pp.108-42

Kettell, B. (2002), Islamic Banking in the Kingdom of Bahrain, Bahrain Monetary Agency (BMA)

Khan, Mohsin, and Abbas Mirakhor (1993), 'Monetary Management in an Islamic Economy', *Journal of Islamic Banking and Finance*, Vol.10, Jul-Sep, pp.42-63

__________, and Mirakhor, A. (1986), 'The Framework and Practice of Islamic Banking', *Finance and Development*, September

Khan, Mohsin S. and Mirakhor, A. (1992), 'Islam and the Economic System', *Review of Islamic Economics*, Vol.2, No.1, pp.1-29

Khan, M. (1987), 'Islamic Interest-Free Banking: A Theoretical Analysis', in Khan, Mohsin S. and Mirakhor, Abbas (ed.), *Theoretical Studies in Islamic Banking and Finance*, Texas, USA: The Institute of Islamic Studies, pp.15-36

Khan, Mohsin S. (1986), 'Islamic Interest-Free Banking: A Theoretical Analysis', IMF Staff Papers, Vol.33, (1), pp.1-27, March

Khan, M.Y. (2001) 'Banking Regulations and Islamic Banks in India: Status and Issues', *International Journal of Islamic Financial Services*, Vol.2, No.4, Jan-Mar

Khan, M.F. (1999), Financial Modernisation in the Twenty-First Century and Challenges for Islamic Banking', *International Journal of Islamic Financial Services*, Vol.1, No.3, Oct-Dec

Khan, M.F. (1991), Comparative Economics of Some Islamic Financing Techniques, Research Paper No.12, Islamic Research and Training Institute, Islamic Development Bank: Jeddah

Khan, Tariqullah and Ahmad, Habib (2001), Risk Management: An Analysis of Issues in the Islamic Financial Industry, Jeddah: IRTI, Occasional Paper #5

Khan, Tariqullah (1995), 'Demand for and Supply of PLS and Mark-up Funds of Islamic Banks – Some Alternative Explanations', *Islamic Economic Studies*, Vol.3, No.1, IRTI

Khan, Tariqullah and Habib, Ahmad (2001), Risk Management: An Analysis of Issues in the Islamic Financial Industry, Jeddah: IRTI Occasional Paper #5

Maroun, Y. (2002), 'Liquidity Management and Trade Financing', in Karim, R. Abdel and Archer, S. (eds.), *Islamic Finance: Innovation and Growth* (pp.163-175), Euromoney Books and AAOIFI

Mirakhor, Abbas (1995), 'Theory of an Islamic Financial System' in *Encyclopaedia of Islamic Banking*, London: Institute of Islamic Banking and Finance

Mulajawan, D., Dar, H.A. and Hall, M.J.B. (2002), 'A Capital Adequacy Framework for Islamic Banks: The Need to Reconcile Depositors' Risk Aversion with Managers' Risk Taking', Economics Research Paper, pp 02-13, Loughborough University

Naughton, S.A.J. and Tahir, M.A. (1988), 'Islamic Banking and Financial Development', *Journal of Islamic Banking and Finance*, 5(2)

Nienhaus, V. (1983), 'Profitability of Islamic PLS Banks Competing with Interest Banks: Problems and Prospects', *Journal of Research in Islamic Economics*, 1(1), pp.37-47

__________ (1986), 'Islamic Economics, Finance and Banking – Theory and Practice', *Journal of Islamic Banking and Finance*, 3(2), pp.36-54

Norman, A.A. (2002), 'Imperatives for Financial Innovation for Islamic Banks', *International Journal of Islamic Financial Services*, Vol.4, No.2, Oct-Dec

Obaidullah, Mohammad (1998), 'Capital Adequacy Norms for Islamic Financial Institutions', *Islamic Economic Studies*, Vol.5, Nos.1 and 2

____________ (1998), 'Financial Engineering with Islamic Options', *Islamic Economic Studies*, Vol.6, No.1, IRTI, IDB

____________ (1999), 'Islamic Financial Options: Potential Tools for Risk Management', *Journal of King Abdulaziz University* (Islamic Economics), Saudi Arabia, Vol.11, pp.3-28

____________ (2000), 'Regulation of Stock Markets in an Islamic Economy', Proceedings of the Third International Conference on Islamic Banking and Finance, August, Loughborough University, Leicester, UK

____________ (2001), 'Ethics and Efficiency in Islamic Stock Markets', *International Journal of Islamic Financial Services*, Vol.3, No.2, Jul-Sep

___________ (2001), 'Financial Contracting in Currency Markets', *International Journal of Islamic Financial Services*, Vol.3, No.3, Oct-Dec

___________ (2002), 'Islamic Risk Management', *International Journal of Islamic Financial Services*, Vol.3, No.4, Jan-Mar

Presley, John R. and Sessions, John, G. (1993), 'Islamic Economics: The Emergence of a New Paradigm', *Journal of Economic Theory*, 1994

Qami, I.H. (1995), 'Regulatory Control of Islamic Banks by Central Banks', in *Encyclopaedia of Islamic Banking and Insurance*, Institute of Islamic Banking and Insurance: London, pp.211-215

Rahman, Y.A. (1999), Islamic Instruments for Managing Liquidity, *International Journal of Islamic Financial Services*, Vol.1, No.1, Apr-Jun

Rosly, A.R. and Sanussi, Mohammed M. (1999), 'The Application of Bay-al-Inah and Bai-al-Dayn in Malaysian Islamic Bonds: An Islamic Analysis', *International Journal of Islamic Financial Services*, Vol.1, No.2, Jul-Sep

Salehabadi, A. and Aram, M. (2002), 'Islamic Justification of Derivative Instruments', *International Journal of Islamic Financial Services*, Vol.4, No.3, Oct-Dec

Sarker, M.A.A. (1999), 'Islamic Business Contracts: Agency Problems and the Theory of Islamic Firms', *International Journal of Islamic Financial Services*, Vol.1, No.2, Jul-Sep

Sarwar, A.A. (1995), 'Islamic Financial Instruments: Definition and Types', *Review of Islamic Economics*, Vol.4, No.1, pp.1-16

Sundararajan, V., Marston, David and Shabsigh, Ghiath (1998), 'Monetary Operations and Government Debt Management under Islamic Banking', WP/98/144, Washington, DC: IMF, September

Sundararajan, V. and Errico, L. (2002), 'Islamic Financial Institutions and Products in the Global Financial System: Key Issues in Risk Management and Challenges Ahead', IMF working paper, IMF/02/192, Washington: International Monetary Fund, November

Udovitch, Abraham L. (1981), Bankers Without Banks: Commerce, Banking and Society in the Islamic World of the Middle Ages, Princeton Near East Paper No.30, Princeton, NJ: Princeton University Press

Udovitch, Abraham (1970), *Partnership and Profit in Early Islam*, Princeton, NJ: Princeton University Press

Uzair, Mohammad (1955), An Outline of 'Interestless Banking', Raihan Publications, Karachi

__________ (1982), 'Central Banking Operations in an Interest-Free Banking System', in Ariff, M. (ed.)

Zaher, T. and Hassan, K. (2001), 'A Comparative Literature Survey of Islamic Finance and Banking', *Financial Markets, Institutions and Instruments*, Vol.10, No.4, pp.155-199, November